BREAKTHROUGH TO DIALOGUE

The Story of Temple University Department of Religion

§

Edited by
Professor Leonard Swidler

Epilogue by
Professor Terry Rey, Religion Department Chair

CONTRIBUTORS

Professors

Mahmoud Ayoub
Thomas Dean
Richard DeMartino
Maurice Friedman
Charles Fu
Roderick Hindery
Samuel Laeuchli
Franklin Littell
Seyyed Hossein Nasr
Bernard Phillips
John Raines
Zalman Schachter
Gerard Sloyan
Ernest Stoeffler
Paul van Buren
Bibhuti Yadav

Students

Steven Antinoff
David Efroymson
John Esposito
Harold Kasimow
Bokin Kim
Kenneth Kramer
Richard Libowitz
Marcia Sachs Littell
John Mawhinney
Kana Mitra
Brian Ortale
Thomas Thompson
Rodger Van Allen
Imtiyaz Yusef

Copyright © 2019 Leonard Swidler

All rights reserved

No part of this publication may be reproduced, distributed, or transmitted in any form or by any means, including photocopying, recording, or other electronic or mechanical methods, without the prior written permission of the publisher, except in the case of brief quotations embodied in critical reviews and certain other noncommercial uses permitted by copyright law. For permission requests, write to the publisher.

The views, opinions, and research expressed in this website/book are those of the authors and do not necessarily reflect the position of iPub Global Connection LLC.

Cover Design by Arewa Abiodun Ibrahim

Cover Photo by Shutterstock

iPub Global Connection, LLC

1050 W. Nido Avenue

Mesa, AZ 85210

www.iPubCloud.com info@iPubCloud.com

US telephone: 484-775-0008

Paperback ISBN-13 978-1-948575-22-5

eBook ISBN-13 978-1-948575-23-2

Welcome Home to iPubCloud.com

You've opened the right book from the iPub international library. You might be a scholar, an avid reader, a mother or father, a teacher, a 'tween or teen, or one of the rest of us.

Welcome home to iPub Global Connection where knights of old and now digital nomads from all over the world meet safely to share ideas, find resources, and support individuals whose voices wish to be heard to create and protect the world for your great, great grandchildren.

We are committed to the empowerment of each and all individuals' contributions to a better world. Often, we feel paralyzed by our limiting doubt that alone we have no ability or opportunity to make any real impact. When that thought comes up, pick up your eraser in your mind's eye and say "backspace, delete." Individually, together, we can and will influence causing the important changes to ensure a habitable world for following generations...a world embracing global citizenship one by one.

How would *you* begin to define global citizenship? One way might be to be open enough to learn about other cultures and peoples so that we can connect with all. There are, of course, many ways—through music, art, blogs, podcasts, philosophy, all of which help children model how to be better citizens.

Here you may find what you're looking for, the idea you'd like to expand...a place to be open, to learn, and to trust.

Read on and become a part of the ongoing conversations. Email a note, comment or share your idea or blog post. Don't keep your views or us a secret. Your voice counts and we care. www.iPubCloud.com.

CONTENTS

Preface Breakthrough to Dialogue 1
Leonard Swidler

State Universities Religion Departments and Temple University Department of Religion 9
Brian Ortale

"In the Beginning . . . ." *History of Temple University's Department of Religion: The Transitional Years* 41
F. Ernest Stoeffler

Bernard Phillips: *An Appreciation* 53
Harold Kasimow

"Remembering Paul" Gedenksymposion Für Paul M. Van Buren Ökumenisches Institut, Universität Heidelberg, Juli 2-3, 1999 57
Thomas Dean

A Global Paradigm Shift *Reflections On Interreligious, Intercultural, and International Development by the Journal of Ecumenical Studies/Dialogue Institute* 89
Leonard Swidler

The Education I Wasn't Supposed To Get, and How I Got Some of It at Temple 119
John Raines

The Years of Early Growth (1965-85) 127
Gerard S. Sloyan

"In Those Days There Were Giants in the Land"...... 148
Marcia Sachs Littell and Richard Libowitz

The Temple Religion Department *An Unscientific Postscript on My Career in Philadelphia* 155
Samuel Laeuchli

From Catholic Ethics to Comparative Ethics 169
Roderick Hindery

Isma'il Al Faruqi: *The Link Between TUDOR and the Muslim World* 179
Imtiyaz Yusuf

Professor Maurice Friedman: *With Gratitude* 201
Kenneth P. Kramer

Dead Man Living Richard Demartino (1922-2013).. 217
Steve Antinoff

"We Wash Your Feet" *Eulogy For Bibhuti S Yadav: July 10, 1943 - October 10, 1999* 243
Thomas Dean

Brief Remembrances 265
Zalman Schachter-Shalomi

Some Recollections of My Years at Temple 271
Seyyed Hossein Nasr

Teaching About Religion on Mark C. Taylor's *New York Times/International Herald Tribune* Op-Ed Essay ... 277
Thomas J. Dean

GRADUATE STUDENTS 315

TUDOR History 317
                Rodger Van Allen

TUDOR Then: Young in the 60's 325
                David P. Efroymson

TUDOR and the Study of Social Justice 341
                John J. Mawhinney, S.J.

Celebrating a Groundbreaking Religion
Department 351
                John L. Esposito

Recollections of a Student From Early Time of
TUDOR 363
                Kana Mitra

Reflections of the Stranger in the Land (Lev 19:34) .367
                Thomas L. Thompson

Looking Forward 385
                Leonard Swidler

Epilogue 387
                Terry Rey

PREFACE
Breakthrough to Dialogue

LEONARD SWIDLER

The title of this volume says it all: *Breakthrough to Dialogue!* That is what *Temple University Department of Religion (TUDOR)* accomplished—almost like Athena, "born full-grown from the head of Zeus"! Only in this case it was not from the head of Zeus, but of Bernard Phillips, the first Chair of TUDOR, which was created in 1962.

TUDOR was the first truly full-fledged interreligious taught department of religion in a public university in the United States, and probably in the world. Yes, there were ancient universities which were established by states, like Cairo's Al Azhar founded in the 10th century, and Oxford in the 11th century, and one of my *alma mater's*, the University of Tübingen in 1477, etc. However, these were all either Muslim or Christian faculties teaching religions from their respective Muslim or Christian perspectives. Other American public universities crept step by step toward such a full-fledged program and faculty, but TUDOR was radically different in that from its' beginning it hired critical-thinking Christian scholars to teach about Christianity, critical-thinking Jewish scholars to teach about Judaism, and similarly with Muslim scholars, Buddhist scholars and scholars from the "outside," i.e., philosophy of religion, psychology of religion, sociology of religion . . .

Like all new "paradigms" it went through several mandatory phases, pretty well skipping the first phase of "being ignored," moving immediately to phase two, "being laughed at." Claude Welsh, from ivy league University of Pennsylvania, and shortly thereafter, one of the founders of the Graduate Theological Union in the San Francisco Bay area, dismissively referred to TUDOR as being built on "the zoo theory." TUDOR's model of "teaching critically from the inside" was at first laughed at, then resisted, as in phase three of an idea. The TUDOR model then quietly moved to phase four where it was imitated everywhere (the highest form of praise!).

Ernest Stoeffler, the only professor to carry over from the old Divinity School of Temple University (the university was founded in 1884, by the pastor of The Baptist Temple, Russell Conwell) described how when after World War II it was becoming increasingly difficult to carry out its' mission of providing education for "workingmen and workingwomen," the university decided to negotiate with the Commonwealth of Pennsylvania to become a *public* university. The university, of course, could not bring its Divinity School into the relationship with the state, and thus started the struggle to form a new body: the Department of Religion within the College of Liberal Arts (CLA). I say struggle because there were those on the faculty who thought that the study of religion could not be done with academic rigor. Professor Ernest Stoeffler in the end prevailed, and in 1962 TUDOR was formally established.

Four years later, in 1966, Temple University became a "state-related" university of the Commonwealth of Pennsylvania. It is clear from Stoeffler's careful history below that many persons among the administration and faculty of Temple University played important roles in helping to bring TUDOR into existence. However, it is also crystal clear that Professor Ernest Stoeffler was the giant who carried the project from almost impossibility to amazing success!

TUDOR was, then, fortunate in having two stalwart visionaries at its beginning. This is when the second creative visionary, TUDOR's first Chair, Professor Bernard Phillips, came into play. He at first made do largely with adjunct hires. He made his first major faculty acquisition in 1964, by hiring Paul van Buren, an Episcopal theologian. Van Buren studied with the then most famous and conservative Protestant theologian in the world, Karl Barth, in Basel, Switzerland. Barth had made the front cover of *Time Magazine* as one of the (in)famous "God Is Dead" theologians!

1966 was an auspicious year for Temple University, for when it formally became a state-related university, it was suddenly flush with funds. That year Phillips added four more full-time professors. The university at large hired well over a hundred new faculty each year starting in 1966 and for the next several years! The new hires were: two *All But Dissertation* faculty (ABD's) Thomas Dean and John Raines, the Co-Editor of the *Journal of Ecumenical Studies* Elwyn Smith, myself, an Editor, and the *Journal of Ecumenical Studies* itself. Elwyn and I were each hired as Full Professors with a $13,000 per ten-month salary, and *JES* was brought on board with an annual subsidy of $50,000—almost four Full Professors' salaries! In 2015 dollars, the 1966 $50,000 *JES* subsidy would be about $400,000!

But the excitement was only beginning. When interviewed, I told Bernard that I would not think of coming to Temple with *JES* without a commitment that several additional Catholic professors would also be hired, as well as Jews, Muslims, Hindus, Buddhists.... I thought that my demand (see the details in my essay below) would kill my and *JES*'s hire, but Bernard said, "Great idea! We'll do it!" and he did in fact do so in the next two years. Whether or not he got the idea from me can't be answered, and really isn't important, because Bernard was the sort of person who was happy to take an idea from anyone or anywhere—from himself or someone else—and run with it if he thought it was a good idea. The TUDOR faculty went from six to ten (plus *JES*!) in 1966, and twenty-one in 1968!

At the same time the graduate student body exploded at an equal rate. In spring 1966, there was one Catholic graduate student (see below the essay by the first Catholic graduate student, Rodger Van Allen), and in two years there were fifty! Remember, it was only December, 1965, that Vatican II ended, with its mandate to "all

Catholics" to engage in dialogue! One story frames what a stunning paradigm shift this was. Catholics in America had for decades been instructed that it was a grievous sin to allow their children to go to a "godless" state university, and thus, in 1966, a Philadelphia Catholic priest—who of course had studied at Philadelphia's St. Charles Seminary before ordination to the priesthood—requested to have a transcript of credits sent to TUDOR so he could study for a doctorate, only to have it denied! He was forced to the subterfuge of having his transcript sent to Catholic LaSalle University's MA program, where he physically picked them up and brought them to Temple!

TUDOR gained another Catholic graduate student in a very serpentine way connected with the Vatican. Below you will read the reflections of Thomas Thompson, Professor of Old Testament, University of Copenhagen, Denmark, emeritus. He came to us at TUDOR because Professor Joseph Ratzinger (a.k.a. Pope Benedict XVI, emeritus) felt that then graduate student Thomas Thompson's prize winning doctoral dissertation on the historicity (really, the lack thereof) of the biblical Patriarchs (Abraham, Isaac, Jacob) was not acceptable to a Pontifical Catholic Theology Faculty. The Catholic Theology Faculty of the University of Tübingen (also my *alma mater* and where I also was Visiting Professor several times) acquiesced, and hence, Thompon was not granted the ThD!

TUDOR's faculty in 1968, and soon thereafter, pulled together a number of "stars" in a wide range of fields. For example, Gerard Sloyan had been the President of the "Liturgical Movement," which during the decades just before Vatican II was the leading intellectual and popular force that helped bring about the massive liturgical reforms of that Council. Sloyan was also the scripture scholar in charge of the then new American Catholic English translation of the New Testament, and had for ten years been the Chair of the Religious Education Department at the Catholic University of America in Washington, D.C. Another addition was Franklin Littell, a Methodist church historian who had spent ten years working with the U.S.

Military High Command and the Protestant Church of Germany, *Evangelische Kirche Deutschland* (EKD), to rid itself of its Nazi penetration and deep-seated Antisemitism.

Richard DeMartino also joined in that period. He was trained as a Japanese linguist during World War II. At the end of the war he served for a year as the personal interpreter of a Japanese general who was convicted of war crimes and eventually executed. Richard then stayed on and studied Zen Buddhism in Kyoto and eventually became the last personal assistant and "amanuensis," first for D.T. Suzuki, and then for Shinichi Hisamatsu, the two most influential Zen thinkers of modern times. He also served as the "interpreter" (in all senses) between Hisamatsu and Paul Tillich, one of the most influential Christian thinkers of the twentieth century. The same period also brought Leonard E. Barrett, an Afro-American who wrote the definitive work on the Rastafarians and covered the Caribbean religions, and Ismail Al-Faruqi. Ismail was the last governor of Galilee under the British Mandate, after which he came to the U.S. and earned his doctorate in philosophy from the University of Indiana. While at TUDOR he brought scores of Muslim students from all around the world to pursue the PhD. Somewhat later, with the outburst of the Khomeini revolution in Iran, he was joined by Seyyed Hossein Nasr, who had been the Academic Vice-Chancellor of Tehran University, and President of the Imperial Iranian Academy of Philosophy.

Then there was Charles Weishin Fu, originally from Taiwan, where he grew up speaking Japanese as well as his native Chinese, and who studied in several American universities, receiving his PhD in philosophy from the University of Illinois. Charles was a prodigiously productive scholar, leaving behind after his relatively early death at 63 over thirty volumes of publications! Zalman Schachter was clearly one of TUDOR's most charismatic professors, having escaped the Nazis the first time from Austria to Belgium in 1938, and then again in 1940 with Stuka dive bombers in pursuit through France. (In 1980, when we stepped out of the airport in Brussels, he said to me: "Len, the last time I looked at this sky, there were Stuka dive bombers in it!"), rejection at the Swiss border, shipping from Marseille to French north Africa, across to Dakar, with ship to South America, and up the Caribbean island chain finally to Brooklyn and the Hassidim; he was also equally at home with Catholics, Zen masters, doing zikir with sufis. Another stunning Jewish TUDOR scholar was Maurice Friedman, the most significant English language scholar of Martin Buber (a personal friend and collaborator of his), as well as an outstanding thinker in the areas of religion, psychology, and literature.

So you can see why, although I had published four books, thirty-five articles and co-founded *JES* with my wife Arlene Anderson Swidler, when I joined TUDOR at age thirty-seven I felt like a young pigmy among giants.

This book also includes a tiny sample of reflections from some of the early graduate students. Although none of the early faculty had doctorates in the academic study of religion—they didn't exist then!—we over the next half century produced many hundreds of them! Now, every year the annual conference of the American Academy of Religion (founded 1964, the same year as TUDOR!) will be deluged with over 10,000 participating scholars—the Past President (2013), John Esposito is a graduate of TUDOR (see his reflections below). Many of those students, especially outside of the West, started whole new networks of departments of religious studies around the world. They were from all different religions. However, by no means did they all stay in academia. One—Young Hoon Lee—became the chief pastor of Yoido Full Gospel Church, the largest congregation in the world (over 1,000,000 members!). Another—Alwi Shihab—became the Foreign Minister of the third largest democracy in the world, Indonesia. Still another—Sunggon Kim—became a multiple-term Member of Parliament of the Republic of South Korea.

A further vital dimension of TUDOR is its intimate relationship with the premier scholarly periodical in the field of ecumenical and interreligious dialogue, the *Journal of Ecumenical Studies* (also founded 1964), and its outreach instrument, the *Dialogue Institute: Interreligious, Intercultural, International* (founded 1978). My essay below further details the development and outreach of the Dialogue Institute.

Let me close by borrowing the words of one of the most influential scholars of Islam in the world today, John Esposito:

> "We celebrate the fiftieth anniversary of Temple Department of Religion and our experiences and memories for many reasons. But these all stem from a visionary experiment and accomplishment: 1) It created in contrast to obtaining a doctorate from a theological faculty in a seminary/university, a unique PhD at a secular university in the academic study of religion; 2) In contrast to most PhD programs with traditional specialty areas within a specific religion, Temple pioneered a graduate program that required a major in one religion and a minor in two others. This approach produced teacher-scholars for late twentieth and twenty-first centuries, trained to teach a world .
> ... The Temple experience offers a 'win-win experience,' innovative program, many dedicated teachers, the study of several religious traditions which trained us to also think, see and analyze comparatively."

In brief: Dialogue and Critical-Thinking.

STATE UNIVERSITIES RELIGION DEPARTMENTS AND TEMPLE UNIVERSITY DEPARTMENT OF RELIGION

BRIAN ORTALE

Context of First U.S. State Supported University Department of Religion

The department of religion at Temple University is affectionately known to some as TUDOR. TUDOR stands for Temple University Department of Religion. The history of the department of religion at Temple has been recounted on various occasions and in various ways. The purpose of this essay is to place TUDOR in the context of the development and history of departments of religion at other state supported, public universities. This essay first will outline the history of the departments of religion at the University of Iowa, Iowa City, the University of Michigan, Ann Arbor, and the University of Florida, Gainesville. In order to place TUDOR in the context of the history at Iowa, Michigan and Florida, this essay will rely heavily upon F. Ernest Stoeffler's "History of Temple University's Department of Religion: The Transitional Years";[1] as well as James W. Hilty's, "Temple University: 125 Years of Service to

---

[1] F. Ernest Stoeffler, "History of Temple University's Department of Religion. The Transitional Years," 2, F. Ernest Stoeffler Papers, Special Collections Research Center, Temple University Libraries, Philadelphia, PA.

Philadelphia, the Nation and the World"[2], and Eric G. Lovik's "Temple: The Story of an Urban University."[3]

Stoeffler begins telling the story of TUDOR by noting that "the history of the Department of Religion at Temple University actually goes back to that day in 1888 when Russell Conwell decided to give instruction to a group of promising but needy young men to prepare them for the Christian ministry."[4] The history of TUDOR indeed begins with Conwell. However, Stoeffler may consider 1888 as the genesis of Temple University since that is the year Temple College was chartered. Lovik indicates that Conwell's offer to give instruction to needy young men to prepare them for the ministry actually goes back to June 1884.[5]

In order to place TUDOR in the context of the development of departments of religion at other state supported, public universities Stoeffler wisely points out an important distinction between Temple, and universities like Iowa, Michigan and Florida. Temple's origin as a private, church related institution makes Temple's story slightly different than the stories of universities like Iowa, Michigan and Florida. Hilty notes the humble origins of Temple saying, "Temple University did not spring from the generosity of a captain of industry or the munificence of a financial wizard. Unlike other multi-purpose universities of today, Temple was not the creation of the state or the beneficiary of federal land grants. Neither did it have roots extending back scores of decades with connections to America's aristocracy; nor was it the vehicle of a religious order or an offshoot of a training institute, as were so many colleges founded in the latter part of the

---

[2] James, W. Hilty, Temple University: 125 Years of Service to Philadelphia, the Nation and the World (Philadelphia: Temple University Press), 2010.

[3] Eric, G. Lovik, Temple: The Story of an Urban University, PDF, Pennsylvania State University, 2005.

[4] Stoeffler, "History," p. 1.

[5] Lovik, Temple: The Story of an Urban University, PDF, Pennsylvania State University, 2005, p. 1.

nineteen century during America's Gilded Age."[6] Temple's origin lay in Conwell's desire to provide an education to working class students whose desire to study for the ministry was complicated by their need to work full time during the day, their lack of education beyond high school, and their inability to afford a college education.

The Founding of Temple University and the Teaching of Religion

Since Hilty notes the humble origins of Temple University and Stoeffler begins with Russell Conwell, a brief description of Russell Conwell and Temple University's humble roots are in order. Russell Conwell, a former Yale student, Civil War captain, Boston lawyer, and Philadelphia minister[7] was the pastor of Grace Baptist Church in Philadelphia.

Conwell was pastoring a church in Lexington, Massachusetts when he was called to lead Grace Baptist Church in Philadelphia in 1882. Grace Baptist Church grew rapidly and sought property for a larger church building. When a suitable property was identified the property began being called The Baptist Temple—the largest church building in North America at the time, at 1800 North Broad Street. Grace Baptist Church and The Baptist Temple were synonymous and held by the same congregation. The only distinctions between the Grace Baptist Church and The Baptist Temple were where the congregation celebrated liturgy and where the congregation conducted Sunday school and other ministries.

When "Charles Davies, a young man working in a print shop, showed up at Pastor Russell Conwell's office one evening after a service at Grace Baptist Church in Philadelphia in June, 1884, requesting to study for the ministry Conwell sensed the urgency of the situation, and he offered to teach Davies and any of his friends

---

[6] Hilty, Temple University, p. 1.
[7] Lovik, Temple: The Story, p. 4.

one evening each week."[8] The numbers of students quickly increased and the Grace Baptist Church created a board of trustees to formalize the endeavor. "When the board conducted its first meeting they named Russell H. Conwell President of 'The Temple College.'"[9]

The Temple College of Philadelphia's humble origins, as Hilty noted, made it different from other colleges founded in the late 19th century. "Temple was not the creation of the state or the beneficiary of federal land grants."[10] In describing The Temple College of Philadelphia's humble origins as unlike those of other colleges founded in the late 19th century, Hilty is undoubtedly referring to the Morrill Acts of 1862 and 1890, and the foundation of public, land grant colleges created by state or territorial legislatures and funded by the sale or use of federal lands. The Morrill Act envisioned colleges dedicated to the military arts, the mechanical arts, and agricultural arts as well as the classical arts and sciences. Conwell's intention to prepare working class young men for the ministry was a very different purpose than the educational mission of land grant public colleges and universities. Still, Conwell's intention to prepare students for the ministry quickly broadened to a mission "to provide instruction best suited to the higher education of people currently employed in a trade; to cultivate a taste for higher and more practical disciplines; and to encourage the working class students the desire to be useful to society."[11] Hilty describes this as "an exemplary model for the democratization and diversification of higher education."[12] Democratization and diversification notwithstanding, the fact that The Temple College of Philadelphia was not called The Baptist Temple College or The Temple Baptist College of Philadelphia is noteworthy.

---

[8] Ibid. p. 1.

[9] Ibid. p. 1

[10] Hilty, Temple University, p. 1.

[11] Lovik, Temple: The Story, p. 2.

[12] James W. Hilty, Interview by Temple University Press, p. 1.

Though Conwell was the pastor of Grace Baptist Church in Philadelphia, and though the classes he first offered one night a week were held in buildings owned by Grace Baptist Church, and though Charles Davies was interested in training to be an ordained Baptist minister, there is no evidence to suggest Conwell or the first board of trustees of The Temple College of Philadelphia ever intended to found a Baptist seminary or to make the college denominational. Lovik identifies The Temple College of Philadelphia as a nonsectarian Baptist College and notes that "a council representing thirty-four Philadelphia Baptist churches met to discuss the future of this enterprise . . . and the general reaction by influential council members was that the venture was too 'wasteful and secular.'"[13]

The Temple College of Philadelphia never had the support or financial backing of the Philadelphia area Baptist churches, and though Grace Baptist Church was one of the largest Baptist congregations in America at that time, Hilty is correct in distinguishing The Temple College of Philadelphia from other private, late 19th century colleges, which were founded through religious orders. The Temple College of Philadelphia was to be, as the council members representing Philadelphia Baptist churches complained, too secular. Indeed, students were admitted "regardless of denominational affiliation."[14]

A final note on the founding of The Temple College of Philadelphia as it relates to the founding of TUDOR is a bit ironic. Though Conwell wanted to prepare Charles Davies and his friends with an education equal to a college education suited to ordained ministry, The Temple College of Philadelphia, initially started in 1884, did not organize a program in religion during its first decade. "Created in 1895, the theological department offered both day and

---

[13] Lovik, Temple: The Story of an Urban University, PDF, Pennsylvania State University, 2005, p. 1.
[14] Ibid, p.2.

evening classes, and after a re-organization of the curriculum it was renamed The Philadelphia Theological School, which led to a five-year Bachelor of Divinity degree. Temple's theological school began offering the Master of Sacred Theology graduate degree in 1903, and a Doctor of Sacred theology was awarded in 1904."[15] The fact that a college initially founded to prepare working class young men for the ministry did not create a theological program for more than a decade may be ironic, but the program that was created and the re-organizing of the curriculum into the Philadelphia Theological School of The Temple College of Philadelphia was very important to the development of TUDOR in two ways. First, the Philadelphia Theological School would later become the Temple University School of Theology which would survive until 1957.

When Temple University School of Theology lost its accreditation from the American Association of Theological Schools, (herein after AATS)[16] it became the Conwell School of Theology in 1961.[17] Secondly, the Philadelphia Theological School would be important to the development of TUDOR because of the shift from a ministry focused degree leading to the Bachelor of Sacred Theology, the Master of Sacred Theology, and the Doctor of Sacred Theology degrees to the academic orientation of the Doctor of Philosophy degree. The Philadelphia Theological School and the Temple University School of Theology, therefore, had both a preemptive and a programmatic effect on the development of TUDOR.

The preemptive effect would be realized in the fact that though Temple University would develop into a comprehensive university separate from the institution founded by Conwell and the Grace

---

[15] Ibid.

[16] The American Association of Theological Schools is now called the Association of Theological Schools.

[17] F. Ernest, Stoeffler, History of Temple University's Department of Religion. The Transitional Years, 2, F. Ernest Stoeffler Papers, Special Collections Research Center, Temple University Libraries, Philadelphia, PA, p.4.

Baptist Church, the common history and affection between the institutions preempted the desire, or need, for the comprehensive university to create a religion program. The comprehensive university had no interest in or desire to compete with or overshadow the theology programs of The Philadelphia Theological School or the Temple University School of Theology.

The relationship between Temple University and the Temple University School of Theology may best be described by Robert Livingston Johnson, Temple University's third president. In the April 1947 issue of *The Conwellian*,[18] Johnson noted "when Temple University was passing through a difficult stage of development . . . a suggestion was made to the Board of Trustees that perhaps the School of Theology had served its purpose . . . and could be dispensed with."[19] President Johnson recounts the story of a trustee, Dr. J. S. Ladd Thomas, who in response to that suggestion insisted that, "the School of Theology was the mother college of Temple University and we could not turn from it now."[20] President Johnson was so impressed with Dr. Thomas' feeling for the School of Theology that when President Johnson had the opportunity to name a dean for the School of Theology he appointed Dr. Thomas to the position.[21] Dr. Thomas' sentiment that the School of Theology was the mother college of Temple University was, in fact, not the most important aspect of this story—rather it was an administrative detail mentioned in the telling of this story. Whatever sentiment perdured between the University and the School of Theology, the fact that the President of Temple University appointed the dean of the School of Theology reveals the administrative power structure between the two distinct institutions.

---

[18] Robert Livingston Johnson, "Our School of Theology – As I see it" The Conwellian Vol. IV, No. 1, April 1947, p.3.
[19] Ibid.
[20] Ibid.
[21] Ibid.

Several other incidents evidence the relationship between Temple University and the School of Theology and what would become the Conwell School of Theology. Stoeffler described several years of struggle to keep the Temple University School of Theology open and accredited while simultaneously attempting to found a department of religion within the College of Liberal Arts. During those years of struggle, between when the Temple University School of Theology first lost its accreditation in December 1957 and the Temple University Department of Religion was established in 1961, three key incidents recorded by the Temple University Board of Trustees demonstrate the relationship between Temple University and the School of Theology. The first incident occurred on 27 January 1961 when the Board of Trustees resolved to support the Conwell School of Theology. The second and third incidents occurred when the Board of Trustees, on two separate occasions, voted to transfer money from the University's holdings to the Conwell School of Theology.

A brief word is in order to clarify these three incidents. When the Temple University Board of Trustees resolved to support the Conwell School of Theology, the support indicated was of an academic nature involving "committee advice on such things as standards for admission, requirements for graduation, appointments to the faculty, and general standards for the operation of the School."[22] This support did not include direct funding for the Conwell School of Theology or any of its programs. Although Temple University seemed only too willing to provide moral and academic support to theological education, funding was not part of the relationship. Indeed, the support Temple University did offer was not gratis. The resolution of 27 January 1961 stated clearly "that

---

[22] Temple University Board Minutes, Sept. 1959 – May 1962, Vol. 22, Vault 1 Range 1A1, p. 3953.

Temple University should be fully compensated for any service rendered to the School."[23]

The other two incidents which demonstrate the relationship between Temple University and the Conwell School of Theology involved the fiduciary duty of Temple University to benefactors and the collection, holding, use, and transfer of funds by the University. On 27 January 1961 and 1 December 1961 the Board of Trustees voted to transfer $7,350.00 and $2,227.45 respectively from the Theology General Fund[24] and from the G. H. Wailes Chair Fund[25] to the Conwell School of Theology. The academic mission and non-profit status notwithstanding, Temple University had a legal duty to transfer these funds if the intention of the donors was to make a gift to the school of theology. The fact that Temple University held these funds suggests more than just the fiduciary relationship between Temple University and the Temple University School of Theology and the Conwell School of Theology. This relationship was also more than historical and affectionate. The relationship must have been one in which the entity of the School of Theology was completely subsumed in the entity which was Temple University; Temple University being the "parent" institution of the Temple University School of Theology and then of the fledgling Conwell School of Theology.

The Temple University Board of Trustees approved the recommendation of the Executive Committee of the Board which outlined "the relationship between the University and the Conwell School of Theology"[26] on 27 January 1961. The resolution of the board acknowledged that "Temple University by tradition and history is interested and has participated in the advancement of theological

---

[23] Ibid.

[24] Temple University Board Minutes, Sept. 1959 – May 1962, Vol. 22, Vault 1 Range 1A1, p. 3956.

[25] Ibid., p. 4016.

[26] Ibid., p. 3952.

education. Because of this historical background and the attitudes expressed by its Founder (Russell Conwell) during formative and developing years, it affirms its desire to encourage and be helpful to any institution devoted to theological education located in the environment of the Temple University campus."[27] The resolution of the Board noted that "inasmuch as it was not possible for the University to continue its direct association with theological education, the Trustees looked with favor upon the organization of the Conwell School of Theology . . . which was inaugurated by trustees and friends of the University and set up as a separate corporation."[28] Though the act of the Board indicated that it was not possible for Temple University to continue its direct association with theological education, the Board further resolved on 27 January 1961 that "for the first five years after the admission of the first class of students, Temple University will confer the Bachelor of Divinity degrees provided that the Conwell School will act only after obtaining the advice of the proper committee named by the President of the University regarding all matters pertaining to the standards for admission, requirements for graduation, appointments to the faculty, and general standards for the operation of the School."[29]

It is interesting that Temple University's board believed it was not possible to continue its direct association with theological education but was willing to confer the Bachelor of Divinity degrees earned in the Conwell School of Theology, a separate corporation, for a period of five years. Temple University's willingness to confer what was considered a professional degree rather than an academic degree suggests a willingness to acquiesce to the needs of the Conwell School of Theology, but not a willingness to lessen Temple University's academic standards. The university would only confer

---

[27] Ibid.
[28] Ibid.
[29] Ibid.

the degrees provided the Conwell School act on the advice of the university regarding matters of academic standards. It will be necessary to return to the issue of professional degrees and academic degrees later. Another interesting aspect of the 27 January 1961 resolution of the Temple University Board of Trustees is the understanding that it was not possible for Temple to continue its direct association with theological education. There is no indication in the record why this was the understanding of the Board. Is it possible that already in the beginning of 1961 efforts were already under way for Temple University to become a public, state sponsored institution? The resolution specifically mentions it was not possible for the direct association with theological education to continue. Nothing in the record explains why the direct association with theological education could not continue. This question will be addressed later, but I turn now to revisit the issue of professional and academic degrees, and the willingness of Temple University to confer the Bachelor of Divinity degree earned at the Conwell Theological School for a period of five years.

That Temple University was willing to confer the Bachelor of Divinity degree for the Conwell School of Theology underscores the second, programmatic, way in which the Philadelphia Theological School would be important to the development of TUDOR. This programmatic development involves the shift from a ministry focused professional degree leading to the Bachelor of Sacred Theology, the Master of Sacred Theology, and the Doctor of Sacred Theology degrees earned at the Philadelphia Theological School, the Temple University School of Theology, and the Conwell School of Theology to the academic orientation of the Bachelor of Arts, Master of Arts, and Doctor of Philosophy degrees offered in the College of Liberal Arts of Temple University.

Another "shift" was also required along with the move from a ministry focused professional degree in theology to the academic orientation of the liberal arts degree in religion. This shift involved the orientation to an undergraduate degree in religion. The Temple University School of Theology and later the Conwell School of Theology were strictly graduate schools of theology. At that time, in seminaries and schools of theology like Temple, the Bachelor of Sacred Theology was a graduate degree conferred only upon those who already possessed either a Bachelor of Arts or a Bachelor of Science degree.

It is worth noting here that TUDOR, which would eventually become both an undergraduate and a graduate program for the study of religion, was developed after a shift occurred from the professional, ministerial degree of the seminary and theological school to the academic degree of the college of liberal arts in the 1960's. It is also worth noting that this shift happened at a time when not more than 50 percent of ordained clergy had a college degree.[30] The lack of a college educated clergy is worth noting in the development of TUDOR because Russell Conwell's primary intention for the founding of Temple College was to prepare students for the ordained Christian ministry who did not have a college degree in a school which prided itself on holding to a nondenominational curriculum.

Since the Temple University School of Theology lost its accreditation in 1957 and the Conwell School of Theology was founded on the grounds of Temple University in 1961, the question needs to be asked, what role did these institutions play? Or, more importantly, why would someone choose to attend these institutions? And, finally, why would Temple University establish a department of religion with an expectation to fulfill the role of the former schools of theology?

---

[30] See studies by E. Brooks Holifield, 2007, God's Ambassadors: A History of the Christian Clergy in America (Grand Rapids, MI: Wm. B. Eerdman's Publishing, 2007), and Glenn T. Miller, Piety and Plurality: Theological Education Since 1960 (Eugene, OR: Cascade Books, 2014).

In 1884 Russell Conwell saw the need to provide an opportunity for a free education which would lead to ordination for a young man who had not been to college and could not attend college during the day because he could not afford to and worked full time during the day as a printer. Very soon Conwell's Temple College of Philadelphia offered day and evening classes, had admission standards and charged tuition. By the time the Temple University School of Theology lost its accreditation from the AATS in 1957, proposals were being presented to establish a graduate school of religion within Temple University. This graduate program, though announced in 1959, never came to be. In 1960 an undergraduate program in religion was to be established to begin in the fall of 1961. After the undergraduate program had been established the graduate program was begun in the fall of 1962.

These bare facts indicate the dates of transition from classes in a pastor's office to a world class department of religion in a comprehensive research university. The facts don't tell the story of the struggle. Nor do they answer the questions about what role Temple College of Philadelphia played, or why someone would choose to attend it or one of the later religious studies versions of Russell Conwell's institution. Part of the story of the struggle to establish a department of religion can be seen through the lens of the Reverend Doctor F. Ernest Stoeffler. Stoeffler is the only full-time faculty member to make the transition from the Temple University School of Theology to TUDOR.

In 1959, Stoeffler wrote a proposal for a graduate program in religion within the College of Liberal Arts of Temple University which would subsume the disaccredited School of Theology. Stoeffler identified the twofold purpose of the graduate program as, "to afford qualified clergymen an opportunity for furthering their professional training by working for an S.T.M. degree and, to provide an opportunity for students of marked scholarly ability to prepare themselves for college or seminary teaching by specialization in certain areas leading to the S.T.D. degree."[31] Though Stoeffler indicates that candidates would prepare themselves to teach in colleges or seminaries, the S.T.M. and S.T.D. degrees were essentially professional degrees more suited to ministry or teaching from a denominational perspective. The predicament of choosing between a professional, ministerial degree and the academic degree was taken away from some candidates who "had to transfer to other seminaries in order to have their degrees recognized for ordination."[32] The choice facing students in the school of theology who chose to remain at Temple was time-sensitive because Temple University was only willing to grant the degrees they sought, S.T.M. and S.T.D., through 1964. Dr. Millard Gladfelter, university provost, announced plans to open a Graduate Department of Theology in 1959 claiming, "In a city of this size, there is a need to serve some men who cannot afford or who do not need to go to a denominational seminary."[33] The need may have been there but Temple University was not willing to fulfill this need permanently. How great this need was, in a city the size of Philadelphia, was an integral part of the struggle to continue the school of theology and establish the department of religion. During the re-accreditation process for the Temple University School of Theology Dr. Daniel D. Williams from the AATS commented, in a letter dated 7 December 1956, on the purpose of the doctorate of theology or the doctor of sacred theology degrees, and questioned if either was equal to the doctor of philosophy degree. Williams indicated there were two purposes for

---

[31] F. Ernest Stoeffler, "Graduate Program in Religion, Proposal, 1959." F. Ernest Stoeffler Papers. Vol/Box 2. Special Collections Research Center, Temple University Libraries, Philadelphia, PA, p. 1.

[32] George Riley, "Temple Plans to Open Graduate Theology School," The Evening Bulletin, Tuesday, 21 April 1959, page 42B. Temple University Department of Religion records, newspaper clipping. KV3A, TEM 1, Special Collections Research Center, Temple University Libraries, Philadelphia, PA.

[33] Ibid.

the professional, ministerial degrees, "one purpose was research for teaching or specialized ministry and the other purpose was as an extension of pastoral training."[34] The purpose of the professional degrees notwithstanding, Temple University seemed intent on developing a department of religion which would grant the Master of Arts and Doctor of Philosophy degrees. Dr. Harry David Hummer, Acting Dean of the School of Theology said of Temple's planned Graduate School of Philosophy and Religion that "we will be the only school in the Philadelphia area which can give a doctorate degree and the local seminaries approve it."[35] Temple's intention was not exactly what the local seminaries would approve, or what Stoeffler wanted. Stoeffler was intent on a continuation of the Bachelor of Divinity degree as a graduate degree. Stoeffler was aware that many students were attracted to the Temple University School of Theology because it offered the graduate Bachelor of Sacred Theology degree, which was required for ordination in certain mainline Protestant churches. Temple University frustrated Stoeffler's desire to see the University grant the graduate bachelor's degree when the proposed Graduate Theology School announced by Gladfelter to open in the fall of 1959 never came to fruition. Instead, on 7 January 1960 the faculty of the College of Liberal arts adopted the following resolution: That the College establish an undergraduate Department of Religion with the appointment of a man possessing all the usual academic qualifications, including a Ph.D. degree, who will

---

[34] Dr. William's Letter, dated 7 December 1956. F. Ernest Stoeffler Papers. Box 2015-49, 2 of 2. Special Collections Research Center, Temple University Libraries, Philadelphia, PA.

[35] Ed Spencer, "Graduate School of Philosophy and Religion to Open Next Semester." Temple University News, 24 April 1959. F. Ernest Stoeffler Papers. Box 2015-49, 2 of 2. Special Collections Research Center, Temple University Libraries, Philadelphia, PA.

offer courses of an academic nature in the History and Literature of Religions."[36]

The resolution to establish an undergraduate department of religion meant an end to the hopes of Stoeffler and others who wished to preserve the Bachelor of Sacred Theology degree and to continue ministerial education at Temple University. In the fall of 1961 Dr. Bernard Phillips was named chair of the newly established Temple University Department of Religion, TUDOR. Stoeffler credits Dr. John Fisher as "the agent for the establishment of an undergraduate Department of Religion within the College of Liberal Arts"[37] because as Chairman of the "Executive Committee of the College he assured the faculty that this was the recommendation of the Executive Committee when he moved the faculty to adopt the resolution for the establishment of an undergraduate Department of Religion."[38] Certainly Fisher is to be credited with bringing the resolution forward and speaking for it from his position on the Executive Committee. However, Dr. Gladfelter, who had been provost when the proposals to merge the Temple University School of Theology with the College of Liberal Arts had first been put forward, and who rose to the presidency of Temple University in the spring of 1959, must surely be remembered for his part in bringing the Department of Religion into the College of Liberal Arts at Temple University.

The resolution to establish an undergraduate department of religion called for the appointment of a man possessing all the usual academic qualifications, including a Ph.D. degree. Stoeffler indicates

---

[36] F. Ernest Stoeffler, "Pre-History – Temple University Department of Religion, Summary of Events." F. Ernest Stoeffler papers Vol/Box 2. Box 2015-49, 2 of 2. Special Collections Research Center, Temple University Libraries, Philadelphia, PA.

[37] Stoeffler, History of Temple University's Department of Religion, The Transitional Years, page 6.

[38] Ibid.

that there was more to the appointment than academic qualifications. For Stoeffler there were additional concerns including "that we must now work toward having the Graduate Program in Religion connected with the newly established undergraduate Department of Religion and that the person hired to chair the undergraduate department must also qualify for the kind of graduate program in religion that will continue to attract students."[39]

I suspect that some of the students Stoeffler was interested in attracting included those who represented Protestant groups. Stoeffler noted that "the S.T.B. program in particular served almost exclusively the needs of Protestant groups, while the university as a whole became increasingly dependent upon state aid."[40] The dependence on state aid, I believe, was a major factor in how TUDOR was established and developed.

Stoeffler was concerned about the S.T.B. program in particular, the ministerial training in general, and the future of the professional graduate programs overall. He was also concerned that "the credentials of the person hired to chair the undergraduate department of religion would transcend the problem that was seldom mentioned, but which was always in the background, namely, whether he or she was going to be a Catholic, Jew, or Protestant, thus presumably affording one or the other of these religious communities an undue advantage."[41] When Bernard Phillips was named chair of the undergraduate department of religion in the fall of 1961 he seemed to be the perfect fit. He was a Jew. Academically, he was trained at the bachelor's and master's level in a large, public university, the University of Minnesota, where he graduated *Summa cum laude* and was inducted into Phi Beta Kappa in 1935. His Ph.D. degree was

---

[39] Stoeffler, History of Temple University's Department of Religion, The Transitional Years, page 6-7.
[40] Ibid, p. 2.
[41] Ibid, p.7.

from Yale University. He was a Fulbright Professor in India, 1950-51 and Japan 1953-54. Professionally, his area of expertise was Oriental Religions and he came to Temple after being professor and chair of the Department of Philosophy at the University of Delaware.[42]

While teaching undergraduates at Temple University in the fall of 1961 Phillips proposed a graduate program in religious studies in which "religion will be studied as one of the humanities, centered around courses in the History of Religions and Religious Thought. The Department expects to observe the highest standards of integrity and impartiality in its teaching. It will make every effort to present the total picture of man's religious life, both in its variety and its common features, and will not undertake to uphold any single point of view or to propagandize for any single faith. It is intended that the faculty shall represent as broad a variety of religious faiths and standpoints as is possible, so that the exposure of students may be a comprehensive one. It is hoped that eventually, the staff will include not only representatives of the major religions of the West, but also of the East as well."[43]

Phillips did much more than teach undergraduates and propose a program of graduate studies in religion during his early tenure at Temple University. Perhaps Phillips' most important endeavor was the creation of a faculty which would uphold the highest standards of integrity and impartiality while representing a broad variety of religious faiths. One of the early additions to the department of religion faculty, Fr. Gerard Sloyan, said of Phillips, "Most influential of all on the department's aims and purposes was the man who assembled the others; Bernard Phillips, a Jew of Minneapolis whose doctorate in philosophy was from Yale University. As a result of

---

[42] Phillips, Bernard, "A Proposed Program of Graduate Study to be Offered by the Department of Religion of the College of Liberal Arts Beginning in the Fall of 1962", p. 3. Temple University Department of Religion Records, Special Collections Research Center, Temple University Libraries, Philadelphia, PA.
[43] Ibid, p. 4.

Phillips' wide reading habits he had become acquainted with the basics of Islam, Hinduism, and Buddhism."[44] The earliest members of the department of religion included Stoeffler, Joseph Weber, and Paul van Buren, who received a bachelor's of sacred theology at Episcopal Theological School in 1951 and was ordained an Episcopal priest in the Diocese of Massachusetts. His doctorate in theology came from the University of Basel in 1957[45]; "T. Patrick Burke, an Australian Catholic who held a doctorate in Catholic theology from the state faculty of the state Munich; Samuel Laeuchli, a Swiss who had studied under Karl Barth in Switzerland, but who, upon coming to the United States, had earned a degree from Union Theological Seminary in New York City; Robert Gordis, a congregational rabbi who had edited Conservative Judaism's revision of its prayer book; Maurice Friedman, who had served on the faculty of Sarah Lawrence College in Bronxville, NY, and was a specialist in the writings of Martin Buber; Leonard Swidler, perhaps the first layperson ever to receive a degree in Catholic theology (from the Pontifical Theological Faculty of the University of Tübingen), as well as a PhD in philosophy and history from the University of Wisconsin; Gerard Sloyan, a Catholic Priest of the Diocese of Trenton, New Jersey, whose doctorate was from the Catholic University of America who was the first Catholic priest to accept a full time appointment at a state related institution;[46] Jacob Agus, a European-born congregational rabbi in a Baltimore suburb who represented liberal

---

[44] Gerard Sloyan, "A Keeper of the Flame," Journal of Ecumenical Studies, 50, 1 (Winter 2015), p.29.

[45] Saxon, Wolfgang, "Paul van Buren, 74, 'Death of God Exponent" Obituary, The New York Times, 1 July 1998.

[46] Pelletier, Annette and Panganiban, Patricia, Gerard S. Sloyan, biography, Talbot School of Theology, Biola University, "Christian Educators of the 20th Century Project." Note: Sloyan may be the first Catholic priest to be professor of religion at a state related institution, 1967; however, Jesuit priest David M. Stanley, was on the staff of the University of Iowa in 1963.

Judaism; and Isma'il al-Faruqi, a native of Jaffa in Palestine who, upon immigration to the U.S., had enrolled in Harvard Divinity School to learn what he could of Christian faith and practice, but who shortly transferred to the department of philosophy at Indiana University, where he earned a PhD"[47]

Before the story of the Temple University School of Theology is further developed into the story of the Temple University Department of Religion it is important to relate the histories of the University of Iowa, the University of Michigan and the University of Florida to the founding of TUDOR.

The University of Iowa

The School of Religion at the University of Iowa was formally organized and incorporated in 1927. This was the first program of its kind at a tax-supported state university in the United States.

In 1921, the University of Iowa considered how religion could take its place alongside science and be taught in a scholarly manner. A plan for a School of Religion called for a program which would be established on "separate foundations affiliated with the University." A grant of $35,000 from John D. Rockefeller, Jr., in 1926, ensured the financial support of the fledgling school for the first three years. The plan, which would eventually be known as the Iowa plan,[48] came

---

[47] Sloyan, Gerard, "A Keeper of the Flame" Journal of Ecumenical Studies, Vol. 50, No. 1, Winter 2015, p. 29.

[48] The Iowa Plan is the title on the 1924 report submitted by R. H. Fitzgerald to Walter A. Jessup, President, The University of Iowa. Records of the School of Religion, RG 06/31, Box 16, Special Collections Department, University Archives University of Iowa Libraries, Iowa City, Iowa. It should be noted that O.D. Foster was the architect of the "plan" which is here referred to as the Iowa Plan. This same plan was outlined elsewhere and early examples of it included an Illinois plan and a Michigan plan.

together formally in 1924. M. Willard Lampe, Ph.D., was named the first director of the School of Religion on 14 March 1927.[49]

The seeds of the school of religion go back as early as 1908 when the university recognized the value of religious education as provided by local clergy on a volunteer basis. With the approval of the Course of Studies Committee the university established a Classification Committee to review syllabi and monitor examinations in elective courses of religious study for university credit.[50] Official bulletins of the State University of Iowa, 1909 – 1910 and 1910 – 1911 entitled Religious Education provided for pastors of churches to teach and students to receive credit up to four hours in one year, and up to eight hours in four years of religious instruction.[51] This program was a definite precursor to establishing schools of religion at public, state universities for two reasons. First, it provided for a review of the academic rigor of the courses presented with the requirement that they substantially meet the standards of the university curricula. This factor would become extremely important for the field of religious studies to be accepted as an academic discipline with the appropriate academic approach to the study of religion. Secondly, academic credit towards the bachelor's degree was awarded for successful completion of the course requirements.

---

[49] M. Willard Lampe, "An Autobiographical Sketch of the School of Religion," The University of Iowa, 1965. Records of the School of Religion, RG 06/31, Box 8, Special Collections Department, University Archives University of Iowa Libraries, Iowa City, IA.

[50] Proposal for religious education, submitted to and approved by the Course of Studies Committee, 28 July 1908, p. 2. Records of the School of Religion, RG 06/31, Box 8, Special Collections Department, University Archives University of Iowa Libraries, Iowa City, IA.

[51] Bulletin of Religious Education 1909-1910, The State University of Iowa, p. 6. Records of the School of Religion, RG 06/31, Box 16, Special Collections Department, University Archives University of Iowa Libraries, Iowa City, IA.

Two important criteria of an established department of religion within a public, state university setting are missing from this early program at Iowa. The first criterion which the religious education program lacked is that the courses were offered outside of the university. In order to be incorporated into the state universities, classes in religion had to be offered on campus without denominational or sectarian bias, alongside and on an equal basis with the other arts and sciences.

The second criterion missing from the program of religious education as outlined in 1908 was that the instructors were not paid by the university. Integration into the public university and acceptance as an integral part of the university curriculum require funding of salaries and programs through, if not by, the universities. The academic study of religion would not be taken seriously if faculty were not able to demand equivalent compensation for their work within the university.

It can be argued that the School of Religion at the State University of Iowa fails this criterion because the salaries of the Protestant, Catholic and Jewish faculty members were paid for by each respective denomination. Still, the program of religious education begun in 1908 served as a good foundation for the development of a school of religion because both programs rested on the support, participation and cooperation of the local churches and synagogues.

The University of Michigan

The history of the department of religion at the University of Michigan begins with the founding of a separate institution, the Michigan School of Religion. On 28 November 1921 two separate meetings were held to put forward the school of religion. One of those meetings was attended by pastors from the city of Ann Arbor; the other meeting was attended by various faculty members of the university.[52] Each of those meetings focused on the plan created by Professor Charles Foster Kent for a school of religion at Iowa State University (*sic*).[53] Kent believed that "conditions were favorable for the establishment of a school of religion at the University of Michigan because more than forty pastors, faculty members, representatives of all the important denominations, including Catholics and Hebrews (*sic*) strongly favored the project of establishing a school of religion."[54] An important aspect of Kent's plan for schools of religion at state universities was the inclusion of and cooperation with local leaders and members of the Protestant, Catholic, and Jewish congregations wherever a school of religion was to be attached to a state university. The representatives from six of the local churches named to the General Committee representing the local Episcopal, Unitarian, Methodist, Presbyterian, Christian and Jewish congregations were identified as professors at the University of Michigan.

The Michigan School of Religion offered its first classes in Newberry Hall on 21 September 1925. "Newberry Hall was situated directly across South State Street from University Hall."[55] This physical separation from the University of Michigan suggests that, though members of the University faculty and administration were

---

[52] Horace L. Wilgus to President Marion L. Burton, 16 November 1922, Box 142 P, Bentley Historical Library, Michigan Historical Collections, Michigan School of Religion, University of Michigan.

[53] Wilgus refers, in his letter to President Burton, of Kent's work at Iowa State University. In fact, Wilgus was referring to the work Kent did at the University of Iowa, Iowa City, Iowa. Iowa State University is the name used to refer to another state university in Iowa which is in Ames Iowa.

[54] Horace L. Wilgus, note to President Marion L. Burton, 16 November 1922, Box 142 P, Bentley Historical Library, Michigan Historical Collections, Michigan School of Religion, University of Michigan, Ann Arbor, MI.

[55] Walter A. Donnelly, et al., editors, The University of Michigan: An Encyclopedic Survey; Walter A. Donnelly, Wilfred B. Shaw, and Ruth W. Gjelsness, eds. (Ann Arbor, MI: University of Michigan Press, 1958.

interested in and pursued a school of religion as part of the University, this was not yet accomplished. One of the stated purposes of the Michigan School of Religion was to provide religion courses for students at the University of Michigan. Students at the University were to receive credit for their courses taken at the Michigan School of Religion from the University of Michigan. Still, the Michigan School of Religion was not part of the University.

The University of Michigan did not take the step to integrate the Michigan School of Religion with the University until 1929. In 1929, President Alexander G. Ruthven appointed Dr. Edward Blakeman Counselor in Religious Education at the University of Michigan.[56] Blakeman started an interdepartmental program of religious studies and also counseled students. The fact that part of Blakeman's responsibilities to the University included the pastoral duty to counsel students does not keep Blakeman's appointment from initiating the religion program at the University of Michigan. The criteria used to determine when a program of religion is incorporated in a state supported university does not exclude extra-curricular activities of a religious, but pastoral, nature. The fact that in 1929 Blakeman, as Counselor in Religious Education, does not offer courses through a department of religion within the University of Michigan is the defining factor which keeps the University of Michigan from claiming to have a fully integrated department of religion at a state supported public university. The University of Michigan will not claim to have done so until the 1970s.

The University of Florida

The history of the department of religion at the University of Florida, Gainesville hinges on the appointment of Delton Lewis

---

[56] Ibid, 1958.

Scudder, Ph.D. as Head Professor of Religion on 12 July 1946.[57] Several issues are identified as problems of religion at the University of Florida as early as 18 February 1942. One of the issues is declining enrollment due to the number of students who leave the university to join the war effort. Though declining enrollment is not specifically a religious issue, the problem of leadership of the religious programs at the University is a religious issue. The leadership of the religious programs at the university is a problem exacerbated by the influx of new programs as a result of the "war situation" and the addition of religious centers adjacent to campus opened by the Methodists, the Catholics, the Episcopalians, the Baptists, and the Presbyterians.[58] While each of these religious centers may adequately address the needs of particular individuals and specific denominations, they create a leadership vacuum. A leadership vacuum is created in that it falls to the university to coordinate the programing of the various religious centers where students from the University of Florida may wish to participate in the religious activities and programs at locations adjacent to the campus. The need to coordinate religious programming is not just a problem for the university regarding off-campus programs. The university must also coordinate the religious programs which occur on campus.

Traditionally, religious programing at the University of Florida, Gainesville was conducted by groups such as the Young Men's Christian Association and the Office of Student Religious Activities. Scudder notes in his 1957 *Study of the Religious Programs at the University of Florida* that "beginning September, 1928, Mr. J. E. Johnson sustained the Y.M.C.A. as a voluntary organization by

---

[57] Delton L. Scudder, "The Religious Program at the University of Florida," p. 6, Series 44, George A. Smathers Libraries. Special and Area Studies Collections, University of Florida, Gainesville, FL.

[58] John J. Tigert, IV, to Clarence P. Shedd, 16 September 1942, UFL Series P76 Box 6, Office of President Tigert, General Correspondence, 1928- 1957.

raising funds for the program from interested donors in the state.[59] Amongst Scudder's papers archived at the University of Florida are notes he made to himself, for himself, of notable figures at the university. One of those notes concerns a John Evander Johnson. Johnson is identified as a General Secretary of the Y.M.C.A. at the University of Florida from 1924 – 1943. During that time Johnson was also Instructor in Bible, 1924 – 1933; Professor of Bible, 1933 – 1943; Director of Social and Religious Activities, 1933 – 1943; and Acting Director of the Florida Union, 1942 – 1943.[60] The record does not specifically identify the Mr. J. E. Johnson of the Y.M.C.A as the same John Evander Johnson listed in Scudder's Biographical Data; but the coincidence is far too compelling to not believe this is the same Johnson. Johnson served the University of Florida as Professor of Bible and Director of the Florida Union. Johnson's death in 1943 created another leadership vacuum at the University of Florida. The record does not reflect anyone else being named Professor of Bible at the University of Florida after Johnson's passing on 24 November 1943. What the record does reflect is that in consideration of the problem of religion at the University of Florida, two separate committees form a joint committee to "formulate recommendations concerning a Department of Religion."[61] One aspect of the problem of religion at the University of Florida that these committees attempted to explore was grasping the size and scope of the problem. The problem of coordinating religious programs remained the same but the problem of declining enrollment due to the war situation was

---

[59] Scudder, "The Religious Program at the University of Florida," p. 4.

[60] Delton L, Scudder, The Religious Program at the University of Florida, 1977, Box 1, AP 7, George A. Smathers Libraries. Special and Area Studies Collections, University of Florida, Gainesville, FL.

[61] John J. Tigert, IV to Townes R. Leigh, Memorandum, 15 April 1946. University of Florida Archives, Records of the President, George A. Smathers Libraries. Special and Area Studies Collections, University of Florida, Gainesville, FL.

reversed; by the end of 1945 the influx of veterans created another problem. That problem involved meeting the needs student veterans who were older, married and often had children.

In coordinating the religious programming and serving the needs of veterans a concern was raised regarding the head of the newly formed Department of Religion being able to teach religion and minister to the needs of the campus community. The character of such a professor became an issue. It was suggested that what was needed was not only someone who was a trained academic but someone who was also ordained in one of the main line Protestant denominations. It was believed that "to establish a chair of religion at the University . . . a man of distinction"[62] is necessary. The person appointed, on 12 July 1946, was Delton L. Scudder, PhD.

Scudder indicates in his study of the religious program at the University of Florida that as Head of the Department of Religion he "assumed the twofold obligation of developing an academic curriculum in religion and a program of religious activities."[63] The Department of Religion at the University of Florida, Gainesville fulfills the academic criteria of an integrated department of religion in a public, state university in 1946. The fact that Scudder accepted or performed ministerial duties above and beyond his academic appointment as professor and head of the department does not keep Scudder from being considered an academically credentialed faculty in an integrated department of religion.

Conclusion

Having considered the histories of the departments of religion at the University of Iowa, established in 1927, the University of

---

[62] Clarence P. Shedd to John J. Tigert, IV, 10 July 1944, University of Florida Series, P7A, Box 25, George A. Smathers Libraries. Special and Area Studies Collections, University of Florida, Gainesville, FL.

[63] Scudder, "The Religious Program at the University of Florida," p. 6-7.

Michigan, established in 1929, and the University of Florida, established in 1946, it is now possible to finally consider the place of the Temple University Department of Religion, in its proper historical context. Several common themes run through the histories of all these schools. All the schools relied on the cooperation of local religious leaders and congregations amongst Protestants, Catholics and Jews. All the schools struggled with academic committees, standards for professors' qualifications, standards for credits and standards for degrees earned. Though the four universities each faced these struggles somewhat differently each university's program was established with the hiring of a single person; at Iowa it was Matthew Willard Lampe, at Michigan it was Edward Blakeman, at Florida it was Delton Lewis Scudder, and at Temple it was Bernard Phillips.

The common themes which run through the histories of the establishment of departments of religion at Iowa, Michigan, Florida and Temple make for a common history which begins at Iowa in 1924 and ends with Temple in 1961. Having studied the record of each of these universities, I find it interesting that only the University of Michigan mentions what was happening at another institution. A committee at the University of Michigan looks specifically at what was at the time considered the Iowa Plan for a school of Religion. The records at Florida and Temple do not indicate any reliance on what had already been done elsewhere, what might have been tried and what proved successful. This is somewhat surprising in an era of "best practices."

In the final analysis, the history of TUDOR is very much like that of the establishment of departments of religion at the University of Iowa, the University of Michigan and the University of Florida. These histories are replete with considerations of basically two criteria: academically qualified and equally remunerated faculty; and courses offered in and on university campuses with credit earned toward a university degree.

There is one major factor which makes the history of TUDOR very different from the histories at Iowa, Michigan and Florida. Though this essay has outlined the establishment of the department of religion at Temple University in the context of the establishment of the religion programs at the three public, state universities, the major factor which makes TUDOR different from these three institutions is that when Temple University founded its department of religion in 1961 it was not legally designated as a state related institution. Temple University, in 1961, was a private university. Temple University was not made a state related institution until 1965.[64] It may be argued that Temple University, legally, remains a private institution. This argument might be taken up at a later time. Certainly, since 1965, Temple University has been identified as a state related institution. Still, TUDOR was established four years earlier in a situation which makes the context of TUDOR quite different from that of the University of Iowa, the University of Michigan and the University of Florida.

Whereas Lampe at Iowa, Blakeman at Michigan and Scudder at Florida had to navigate a path toward the full integration of their respective departments of religion at public, state universities, TUDOR developed out of the disintegration and disaccreditation of the Temple University School of Theology and the need to reintegrate the study of religion in a comprehensive university increasingly dependent on state aid. This meant that the programs in professional, ministerial education at the Temple School of Theology had to be reenvisioned and revised to be integrated into the academic study of religion in the College of Liberal Arts at the state related Temple University.

The irony of TUDOR's history, in the context of the histories at Iowa, Michigan and Florida, is that whereas Lampe, Blakeman and Scudder were all simultaneously tasked with both the academic study

---

[64] Temple University Commonwealth Act, 24 P.S. § 2501-1, 1965.

of religion and the duty to offer programs of religious exercises, each of these men being both academically trained and ordained clergy separated them from Phillips, at Temple, who was a layman at a private university and did not have the dual roles of professor and pastor. Temple, the private university, accomplished in Philadelphia what had not been possible at Iowa, Michigan and Florida, the establishment of a department of religion which fully honored the American tradition of the separation of church and state.

Bibliography

Donnelly, Walter, A., Wilfred B. Shaw, and Ruth W. Glelsness, eds., *The University of Michigan: An Encyclopedic Survey* (Ann Arbor, MI: University of Michigan Press, 1958)

Hilty, James, *Temple University: 125 Years of Service to Philadelphia, the Nation and the World* (Philadelphia, Temple University Press, 2010).

Hilty, James, Interview by Temple Press: https://www.temple.edu/tempress/authors/2033_qa.html

Holifield, E., Brooks, *God's Ambassadors: A History of the Christian Clergy in America* (Grand Rapids, MI. William B. Eerdman's Publishing, 2007).

Johnson, Robert, Livingston, "Our School of Theology – As I see it." *The Conwellian,* Vol. IV, No. 1, April 1947.

Lampe, M., Willard, "An Autobiographical Sketch of the School of Religion, The University of Iowa, 1965." Records of the School of Religion, RG 06/31, Box 8, Special Collections Department, University Archives, University of Iowa Libraries, Iowa City, Iowa.

Lovik, Eric, G. *Temple: The Story of an Urban University.* Pennsylvania State University, 2005.

Miller, Glenn, T., *Piety and Plurality: Theological Education Since 1960* (Eugene, OR, Cascade Books, 2014).

Phillips, Bernard, "A Proposed Program of Graduate Study to be Offered by the Department of Religion of the College of Liberal Arts Beginning in the Fall of 1962". Temple University Department of Religion Records, Special Collections Research Center, Temple University Libraries, Philadelphia, PA.

Riley, George, "Temple Plans to Open Graduate Theology School," *The Evening Bulletin,* 21 April 1959. Temple University Department of Religion records, KV3A, TEM 1, Special Collections Research Center, Temple University Libraries, Philadelphia, PA.

Scudder, Delton, L., "The Religious Program at the University of Florida." Series 44, George A. Smathers Libraries. Special and Area Studies Collections, University of Florida, Gainesville, Florida.

Spencer, Ed, "Graduate School of Philosophy and Religion to Open Next Semester." *Temple University News,* 24 April 1959. F. Ernest Stoeffler Papers. Box 2015-49, 2 of 2. Special Collections Research Center, Temple University Libraries, Philadelphia, PA.

Sloyan, Gerard, "A Keeper of the Flame," *Journal of Ecumenical Studies,* Vol. 50, No. 1 (Winter 2015), pp. 29-36.

Stoeffler, F. Ernest, "History of Temple University's Department of Religion. The Transitional Years." 2, F. Ernest Stoeffler Papers, Special Collections Research Center. Temple University Libraries, Philadelphia, PA.

Stoeffler, F., Ernest, "Graduate Program in Religion, Proposal, 1959." F. Ernest Stoeffler Papers. Vol/Box 2. Special Collections Research Center, Temple University Libraries, Philadelphia, PA.

Stoeffler, F., Ernest, "Pre-History - Temple University Department of Religion, Summary of Events." F. Ernest Stoeffler papers Vol/Box 2. Box 2015-49, 2 of 2. Special Collections Research Center, Temple University Libraries, Philadelphia, PA.

Temple University Board Minutes, Sept. 1959 - May 1962, Vol. 22, Vault 1 Range 1A1. Special Collections Research Center. Temple University Libraries, Philadelphia, PA

"IN THE BEGINNING...."
History of Temple University's Department of Religion: The Transitional Years

F. ERNEST STOEFFLER

The history of the Department of Religion at Temple University actually goes back to the day in 1888 when Russel Conwell decided to give instruction to a group of promising but needy young men to prepare them for the Christian ministry. For more than twenty years the institution of learning which resulted from that decision was supported by private funds, including the proceeds from preaching his famous sermon *Acres of Diamond*. In 1911 the Founder was forced to seek public assistance, which was given in slowly increasing amounts. As we shall see, this progressive dependence on public funds became an important factor in the development of the Department of Religion.

The result of Conwell's original dream was the eventual establishment of what came to be called Temple University School of Theology. Under the leadership of Dean J. S. Ladd Thomas, the School of Theology reached its peak enrollment of 280 students in 1956. At the time they represented twenty-two Protestant groups. More than half of these students were in various stages of progress toward a Master of Sacred Theology (STM) or a Doctor of Sacred Theology (STD) degree. The faculty consisted of nine full-time and six part-time instructors, most of the latter having been drawn from the ranks of professors with national reputations who had retired from other institutions.

In the spring of 1956 the School of Theology was visited by a team representing the American Association of Theological Schools (AATS) for the purpose of evaluating its total operation. On April 22, 1956, a lengthy report of the visiting team, written by D. D. Williams, was forwarded to Dean Thomas. As one would expect, the visitors were critical of the School of Theology with respect to various points, notably its program. It especially raised questions about such matters as faculty load, course structure (all courses being only two hours), and particularly the attempt to carry on a doctoral program of considerable size with a group of eminent, though only part-time scholars.

Alerted to the deficiencies pointed out by Dr. Williams, the Temple Administration made an attempt to correct them. A faculty committee consisting of Dr. Richard Kroner, Dr. Howard Slaatte, and me as chairman, consulted with various theological faculties. On October 12, the committee agreed upon a completely revised Bachelor of Sacred Theology (STB) program which, with some changes, was adopted by the faculty of the School of Theology on November 1, 1956.

Much more difficult for the University Administration was the matter of dealing with the remaining problems. One was the creation of a separate theology library upon which the AATS insisted. At considerable expense such a library was established about one block away from the University Library, though it contained only ca. 15,000 volumes. The most vexing problem, however, was the matter of faculty load. The STB program in particular served almost exclusively the needs of Protestant groups, while the university as a whole became increasingly dependent upon state aid. Hence, funding the salaries of additional full-time faculty members would take considerable time and effort. Even as it was, the university had projected for the coming year a subsidy of $513 for every full-time student in the School of Theology.

Because of this situation the faculty of the School of Theology became increasingly apprehensive about the future of an STB program, which would of necessity have to continue to be specifically designed to serve a Protestant constituency. Thus, in a memo submitted to the School of Theology faculty in the beginning of 1957, the writer suggested among other things the need for a graduate program which "should be an autonomous unit within the structure of the university." His hope was that this could be done with the cooperation of the Graduate Council. Requested by Dean Thomas to pursue the matter further, an informal discussion involving our theological faculty members about a graduate program in theology (as yet, the word "religion" was not used) was held January 23, 1957. The upshot of that discussion was that our graduate degrees must continue to be essentially academic, though a professional STM might be considered. This was our response to various suggestions by alumni and others (faculty members of neighboring seminaries) who had advised us that we might consider giving Master of Theology (ThM) and Doctor of Theology (ThD) degrees, which would be essentially professional in nature. We rejected this suggestion because it again seemed to be an option which would serve in the main the Protestant community.

At the same time, we decided to find out whether there might not be instructional collaboration between the graduate faculty of the School of Theology and the graduate faculties of other units of the university, as well as those of neighboring institutions. We further explored the question as to whether the graduate faculty of the School of Theology might henceforth work under the aegis of the Graduate Council of the university. The whole set of problems was to be discussed with Provost Millard Gladfelter at a future meeting.

The requested meeting was held on February 26, 1957. Though the School of Theology faculty appreciated the efforts of the Administration to meet the AATS conditions for continued accreditation of the STB program, it was apprehensive about the possibility of funding it under prevailing conditions. Hence the bulk of the discussion was focused on the need for a graduate program in the religious field which could be shaped to serve a much broader purpose. While it was decided to continue upon established lines regarding the STB and the STM levels, the decision was also made that steps shall be taken "to set up a graduate department of religion (this word used for first time) working under the Graduate Council of the University which would guide the work toward the PhD degree." The minutes of that meeting with Provost Gladfelter further state, that "this committee could ask the Dean of the College of Liberal Arts regarding the formation of a department of religion." (Spring 1957) This subcommittee, later referred to as "special committee," and finally as "graduate committee," was admonished to "begin working at once."

The graduate committee members were originally Dr. Richard Kroner, Dr. Howard Slaatte, and me. Since I brought the matter before the faculty, I was asked to be chairman, and remained so during the entire transitional period.

Not being able to proceed on both the graduate level and undergraduate level at the same time, the committee decided to give priority to the establishment of a graduate program. Our reasoning was twofold: on one hand we felt, as previously indicated, that such a program would best serve the needs of the broader community. On the other hand, we still had over 60 students in the School of Theology who looked forward to advanced degrees, many of whom, we felt would be drawn into such a program. Hence the next few weeks were spent acquainting ourselves with the graduate programs in religion of other institutions, including Yale and Union Theological Seminary. On May 7, 1957, our collection of ideas "Proposals for a Graduate Program in Religion at Temple University" was ready. They were adopted by the faculty of the School of Theology and forwarded to Provost Gladfelter, Dean Caldwell of the College of Liberal Arts, the Executive Committee of the College of Liberal Arts, as well as a number of professors in that college. Having been encouraged to proceed, the faculty of the School of Theology formally asked Provost Gladfelter on June 5, 1957, to try "to institute a cooperative PhD Program in Religion."

The request was accompanied by an eight page, closely spaced set of proposals. This was forwarded to the Graduate Council of the university, which eventually formed a special committee, chaired by Dr. James Harrison, to deal with the matter. On October 5, 1957 came the first response from Dr. Harrison, asking many questions. Among them was the query as to why we wanted to require German and French rather than Greek and Hebrew, and how we would restrain the program from developing along narrow denominational lines. During the rest of the fall semester of 1957, much time was spent discussing with Dr. Harrison and others of the Graduate Council various details of the projected program and trying to allay the fears and apprehensions of members of the Liberal Arts faculty. In due time the whole effort ended in frustration.

In the meantime, the worst fears of the faculty of the School of Theology were confirmed when the AATS dropped it from the list of accredited theological institutions on December 7, 1957. This had been done without previous notification either of Dean Thomas or President Robert Johnson. It was a rash action which, because of its disastrous effect on Temple, caused the AATS to revise its procedures in the direction of a more cautious approach to enforce its standards. It meant, of course, that during the spring and fall semester of 1958 many of the STB students were forced to transfer to other institutions. Most of the rest declared their intention of doing so before the spring semester of 1959. In addition, Dean J. S. Ladd Thomas and Drs. Andrew Blackwood and Richard Kroner were scheduled to retire in June of 1958, though the latter was persuaded to postpone his retirement. To the faculty it was quite clear that this was the end of any viable STB program at Temple. Yet, on the part of the trustees there remained the hope that somehow it could be continued. Hence a new dean, Dr. Aaron Gast, was eventually chosen to replace acting dean Dr. Harry Hummer, and the school was renamed Conwell School of Theology. The Conwell School continued on the Temple campus for some years, a testimony to the genuine concern on the part of many of the trustees to carry on a program of theological education growing out of Dr. Conwell's original vision. In due time the Conwell School united with the Gordon School of Theology and is today a flourishing institution under the name of Gordon Conwell School of Theology.

Perceiving the plight of the School of Theology, and the apparent failure of the projected cooperative PhD program in religion, the faculty of the philosophy department, led by Drs. John Fisher and Sydney Axinn, decided that the religious heritage of Temple could best be preserved by instituting an MA program in philosophy and religion. During February of 1958 Drs. Axinn and Fisher, and Dr. John Skinner of the School of Theology faculty, together with myself, met several times to discuss details. On March 25, 1958, at a meeting with Provost Gladfelter and Dean William Caldwell of the Liberal Arts College a definite proposal was discussed, which was eventually adopted by the Liberal Arts faculty. The MA Program in Religion and Philosophy was to begin in the spring of 1959, and an announcement of it was printed and distributed. Applicants, however, were few.

About the same time (Spring 1958) it was decided by the Administration that the STM and STD programs were not to accept any new applicants, and somewhat later that they were to be discontinued altogether by 1960. These programs in which ca. 70 students were still enrolled, or had applied to be enrolled, were to be administered by me, who as "chairman of the graduate committee" was now working directly under the authority of the Provost of the university. The task of "finishing out" these programs was made difficult because on May 20, 1958, the faculty of the School of Theology, including the myself, were notified by President Johnson that if the School of Theology were to be dropped or reorganized (something which had become a virtual certainty), their "status with respect to tenure would of necessity be terminated." When the decision to reorganize was eventually reached all fulltime faculty members of the former School of Theology, with the exception of the chairman of the graduate committee, were notified that Temple's contractual relationship with them would end as of June 1958. It was understood, however, that they could be temporarily employed on an adjunct basis.

By the fall of 1958, the lack of student interest in the Master of Arts Program in Philosophy and Religion became generally apparent. Consequently, a special alumni committee of the now defunct School of Theology, upon which the chairman of the graduate committee was also invited to serve, contacted some thirty religious leaders in the area. Regarding this survey, the secretary of this committee reported among other things that "overwhelmingly the opinion of most persons interviewed was the great need for an Interdenominational School of Theology or Religion on the graduate level" (past the Bachelor of Divinity, BD, level). This information was forwarded to Dr. Alexander Mackie, chairman of the appropriate trustee committee, Bishop Fred Pierce Corson, President of the Board of Trustees, as well as Dr. Robert L. Johnson, President of the University, and Provost Dr. Millard Gladfelter. An array of similar opinions by others was brought to the attention of the Administration. The basic intention of all of this effort was to insure the continuance of a graduate program in the field of religion, rather than in religion and philosophy, at Temple.

The first ray of hope came on January 23, 1959, when Dr. Mackie's committee recommended to the Board of Trustees the following resolution: "Resolved, that the Board of Trustees authorize the administrative officers to proceed with the reestablishment of graduate programs in religion and philosophy and the formation of plans that would develop a program and faculty of high quality and excellence." The resolution was forthwith approved by the Board. The importance of this resolution to some of us lay in the fact that it spoke of "the reestablishment of graduate programs (plural) in religion and philosophy." We interpreted that to mean programs in addition to the already approved MA degree in Philosophy and Religion.

The result was a period of considerable confusion. On April 24, 1959, the *Temple News* announced, "Graduate School of Philosophy and Religion, to open next semester, will be the only school in the Philadelphia area which can give a doctorate degree and the local seminaries approve it," it was asserted. "Plans have also been made to offer courses leading to a Master of Arts degree in Philosophy and Religion," the article continued. At the same time the writer of this paper was in charge of the STM and the STD programs which were to be phased out in 1960, but which some of us now regarded as having been given a new lease on life by the above mentioned resolution of the Board of Trustees. In addition to this, some members of the Board of Trustees still clung to the hope that a school of theology leading to a Bachelor of Divinity degree could somehow be brought into existence. As a matter of record, the Graduate School of Philosophy and Religion projected by the *Temple News* never became a reality.

In the hope of clearing up various misconceptions, which understandably abounded, a consultation was arranged with the deans and presidents of neighboring seminaries. It was held on October 9, 1959. At that time I announced to the assembled dignitaries that at Temple now had two graduate programs, one in Philosophy and Religion, leading to an MA, and one in Religion. The latter was reported to lead to a master's degree in three areas, namely, practical theology, history of religions, and religious thought, and a doctor's degree given in two fields—religious thought and the history of religions. The degrees offered were of necessity still designated as STM and STD. What was not stressed was that this program in religion was currently carried on with three full-time and two part-time professors, and that as yet it was not anchored in any college, or even in the Graduate School. Instead, it operated directly under the authority of the Administration. Approximately seventy students were registered in it.

During the fall of 1959, a number of things became very clear to those of us who were concerned about graduate work in the field of religion at Temple:

1. That there was a very great demand for a graduate program in religion at Temple.
2. That such a program had to be anchored in the College of Liberal arts.
3. That to bring this about the help of sympathetic members of the Liberal Arts faculty was essential.
4. That this would necessitate giving MA and PhD degrees acceptable to the Liberal Arts faculty instead of theological degrees based on traditional patterns of study.
5. That the new faculty members who would need to be employed would have to have credentials acceptable to the Liberal Arts faculty.
6. That it would be necessary to establish a department of religion in the College of Liberal Arts, as had already been suggested by the faculty of the School of Theology in the Spring of 1957.

While all this seemed quite obvious to some of us, there was by no means universal agreement with such a course of action. Some members of the seminary faculties in the Philadelphia area tended to think along more traditional lines. Most of the alumni of the School of Theology gave much less than enthusiastic support. Within the faculty of the College of Liberal Arts, feelings about the matter ran the gamut from indifference to intense opposition. Dr. Gladfelter, however, who had become president of the university during the spring of 1959, began to favor the idea. Thus, efforts were now directed toward creating as much understanding of and sympathy with our goals within the faculty of the College of Liberal Arts as possible.

The agent for the establishment of an undergraduate Department of Religion within the College of Liberal Arts was Dr. John Fisher. At a meeting of the College faculty on January 7, 1960, he moved the faculty to adopt the following resolution: "That the College establish an undergraduate Department of Religion with the appointment of a man possessing all the usual academic qualifications, including a PhD degree, who will offer courses of an academic nature in the History and Literature of Religions." He assured the faculty that this was the recommendation of the Executive Committee of the College, of which committee he was chairing at the time. The minutes of the meeting record various objections to such a move, but in the end the motion was passed 29-19. Needless to say, this was a monumental step forward.

The immediate result was that some of us (Fisher, Axinn, Hummer, Stoeffler) were asked by the Administration, and presumably the dean of the college, to find the person who would meet the qualifications of the motion of the Executive Committee. To those of us who were connected with the Graduate Program in Religion this meant two things: First, that we must now work toward having that program connected with the newly established undergraduate Department of Religion, and secondly, that the person hired to chair that department must also qualify for the kind of graduate program in religion that will continue to attract students. On the basis of opinions advocated by some members of the Liberal Arts faculty this could by no means be taken for granted. We were cognizant, furthermore, of the fact that the credentials of this person would also have to transcend the problem that was seldom mentioned, but which was always in the background, namely, whether he/she was going to be a Catholic, Jew, or Protestant, thus presumably affording one or the other of these religious communities an undue advantage.

While this search was going on, and in order to promote the idea of a continuing Graduate Program in Religion, another meeting of the heads of neighboring seminaries was called March 23, 1960. Hoping with somewhat foolhardy optimism that this program would eventually be joined with the undergraduate Department of Religion in the College of Liberal Arts, we now boldly talked about a PhD program in Religion, centered in the areas of history of religion and religious thought, thus brushing aside the repeated suggestions coming from that quarter of a more traditional ThM and ThD program. A committee was formed, consisting of Drs. Fisher, Axinn, Huganir (Dean of the Graduate School), and me, to discuss the details of such a PhD program. My additional concern at the time was stated in a letter to Dean Huganir on August 17, 1960. It said, in part: "In establishing a PhD program in religion we must consider the point of view of theological educators along with that of liberal arts people." Behind that statement lay various pressures coming from the Liberal Arts side to shape the projected Graduate Program in Religion in a way that would make it a religion program in name only.

Through the year 1960 the search for a chairman of the mandated undergraduate Department of Religion in the College of Liberal Arts continued. It ended in the office of Vice-President for Academic affairs, Dr. Paul Anderson, when it was decided to bring Dr. Bernard Phillips on board. His credentials, as well as the interview we had with him in Dr. Anderson's office, seemed to meet both the concerns of the Liberal Arts faculty and of those of us who were in the still existing Graduate Program in Religion. Thus Dr. Phillips joined the Liberal Arts faculty in the fall of 1961. During the fall semester he taught only undergraduate courses, but his strong and resourceful leadership quickly became a major factor in bringing the existing Graduate Program in Religion and the undergraduate Department of

Religion in the College of Liberal Arts together. This marriage took place during the spring semester of 1962. Thus, on April 13, 1962 I wrote a letter to Dr. Gladfelter which in part read as follows:

> Dear President Gladfelter: Yesterday Dean Smith has finalized my appointment to the faculty of the College of Liberal Arts and Sciences. This brings to an end a long period of uncertainty with regard to my place at Temple.... It is a source of deep satisfaction for me to find that the Department of Religion in the College of Liberal Arts has become a reality. Its basic structure is the sort of thing I had long envisioned and I sincerely believe that we are on the right track.... I take the liberty to address to you this note since it was under your direction that I first began to dream about and work for such a program.

With the establishment of a Department of Religion as we now have it (February 1962) the problems of those of us who were concerned about religious studies at Temple did not cease. They were simply shifted to another level. But the strong leadership of Dr. Phillips, and all those of who gradually came on board, beginning with Joseph Weber and thereafter Paul van Buren, made it a joy to have a part in one of the very significant academic developments in our country. What the future holds is largely in their hands.

BERNARD PHILLIPS:
An Appreciation

HAROLD KASIMOW

According to the Baal Shem Tov, the founder of Hasidism, all human encounters have significance. The truth of this teaching was borne out in my own life by the profound effect that several remarkable teachers had on me as a graduate student in the Religion Department at Temple University from 1967 to 1972. Among them were Maurice Friedman (my dissertation advisor), Robert Gordis, Jacob Agus, Gerard Sloyan, Ismail al Faruqi, Leonard Swidler, Thomas Dean, Richard De Martino, Ernest Stoeffler, Roderick Hindery, Franklin Littell, and Alan Lazaroff. But it was Bernard Phillips who was my mentor and role model. I have been living with his spirit all of my academic life. By the time I met him in 1967, he said that he was more interested in finding saints, that is, truthful people, than in finding the truth. He told me that from the faces of truthful people the sun shines. Whenever I was with him I felt that the sun was shining.

It was through Phillips that I became enticed by Asian religions. He introduced me to Hinduism, Buddhism, Chinese thought, and Sufism, the mystical dimension of Islam. I can still remember how I was taken by some of the Hindu teachers such as Sarvepalli Radhakrishnan, Ananda Coomaraswamy, and especially Swami Vivekananda. I was especially moved by a statement that Vivekanada made at the World Parliament of Religions on September 11, 1893: "I am proud to belong to a religion which has taught the world both tolerance and universal acceptance. We not only believe in universal toleration, but we accept all religions as true."

Everything that I was studying with Phillips was new to me. Yet at the same time it corresponded to my own religious views, which I learned from my great teacher Abraham Joshua Heschel as an undergraduate at the Jewish Theological Seminary in New York City. Heschel said, "In this aeon diversity of religions is the will of God," and "Holiness is not the monopoly of any particular religious tradition…The Jews do not maintain that the way of the Torah is the only way of serving God." He also said that religion is a means, not an end. According to Heschel the aim of religion is to transform us, to have concern for others, which makes us truly human. It seems to me that what was most critical for Heschel, as for Phillips, was not what religion a person belonged to but how human he or she really is. What is most significant is not what tradition a person follows but how he or she lives life.

Bernard Phillips created the vision for the graduate program of religion at Temple University, hiring representatives of each of the major world religions to teach their own traditions and at the same time to also be critical of them. Phillips wanted people who could train students broadly in the history of religion, in comparative religion, and in comparative mysticism. To his great credit, he brought in teachers whose views were radically different from his own. He encouraged me, a Jew (and Holocaust survivor!—Swidler), and John Esposito, a Catholic, to take courses with Ismail al Faruqi, one of the outstanding Muslim teachers in America of traditional Islam, even though al Faruqi was very critical of Sufism, which was dear to Philips.

I believe that the vision Phillips tried to create at Temple University is the one articulated by Ananda Coomaraswamy, who said that ideally the great religions would be taught by those who confess them. For Phillips, to really know a religious tradition one must live that tradition. So, while he was studying Zen Buddhism, he lived in Zen monasteries in Japan, spending a year there while editing a book on D. T. Suzuki. When Phillips became interested in Sufism he traveled to Algeria to find an authentic Sufi, whom he later invited to lecture in the United States. What was key for Phillips was that you must make your religion your own.

For Phillips the spiritual approach to religion required the complete giving of oneself to the task or the person who is before you. Phillips, who was influenced by Martin Buber, used many Hasidic tales in his writings to present his vision of authentic religion, especially tales that stressed the hallowing of the everyday and tales which illustrated that the most important thing in life was to be fully present to what you are doing at this very moment. He defined religion as the love of life. For him the truly religious person was the lover of life, and to love life means to be in creative union with life: "Love is the perception of the infinite in the finite."

I am deeply grateful to Dr. Phillips. He has played a major role in how I teach comparative religion and in my becoming active in dialogue with members of other religious traditions. I also realize that a number of the crucial touchstones of reality for Phillips have become touchstones for me. I try always to remember his caution:

> The danger in reading too much about the spiritual, and the danger in attending too many conferences on the spiritual life, is that one may come to imagine that hearing about the truth, talking about the truth, thinking about the truth, reading about the truth is the same thing as the living of the truth.

"REMEMBERING PAUL" GEDENKSYMPOSION FÜR PAUL M. VAN BUREN ÖKUMENISCHES INSTITUT, UNIVERSITÄT HEIDELBERG, JULI 2-3, 1999

THOMAS DEAN

I. Introduction

You are gathered today to honor the memory of *Paul M. van Buren*, your co-worker at the *Ecumenical Institute* in Heidelberg over the last decade, at the *Shalom Hartman Institute* in Jerusalem for a decade, and my colleague in the Department of Religion at Temple University in Philadelphia for twenty years. We come together to celebrate his career among us and in so doing to renew our own dedication to the life of teaching and scholarship, and to the struggle for religious and national reconciliation, to which he was so passionately devoted and which he so splendidly embodied until the very end.

Paul Matthews van Buren was born in Norfolk, Virginia on April 20, 1924. He died—for his family and for us, all too soon—in a hospital near Little Deer Isle, Maine on June 18, 1998. His ashes were scattered at sea off the coast of Maine. Death was due to cancer, a disease that had afflicted him even before he had come to Temple University thirty years ago. Ironically, it was the effects of the radiation treatment which had overcome the disease years earlier that rose up these many years later to strike him down. Such are the mysterious ways of illness and "cure," life and death.

I knew Paul van Buren, as for the most part we know each other, in a context limited primarily to our shared life in an academic department in a large, impersonal, urban university. It was in that setting that I formed my impressions of him as a brilliant scholar, challenging teacher, respected chairman, and engaging colleague of the highest personal, intellectual and academic integrity. He practiced excellence in all that he did and worked tirelessly to help his department meet the same high standards. On his shoulders above all rested the claim that our department had to achieve national and international recognition as a place where serious work could be done. His colleagues and students alike held him in the highest esteem. He was our shining prince.

II. His Background

Before we recount the story of Paul's career at Temple for those who knew him as a colleague in another venue, it may be of interest to hear something of his education and career before he came to Temple in the fall of 1964. The son of a graduate in engineering from the U.S. Naval Academy at Annapolis, Maryland, Paul van Buren was born in 1924 in Norfolk, Virginia, a navy town on the coast of the Atlantic Ocean. Shortly thereafter his family moved to Staten Island in New York and then to Glendale, Ohio. After graduating from high school, he served during World War II for a year as a seaman in the United States Coast Guard Reserve and then as an aviation cadet in the Naval Air Force from 1942 to 1945. After leaving the Service in 1945 he attended Harvard University where he majored in Government, specializing in political theory, receiving a bachelor's degree *cum laude* in 1948 (class of 1946, delay due to three year's war service). This was followed by a Bachelor of Divinity *cum laude* from the Episcopal Theological School in Cambridge, Massachusetts in 1951. In that same year he was ordained an Episcopal priest in the diocese of Southern Ohio. He earned his doctorate in theology under Karl Barth at the Universität

Basel, *summa cum laude*, with a dissertation on Calvin's doctrine of reconciliation—foreshadowing what was to be a lifelong concern academically and practically. It was published in 1957 as *Christ in Our Place: The Substitutionary Character of Calvin's Doctrine of Reconciliation*.

After Basel and prior to taking his first teaching position, Paul served first as the co-rector of St. Thomas Episcopal Church in Detroit, Michigan, from 1954 to 1956, then curate of St. Paul's Cathedral in Detroit from 1956 to 1957, and later as a theological advisor to the Detroit Industrial Mission, working in the poor sections of the city.

Paul assumed his first teaching post as an Assistant Professor of Systematic Theology at the Episcopal Seminary of the Southwest in Austin, Texas in 1957, where he was promoted to the rank of Associate Professor of Systematic Theology in 1960. There he came to know a young German theologian who was teaching at a nearby seminary. His name was Dietrich Ritschl [Dietrich was also the first Book Review Editor of the *Journal of Ecumenical Studies*, 1964-; Swidler]. After teaching systematic theology there for seven years, Paul came to the Department of Religion at Temple University as an Associate Professor in the fall of 1964

In a memo in 1965 responding to Temple University's request for biographical information about one of its newest faculty members, Paul wrote: "The above list of facts is all correct and says almost nothing about me. The facts of my life which provide far more information, however, are not so simply listed. It would start, I suppose, with a very normal youngster of moderately affluent and proper background who began to wake up during a monotonous stint with the Navy during a monotonous war, who had only two and a half years left of college to make something of, who was led by one professor into an interest in theology which was not quite killed in seminary and led him to three exciting years with Professor Karl Barth in Switzerland, the effects of which took some time to wear off. I only discovered Ludwig Wittgenstein at the point in life in which I had begun to realize that life is something to be lived in the present, that living is not quite the same thing as accomplishing, being not quite the same as doing. This led to a course of exploration in which I suppose I shall continue for the rest of my life, exploring persons, human life, and human thought, one puzzling piece of which is that which we identify (not knowing quite what else to do with it) with the tag 'religion.'" In fact, because of something that happened to him in the 1970s, it was to be the effects of Wittgenstein that eventually wore off while the works of Barth returned to provide him with new stimulus for the remainder of his theological career.

His wife, Anne, supplied some interesting footnotes to Paul's commentary on his own biography. Paul, she says, was only an "indifferent student" when he first went to college. However, apparently to relieve the monotony of military service, he ended up spending a good deal of time in the base library where he discovered the works of Harold Lasski, the socialist English political theorist. When he returned to Harvard to finish the "only two and a half years left of college," a period which all of a sudden seemed too short for the intellectually awakened young scholar, he chose to focus on political theory.

Even so, as his college days were drawing to a close he apparently had no further academic ambitions. Challenged by his Presbyterian (i.e., Calvinist!) future wife, "What are you going to *do* with your life? What are you going to *contribute* to people?" he opined he would become a boat designer and builder, work that would bring him back to his beloved Atlantic Ocean—and as for service to humanity, well, he could always be a Boy Scout leader!

But the story took an unexpected turn. At about the same time Paul went through an important personal experience, perhaps on the order of a conversion experience. At the funeral service for Paul's maternal grandmother, his grandfather, Paul Matthews, an Episcopal bishop and Paul's namesake, read the famous passage from I

Corinthians 13 ["If I have all the eloquence of men or angels, but speak without love, I am simply a gong booming or a cymbal clashing.... In short, there are three things that last: faith, hope and the greatest of these, love."— Swidler] It must have struck home, because the next day young Paul went to his grandfather and told him he had decided to enter the ministry.

This happened in the summer before his senior year. Back at Harvard in the fall of 1947 Paul needed a subject for his senior thesis. His senior tutor, Samuel Beer, asked him what he was planning to do in life and when Paul said he was planning to enter the ministry, Beer handed him a book by the then most popular American theologian and political thinker, Reinhold Niebuhr. It was Niebuhr's magnum opus, *The Nature and Destiny of Man*. His appetite for theology by now whetted, Paul wrote his senior thesis on Niebuhr's doctrine of the nature of man.

At seminary he steeped himself in the great classical and reformation theologians, and in the great twentieth century theologian who had attracted the attention of Americans after WWII, Karl Barth. Paul began to entertain something that no one else in his family had ever done—to work toward a doctorate. But if he was going to undertake such a project, he wanted to study under the best theologian available. For Paul this could only mean one thing: after finishing his seminary studies he would have to go to Europe to pursue his doctoral studies with Karl Barth. In fact, Paul van Buren became the first Episcopalian or Anglican to study under Barth.

(A side note: According to Anne, Paul said to her, "I want to study with Barth because he's the best. If I lived in Origen's time, I'd study with him, even if he was considered a heretic." Anne added, "Paul admired Origen but didn't agree with him"—an interesting foreshadowing of Paul's rather different but fascinating and complex back-and-forth relation to Barth's *oeuvre*!)

Perhaps Anne can tell those of you gathered in Heidelberg stories about Paul's adventures as an American graduate student, initially entirely innocent of German, trying to get up to speed linguistically in order to be accepted as one of Barth's *doktorande*!

III. How He Came to Temple University

You may be interested to know how Paul came to Temple from the Episcopal Seminary of the Southwest in Austin, Texas. Paul's controversial book, *The Secular Meaning of the Gospel*, came out in 1963. When he finished writing it, he decided he wanted to teach in a secular university and went to the professional meeting of the *American Academy of Religion* that year in order to find such a job. There he met the chair of Temple's Religion Department, Bernard Phillips. In those days there was nothing like what we now call a "national search." Rather, Phillips, knowing of Paul's availability, talked with him further about leaving the world of the theological seminary and coming to the world of a secular university department of religion. In a letter of recommendation for Paul written at the time, Gibson Winter noted that "Paul has a fine analytical mind and will probably make one of the significant contributions in the field of theology." He added, "He is not a conventional thinker and probably should have the freedom to work in a university context."

Winter also observed, "If Paul has any faults they are those of forthrightness. This kind of honesty is an absolute prerequisite in a scholar but can often be disturbing to the religious establishment. I think that other members of the Department of Religion would find him a refreshing colleague in their inquiries." Truer words were never spoken, and it is one of the reasons, among many others, why his colleagues and students at Temple came to value him!

In his response in January of 1964, Paul indicated that he was "definitely in the market for next fall." However, Temple's Department of Religion was an unknown quantity, having come into existence only two years earlier. At the time there were only three full-time faculty members in the department. Thus, in his response Paul asked for "whatever written material you may have that would explain the department of religion and its relationship to the rest of the university, as well as whatever information you could give me about not only the present state but also the future prospects or plans for the department." Of course, it was this exciting, young, controversial and decidedly nontraditional theologian who would prove central to the department's "future prospects or plans."

Indeed, Bernard Phillips was a persuasive empire builder. In the early heyday of the department in the 1960's, shortly after he brought Paul van Buren to Temple, he also managed to bring such luminaries as the Protestant patristics scholar, Samuel Laeuchli; the Protestant Free Church and Holocaust Studies historian, Franklin Littell; the Catholic editor of the *Journal of Ecumenical Studies*, Leonard Swidler; the Catholic New Testament scholar, Gerard Sloyan (Swidler and Sloyan participated in reshaping the text of the Oberammergau Passion play to eliminate its antisemitic remarks); the Jewish Buber scholar, Maurice Friedman; the Islamics scholar, Isma'il al Faruqi; the African religions scholar, Leonard Barrett; and the Chinese philosophy scholar, Charles Fu—to name only some of those who were internationally known scholars By 1967, in three short years, the department had grown from a faculty of three to one of sixteen [twenty-one by 1968 – Swidler]. The central figure in its growing national and international prominence and its claim as a uniquely ecumenical, multi-religious venue for the scholarly study of religion was Paul M. van Buren.

Already in his initial correspondence with Professor Phillips in January 1964, Paul made it clear that one of his major concerns was "how much time would be left for study and writing, and in that connection, the university policy on sabbatical and other leaves for research and writing." In a letter of February 1964 Paul returned to this question. He wished to talk further with Phillips "and other powers-that-be who would have some say about research grants, special leaves for research, reduction of teaching for research, etc." This was to remain one of his main preoccupations throughout this teaching career. Paul was a dedicated classroom instructor second to none, but his primary passion and commitment was to his own scholarly work. Temple, a large bureaucratic and public entity beholden to the state legislature, was not always as understanding of this as could have been wished. However, as can be seen from the list of Temple-sponsored research grants and study leaves on his curriculum vitae, for the most part Paul prevailed in his efforts to secure time and space for his own work. For this, the scholarly and religious world will always be grateful.

In a letter asking the dean of the college to authorize bringing Paul to campus for an interview, Professor Phillips gave more of the background that had led to the invitation, including what he saw as Paul's contribution to the department's work and its future. At the same time the letter reflected his appreciation of Paul's situation and Paul's wish to find time for his own research.

> At the meeting of the American Academy of Religion in December I had the chance to meet Dr. Paul van Buren, whose book, *The Secular Meaning of the Gospel*, published last year, has brought him into prominence as one of the most promising younger Protestant thinkers in America today. Professor van Buren is at present teaching at the Episcopal Theological Seminary in Austin but finds the atmosphere too confining for his thought and wishes to find a position in a university. He is a creative and critical thinker with a great zeal for scholarly publication and most of his questions concerning the position here had to do with the opportunities he would have to do research and writing. He would be a real asset in our graduate program and would also nicely supplement the courses now offered in the area of Religious Thought. I am sure that his name will grow and that he would reflect glory on Temple if we can get him.

After Paul's visit later that month, Professor Phillips wrote him to discuss an appointment at the rank of associate professor and a salary of [the munificent sum!] of $11,000.

Things soon hit a snag, however. In a letter of March 5th to Professor Phillips, Paul reported that not only had the dean of the Episcopal Seminary of the Southwest made a counter offer meeting Temple's salary but also proposing to promote Paul to the rank of full professor; furthermore, it seemed that Temple University was not the only institution interested in this hot new young theologian. On March 2nd Paul had gotten a phone call from the dean of the Church Divinity School of the Pacific in Berkeley, California that followed up on a conversation Paul had had the previous month with the dean of the Graduate Theological Union which was being put together from the faculties of six theological schools in the San Francisco area. With characteristic frankness, Paul indicated that he was still interested in "the idea of Temple and your department," but not if it would involve sacrifice of tenure and income. Again, he asked about assurances concerning the possibility of a leave of absence early in his career at Temple.

The very next day, March 6th, Paul sent a follow-up letter reporting that an offer had come through from the two California institutions. Its strengths: a larger salary than Temple's, full moving expenses, the imminent possibility of an even larger salary figure, and "participation in a very strong and interesting graduate faculty." Its weaknesses: "moving further west rather than back to a part of the United States with which I am more familiar, and the fact that half of my job would be within a denominational seminary." He added: "For me, then, the pros and the cons are both quite strong." He promised Phillips that "I will not prolong this more than a week."

Phillips' reply of March 9th was interesting. He could not meet the higher salary offer, nor could he guarantee a study leave during the first three years of the appointment. He said he did not envy Paul's having to decide between the alternatives confronting him. And while he could not presume to tell Paul what to do, he could only note that "the choice seems to be basically one between a university situation with its advantages and disadvantages and a seminary situation with its advantages and disadvantages. In the end, where one cannot have everything, one must decide what it is that one wants most of all. And that's not always an easy decision to make."

Sometime during the following week, Paul, as promised, had made his decision. His letter of March 18th is for the first time addressed to "Dear Professor Phillips, or if I may, Dear Bernard." In his reply of March 23rd, Bernard for the first time writes to "Dear Paul." Paul van Buren was coming to Temple.

In an interview in 1966, Paul was asked whether there had been a connection between his book, *The Secular Meaning of the Gospel* and the change in his thinking that it represented; and his decision to leave the world of the theological seminary and move to the world of the religion department in a secular university. Paul answered, "I suppose the book indicates the kind of interests and a certain way of going at the theological problem which I felt could be more fruitfully carried out in the context of a university than in the context of a seminary. That is, I wanted to be able to go at the problem in ways in which the problem posed itself for me rather than as a way it would be posed for me by satisfying the theological curriculum appropriate for men studying to go into the ordained ministry."

IV. His Academic and Teaching Career at Temple University

In arranging for Paul van Buren to come to the Department of Religion at Temple University, Bernard Phillips succeeded in landing not only "one of the most promising younger Protestant thinkers in America," but also, as I have already indicated, "a dedicated classroom instructor second to none." This emerges clearly from the Annual Faculty Reports he submitted to the dean. These reports, required of all faculty members, listed such things as publications, scholarly work in progress, service to the university, and a category labeled "Teaching." Most faculty contented themselves with simply listing the courses they taught that year. Not Paul. From the very first year he wrote extensive analyses, frankly evaluating his own teaching success or lack thereof, and pulling no punches in his assessment of the quality and work of his students, undergraduate and graduate alike. Some sample comments over the years:

1964-65: "I have not even begun to hit my stride in undergraduate teaching. I find it exceedingly difficult to hit or even find the optimum level for classes containing freshmen who cannot write a well-constructed paragraph and have never, apparently, written an essay, and seniors who are able to do outside work on their own and contribute from their own work in discussions and papers. I find I have a great deal to learn in this area, but that this is coming as I have more experience with it.

"As for the graduate teaching, I can say quite simply that what I have been trying to accomplish is to get the students to read and think critically, to see the strengths and weaknesses of any argument, to refrain from taking sides on an issue until they have explored the question from a number of angles.

"A good deal of my teaching occurs outside of the classroom. At the request of a group of our advanced graduate students, I have been leading an informal colloquium in which we discuss in depth some of the major problems in contemporary religious thought.

"As the graduate program in Religion settles down, it should be possible to exercise more discrimination in selecting students. I would judge that maybe a quarter to a third of those now studying with us are not really up to a serious doctoral program and will not make the grade. I am delighted to find, however, that our top students are of a caliber that would be outstanding in any graduate program in the country."

1965-66: "This year has been for me the best year yet as far as teaching is concerned. I am not entirely sure why it is that I have found it so much more exciting or that the response of the students seems to have been so much better. The second wind I have seem to have acquired was due in part to the fact that I had a group of able students, in part to the fact that I had done a good bit of work on the material of our research, in part due to the fact that after a year and a half at Temple, I seemed to begin to hit my stride here."

Speaking of his participation in helping to develop a new foundation course for all further graduate work in religious thought, he said that "I find this time well spent, as it is going to go a long way in setting the tone of our particular emphasis in this department in making a graduate program we can be proud of."

In addition to his regular instructional duties, Paul had also given guest lectures at ten other academic institutions that year. Noting that this represented less than ten percent of invitations he had received "during a year in which a great deal of mostly unfounded publicity attended some of us involved in contemporary religious thought," he observed that "the time given to these outside lectures was given not in order to 'contribute to my professional development,' but as a service to the department and our graduate program—i.e., I judge that the time was not wasted and helped the standing of the department and of our program as one devoted to the serious critical study of religion, rather than as a center of flamboyant theatricals in up-to-datism." Throughout his career Paul continued to perform this service for the department.

1968-69: Paul described this year as "a fundamental turning point" in his teaching. "I have defined my major goals to my students during the past year as seduction, not rape. I have quite openly warned them that I was out to convert them to a way of seeing problems of thought as being problems in the working of our language. So important do I consider this shift in our thinking about language, so fundamentally do I think that this way of seeing these problems is part and parcel of the actual role or function of language in our actual lives as linguistic beings, that I do not see much point in turning to specifically religious questions until we find out what sorts of things different sorts of questions are in human life.

"All this is by way of saying that 1969 has been a fundamental turning point in my life as a teacher. Never before have I found teaching to be so exciting, so exhausting and so rewarding. I have gotten into contact with the minds and thoughts of students in a way which I never have before. It surely has something to do with the next spirit in the air these days (Thomas Dean note: the days of protest against the Vietnam War), for it is an important part of what I am doing in teaching that I find I stand very close to the students in their criticisms of our society and in their quest for a new form of life. To put it in a word, I think they are great.

"It is, as I keep reminding them, their education, not mine, which is at stake after all, although in another way, this year has been an education for me, an education in a new sort of flexibility in style, openness and defensiveness in spirit, and the sheer delights of watching now one, now another student begin to get turned on intellectually and start doing some thinking on their own."

1972-73: But things were about to change. The country, and with it Paul, had grown dispirited. In the fall of 1972 Paul had sent a memo to his colleagues in the area of religious thought proposing the formation of a "continuing seminar in the problems *of*, as well as problems *in*, the study of religious thought." His hope was to persuade his colleagues to join with him "to explore problems in religious thought in a cross-religious, cross-cultural, cross-philosophical-traditions setting, for our mutual edification." He saw the merits of such a seminar being "to learn how different problems present themselves differently in different traditions." But it would require of his colleagues to commit to "the task of trying to listen, understand, and make yourselves understood by colleagues who share no more nor less than genuine puzzlement about religious thought." He seemed to be searching for new stimuli for his own thinking, as if he just about exhausted what he wanted to do in the area of linguistic analysis of religious language, the subject of his two most recent books. (see below: V. His Publications)

As he put it in his annual report in the spring of 1973, "I have been casting about for where to turn next and must report that I have not come up with an answer. Whether it is turning 49, post-publication (of the book) depression, the uninspiring results of teaching poorly equipped students this semester, or the effects of the cultural climate, for whatever cause, I find myself feeling at loose ends about my job and my work. I find this psychologically inadequate and, for me, a novel and unpleasant state of affairs. Like it or not, however, I find myself getting a bit tired of the philosophy of religion, at which I have been working for a dozen years, and not even convinced as I once was that education is so valuable an occupation. Maybe the political campaign and its Watergate aftermath have been getting to me and making me cynical. I am not giving in to this mood and it may pass, but in all honesty, I find it remarkably difficult to think concretely and positively about my future development. However, it may be that this year will have fitted into it, I cannot at this time see what its contribution has been." His intellectual and spiritual crisis, if that is what it was, was clearly related to what was going on in the world around him, not only the department, or the university, but also society.

His annual report to the dean that year makes for gloomy reading. "To place what I have been doing and what has been happening to me during this year in the context of my department and then in the larger context of the college—and indeed, why not in the larger context of our society—is to place them in a time of hesitation, uncertain direction, and doubt. There lurks ever present in the wings the economic squeeze, the feeling that we have to get by on what we have, or rather, stretch our limited talents and assets to prove to a world (that can live very well without us) that we should at least be tolerated. The climate, undoubtedly, has hardly been propitious for higher education, least of all for an institution such as ours which is still struggling to rise out of a past more nearly associated with public secondary education, in its goals, ambitions and self-understanding.

What is so terribly debilitating, however, is to live with the double-standard of paying lip-service to an academic image that is belied by our actual life and work. The same duplicity and fraud that permeates our society also permeates the life of Temple.

"And the department? Well, in all frankness, the same applies. There has been some sound consolidation this year, and we are slowly but surely bringing order into the chaos resulting from seven years of absurdly rapid growth and hardly the most responsible leadership. Anyway, it is clear that there is not a first-rater among us, not one. We have some who are perfectly good second-raters, and perhaps two at lower ranks who may yet turn out better than that, but we have talked too much of 'stars' and 'names' without in fact being able to point to one whose standing is recognized in his fields as a first-rate scholar. What we do have that is important is a pretty good program and a faculty wide and diverse enough to make for programs that are quite a bit stronger than the individuals who teach in them."

1974-1976: But another change was about to take place, one with exciting consequences for Paul, and one that was to open up a path that would engage him with renewed energy, passion, and commitment for the rest of his life. In the fall of 1974 Paul van Buren "moved up" to administration. He agreed to serve as the chairman of the Department of Religion. Despite the fact that the move was not envisaged as way to solve the above-mentioned intellectual or spiritual crisis—in fact it was probably intended simply as a way to gain temporary breathing space while he figured out what he wanted to do next— it was a move destined to have a dramatic impact on his subsequent career as a thinker. As he recalled it seven years later, "I had reached the limits of what I could do to understand religion with the help of Ludwig Wittgenstein, and I was not impressed with the results. I found instead that I was becoming increasingly bored by philosophical analysis. I therefore gave in to the urging of colleagues and accepted something I had avoided all my life: administrative work. I took the chairmanship of the religion department at Temple

University in 1974." To accept the post, he had to turn down a coveted study leave for the academic year 1974-75, but given the fact that he was at complete "loose ends" about the next stage of his scholarly career, perhaps it was not such a difficult decision after all. In any case, what he could not have foreseen was that this temporary step aside into administration would open up the whole world of Judaism in a totally new way, in a sense for the very first time.

By the end of his two-year term as chair, Paul van Buren had come to another major decision. Fired by enthusiasm for the new theological vista that had opened before him, but disenchanted with the academic situation at the university, on the other, in the fall of 1976 he wrote to the new chair: "Basically, I have decided that I shall not return to Temple full-time. I want to live with Anne (she had an academic position at Tufts University in Boston), and I want more time to work on theology." To the dean he said, "May I add that I am having the time of my life, on some days getting in up to 8 even 10 hours of reading and note-taking, which has sent me to the oculist, but which is proving the most stimulating, exciting time of my life. I have a terrible itch to start putting things together on paper, but with a book published last month, I am trying to restrain the urge to write until I have built a broader and deeper foundation." Clearly a corner had been turned in his life and his research, and he was eager to proceed full steam ahead. The alternatives, as he saw them, were either to resign from Temple or to renegotiate his relationship with Temple.

Reluctant to lose Paul, "both in terms of his international reputation as a creative scholar and as a colleague in the work of the department," the chair urged the dean to approve Paul's proposal for a reduction to what would in effect be a half-time appointment, focused on graduate teaching only. The dean readily agreed, and so Paul was to continue his relationship with the department for another decade until his "early retirement" in 1986.

(For a partial list of the graduate seminars Paul taught at Temple University from 1964 to 1986, please see the Appendix at the end of this document.)

During his tenure in the Department of Religion at Temple University, Paul van Buren also served as a visiting professor/lecturer on numerous occasions at other universities and theological faculties both in America and abroad. Simply to list them is to give you some idea of the esteem in which he was held outside Temple: Guggenheim Fellow and Fulbright Senior Lecturer at Oxford University, 1967-68; Visiting Professor, Princeton Theological Seminary, summer 1973; Visiting Professor, Andover Newton Theological Seminary, spring 1980; Visiting Professor, Harvard Divinity School, spring 1981; Senior Fellow, National Endowment for the Humanities, 1982-1983; Visiting Professor, Union Theological Seminary, New York, spring 1984.

V. His Research and Publications

Paul van Buren authored numerous publications and scholarly presentations at academic conferences, research institutes, and religious venues in America and abroad. As one scholar noted, "Over the past forty years Paul van Buren has let the gospel coax him, with an abandon reminiscent of the holy recklessness of his New Testament namesake, into theological minefields. The record of his writings reads like a chronicle of the central theological issues of our time." One could go further: Paul's works not only reflected but also shaped and are still reshaping the landscape of contemporary Christian thought and interreligious relations. An overview of his book length works may give a sense of the intellectual, spiritual and ecclesial concerns and the fascinating development of this remarkable, passionate, and original theologian, philosopher and religious thinker. In addition to his study on Calvin, Paul published eight major works.

His second and perhaps most well-known work was *The Secular Meaning of the Gospel* (Macmillan, 1963). In it, Paul attempted to reconstruct "God talk" in terms of a faith focused on the ethical behavior of the historical Jesus. Taking his point of departure from Bonhoeffer's view of Christianity "come of age," and employing the philosophical method of linguistic analysis with its focus on speaking meaningfully about God in what seemed an increasingly "secular" age, he worked out an entirely original interpretation of the gospels which, one commentator noted, "bridged linguistic analysis, demythologizing with its existentialist background, and classical theology as restated in recent years by Bonhoeffer and Barth."

What had happened to transform this student of the neo-orthodox theologian Karl Barth into the secularizing *infant terrible* of the American theological scene? While at the Episcopal Seminary of the Southwest Paul attended a seminar at the University of Texas on Wittgenstein given by the philosopher William Poteat. Up to that time Paul had always been opposed to philosophy—a legacy of his days under Barth and the suspicion of speculative metaphysics or anything hinting of "natural theology." But Wittgenstein's understanding of philosophy as linguistic analysis was a whole different ball game and for Paul it opened up a new vista for how philosophy could be placed in the service of religion. In any case, Paul resolved to recast the traditional supernatural language of theology into the "ordinary language" of the secular age.

This book earned him overnight celebrity nationally and internationally, in both the theological world and the media, as one of four principal American Christian theologians identified with the "Death of God Movement." The "movement" made *Time Magazine*'s April 8, 1966 cover: (link time.com/time/covers/0,16641,19660408,00.html and the others were Thomas J. J. Altizer, William Hamilton, Gabriel Vahanian). One reviewer said that it was "a courageous, naughty, important and disturbing book which, if its main vision is a true one, will make it very difficult for us to swallow whole the Bible, the *kerygma*, Chalcedon and Christendom in the old pious way." The book was subsequently translated into German, Dutch, Spanish, Italian and Norwegian.

Paul himself refused to be included in this alleged "movement." In a letter in 1966 to the president of the university, prepared at the latter's request, Paul wrote as follows: "The 'God is Dead Movement' is an invention of imaginative journalists seeking sensational slogans. It certainly is not a phrase I am given to using myself, its meaning being exceedingly ambiguous. My own work has been focused in recent years, not on the old question of the existence of God, but on the far older question of man's puzzling language about God. By exploring various ways of taking this language, I am seeking and testing interpretations of religious faith which would not be wholly incompatible with the understandings of life which are characteristic of the age in which we live. That this complex and constructive work has been interpreted by poorly informed journalists as simple and negative is a matter I regret but over which I have been able to exercise no control. When the sensationalists have tired of this game and turned to other matters, the deep and important questions of human faith and life will remain. Until that day, it is a time for a sense of humor and patience on the part of those who care about the human spirit."

Asked in 1966 whether he would nevertheless claim for himself the name of "a God is dead theologian," he replied: "Well, the expression is logically absurd. It is a contradiction in terms, strictly, to say that God is dead. One might argue that there never has been a god; or one might say that the way in which Christian theology has spoken of God is such as to lead one to suspect it does not refer to anything; or one might say the way Christian theology has talked about God has been misunderstood by those who think it refers to something. In any case, that about which theology has spoken doesn't fall into a category in which being dead and alive seem to apply."

In his next two books, *Theological Explorations* (1968) and *The Edges of Language: An Essay in the Logic of a Religion* (1972), Paul further extended his philosophical analyses by drawing on the work of William James and Ludwig Wittgenstein, crafting a typically innovative and sophisticated examination of the implications of linguistic analysis and American pragmatism for rethinking the meaning and logic of theological and religious discourse.

Theological Explorations. It might be interesting to pause for a moment and look into the workshop of a thinker to see the process by which the 1968 book emerged. Already in his 1964 correspondence about the Temple position Paul had briefly mentioned to Bernard Phillips the book he was working on subsequent to *The Secular Meaning of the Gospel*: "I now want to explore the meaning of secularism, as a religious category, and of the phenomenon or phenomena of modern culture to which the religious use of the term applies as they would be seen from non-religious perspectives."

One year later, in his annual faculty report in 1965, he reported having finished three-fifths of a manuscript consisting of "a series of connected essays which attempt to break out of the dichotomy of theism versus atheism by setting the problem of religious faith and religious discourse in a setting which, although not exactly new, is certainly not conspicuous in contemporary theology. That is, I have tried to argue that religion may be understood as a function of the human imagination, that faith is related to knowledge as imaginative insight, and that the language of faith makes more sense when compared to the function of poetic language than when it is taken as prose. This book, then, will serve as the development of a hypothesis about the character of religious belief, namely that religion can be fruitfully studied by focusing on the role of imagination in human life, a hypothesis to be tested and perhaps modified through further study."

That he had undertaken a series of "theological explorations" into "a hypothesis to be tested and perhaps modified through further study" and that he was engaged in a rigorous intellectual effort that was not only creative and original but also unsparingly honest and self-critical, may be seen in his faculty report for the following year in 1966. For the first time the name of William James enters the picture alongside that of Wittgenstein, and with that a need to begin re-thinking things all over again. "Perhaps I should report," he tells the dean, "that the manuscript on which I was working at this time last year was about two-thirds finished when I reached a point of sufficient dissatisfaction with the way it was going to abandon it in February, 1966. I found that I was hung up between an aesthetic and a metaphysical approach to the character of religious language. The work I have done on Wittgenstein and especially on James has helped clear the air for me to some extent and I believe I shall be in a position by the end of this spring to define a fresh attack on the problem of the way in which religious language can be interpreted." The book that finally emerged in 1968 was to be "a tripartite exploration of the pluralism of William James, the metaphysics of Ludwig Wittgenstein, the metaphysical assumptions of theism, and the ways (of more than one sort) in which these are interrelated."

The Edges of Language. By the time he wrote his faculty report in 1968 (after a year's leave as a senior lecturer at Oxford), Paul was already hard at work on his next book, the 1972 study on the "logic of *a* religion." It was an effort to work out the implications for the philosophy of religion of Wittgenstein's later works. "Within the area of the analytic philosophy of religion, my research continues at the point of intersection of the philosophy of religion, moral philosophy and metaphysics. Specifically, my research is centered now on ideals, whether or in what way they may be considered moral (i.e., how or in what way they may be said to be guides to conduct), and whether or in what way holding an ideal commits one to holding specifiable beliefs about how things (or the world) is. The other side of this research is the question of whether or in what way the religious 'object' may be regarded as an ideal."

A year later he now described this project with more specificity as "An analysis of non-theistic 'Christian' religion in contemporary western culture. The project is an analysis of the use of language in one particular and identifiable religious position in western culture today, that of non-theistic 'Christianity.' The analysis will show to what extent religious beliefs of this sort are moral beliefs, and to what extent they are metaphysical beliefs, thereby clarifying the role of this particular religion in this particular setting. Such an essay in the analytic philosophy of religion will challenge most of what is being done in this field by arguing that failure to identify, locate and date, to fix clearly in one or another historical and cultural context the so-called 'religious utterances' to be analyzed vitiates the whole analysis. To analyze an ahistorical 'utterance' is to analyze what could not possibly be a religious utterance at all, but only an abstraction."

In his 1970 faculty report, the new book still two years away from publication, Paul had once again arrived at a new discovery in his thinking about the project. "After worrying away at it for some years, I have in the last month made a real breakthrough and come up with a new theory about the linguistic placing of religion, which I can now see I was closing in on during last spring and especially in work this summer. I think I'm on to something really hot, to be worked out in detail during the coming study leave."

Though Paul's philosophical exercises in the analysis of religious language in these two books by now seemed far removed from the doctrinal labors in dogmatic theology he had pursued under Karl Barth, in fact for Paul there was still a connection. In answer to another question in that 1966 interview, "What is the task of the theologian?" Paul had said, "I learned a good deal of my theology under a certain broad definition of the theological task which seems to be on the whole satisfactory: that is, the theologian is one who is engaged in the analysis and investigation of the church's language about God. That would also include many other things that are related to that 'speaking.' In that sense, I consider myself to be a theologian, still engaged in the problem of trying to understand this language and to see how it goes."

In his faculty report in the spring of 1972, with *The Edges of Language* in galleys, Paul was still planning to continue his research in the analysis of religious language, now focusing on the early work of Wittgenstein and its implications for the concept of limits. But this was about to change.

The Burden of Freedom: Americans and the God of Israel. 1976 marked the appearance of a book that heralded an entirely new and totally unexpected development in Paul's scholarly work and indeed in his life-work as well. It appeared to those of us who had been following his work in the logical analysis of religious language a complete *volte face*—a "turning" (*Kehre*), and indeed a "returning," not just a "return," a *Wiederkehr*, but a *Wieder-Kehre* to the classical language of theology *a la* Barth. It was a book that seemed to mark the abandonment of over a decade and a half of work, the period of what one could call "the early van Buren," and that inaugurated the period of "the later van Buren"—the work that in fact was to occupy him for the remainder of his life. For it was in this year that his book, *The Burden of Freedom: Americans and the God of Israel,* appeared.

Writing in a straightforwardly theological way about "freedom, both God's and man's," Paul affirmed the continuing validity of Judaism and its significance as posing a challenge, in America's bicentennial year, to what he saw as Christianity's subjugation to American culture. But the argument cut deeper and went further: "Confronted by the facts of Jewish renewal, the existence of the state of Israel, and the Holocaust out of which these came," Paul wrote, "a few Christians have begun to speak of Judaism in tones markedly different from those which have characterized the first nineteen centuries of the life of the Church.... one began to hear voices calling into question the long-sanctioned anti-Judaism of the churches."

To understand what had happened in the interim between 1972 and 1976 that had brought about this dramatic *intellectual* and indeed *spiritual* change, it is necessary to make a detour through his *administrative* work as chair of our department during the, for him, fateful years 1974-1976.

The year he became department chairman, one of Paul's first duties was to launch a search for a new professor in the area of Jewish studies to replace our departing colleague, Maurice Friedman, the Buber scholar. In an essay entitled "Probing the Jewish-Christian Reality" that appeared in the *Christian Century* in 1981 (June 17-24 issue) in a series entitled, "How My Mind Has Changed," Paul described what happened. Let him tell it in his own words:

> My change of mind in moving from philosophy of religion to the task of systematic theology came roughly in the middle of the decade (the 1970s). I had reached the limits of what I could do to understand religion with the help of Ludwig Wittgenstein, and I was not impressed with the results. I found instead that I was becoming increasingly bored by philosophical analysis. I therefore gave in to the urging of colleagues and accepted something I had avoided all my life: administrative work. I took the chairmanship of the religion department at Temple in 1974.
>
> The first and primary job confronting me was making two appointments in Judaism to replace Jewish colleagues who had left us for other institutions. The process took two years, and I spent a good deal of that time talking with Jewish scholars, reading about Judaism, and reading the works of and finally interviewing candidates. All of those other contacts with the world of Jews and Judaism opened my eyes to something I had been looking at somewhat casually all along but had never really seen: Israel, the Jewish people, the people of God, was definitely alive. 'The synagogue,' 'Jewish legalism,' and all those old slogans of our theological tradition came tumbling down like the house of cards they were. In their place, actual Judaism, the living faith of this living people of God, came into view. I was fascinated.
>
> I was more than fascinated. In the midst of my administrative chores taking more and more of my time, I was set to thinking

furiously. I was far more than fascinated; I was back at my old discipline, wrestling with fundamental issues of systematic theology. What would Christian theology look like if it were corrected at so central a point? Would it even be recognizable as Christian theology?

Whatever my earlier difficulties in understanding the use of the word 'God,' I found that if I were to get anywhere with the problem now confronting me, I had to accept myself as a member of one of those two linguistic communities and therefore to speak with them of the God of whom they both spoke. My older problems did not receive any direct answers. They simply receded into the background, or rather the position from which I had been asking them was no longer one on which I could stand if I were to take seriously this new (or very old) problem. All the old problems remained, but they now appeared to be philosophical problems, not half so burning as the theological ones. I had run into a paradox and an incoherence that made the philosophical ones seem positively trivial. The last third of the decade of the '70s was spent digesting, digging deeper and formulating for publication the results of the change of mind that took place during the middle third.

As Anne summed up the situation, at the time of his crisis Paul had decided that ordinary language analysis was not enough, that more was going on in religion than philosophy could express, and that to understand religion one had to take part in what was going on in the congregation. In Wittgensteinian terms that Paul might have used, one had to take part in the "language game" and become a member of the "linguistic community" where religious language was actually used. For Paul this meant returning to what he trained under Barth to do—to serve as a "church theologian."

By the fall of 1976 Paul was deep into what was to become a three-volume effort at rethinking the entire theological relationship between Christianity and Judaism. As he reported in a letter to Franklin Littell, the new chair of the department, "I'm deep into Barth's *Israellehre*, and it goes so centrally into his doctrine of God, election, Christology, etc. that I am staggered at the task which I have set myself. Reworking all those interlocking and deep problems is going to be quite a job! The real difficulty in Barth's thought is that he clearly never seems to have been thinking about or talking to living Jews. His *Israellehre* is dialectical, when it needed to be dialogical. Yet for all that, he is the first to have tackled the problem, and for all its short-comings, he did make Judaism a crucial item right within the agenda of serious theology. That was surely an absolute *novum* in the whole history of the Christian theological tradition and one that has still not been sufficiently appreciated." Paul van Buren would see to it that that situation was rectified, but of course in his own creative and original way.

To continue with his 1981 narrative: "In my last conversation with Karl Barth, in 1961—a conversation that was for both of us in some ways painful—I asked him what he expected of his former students, seeing that he was so dissatisfied with what I was then doing (i.e., developing what was to be *The Secular Meaning of the Gospel*). Barth's answer was that every page of his *Dogmatics* was in need of improvement and that we should set to work to make it better. I took him to mean that we should be devoting ourselves to writing footnotes on his work. Instead, I took another path which led to some dozen years of working in analytic philosophy of religion, and that was where I was when the '70s began. By the end of the decade, however, I was at work at the task that Barth had asked of me, not as I then heard it, but as I now hear it. The dogmatic or systematic theological work of the church, of which Barth's *Church Dogmatics* is a distinguished crown, is indeed in need of serious correction on every page, and with the years that remain, I mean to continue the task of trying to improve it."

"Let me conclude with three points the clarification of which will help define how my mind has changed in the past decade. The points are that I am now a Christian, doing systematic theology, not 'Holocaust theology.'

"First, I am a Christian, not a Jew. The more I learn about Judaism and the Jewish people, the clearer it becomes that I am not a

Jew, not an 'honorary Jew,' not a Jew by adoption or election. I am a gentile, a gentile who seeks to serve the God of Israel because as a Christian I share in the call of that God to serve him in his church, alongside, not as part of, his people Israel. As a gentile I am bound to that God not by *Torah* but by Jesus Christ.

"Second, I have returned to the work I left off in the beginning of the '60s, the self-critical task of the church called systematic theology. I have now found a new lens, Judaism, through which to carry on this work, but I am finding Karl Barth once more to be a superbly stimulating and helpful teacher, especially at the points where I must disagree with him. He is proving to be a better guide than Calvin, Luther, Thomas, Augustine, Athanasius or Irenaeus (with all of whom he was in continuous dialogue) because he was both more thorough and more rigorously systematic down to the smallest detail." (Anyone who has seen Paul's meticulously organized sailboat at his home on Little Deer Isle, or the finely constructed model wooden ship he built from scratch accurate down to the last detail, will recognize in his words of praise for Barth a reflection of those same qualities that pervaded every page of his own intellectual work.)

"Finally, I must say that I do not in any way conceive of myself as a Holocaust theologian or a theologian of the Holocaust. The horror of the Holocaust has surely opened the eyes of many Christians to the reality of the Jewish people. I have told the story of how my eyes were opened, which was not by way of the Holocaust. What Christians need to see, in my judgment, is not the Holocaust, but that which lives after and in spite of the Holocaust, the living reality, "warts and all," of the Israel of God, the Jewish people. The reality of the Jewish people, fixed in history by the reality of their election, is as solid and sure as that of the gentile church. That is what I ran into and had to see, and that is what accounts, as far as I can tell, for how my mind changed in the past decade, and my agenda for the future."

Thus by 1976 the reality of the Jewish people had become the cornerstone for Paul van Buren's reconstruction of Christian theology itself. With this new direction set in his scholarly work and increasingly in his other professional activities as well, Paul entered into a period of intensive intellectual labor throughout the decade of the 1980's that resulted, one after another, in the three books that make up his enduring contribution to the theology of Jewish-Christian relations, called by one scholar "the most promising theological undertaking of the present generation"—his trilogy entitled *A Theology of the Jewish-Christian Reality*: Part I, *Discerning the Way* (1980); Part II, *A Christian Theology of the People Israel* (1983); and Part III, *Christ in Context* (1988).

(Plans for a fourth volume, in which he would have extended his analysis to the third Abrahamic tradition, Islam, and possibly the relation of Christianity to other religions, were dropped after Paul concluded that he simply did not know enough about the subject to continue the project.)

In a summary of his work up to 1984 after the first two volumes had appeared, he reported to the then chair of the department, Gerhard Spiegler, "My research efforts over the past few years have been the continuation of the project that I defined for myself in the course of studies undertaken during a study leave in 1976-77—to develop a thorough, coherent and systematic analysis and presentation of the implications for Christian theology of recent official church pronouncements affirming the eternity of the covenant between God and the Jewish people. This radical reversal of church teaching of over eighteen centuries duration, having been made during the past two decades by Roman Catholic and Protestant churches, on both sides of the Atlantic, entails a reworking of every part of Christian theology if it is to regain coherence. This is the project on which I have been working for eight years." Looking forward to his third volume, which was to be on Christology, he added, "If the church's teaching is to be coherent, it will have to develop an understanding of Jesus Christ that does justice to the Jewish as well as to the Christian reality. The questions of whether this is possible and whether traditional Christology is inherently anti-Judaic are becoming matters of increasing debate and stand at the heart of Jewish-Christian dialogue." He proposed "to clarify the issues and explore the criteria for a Christology adequate to the relationship between the church and the Jewish people."

His trilogy distilled Paul's long engagement with Judaism, begun with that fateful personnel search in the early 1970s for a new professor in Jewish Studies, and continued in his discussions throughout the 1980s with rabbinical scholars and Jewish thinkers at the Shalom Hartman Institute for Judaic Studies in Jerusalem. He was Director of the Center for Contemporary Theology from 1982-1987 and Co-Director of the Center for Religious Pluralism from 1987-1992, working to build bridges and promote reconciliation between Christianity and Judaism.

Paul's last book, *According to The Scriptures: The Origins of the Gospel and the Church's Old Testament*, was completed before his final illness and appeared posthumously this past October (Eerdmans, 1998). In it he demonstrated how the early Christians, themselves Jews, understood the death of Jesus through Jewish methods of biblical interpretation. The early Christians received a gospel "according to the scriptures"—the scriptures of the Jewish tradition, that is. Their reading of the story of the binding of Isaac (Genesis 22) helped them "discover" the good news, which meant that Christianity was located not in the "New" Testament but in what, once the discovery was made, could be called the "Old" Testament. Thus, Paul restores the normative status enjoyed by the Old Testament in the community that discovered the gospel by reading old stories in the light of new problems—a practice deeply rooted in the tradition out of which both Christianity and contemporary Judaism grew. Reclaiming that tradition, he argues, would not only enrich Christianity but also enable more constructive dialogue in a world of more than one religion, in which God's love is not restricted to a single people.

Did Paul have other projects in mind? According to Anne, he intended to turn his imaginative attention and analytical powers to another Christian writing that had always puzzled him, the Gospel of John, which he had by his bedside. It is fascinating to speculate what this original and provocative thinker would have turned up that would once again have turned upside down much of previous speculation about that enigmatic text.

In summary, Paul van Buren's work over the last two decades of his life represented perhaps the first attempt in the two-millennial history of Christianity to integrate the ongoing witness to God of the Jewish people into the self-critical reflection of the Christian church, while seeing Christian confession of the continuing validity of the covenant between God and the Jewish people as an intrinsic component of the Church's faithfulness to Jesus Christ.

How far he had come from the "secular meaning" of the gospel! And yet how faithful had this "nontraditional theologian" remained to his lifelong task of calling his fellow Christians to a deeper understanding and truer witness to that gospel?

(NB: In 1997 the first full-length study in English of Paul's work appeared in a book by James H. Wallis, *Post-Holocaust Christianity: Paul van Buren's Theology of the Jewish-Christian Reality* (University Press of America). It covered the entirety of Paul's work from his first two works, *Christ in Our Place* and *The Secular Meaning of the Gospel*, through his two works in the late 1960s and early 1970s in analytic philosophy of religion, *Theological Explorations* and *The Logic of a Religion*, and concluding with his 1980s trilogy, *A Theology of the Jewish-Christian Reality*.)

VI. His Post-Retirement Career

Paul remained active as a thinker and writer after his retirement from Temple University in 1986. Not only did he publish the final volume of his trilogy on *A Theology of the Jewish-Christian Reality*, a complete work on *According to the Scriptures*, and contribute over two dozen articles or chapters to major journals and books in his field, he also continued his ecumenical activities at the Hartman Institute in Jerusalem which he had begun in 1982. In addition, as you know better than I, he became your co-worker at the Ecumenical Institute at the University of Heidelberg, where he also served as *Honorar Professor für systematische Theologie* from 1987 until his death. I am not sure that "retirement" is the best word to describe Paul's life and career after he left Temple!

During that same period Paul also served as president of the American Theological Society (1988-1989), Founding Scholar of the Abrahamic Accord of the Diocese of Rhode Island (1988-1998), member of the Presiding Bishop's Committee on Christian-Jewish Relations (1987-1992), and on the advisory boards of the International Conference of Christians and Jews (1993-1998), the Center for Jewish-Christian Studies and Relations, General Theological Seminary, New York (1988-1990), and the Institute for Christian-Jewish Studies, Baltimore, Maryland (1987-1998).

In 1990, in recognition of his service on behalf of Jewish-Christian relations, he received the Sir Sigmund Sternberg Award of the International Conference of Christians and Jews.

VII. Those He Leaves Behind

In addition to his wife of fifty years, Dr. Anne Hagopian van Buren (PhD, Bryn Mawr College), a retired professor and scholar of Renaissance art history, who divides her time between homes in Little Deer Isle, Maine, and Paris, France, Paul is survived by two daughters, Alice van Buren, 47, a writer, journalist and artist living in Santa Fe, New Mexico, and Ariane van Buren, 45, a PhD in Ecological Economics working for the Center for Corporate Responsibility in New York City, and two sons, Philip, 43, a Presbyterian minister and law student at New York University in New York City, and Thomas,

40, of Hastings-on-Hudson, New York, an ethnomusicologist working for the Center for Traditional Culture and Music in New York City.

Perhaps Anne will not mind if I share one vignette with you. On a visit to their beautiful home overlooking the Atlantic Ocean on Little Deer Isle in Maine, I noticed a little cabin tucked away in the piney woods a short distance from the main house. It was outfitted as a separate study, the sort of private little workplace any one of us would have given our eye teeth to occupy. I wondered which of the two van Buren scholars, Paul or Anne, had prior claim to this marvelous hideaway. As it turned out, the two scholars took possession of it in alternate years. Of course!

Now the little study in the woods will echo to the footsteps of only one of the two van Buren scholars—a thought which brings with it immeasurable sadness but also, I hope, dear Anne, a small measure of happy and comforting memory as well.

VIII. Concluding Salute and Farewell

And so, dear Paul, we, your colleagues and co-workers, thank you one last time for your life among us. We were honored and proud to have known you and to have been able to call you colleague and friend. May we too, in the time given to each of us, measure up in some small way to your shining example of devotion to teaching and thinking, and to the cause of reconciliation among faiths and peoples, which you so passionately and splendidly embodied until the very end. We salute you. We miss you. We bid you a loving and final fare-well.

A GLOBAL PARADIGM SHIFT
Reflections on Interreligious, Intercultural, and International Development by the Journal of Ecumenical Studies/Dialogue Institute

LEONARD SWIDLER

1. A Global Shift in the Making

In the wake of the bifurcated World War the first half of the twentieth century, the world attempted in the 1950s to reestablish "normalcy," only to be met with the major paradigm shift of the multiple upheavals of the 1960s:
- the Civil Rights Movement
- the Second Wave Feminist Movement
- the Anti-War Movement
- the world-wide Student Movement
- the election of the Two John's (Catholic President John F. Kennedy and Pope St. John XXIII)
- the Catholic Vatican Council II (1962-1965)
- and Temple University ceased being a Baptist-related private university and became a state-related public university—with an academic department of religion unique in the world…

These reflections are about the role that I, my wife Arlene ("Andie") Anderson Swidler, the *Journal of Ecumenical Studies,* and Temple University Department of Religion played in that major paradigm shift.

2. Len and Andie's Roles

First, how I got involved: My father, Samuel Swidler, was a Jewish lad of fifteen from Western Ukraine when in 1912, he came by himself to America, picked up perfect English—along with his knowledge of Hebrew, Yiddish, Ukrainian, Russian, Polish, and German—and eventually married my Catholic mother of Irish descent. I was born on January 6 of the auspicious year 1929, the beginning of the Great Depression (like Louis XIV, I could say: *Apre moi le deluge!*). I subsequently had twenty-five years of Catholic education, including an advanced degree in Catholic theology (*Sacrae Theologiae Licentiatus, STL*) from the Pontifical Catholic Theology Faculty of the University of Tübingen (founded in the fifteenth century), quite possibly the first layperson ever to receive a degree in Catholic theology, as well as a PhD in History and Philosophy from the University of Wisconsin.

Andie and I spent the first years of our marriage in Germany as I completed my STL and the dissertation research for my PhD. We returned to the US in 1961, to teach at Duquesne University, Pittsburgh. She taught English and I taught History. My research had been on the dialogue that began in Germany after World War I between Protestants and Catholics called the *Una Sancta Movement*.[1] Andie and I shared all the major aspects of our four years in Germany in various degrees and ways: birthing and raising our first child, teaching (part-time for myself and eventually full-time for her) to support ourselves, soaking ourselves in Germany and Europe, and researching my two dissertations (PhD and STL).

Hence, when the Second Vatican Council totally reversed the Vatican stance against dialogue with non-Catholics, Andie one day said to me, "There is no scholarly periodical devoted to ecumenism

---

[1] See Leonard Swidler, The Ecumenical Vanguard (Pittsburgh: Duquesne University Press, 1965).

and dialogue, perhaps we should start one." And so we did. The first issue of the *Journal of Ecumenical Studies (JES)* appeared in 1964. We invited Elwyn Smith from the Presbyterian Pittsburgh Theological Seminary to be Co-Editor along with me, and we made Andie Managing Editor.

The first issue started with a bang! It included articles by Catholic *Enfant terrible* Hans Küng, and his then friend and colleague Joseph Ratzinger (now Pope Emeritus Benedict XVI).[22] That first year the subtitle of *JES* was *Catholic, Protestant, Orthodox*, but before the end of the second volume it was dropped because we had already taken on our first non-Christian Associate Editor, Rabbi Arthur Gilbert.

3. Duquesne University—"Just Fine, Thank You!"

Things were going swimmingly in 1965 at Duquesne University. Andie and I had launched the *Journal of Ecumenical Studies (JES)*, Vatican II and all its daily excitement was coming to a thunderous climax, and I was heavily involved with Father Henry Koren— Founder of Duquesne University Press, Chair of the Philosophy Department, world-famous for phenomenology and existentialism — in working to reinvent the Theology Department from a sort of unacademic catechism class to a serious academic enterprise. I had also set up a radio program with the Duquesne University FM station, interviewing interesting persons and visitors from the area.. It was there that I interviewed Lowell Streiker, a young scholar who was teaching in the newly established (1964) Department of Religion at Temple University (which was to become a state-related university in

---

[2]Hans Küng, "The Historical Contingency of Conciliar Decrees," trans., Erica Strasser, Journal of Ecumenical Studies, 1, 1 (Winter, 1964), pp. 109-110; Joseph Ratzinger, "The Ministerial Office and the Unity of the Church," trans., Howard Bleichner, Journal of Ecumenical Studies, 1, 1 (Winter, 1964), pp. 42-57.

1966). We had just published an essay of his, "The Modern Jewish-Christian Dialogue," in *JES*,[33] and I was so positively impressed by him in the radio interview that I urged him to apply to join our Theology Department (I was acting as "recruiter" for Father Koren). He said he would think about it. A couple of days later I received a phone call from Lowell, saying that when he spoke to the Chairman of the Religion Department at Temple University, Bernard Philips, a Jewish philosopher, Bernard responded by offering to hire me, my Co-Editor Elwyn Smith, and the *Journal of Ecumenical Studies!*

Well, I was not at all interested since I was so deeply involved in the exciting things at Duquesne University, but Elwyn, who was a professor at Pittsburgh Theological Seminary, a Presbyterian seminary, was really eager to get into a university, and kept pushing me to go with him for an interview. Eventually, I reluctantly told Elwyn that I would go just for his sake, but that I would tell Bernard Philips that I would not even consider coming unless he made a firm commitment to hire not just one Catholic (me), but several, and further, that he would also hire Jews, Muslims, Hindus, and others. I did not want to be a "token Catholic." This was a fantastic dream idea at that point, and I thought such a demand would kill the offer to this troika, Swidler, Smith, *JES*, and allow me to happily stay at Duquesne University.

It must be recalled that up until that time religion, or rather, theology, in the US was almost always taught by Protestant theologians. Think Harvard, Yale, Princeton, University of Pennsylvania, Columbia, Chicago University, Stanford.... There were Catholic colleges and universities, of course, where whatever passed for the teaching of religion was—confirmed by my personal experience at St. Norbert's College (1946-1950)—often non-credit, glorified catechism taught (in my time—jokingly—to classrooms of

---

[3] Lowell Streiker, "The Modern Jewish-Christian Dialogue, *Journal of Ecumenical Studies*, ital II, 2 (spring, 1965), pp. 179-188.

combat-hardened World War II ex-GIs!) by Catholics. It was precisely that tsunami of ex-GIs after World War II that helped bring Catholicism "of age" in 1950s' America. Along with the World War II experience in general, this led to taking the study of theology more seriously in US higher education by both Catholics and Protestants—but it was still religiously segregated.

That all began to change drastically as the world moved into the Baby-Boomer generation with its civil-rights movement, the anti-war movement, and the student-rebellion "Light-up/Turn-on/Drop-out" movement. Part of this break with the past worldwide paradigm shift was the opening-up of religion, most dramatically expressed by the Catholic Church's Vatican Council II in which "all" Catholics were told to engage non-Catholics in dialogue, even "taking the first steps." All this was very, very new and giddy-making (my "demand" to Bernard Phillips doubtless a manifestation of the latter). At that time there was *one* significant Catholic scholar teaching Catholicism at a non-Catholic university—Christopher Dawson at Harvard, Professor of the newly established (1960) Stilman Chair of Catholic Studies.

4. Coming to Temple University Department of Religion (TUDOR)

However, much to my utter surprise, when I presented him my demand, Bernard responded, saying: Great idea! We'll do it! He then presented me with a concrete offer: Full Professor, a nine-month salary of $13,000, a lightened load of one undergrad and one grad course each semester, and a $50,000 annual subsidy for *JES* (the equivalent of at least $400,000 in 2013 dollars!). I still was not persuaded—even though at Duquesne I was only an Associate Professor earning $9,500 with a 12-month commitment. I planned to go back to my Dean and tell him about the offer, and expected that he would say that while they of course could not match those finances, they would instead offer me a raise to perhaps $11,000 (which I would have accepted). However, I was utterly surprised once again.

The Dean said to me, "Gee Len, I don't see how you can turn that offer down."

It never occurred to me then that my working so closely with Father Koren with his amazingly energetic and "liberal" agenda might have made me *persona non-grata* to his conservative opponents within the Holy Ghost Fathers. Consequently, it never occurred to me to speak with Father Koren about the matter. How naïve! I will never know—had I spoken with him....? Well, after consulting with Andie, I decided to accept the offer—much to Elwyn's delight, of course. Thus, *JES* and I came to Temple University Department of Religion (TUDOR).

Looking back now, I can see why Bernard went after me and bought my demand. In the *JES* issue before the one with Lowell's essay, I see now that I had published an editorial on "Religion and Higher Education,"[44] which had laid out in positive form my demand to Bernard Philips—long before I was invited to visit there, or even knew about Temple's existence. I opened my editorial by writing:

> The Christian churches and synagogues face a common problem in higher education: how to make religion and theology relevant and effective in the lives of university and college faculties and student bodies, and through their leadership in society at large.... (To date, their efforts) are really only manifestations of religious tokenism. (Rather,) should we not as quickly as possible shift our emphasis in the area of higher education to where it will be most effective? Should we not expend most of our efforts where most of the students are, the secular campuses?
>
> Over ninety percent of the college and university students in the next two decades will receive their education on secular campuses. It is obvious, therefore, that thousands of trained men and women, lay and clerical, must be sent to these campuses.... Theology must be taught as an intellectual discipline by men and women who are the scholarly peers of professors in other disciplines. Only thus will it be

---

[4] Leonard Swidler, "Religion and Higher Education," Journal of Ecumenical Studies, II, 1 (Winter, 1965), pp. 97-99.

able to meet the intellectual and moral challenges of the intellectual community and our society at large which is so greatly influenced by college graduates. Here is where the best theologians among the clerics belong. However, since theology is not an exclusively clerical sphere there should also be laywomen and laymen who are trained theologians teaching in these university theology programs, which should not remain extra-curricular, but which must be as academically recognized as chemistry, philosophy, and history.

Today, as I review my words from 1965, I am struck by how prescient I unconsciously was at that time. It was only the following year, 1966, that Temple University, with its newly established Department of Religion, would become a "secular" university—and me and *JES* would be part of it! I even strongly urged that the interreligious structure of faculty—which, after Bernard Philips accepted my "demand" (of course, he might well have gone in that direction even without it), did in fact become the mark of Temple University Department of Religion (TUDOR). I was careful to include a non-believing perspective as well:

> These theology faculties should never be exclusive.... What are needed are ecumenical faculties including Protestant, Catholic, Orthodox, Jewish, and world religion scholars. It is in an intellectual, ecumenical setting that all theology can become most profound and most relevant, when it must constantly meet the challenges and problems of all the disciplines and all the faiths—and unfaiths.... large numbers of men and women must be sent off to be trained in theology in first-class fashion. Secondly, every avenue of approach to the setting up of these ecumenical, theological faculties on secular campuses must be investigated and heavily trafficked...The churches and synagogues must extend every effort to produce scholarly theologians in numbers and encourage them to form these ecumenical faculties.

That is exactly what happened at TUDOR, starting at its inception as a state-related university in 1966. That year the number of TUDOR faculty went from six to ten, and in another two years, to twenty-one! The one really famous theologian on the faculty at that time was Paul van Buren, an Episcopal priest who earned his doctorate at the University of Basel, Switzerland under the world-famous theologian, Karl Barth. Shortly after I published the *JES* editorial, Paul appeared on the cover of *Time Magazine* as one of the four (in)famous "God Is Dead" theologians.[55] It is ironic that he studied under "conservative" Karl Barth, considering he then went in a completely opposite direction intellectually.

Bernard Philips kept his word about hiring more than just one Catholic theologian. I quickly suggested Patrick Burke, a young Australian priest who had earned his doctorate in systematic theology at the Catholic Theology Faculty of the University of Munich (where I had been in the late 1950s and Patrick came in the early 60s). Patrick had earlier tried to get me hired as Dean of the Iowa School of Theology, where he was teaching at the time. Patrick quickly suggested to Bernard Father Gerard Sloyan, widely known then in Catholic circles as the President of the "Liturgical Movement" (the engine for Catholic reform in the U.S. in the years leading up to Vatican II) and a New Testament scholar. Shortly after they both were hired, Roderick Hindery, a recently laicized American Benedictine monk, was hired in the area of comparative ethics. So, within two years there suddenly were four Catholic scholars on the TUDOR faculty. In the same time period we also hired Buddhists, Hindus, Jews, and Muslims.

Of course, because of Vatican II, Catholics were suddenly "hot numbers," and this was true on the student level as well. On the undergraduate level Temple University in the middle 60s was known as both the largest Jewish and largest Catholic university (!) in terms of numbers of students. I remember well that in those days our general introductory classes (called "Religion and Human Life")

---

[5]See:http://www.time.com/time/magazine/article/0,9171,9413410-1,00.html, the October 20, 1965 issue of Time Magazine—accessed June 14, 2013.

would normally be 40% Catholic, 40% Jewish, and 20% Protestant. In 2016 the percentages would be about 23% Catholic, 3% Jewish, 20% Protestant, and the rest a wild world assortment, including self-proclaimed agnostics and atheists (often my best students!).

5. *Journal of Ecumenical Studies*
Dialogue Institute: Interreligious, Intercultural, International

Let me here say a word about the relationship of *JES* to TUDOR, and later the *Dialogue Institute: Interreligious, Intercultural, International*. The Religion Department had no direct control over *JES*, which had its own editorial board, though for the first few years both my Co-Editor Elwyn Smith and I were given a teaching schedule that was one course lighter per year—but quickly that was extended to all of TUDOR's full professors. The annual $50,000 came from the University, not through TUDOR. Some TUDOR faculty members were on the *JES* editorial Board, but that was a result of *JES* invitation. Thus, both *JES* and TUDOR benefitted from each other, but were structurally independent. When Elwyn, *JES* and I came to Temple University in July, 1966, we were able to set up an office and hire two Editorial Assistants: Catherine Berry Stidsen and Val Rementer. We produced large-page and voluminous issues four times a year (at Duquesne it was three times a year), and even paid the authors honoraria!

When the 1973 oil crisis hit, I was called in by the Provost (Gerhard Spiegler at that time, and later Chair of TUDOR) and told that *JES* had two years to wean itself from its annual $50,000 subsidy down to a break-even budget! That was about the time when both Paul Mojzes and Nancy Krody came on the staff. Paul soon became Co-Editor (also, like me, *pro-bono*), taking Elwyn's place. Elwyn had left to teach elsewhere and the page size and length of each volume was trimmed in a variety of ways to meet the "drop-dead" zero-budget (which "gap" I increasingly bridged each year, until in the 1990's *JES* became a nonprofit Non-Governmental Organization (NGO)). Andie continued her involvement with *JES* in a variety of ways, at times serving as Education Editor, at times editing special issues, for example, "Human Rights in Religious Traditions" (*JES* 19 [Summer, 1982]), and "Marriage in the World Religions" (*JES* 22 [Winter, 1985]). Some of these were also published simultaneously by trade publishers. Cruelly, Andie was stricken by Alzheimer's in 1991, and died at home (where she had remained under my eye and care—increasingly along with the help of others—for seventeen years) in 2008.

Early after my arrival at TUDOR, I was invited to join a Pennsylvania Commonwealth committee to oversee the implementation of a Pennsylvania law passed in the mid-60s. This was shortly after the US Supreme Court decided in the 1963 Schempp vs. Abington (a suburb of Philadelphia) case that public school pupils could be taught *about* religion. In fact, a couple dozen public high schools around the state very successfully taught such courses—until the 1973 oil crisis, which financially drove out all courses not required by state law. Before that happened, I tried to arrange collaboration with the Temple University College of Education, (COE), but I was too late, and my subsequent attempts to work with COE to train high school teachers to properly teach such courses has found no support to date. Perhaps in the future…?

In 1978 I formalized, at least in name, the various activities I occasionally organized—to put into practice, so to speak, the theory that was published in *JES*, and the name that in the end was settled on was the *Dialogue Institute: Interreligious, Intercultural, International (DI)*. In 1978, it was the participation in the Scholars Trialogues (Jewish-Christian-Muslim Dialogue) that Eugene Fisher and I were asked to put together by Sargent Shriver (founder and first president of the Peace Corps).[6] If you read the two fulsome reports listed in the previous footnote, you will gain some idea of the huge effort, first by the Kennedy Institute in Washington, D.C., and then, starting in the 1990 until 2008, by *JES* invested in the "International Scholars Abrahamic Trialogue" (ISAT).

From 2008 onward, the DI/*JES*, having become a non-governmental organization at Temple University a decade before, initially had one full-time staff person. This grew to a staff of five and an annual budget of $1,000,000 in 2009. It focused on two U.S. State Department funded training programs bringing twenty students from Egypt, Lebanon, Iraq, Saudi Arabia, Jordan, Turkey and five Southeast Asian countries (Indonesia, Malaysia, Myanmar, Thailand, the Philippines), and eighteen scholars from eighteen countries, for training for five or six weeks respectively on American religious pluralism and Democracy.

5. TUDOR Largest (Greatest?) Graduate Religion Program in the World

It was on the graduate level where the revolution of Vatican II was most dramatically reflected. When I arrived in the fall 1966, there was only one previous Catholic graduate student in TUDOR, Rodger Van Allen. Rodger became my advisee, wrote his dissertation on the history of *Commonweal*, a major American Catholic intellectual periodical, and went on to become professor of theology at Villanova University, a large Catholic university in the suburbs of Philadelphia. He is still teaching there as of 2016. A group of about

---

[6] For the years (meeting semi-annually) 1978-82, see Eugene Fisher, "Kennedy Institute Jewish-Christian-Muslim Trialogue," *Journal of Ecumenical Studies*, vol. 19, no. 1 (winter, 1982), pp. 197-200. For the years of the late 1990s to 2008 see Leonard Swidler, "Trialogue: Out of the Shadows into Blazing 'Desert' Sun!" *Journal of Ecumenical Studies*, vol. 45, no. 3 (summer, 2010), pp. 493-509.

seven Catholic doctoral students came with me that fall, 1966, and by 1968, there were fifty Catholic doctoral students in TUDOR! Vatican II had told Catholics to go and investigate the world—and scores of them did by coming to study religion at the "secular" state university, Temple!

My first graduate seminar was on Vatican I, but my second one—on Vatican II—was quite unusual. Let me recall one interesting aspect of that first graduate seminar I ever offered. For the first assignment, I asked each student to pick a topic he (they were all he's) wanted to research and to then work up a thorough bibliography. There was one German student—Peter Schreiner (son of a family friend who came to pursue an MA with TUDOR)—in the seminar who proceeded in stereotypical German fashion to gather a seemingly unending bibliography. After about 200 plus entries, one of the American grad students in panic told him that the Americans wanted him to please stop!

The graduate seminar I offered the second semester was a follow-up on Vatican II. I don't remember the exact number of students, but I recall that all were Catholics save one, who was a Protestant pastor who had spent many years in the Philippines. What made it unusual was that we, as a seminar, had access to all the documents of Vatican II as they developed in their various stages. This happened because I had quickly become friends with Father William Leahy. He was a young priest of the Philadelphia archdiocese who had finished his doctorate in theology in Rome just before the beginning of the Council and was appointed by Cardinal Krol of Philadelphia as an "expert" (*peritus*) to Vatican II. He was subsequently made a secretary of the Council. That meant that he received all the different versions of each document (*shema*), so that looking at them chronologically revealed a lot about the forces at play in the Council. Since all the documents (*schemata*) were in Latin, they were closed books to the average American graduate student, but not to young Catholic priests of the 1960s since they had been soaked in Latin in their philosophical and especially theological studies. All of the textbooks were in Latin!

Consequently, each of the graduate students chose a Vatican II document (the close of the Council was only a few months in the past then!) and had the opportunity/burden of going through all of its permutations to write an analysis for the seminar. I am sad to say that I did not save any of those seminar papers.

TUDOR was unique in several ways. It was the first state university (1964) to have a full-fledged department of religion. There were of course departments of theology at many private universities, including our neighbor in Philadelphia, the University of Pennsylvania, founded by Benjamin Franklin in the eighteenth century. It was basically a Protestant theological faculty, as were basically all the others. There was the "halfway house," for example, of the School of Theology at the University of Iowa where the faculty was hired and paid for by the several religions, and the courses were then recognized by the University. I mentioned that Pat Burke had arranged for me to be interviewed as a candidate for Dean of the Iowa School of Theology. However, in the end they hired one of their own, George Forell, who was a spell-binding lecturer at Iowa. Eventually, the School of Theology was incorporated into the University—but that was only after TUDOR led the way.

I should say something further about the extraordinary faculty of twenty-one members that Bernard assembled by 1968 or soon thereafter. Only three of the six faculty at Temple when me and the other three new-hires arrived in 1966 remained by 1968: Ernest Stoeffler (Protestant History and Theology), the one former member of Conwell School of Theology faculty, Bernard himself (Religious Mysticism), Paul Van Buren (Contemporary Christian Thought). Allen Cutler and Lowell Striker did not remain and the sixth's name eludes my memory. Two others came in 1966 besides Elwyn Smith (Protestant Thought) and myself (Modern Catholic Thought and Interreligious Dialogue), namely, Thomas Dean (Religious Thought) and John Raines (Social Ethics), both young ABDs. The faculty of 1968 included the three Catholics already mentioned—Patrick Burke (Modern Catholic Theology/Philosophy), Gerard Sloyan (New Testament and Catholic Theology), and Roderick Hindery (Comparative Ethics)—as well as Franklin Littell (Church-State Relations and Holocaust Studies), Richard DeMartino (Zen Buddhism), Leonard Barrett (African and Caribbean Religions), Samuel Laeuchli (Christian Patristics), Ismail al Faruqi (Islamics), Bibhuti Yadav (Indian Religions), Maurice Friedman (Religion and Literature and Buber Studies), Robert Gordis (Hebrew Bible), and slightly later Charles Fu (Chinese Religions and Buddhism). In addition to me and Smith, I was also responsible for hiring Patrick Burke, Franklin Littell, and al Faruqi—and later, in the wake of the 1979 Khomeini Iranian revolution, Seyyed Hossein Nasr.

Speaking of personnel matters I was responsible for, at least in part, rose from my interest in teaching at Temple University Japan (TUJ) for a year. Tom Dean, who was likewise interested in Japan, proposed that he would serve as Director of Graduate Religious Studies for a year, during which time I could go to Japan, if I would take over the position when I returned so he could go to Japan. I agreed. I became Director of Graduate Religion Studies, a position I held from 1991-1993. When I started, I went through all the graduate student files and brought everyone in line, performing several "rescue operations" in the process. For example, Brian Victoria was at the dissertation stage and had been a student of Charles Fu. Unfortunately, Charles was going through a difficult personal time, and Brian was caught by the waves caused. So, I took over as dissertation advisor. He finished spectacularly. His dissertation on the complicity of Zen Buddhism (of which he is also a certified Roshi) in the imperial wars of twentieth-century Japan (it was favorably reviewed in the *New York Times*) was the cause of the two major Zen institutions in Japan publicly expressing their apologies. A second successful "rescue operation" was Racelle Weiman, an

American/Israeli who was working with Franklin Littell. Because of personal circumstances, she was far over the time limit, and had to reapply and retake her Comprehensive Exams. I took over the position of Advisor, and arranged for the written Comprehensive Exams to be taken at the University of Haifa, where Racelle was teaching, and for the oral Comprehensive Exams to be taken in my hotel room in Washington D.C. during the annual meeting of the American Academy of Religion with Professors Sloyan, Littell, and myself examining. She went on to become the Founding Director of the "Center for Holocaust and Humanities Studies" at Hebrew Union College in Cincinnati, and later the first Director of the "Dialogue Institute: Interreligious, Intercultural, International" at Temple University. Slightly less dramatic was the "rescue operation" of Steve Antinoff, who was a student of Richard DeMartino (see Steve's essay about Richard in this volume). Steve was teaching in Temple University Japan (TUJ), as was Tom Dean, who served on Steve's dissertation committee. I arranged, during a trip through Tokyo on my way to Korea, to complete Steve's oral Comprehensive Exam at TUJ with Richard via telephone from the States.

I promoted the TUDOR doctoral program vigorously while Director of Graduate Religion Studies with various forms of advertising. Having done doctoral studies in Germany, I was very aware that the vast majority of German PhDs in theology did not end up teaching at universities; in fact, only a small percentage did. Most simply found appropriate work in the "real world." I made the case to potential American and international doctoral students that university-level teaching was not the only prospective gainful employment available to religion PhDs (e.g., ethics officers in corporations or hospitals, NGOs, religious organizations, governments....). As a result, thirty to thirty-five new doctoral students came each fall semester I was the Director (meaning that seventy were admitted, but only about half actually came—usually because of financial considerations). Consequently, during those years and immediately following, TUDOR had normally 165 active doctoral students—doubtless the largest religion PhD student body in North America, and probably in the world! My successor as Director, Shiganori Ngatomo, continued the same policies, with similar results.

Unfortunately, matters took a decided turn for the worse in 1996, when James England was hired away from Swarthmore College and made Provost. He then set about downgrading many graduate programs of the University. He unilaterally mandated that TUDOR immediately cut its intake of doctoral students by more than half! At that time TUDOR had thirty teaching assistants, which of course meant that seven or eight were available to redistribute each year to the incoming thirty-five doctoral students. By my higher mathematics analysis, that meant that twenty-seven of the yearly new students were tuition-paying doctoral students. I then sat down and figured out conservatively the financial loss of funds from the forbidden doctoral students. I simply multiplied the annual tuition for in-state students by the missing twenty-seven students for the first year. I then added the same amount for the second year—plus the same amount for the first "cohort's" second year of tuition. The same also was true for the third year, plus, of course the second cohort's missing second-year tuition. All in all, figuring very conservatively, over a three-year period, Temple University lost $500,000 (1990s dollars!). That would have paid the salaries for at least three to four new professors for those three years—which the University was throwing out the window.

I sent all that carefully laid-out data to Provost England, asking what his rationale for the demanded cut in graduate students was. I eventually received a curt "send it up the chain of command" reply. Unfortunately, neither our Chair nor our Dean went to bat for our graduate program, which consequently has continued to be seriously weakened.

Thus, while the first half of the 1990s drew the highest number of TUDOR doctoral students (165), it was also a devastating decade for the faculty. It was during the 1990s that many of our outstanding older faculty left, retired, or died, and were—or were not—replaced by younger scholars. We lost, e.g., Gerard Sloyan to the then prevailing law of mandatory retirement (age, 70)—who as of 2014 was still teaching at the Catholic University of America and Georgetown University at age 94, and still publishing scholarly articles and books. Richard DeMartino retired to care for his slowly dying mother; Zalman Schachter took early retirement to go live and teach in Israel (which plan, unfortunately, was not eventually realized); Charles Fu was hired away by his homeland Taiwan, and was building a fantastic bridge of cooperation with TUDOR when he suddenly died from post-surgery infection for what turned out to be a benign tumor; Gerhard Spiegler was hired away as a College President; Patrick Burk went into American politics with the Libertarian Party, Bibhuti Yadav died of a stroke; slightly earlier (1986) Ismail al-Faruqi and his wife Lois (who also taught part time in TUDOR) were murdered by an African-American convert to Islam (Ismail had taught him while he was in prison); Thomas Dean took early retirement so his wife could accept a tenure-track teaching position in a Midwest college; Paul Van Buren retired to work in Israel, and died later of a recurrence of cancer, and John Raines retired in 2011, but could not stand the boredom, and returned to teach one course per semester until his death in 2017. As of 2019, the *fifty-third* anniversary of the founding of Temple University becoming a state-related university, and TUDOR's Golden Anniversary plus tree, I am the only full-time teaching faculty member from that early cohort.

6. The Baptist Temple Pressed Into Service

Today we have multiple halls where large numbers of students can gather for classes or other events. However, in the early years after Temple became a state-related university in 1966, there was only one large space, and it didn't even belong to the university: The

Baptist Temple on Broad Street. Today it is part of the university and has been renovated into a splendid performance and lecture auditorium, but at that time it still belonged to an active church congregation. It was a wonderful facility even then, holding up to two thousand people. TUDOR made use of it at least four times in the first decade of its existence; I organized three of the events.

The first was the most awesome. It took place in the spring semester of 1968. My wife Andie had translated from German to English at least two of the books of the then world-famous Catholic Moral Theologian Bernard Häring. During the summer of 1967, when the enthusiasm of Vatican Council II (1962-65) was still in full bloom, Andie and I both taught at a summer conference in Washington, D.C., along with Häring. I asked him what he would be doing the next year, and he said that in spring he would be teaching at Union Theological Seminary in New York. Practicing my chutzpah, I asked him if he would be open to coming down from New York one evening each week to teach a course at TUDOR. He said yes!

After making all the necessary arrangements, I sent word abroad that the course could be for credit or free. As a result, 650 persons signed up for the course! At that time the only place large enough to hold the crowd was The Baptist Temple. So, every Monday night 550 nuns—still wearing their "penguin habits"—flocked to the church (plus an additional 100 priests and laity). It seemed that each of the nuns brought along a small tape recorder. When asked about them, each replied that they had groups of 20-50 people back home (they came from southeastern Pennsylvania, south New Jersey, and northern Delaware) for whom they played them and subsequently discussed each week—meaning that twenty to thirty thousand Catholics were hearing and discussing Häring's lectures!! That first evening I attended with Prof. Ernest Stoeffler, Protestant church historian on our TUDOR faculty—originally from Germany, the land of the Reformation. When Father Häring went to the podium and said "Good Evening," all 550 of the nuns responded in one sing-song voice: Good *Ev*e*ning Fa*ther! I thought Ernie would have a heart attack! The Reformation has been undone!

Largely because Andie was so familiar with Häring's thought, she was hired to serve as his "Assistant" for the course, and had three graduate student TAs working under her to help handle the paper work and grading. I went every Monday night, and after the first two weeks, Andie arranged for groups of twenty-five to meet with Häring for an hour ahead of time at the nearby Newman Center. Andie and I and a guest or two got to have dinner with him before the class each week. At the end of each class (which lasted two hours) he prayed—for things like: "O Lord, give Cardinal Krol (Philadelphia's arch-conservative archbishop) the wisdom to see …. and the strength carry it out." When dealing with the Vatican II document on the *Church in the Modern World* (the whole course was on Vatican II), he would relate why certain wording was the way it was because of a struggle in the drafting committee, and he would at times remark, "When I wrote these words, I meant…. ☐." It was like listening to a Hebrew Bible prophet speaking in front of you! He was fearless. When I later read his war memoirs, I understood better. Among other escapades, as a medic with General von Paulus' doomed Sixth Army at Stalingrad, the men in his unit came to him and pleaded that he was the only one who could lead them out through the pincers movement closing behind the Nazi army. He said he would try on two conditions: they release the Russian prisoners unharmed, and lay down their weapons. Fortunately, coming east with the German invasion he had left behind him a train of Ukrainian households that he, both as a Catholic priest and as a medic, had befriended. He succeeded. He later wrote this about this experience:

> As we broke out of the ring around Stalingrad—without weapons—Russian peasants gave me their sleighs and horses so I could take a substantial number of wounded with me. Without the kindness of the Russian populace at that time we would have starved and frozen to death—and had we survived, we would have been

taken prisoner. When at the capitulation of our armies I became a Russian prisoner of war, courageous Poles freed me from prison and without any higher approval made me their pastor.

It was amazing to learn at his feet.

There were two other occasions in the very late 60s and early 70s when we had to press into service the Baptist Temple. One took place when I invited Professor Hans Küng to lecture, as again there was no hall large enough to contain the crowd. The second was similar when Professor Edward Schillebeeckx came to lecture—the crowds overwhelmed all other available halls, except The Baptist Temple. Over a thousand came for each of them! All three of these "rock-star" theologians were indeed theological stars at Vatican II, and hence were household names, especially among Catholics.

The one other time TUDOR made perforce use of the Baptist Temple was when through Ismail al-Faruqi we invited the head of the "Black Muslims," Wallace Muhammad. Sitting there in the Baptist Temple surrounded by the hundreds of Black American Muslims, I *felt* like I really was in a Baptist church! Wallace's lecture, that is, "sermon," reflected a "low Christology" with which I personally felt very comfortable, while all around me the "congregants" were interjecting and shouting "Allah Wakbar!" instead of "Alleuja!" (they both mean "Praise God," one in Arabic and the other in Hebrew).

7. German, Germany, and TUDOR

TUDOR has had over the years an extraordinarily broad and deep relationship with German scholarship—which makes a lot of sense since outside of the English language the greatest amount and greatest quality of research in the fields of religion and philosophy have been written in German since the eighteenth century. Of the early core of TUDOR's initial extraordinary faculty, seven either had German degrees or whose mother tongue was German. To begin, the "Founding" professor Ernest Stoeffler was from Germany. The others were Gerhard Spiegler, whose mother tongue was German, as well as Samuel Laeuchli from Switzlerland, and Zalman Schachter, who was raised in, and fled from, Vienna. Then there were the German-trained *Ausländer*: Paul van Buren, whose doctorate was earned under Karl Barth at Basel, Switzerland, the Australian Patrick Burke, who earned his Doctor of Theology at the University of Munich, Franklin Littell, who spent nine years in Germany at the end of World War II renewing the *Evangelische Kirche Deutschland* of Nazi muck, and me with my Catholic Theology degree from Tübingen.

Over the years TUDOR sponsored a lecture series *auf deutsch*, and put on a quite stunning *Ringvorlesung auf deutsch* (Lecture Series of twelve weeks in German) of lectures on Jewish-Christian Dialogue by twelve professors held in the Religion Department in Spring of 1980. I personally also offered several semesters of graduate seminars on doing research in German. We spent all our time in the research section of the main library working our way through all the German language reference tools there, which are neglected at their peril by religious studies scholars.

This is also probably a good place to note that TUDOR was always strong in its expectations of its graduate students. We required two languages of scholarship besides English and any necessary primary languages. The two languages of scholarship were almost always German and French simply because that is where the current scholarship was to be found in almost all areas of religious studies. For example, if someone was going to concentrate on Islam, s/he had to know the primary language, Arabic. However, the vast majority of critical scholarship published today on matters Islamic are mainly in English, German, and French. Without knowing them, a scholar of Islamics is going half-, or more, blind!

In those early halcyon years when the TUDOR faculty was, with just a few exceptions, made up of "world stars" in their respective fields, we demanded that the graduate students and majority of faculty attend and participate in intense lectures (by insiders and outsiders) and discussions, held usually once a month. They generated a true community of scholars!

Then there were the extraordinary student and faculty exchanges I set up with the University of Tübingen and the University of Hamburg, and eventually all the universities of West Germany. Several faculty members from Tübingen and from Hamburg taught one or more semesters at TUDOR, and I and other TUDOR faculty taught multiple semesters at those two universities. Doubtlessly even more significant was the exchange program for ten German students to come to TUDOR every year for a year. That program led to joint seminars on Jewish-Christian dialogue with the Reconstructionist Rabbinical College and the Lutheran Seminary, which were always heavily peopled by the exchange German graduate students. Perhaps sixty percent of the ten German students each year earned a TUDOR MA, and a further perhaps eight or ten stayed and did a doctorate with us.

There were perhaps two "capstone" programs with Germany. For the 1979/80 academic year I wrote to sixty university faculty members all over Europe with the proposal described just below. The responses were uniformly negative from France, Spain, Holland, Italy, Sweden, Switzerland, Austria and Rumania. However, instead of just one or two positive responses from Germany there were thirteen! Nine were universities: Freiburg im Br., Tübingen, Heidelberg, Bonn, Duisburg, Münster, West Berlin, East Berlin, and Regensburg. An additional four came from Catholic and Protestant Academies (conference centers), Aachen, Arnoldshain, West Berlin, and East Berlin. Temple University would conduct a graduate seminar on Jewish-Christian relations in fall 1979 and spring 1980 in conjunction with the German universities, after which we would come to Germany/Austria for face to face dialogues. We were four professors (Sloyan, Catholic; van Buren, Episcopal; Schachter,

Jewish; and Swidler, Catholic), and thirteen graduate students, six Jewish, four Protestant, and three Catholic.

We travelled together for over one month, the funding coming from a special grant from the West German Foreign Office that I was able to solicit. The impact on the Americans was stunning but the effect on the Germans was staggering! A glimpse of it may be found in the Special Issue of the Journal of Ecumenical Studies devoted to it. Just a word on how it began. We flew first to Brussels on Sabena Airlines because that was the closest to our first destination, Aachen, Germany. As we waited for the arrival of our luggage, Zalman and I walked out to the front of the airport to check on our bus. As we came out, Zalman looked up and said, "Len, the last time I looked at this Belgian sky it was full of Stuka Dive Bombers." I knew what Stukas were, but I had never experienced them screaming down preparing to drop their bombs on me. Moments like that occurred all throughout the trip—life-shaping!

Zalman was born in Galicia, Poland, and grew up in Vienna. After the *Anschluss*, the Nazi takeover, in 1938, of Austria Zalman's father smuggled his family to the Belgian border, only to be betrayed and left standing by the smuggler. He later tried again, and this time succeeded, giving them two years breathing before the Stukas and the Blitzkrieg roared in. Zalman and family fled south before the invading armies to Switzerland, only to be refused entry. The father was eventually able to get the family on a French boat in Marseille, across the Mediterranean to French North Africa, across the hump of Africa to Dakar, via ship to South America, and then Caribbean island-hopping until they at long last landed safely in Brooklyn. This "going home again" for Zalman, and all of us with him, was an irreplaceable experience. This was indeed Deep-Dialogue!

8. *Jews and TUDOR*

Quite independently, the Reconstructionist Movement within Judaism wanted to start its own seminary and wanted to do so in conjunction with a university. Intimate to this planning was Rabbi Arthur Gilbert, who knew about the Swidler/Smith/*JES* move to Temple, and so approached Swidler about a possible collaboration. The upshot was that the Reconstructionist Rabbinical College was set up physically contiguous to Temple and arranged that they would accept students for rabbinical training only if they were at the same time accepted into the TUDOR doctoral program. This provided a steady flow of bright Jewish graduate students in TUDOR, while the religious spread of the faculty also drew a wide range of students from different religions and cultures.

It was while teaching at the Catholic Duquesne University in Pittsburgh (1960-66) that I first became involved with interreligious dialogue by working with Rabbi Arthur Gilbert, the Executive Director of the "Committee on Religion in the Social Studies Curriculum," sponsored by the *National Conference of Christians and Jews*, 1964-65. I mentioned earlier that *JES* took on its first non-Christian Associate Editor already before the second volume was finished, in 1967. That Associate Editor was Rabbi Arthur Gilbert. Arthur was trained in Reform Judaism and worked most of his adult life in the field of interreligious dialogue, working for a number of years during the 1960s for the *National Conference of Christians and Jews (NCCJ)*. During that period he was the Executive Director of the "Committee on Religion in the Social Studies Curriculum" of the *NCCJ*, and that was when I met him at Duquesne University. I invited him to become an Associate Editor of *JES*. It was in that same period that Arthur also became intimately involved with the Jewish Reconstructionist Movement, founded by Rabbi Mordechai Kaplan and Rabbi Ira Eisenstein in the 1930s.

Various trajectories came together in the latter 1960s, with Vatican II and its commitment to Dialogue, the beginning of the Second Wave of Feminism with Betty Friedan's 1963 book *The Feminine Mystique,* the Civil Rights Movement, TUDOR being founded in 1964, adding Rabbi Gilbert to the staff of *JES* in 1965,

Temple University becoming a State-Related university in 1966, Swidler and *JES* joining TUDOR in 1966, and Rabbi Gilbert joining the Reconstructionist Movement administration in 1967.

Ira Eisenstein and Arthur Gilbert were the major figures planning the establishment of a Rabbinic Seminary for the Reconstructionist Movement in the late 1960s. When it was founded in 1968, Ira was the first President and Arthur the first Dean. They decided that they wanted to found the seminary in a close relationship to a major university. Serendipitously—or providentially?—Arthur knew of my and *JES*'s move to TUDOR and Chair Bernard Phillips' commitment to gathering a faculty of Jewish, Christian, Muslim, Hindu, and Buddhist-trained scholars, and so telephoned me to ask whether there might be an openness to exploring a relationship between a newly founded Reconstructionist Rabbinical College (RRC) and TUDOR. I assured him that Bernard would not only be open, but enthusiastic. The result was that the RRC bought property on North Broad Street adjacent to Temple University and mandated that for acceptance to study at RRC a student would have to be simultaneously accepted into the Ph.D. program at TUDOR! Thus, for about the next two decades TUDOR had a constant trove of highly trained Jewish doctoral students. Unfortunately, this arrangement was taken so for granted that when a new RRC president came in we let him get so far into land negotiations in the suburbs that the physical move of the RRC could not be hindered, which sadly soon also led to the loss of the mandated Jewish TUDOR doctoral students.

9. Recollections of the Early Relations of TUDOR and RRC

Sheila Hindery, the wife of Professor Roderick Hindery, took on the job as general factotum when the Reconstructionist Rabbinical College (RRC) set itself up physically in a large brownstone at Broad and Susquehanna streets, just three blocks from TUDOR's initial home. She reported in a letter recently that "it seemed ideal to (Rabbi) Arthur (Gilbert), especially its proximity to Temple. Setting up files for students, including admission documents, referrals, etc., kept me fully occupied. We had many drop-in visits by TUDOR religion faculty, e.g., Robert Gordis, Jacob Agus, etc., as well as world-renowned Jewish scholars whose names now escape me. Mordecai Kaplan (Founder of Reconstructionist Judaism) and Ira Eisenstein (Kaplan's son-in-law and first President of RRC) visited. The latter was with us quite frequently. Noam Chomsky's parents visited us once. The kitchen at the RRC, of course, was kosher. I recall ordering meals for visiting faculty and others occasionally.

"Arthur had an infectious enthusiasm, greeting people in the first-floor reception area. Commuting from New York and his home on Riverside Drive took a toll on him throughout the year. When I heard of his heart attack while jogging in New York I was not surprised. I recall warning him that he was burning the candle at both ends. (He was also a part-time teacher at Manhattan College.)

"As for Temple University, I found the milieu at the Department exciting, especially the early years from 1968-1982. There was a spirit of adventure in the air: the breath of ecumenism as exuded from the likes of Len Swidler, the charisma of dear Bernard Phillips, the exotic presence of scholars from eastern religious traditions, the sense of hope enkindled by the recent Vatican Council, and the felt expectation that big things were going to happen at the Department of Religion.

"Prima donnas and struggling junior faculty rubbed elbows in the crowded brownstone on Broad St. And, too, the politics of the day challenging the legitimacy of the Vietnam War, the emergence of feminism, and the civil rights movement contributed to the atmosphere everyone breathed.

"As the wife of a professor, I shared in many of the ups and downs of the department over the years. Hosting department gatherings, attending lectures on occasion, participating in picnics, etc. gave me a feel for the department's evolving ethos. As 'Harvard on the Delaware,' Temple's Department of Religion was never a zoo, as a competing university would have it. Rather it was a picture window projecting a panoramic view of the world's religions by men and women who dedicated their lives to revealing the richness of the human spirit."

10. TUDOR, TUJ and Journalism

There was at least one other expansive foray that I undertook for TUDOR—at Temple University Japan. Marvin Wachmanan inveterate internationalist while president of Temple University, started *Temple University Japan (TUJ)* in 1982 *www.tuj.ac.jp/about/japan-campus/*. Over the next ten years almost two dozen American universities and colleges established some kind of presence in Japan, but by the twenty-first century, all but Temple had folded. Today it is a strong, expanded TUJ which is recognized by the Japanese government (it took a decades-long fight to attain that!), with over 3,000 students and a variety of undergraduate and graduate programs.

I taught at TUJ in the summer of 1987, and fell in love with it, so that Andie and I arranged to teach at TUJ for the summer and academic year of 1990-91. One of the things I did then was to set up a Master's in Religion program, and taught the first graduate seminar in it. I know of at least one student who in fact finished the MA in Religion at TUJ. Unfortunately, without regular TUDOR faculty presence the program fell into abeyance. One could note that no one else was willing or interested to carry the project on, or that as a "serial entrepreneur" I failed to set up the necessary structure to ensure its continuance.

Another success/failure of mine at TUDOR was setting up a joint Master's program in religion and journalism. The reason for such a program was obvious to anyone who watched TV, listened to news on the radio, or read newspapers: the coverage of religious matters was miserable. What I proposed in 1987 was put into action when I was Director of Graduate Religion Studies 1991-93. The requirements for the program were as follows:

RELIGION AND JOURNALISM
Two Master's Options

1. The MA in Religion and Journalism or the MJ in Journalism and Religion be chosen by the student either at the beginning or at least before the completion of the program, although the program followed would be precisely the same.
2. The necessary Departmental prerequisites for whichever program chosen (including 1100 GRE minimum for the Religion and Journalism MA).
3. A minimum of 18 graduate credits in Religion at Temple.
4. A minimum of 16 credits in Journalism at Temple.
5. A 4-credit course in Religion & Journalism taught jointly by faculty from the two Departments.
6. A four-credit research/writing seminar conducted jointly by faculty from the two Departments—essentially a research and thesis-writing project under the guidance of regular meetings with the faculty and other grad students.
7. A total of 42 credits.
8. Since this is not an academic research-oriented degree, there is no foreign language requirement.
9. The Religion Department may wish to shift its proseminar requirements to 3 religious traditions (including Judaism and Christianity), social scientific methods, and religion in America.
10. A joint Religion and Journalism Committee be set up to be responsible for the program and students, and, *very important*, the promotion of the program nationally and recruitment and placement of graduating students.
11. As this program progresses, the feasibility of expanding it to include a joint Master's program (if then thought desirable) and doctoral program will be investigated by the Committee.

May 3, 1987, Leonard Swidler

In fact, at least one student took the program and earned an MJ with a religion emphasis. However, the necessary structure was not put into place and the program subsequently withered—through the lack of faculty interest, and my failure as a serial entrepreneur.

10. TUDOR and Now

Here we are in the year 2019, more than a half century after the founding of TUDOR (and, as it happens, also of the *Journal of Ecumenical Studies*), and more than a half-century into Temple University's formally becoming a State-Related University of the Commonwealth of Pennsylvania and my arrival at TUDOR (both, 1966). What a fantastic and enormously productive fifty-plus years! A whole new paradigm of how to study religion was launched, at first ridiculed, and long since almost universally imitated. Were they here now, Ernie Stoeffler and Bernard Phillips would doubtlessly be extremely pleased to review the extraordinary past half century and the equally extraordinary role TUDOR has played in it—and will continue to play in the future. Andie and I are extraordinarily pleased to have had a role in it—and will continue to have in the foreseeable future, *Deo volente*—God Willing!

THE EDUCATION I WASN'T SUPPOSED TO GET, AND HOW I GOT SOME OF IT AT TEMPLE

JOHN RAINES

I was hired by Temple University and joined the faculty of the Department of Religion in the Fall of 1966. I had yet to finish my dissertation at Union Theological Seminary and so came to Temple as an Instructor. A year later with my dissertation in hand I was promoted to Assistant Professor. I would remain at Temple, teaching undergraduates and graduates, for the next 46 years.

It was a heady time in the history of the Religion Department. Tom Dean, also from Union, and I were soon to be followed by new tenured and tenure-track additions, so that by the middle 1970s we had become a department of over twenty full time professors and thus the largest non-seminary connected faculty teaching religion in the country. And it was religion we taught, not theology. Of course, we studied and taught the major texts from the various Western traditions, just as we studied the classic texts of the Eastern or Wisdom traditions. But at Temple we studied them as part of the rich heritage of insight into the human condition embedded in those texts and traditions. That is to say, we taught religion not dogmatically but descriptively. Religion was for us a *human* enterprise.

Back then, this was a sharp departure even from the liberal Protestant tradition that Union Seminary represented. I was doing graduate work there in the 1960s and Karl Barth, with his austere Reformed Christianity, was all the rage for some of my student colleagues. Barth, following up on John Calvin's insistence upon "total depravity," argued that because of sin, human religions were naturally and inevitably idolatrous, a fate that only Reformed Christianity, with its profound grasp upon the disastrous results of the Fall, could and occasionally did escape.

The arrogance of that claim seemed mostly missed by many of my Union colleagues, some of whom were obsessed with finding "certainty" in their faith endeavors. I remember one asking me, full of passion and yearning, "where can we put our foot down except on the Bible?" (as interpreted by Barth). I replied, "Try putting your foot down on the earth!" Yes, even back then I was beginning to sense that the search for "certainty," for "confident conviction," for the "voice of authoritative authority," was a misplaced search and should be abandoned in favor of a more modest ambition. But even Union, with its powerful attraction to Jewish scholars like Buber and Heschel, remained quietly proud of its own history and reputation as this country's leader in the progressive but distinctively Protestant religious movement. It was, back then, the voice of the Protestant Establishment that still commanded the culture - at least of the East Coast.

It was symbolic of this hegemony that President Eisenhower came to the upper West Side of Manhattan in the late 1950s to lay the foundation stone of what would soon become known as "the God Box," located just across the street from Union. This building would, for a while, house the national headquarters of all the mainstream Protestant denominations. God's "Box" was Protestant.

It was with this mixed Protestant intellectual heritage that I came to Temple in the Fall of 1966. And that was the beginning of a big change. Because of Vatican II (1962 – 1965) and its spirit of openness to the modern world, a regular tidal wave of very bright Roman Catholic lay and religious poured into our doctoral program. Soon, these would be followed by a similar inundation of Muslim graduate students brought from around the world by the amazing charismatic and entrepreneurial skills of Ismail 'al Faruqi. The student mix in my graduate seminars looked nothing like the student mix at Union, or at Harvard, Yale, or Princeton. I was learning how to teach folks whose cultures I had previously hardly known. In my mind the Protestant Establishment was beginning to drift away. Little did we Protestants realize back then that this eclipse was happening not just in minds like my own but in our nation as a whole.

Shortly after I was hired my senior colleague Ernest Stoeffler told me that I was hired "to carry forward the work and spirit of Reinhold Niebuhr," for whom I served as class assistant at Union in the early 1960s. My discipline was called "Christian Social Ethics" and its task was to address "the powers that be" with the critical voice of the Hebrew prophets. I had been born in 1933 into those "powers that be," enjoying a childhood, an original and originating identity, and view of the world as a privileged member in waiting of that Protestant Establishment. It included private schools, private country clubs, an elite college and, yes, a confident and elite graduate school.

But I acquired an unexpected adulthood when I joined the Civil Rights Movement in 1961 as a Freedom Rider. Along with two blacks and another white I would (for the first but not the last time in my life) be arrested in the "white waiting room" of the Little Rock Trailways Bus Station. We were charged with a "threatened breach of the peace." Judge Quinn Glover, a white guy of class privilege just like me, took us into chambers before finding us guilty and sentencing us to six months in prison. He said, "I know the Supreme Court has ruled that you had a constitutional right to be in that waiting room. But I'm going to find you guilty because if I don't, I won't get reelected and the guy running against me is worse on niggras (sic) than I am."

What a defining moment in my still young and unfinished selfhood. For the first time in my life I was standing outside of power and regarded by power as a threat. And power had the power to punish me for that. That moment became the opening of a whole new adulthood where my teachers would be black civil rights workers in the South who would begin for me a second education I wasn't supposed to get and didn't even know I needed. Power, privilege, law and order—the land I inherited and inhabited—was for me no longer anchored in the taken for granted world of everyday reality, but instead must be met with a sustained hermeneutic of suspicion. I was becoming a subversive reincarnation of my birth self!

In my earlier credentialed and credentialing education I had been taught much (of course) about Protestant Christianity, less (much less) about Roman Catholic Christianity, a tiny bit about Jewish religious beliefs and practices, and nothing whatsoever about Islam. This absence in my graduate instruction instructed me (without saying it) that there was in the minds of the academic establishment nothing of importance we religious scholars of the West needed to learn about Islam.

Then I bumped into Ismail 'al Faruqi, or better he bumped into me! He was becoming noted (notorious?) in the scholarly world for his project called "the Islamization of knowledge." At the time I was reading postmodern critics like Foucault and Bourdieu who taught me that scholarship was best understood as a business enterprise and knowledge as a field of contestation where power and legitimacy were at stake. Could it be that the academic enterprise of the West was complicit with the colonial ambitions of the West—ambitions that continued in the so-called post-colonial world and remained alive and well—namely, the attempt to occupy not just the land and economy but the hearts and minds of the "still developing" world?!

I began to learn from my Muslim students and colleagues to draw into question the whole popular language of dividing the world into the "developed" and "developing" world. I began to suspect the arrogance and ignorance that was embedded in that way of dividing and inscribing the world. It helped that I was reading scholars who were critical of the established scholarly enterprise. But what really brought the lesson home was the obvious intelligence and moral seriousness of the followers of Islam, who were my students and friends. What was the Western academy teaching them when their reality as "still developing" and our own reality was already "developed?" If we, the West, are "developed" that must mean we have realized the Promise of the Enlightenment and have mastered the game of modernity. The other "still developing" only need to learn from us to join in that happy future. The "still developing" certainly had nothing important to add to the discussion. We knew the way; all they had to do was follow the path we had already forged. That misplaced self-importance became and remains the logic of the International Monetary Fund and The World Bank.

What had started for me on the dusty roads of the Jim Crow South was broadening into a hermeneutic of suspicion directed at the whole language of development that was, rather obviously, developing a world of a few very rich winners and many losers and a recommended consumer lifestyle that was environmentally unsustainable. I was going decidedly Left just as the intellectual establishment, including many within my own discipline of Christian Ethics, were going Right—into the ethics of the professions (law, medicine, business) or the theological tragic sensibility of Hauerwas and his "resident aliens." But clearly, we humans were and are not "alien" in any fundamental sense or, as Darwin saw, we would not have become "residents" in the first place. I became convinced that we ethicists—Christian, Muslin, Hindu, you name it—had to humble ourselves to the this-worldly task of species preservation. And that species' task involved cooperating across vast doctrinal and ritual differences as we discovered our new fellow travelers spread widely across the world were driven by the same vision of crisis. Below and behind our religious differences we are humans absolutely dependent upon the thick living network of materiality that modernity treated as "raw stuff" to be used and then thrown away. (There is in fact no "away" there. We drink the same water and breathe the same air as Buddha and Moses did.) The dual task of economic and ecological justice—two sides of the same coin—opened for me a radical "dialogue of civilizations." And I was not alone there. In the 1980s and 1990s Temple University and the Department of Religion fell upon hard times. Undergraduate enrollments shrank, budgets had to be cut, and retiring faculty were not replaced. Starting out at a high of 22 full-time faculty members, our department retrenched and at one point numbered only 9. Then, with the new millennium, the students started to return in a big way! Life in the city became less a threat and a danger than an invitation into the energy of a rich and vibrant urban culture.

The department started to rebuild. But would it, could it, preserve its original and originating identity? Now, well-endowed universities began to follow the path we at Temple had earlier forged in seeing and studying religion as a human endeavor to be explored not doctrinally or dogmatically but descriptively. We were becoming a department of religious anthropology. But were we losing our critical edge on issues of justice—even as the world was becoming every year more and more unequal in terms of income and wealth, and thus more and more concentrated in terms of how power worked. The Occupy Wall Street movement signaled a deep hunger, and it quickly spread worldwide. But it found little welcome in the academic world and certainly no home there. It was the business and engineering schools that got the shiny new buildings and the bragging rights of academic administrators. How ironic, the very financial system that was responsible for the Great Recession was being looked to by more and more of our best and brightest as the likely source of future employment, as if there was only one game in town and they had better learn to play it. Their mentors became the ones they used to despise. An impractical practicality became popular.

But the hunger was still there. There is a blessed itch out there that this generation cannot scratch away. But the change required for economic and ecological justice to prevail seemed so daunting as to invite a kind of lethargy of hope. But that kind of sad disappointment is possible only for the relatively privileged. The single mother in rural Africa trying to keep her children from starving under the conditions of absolute poverty is too busy trying to keep herself and her kids alive day after day to be disappointed. The demands of survival focus her energy and her efforts and consume her attention.

It is, I think, an accurate metaphor for where we find ourselves as a species, and our precarious promise of a tomorrow. Known or unknown, acknowledged or ignored, our species is that struggling young mother. So we, as she, must try.

Significant change, precisely because it is significant and would change the way the world works, always appears impossible until in retrospect it seems inevitable.

THE YEARS OF EARLY GROWTH (1965-85)

GERARD S. SLOYAN

I had been the chairman for ten years of a religion department in a graduate school of arts and sciences that had achieved a certain eminence on the national scene. The Catholic University of America was founded in 1889 as a school of graduate studies only, as were Johns Hopkins and Clark Universities. Like them, however, it shortly added an undergraduate college for men to prepare them for graduate work. A difference at Temple College was that not long after its founding in 1888, women were admitted.

The academic department I served as head brought it to the attention of not only the numerous fledgling graduate departments of religion and theology around the country but also, uncomfortably, to that of its internal near neighbor, the School of Sacred Theology. That school, which was as old as the university itself, awarded degrees to young men preparing for priestly ministry and, at the graduate level, men already in priest's orders. Seven or eight years before 1966, the initial date of the memoir to follow, Brothers in teaching congregations were admitted to theological study and five years later two religious Sisters. Meanwhile, the number and quality of candidates for the MA and PhD in the study of the Bible and theology in the adjacent School of Arts and Sciences was steadily on the increase. This caused a certain discomfort for the older school. The Theology faculty attempted to relieve their discomfort by an administrative coup that would absorb the students for the PhD but not the MA or all the college students who were taking eight semesters of required religion courses.

At the same time, something roughly comparable was taking place in north Philadelphia. Temple University had long had a School of Theology but not in the Baptist tradition of its founder Russell Conwell. It was generically evangelical Protestant in character and prepared degree candidates chiefly for the mission field, who then sought ordination from their respective churches. When Herman Gladfelter, a Lutheran layman, sought and received state related status for the university, he knew that a confessional institution could not continue. He therefore inaugurated a department of religion qualified to offer degrees at the three levels.

When the attempt at the snatch of a graduate student body was made for a third time in the course of several years at The Catholic University by the route of Church politics, I began to make inquiries about an opening for a young full professor with a respectable publication record. Fordham University and The University of Notre Dame offered me a position in their then weak religion departments. One evening in winter of 1967 I received a telephone call from T. Patrick Burke, a colleague at The Catholic University of America who had just come off the train from Philadelphia. The message was, "I have been offered a job by the chairman of the religion department at Temple University and he's looking for another Catholic." I had known something of Temple as a commuter school with a law faculty but little else about it, and was not attracted by the prospect of a position there. Later though, having learned that a friend, Daniel Callahan of the Hastings Center of health research, was offering a graduate course in its religion department, I got in touch with him. He told me that the chairman, Bernard Phillips, was building something of scholarly importance by adding to the already hired Paul Van Buren and Leonard Swidler, whose names I was familiar with, a number of adjuncts like himself, including a Swami Nikilinanda and Richard Kroner, a retired European professor of academic repute. Dan Callahan was enthusiastic at the possibility of my being offered a job at Temple.

On the basis of that recommendation I contacted Professor Phillips and relayed Patrick Burke's message, asking if I might come for an interview. He said yes, by all means. When I arrived, my enthusiasm was dimmed somewhat by learning that the department's offices were in a row house on Broad Street immediately north of Conwell Hall. Phillips, however, offset the impression by proving to be more than gracious. In a visit with him I was told the history of Russell Conwell's foundation of a college he named for his Grace Baptist Church well east of Broad Street, later simply The Baptist Temple. This energetic pastor intended the college to be for working Philadelphians of both sexes who could never aspire to a University of Pennsylvania, Haverford, or Swarthmore education. Phillips went on to explain Temple's recently acquired state-related status and the circumstances of the founding of a religion department. He then surprised me by booking me for two other interviews. The first of these was with the acting president, Paul Anderson. Phillips stayed for a three-cornered visit while Anderson explained how his predecessor, Herman Gladfelter, had successfully achieved Commonwealth-related status for Temple a few years before on the same date as for the University of Pittsburgh, equally a private institution. The reasons were obvious, Anderson said. The Commonwealth of Pennsylvania had only one institution of higher education, the Pennsylvania State University, which meant that people of college age who sought an education at the lower fees of public colleges were enrolling in adjacent state institutions. There were numerous public teacher training colleges in Pennsylvania and even more Catholic and Protestant foundations, but the state had clearly not been meeting its educational responsibilities. Hence, the adoption of Temple and Pittsburgh under the administrative and fiscal control of the state governor and legislature.

I was favorably impressed by Anderson's modest demeanor but even more that Phillips had brought me for an interview with him. We went next to visit with the college dean, Rohten Smith, who explained the recent inaugurating of graduate degrees in the departments that had the faculty strength for them. I had made sure that Temple's religion department was awarding the MA and PhD before I first got in touch with Bernard Phillips. He then turned me over to his strong right arm, Ernest Stoeffler, who I later learned was the sole faculty member of the School of Theology Phillips had retained for the newly founded Department of Religion. Professor Stoeffler brought me to lunch in the faculty club housed in the suites of a former funeral home on Broad Street. His warmth of manner was not in contrast but more in complement to Phillips' brisk tone in conveying factual data about the university and the department's setting in it.

After lunch I was brought back to the department to be introduced to two faculty members in turn, Leonard Swidler and Thomas Dean. Swidler I had known by reputation as a Duquesne University professor with whom I had the work of Catholic higher education in common. He clued me in on his co-founding with Elwyn Smith, who had left the Pittsburgh Seminary faculty to join Temple's simultaneously with him, of *The Journal of Ecumenical Studies*. Swidler told me that his wife Arlene had done much of the editorial work. The two men had been hired in the previous year and their fledgling publication brought to the Temple campus as part of their appointments to the faculty. The Tom Dean interview, and it was that, I found amusing. But I took care not to convey this to the interviewer. This earnest young man with a shock of unruly blond hair began immediately to engage me with a series of questions. The first was to ask what I thought of St. Anselm's ontological argument. I had trouble keeping from smiling as I realized what was going on. I, who at forty-seven and a professor of New Testament had conducted numerous interviews as a department head with priest applicants for faculty positions, was being interviewed, and on a subject out of my field. By luck I had conducted a seminar with PhD candidates a few years before in which we explored a number of landmark theological writings. The *Proslogion* in English translation was one of them—I had never tackled the *Monologion*—and so I put the best face I could on my remembered knowledge. The meeting ended amiably. I was impressed with my questioner's philosophical learning, which the monk of Bec and later archbishop of Canterbury thought of as theologically suitable for dialogue with Jews and Muslims. I never learned what Dean thought of my philosophical grasp. Before joining up with Professor Phillips in late afternoon I took a private walking tour of the campus and tried to identify Sullivan and Mitten Halls by their use, as well as a number of others of more recent construction and quite good architectural design. All this added to the good impression made by the men—no women—I had conversed with earlier in the day, and convinced me that both university and department were "go-ahead" enterprises. If I came to Temple I was sure it would be in conjunction with female students and faculty as was the case in all my Washington years. I had worn my black suit and Roman collar that day, normal street dress for the Catholic clergy, and no one remarked on my status besides the academic, which cheered me. The interviewers took me for the university professor that I was and were not put off by my clerical state. I was aware at the time of two priests who had had visiting appointments of a semester or a year at universities that were not Church related: John Courtney Murray of a rural Jesuit seminary faculty, who had been influential in the framing of the Second Vatican Council's "Declaration on Religious Liberty," at Yale, and Bernard Häring of the Congregation of the Most Holy Redeemer of a theological faculty allied with Rome's Gregorian University, at Brown. If I came to Temple, I knew I would be the first priest in the country to have a tenured appointment at a university not conducted by the Catholic Church. More importantly, Temple was the first public university and probably the only university of any sort in the country to teach in academic fashion the full spread of the world's major religious traditions.

In the car driving me back to the airport where he had earlier come to get me, Bernard Phillips looked straight ahead at the road and said in a somewhat hesitant tone that he was able to offer me a faculty position, and if I accepted would I find sixteen thousand five hundred dollars acceptable? For someone who had been a full professor three years at thirty-six hundred dollars, room, board, and laundry (the Catholic University of America had long settled on sharply dis-counted salaries for priests and vowed Brother and Sister faculty members), it was a remarkable sum in terms of where the U.S. dollar stood in the 1960s. I had not imagined that an offer would be made on the spot. Taken by surprise, I might have wished to give an immediate acceptance but said I would write my decision within a week or ten days. I was not self-importantly taking the invitation "under consideration" but knew that I had to get the permission of the Bishop of Trenton to make the move. This had nothing to do with money since diocesan priests are in charge of their own finances, having only to repay at ordination the cost of the six years of seminary education. The three years of my pursuit of a Ph.D. had been taken care of by the people of the Diocese of Trenton without their knowing who I was or what work the bishop of the time meant to put me to. The matter was otherwise. At the point of ordination a diocesan candidate had to make a promise to the current bishop that he would be obedient to him and his successors and would, with the help of God's grace, go unmarried for life. Trenton's bishop of the time had been my seminary professor of doctrinal theology, lecturing in Latin. I asked for a date regarding a fairly important matter and he invited me to his home for the evening meal. He had released me seventeen years earlier for service in the national Catholic university and probably supposed that my question was somehow in the same order. After a brief exchange in his study after supper, he said quite matter-of-factly, "Why, yes, go if that's what you want to do."

Later that summer I found a first-floor apartment near Head House Square, knowing only one other person in Philadelphia besides its archbishop. That was a man I had worked with at a meeting of some 13,000 people four years before in the city's Civic Center, a National Liturgical Week sponsored by a group of which at the time I was the president. It would be a challenge to know only one person after having been in close contact with many hundreds in the seventeen years in Washington. On that first night in a strange city I wandered out and, under a full moon, sat on a stone bench in Old St. Mary's cemetery on Fourth Street, quite desolate, wondering what I had gotten myself into. Early the next morning I was on the city subway making a change at City Hall, going north. As I climbed the steps at Montgomery Avenue (later Cecil B. Moore), I looked up to see Sister Charles Mary Fahy of the Congregation of Notre Dame de Namur. This time, remarkably, she was dressed in a two-piece wool suit and not the black habit with white trim and black veil I was familiar with. I knew that the Church of the West had recently undergone many cultural changes besides ritual language. But why was she here in Philadelphia and not in the halls of Trinity College preparing for another school year armed with the Master's degree toward which I had helped steer her? The answer was obvious. She was headed toward registration for classes leading to a PhD in religion. When I reached the department offices I immediately closeted with Dr. Phillips and we talked about course offerings and schedule. He proposed one course each with undergraduates by day and graduates by night. Thinking that I could not propose anything in professedly Christian studies (which proved not to be the case) I suggested two courses in the Bible: the Old Testament with the college class, something I had done many times before, and a New Testament course with graduates. Assured that if I taught both critically there could be no Church/State problem in a tax-supported university, I need not have worried. Very shortly I learned that my first Jewish colleague was teaching rabbinic Judaism freely and the chairman Buddhist or Hindu thought with equal liberty. I also continued to come to the campus in the clergy attire of my previous twenty-three years.

I am not sure whom I met among my fellow department members that first day but within the week I was in conversation with Stoeffler, Swidler and Dean, and then the other men already on the faculty. Paul Van Buren, ordained to ministry in the Episcopal Church and a student under Karl Barth at Basel, was on a sabbatical leave so I did not meet him for a year. There was, however, John Raines in religious ethics who had completed work for his PhD at the Union Theological Seminary not long before. Thomas Dean had done the same, but memory tells me that neither his degree nor Raines's had yet been awarded. I met a cheerful young man named Alan Cutler, a Jew but not a teacher of Judaism, rather of Islam. There were three others who had completed course work at Temple but were writing dissertations. They were Leonard Barrett, a native Jamaican and an ordained Methodist minister, whose doctorate would be in cultural anthropology, and two who were PhD candidates in the department where they were already teaching college students. They were Richard DeMartino, a Brooklynite who in the Navy had come abreast of the Japanese language and privately immersed himself in the Zen Buddhist tradition, and Lowell Streiker, of Jewish family, who had become a Lutheran Christian.

Four others had joined the religion department faculty along with me: Samuel Laeuchli, a native of Basel, who upon coming to the States, had taken a doctorate at New York's Union Theological Seminary; Rabbi Robert Gordis, who journeyed to Temple for his classes while maintaining a congregational pulpit in Far Rockaway, Long Island; Patrick Burke, a native of Toowoomba, Australia, whose first appointments after doctoral study in Europe were in the University of Iowa's famed religion department supported by Rockefeller money and at St. Xavier in Chicago, a Sisters of Mercy college for women; and lastly Maurice Friedman, an Oklahoma native most recently at Sarah Lawrence College in Bronxville, New

York. We were all happy to get to know each other and did so by direct conversations and circuitous inquiry. Burke was the only formal Christian theologian among the new arrivals but among those already there, Van Buren and Swidler would be numbered. The latter had earned a Licentiate in Theology after a year of study in the Catholic faculty of Tübingen University. His earlier degree was a doctorate in history from the University of Wisconsin.

I thoroughly enjoyed the first two classes I taught, having had Jewish and Protestant students in numbers seated before me for the first time. The eight or nine graduate students included two Catholic Sisters, a Filipina female member of a Secular Institute known as the Ladies of the Grail, and a Greek orthodox priest. Only the last was in the course as part of his pursuit of the MA, which was just as well because only he and the Filipina woman had the intellectual equipment and training for it. The others were "sampling" a new Catholic professor. On the college front where some twenty-five or thirty were enrolled (one semester of religion or philosophy study had lately become a BA requirement), I was struck by the intelligence of two Jewish students in particular, a young woman and a man. Her family name was the same as that of a man who with his partner O'Hara had a corner on the high school uniforms for girls market in the Catholic schools of that city. But no, that was not her family. After two months of exploration of the five books of Moses I proceeded toward the pre- and postexilic prophets in historical fashion. At that point the lad raised his hand in the middle of a critical exposition to say, respectfully, "That's not the way our rabbis taught it." "What way was that?" I asked and he responded, "By telling us *midrashim*," the homiletic elaborations on the text rather than the text itself. I said rather lamely that I was not capable of that method and when I taught the Christian Scriptures it was not the academic custom to do so by way of the legends of the saints, some of which conceivably conveyed the core of certain scriptural passages. He was unmoved. But I think I retained his friendship.

Later, I learned, he went on to the Jewish Theological Seminary in New York and was ordained to the rabbinate of Conservative Judaism. The young woman proceeded from the graduation platform to the newly founded Reconstructionist Rabbinical College adjacent to the Temple campus, where I taught her again, this time in a graduate course in some aspect of Christianity.

The listing of new department faculty in the fall of 1967 provides a cue to listing another four who joined us one year later. There was not faculty consultation or interview of candidates. Bernard Phillips did it all, as I had done in a department headship. That was the way of academic life forty-odd years ago. Our new colleagues were Franklin H. Littell, the former president of Iowa Wesleyan College; Jacob Agus, a distinguished congregational rabbi and lecturer at Baltimore Hebrew College; Isma'il al Faruqi, a Palestinian Muslim whose doctorate in philosophy was from Indiana University; and Roderick Hindery, a Benedictine monk of Conception Abbey in Missouri. The last-named appointment is part of a story worth telling.

In the spring of 1968 Professor Phillips' application for a semester's study leave was approved and he asked Ernest Stoeffler to assume the duties of chairman in the upcoming semester. He asked me to act as director of graduate studies in Stoeffler's place. Phillips set me up in his own office and went off to Asia for some field research on Hindu or Islamic life. Continuing to teach with an added undergraduate section, I immediately began to explore the files on currently enrolled graduate students. They were fat with the records of men, largely Protestant clergy of the Delaware Valley, who had not been enrolled in either the previous or the current year. They had taken most of their courses with Drs. Phillips, Stoeffler, and the not yet Dr. DeMartino. I invited all fifteen or twenty of them to the campus for an interview, asking if they wished to continue for the Ph.D. in religion, and if so to register for course work in the fall. If their ministerial duties had proved too demanding, then resignation from the program was indicated.

They did not take my two options kindly. In general, they let me know that they had been assured that academic exposure to several religions of the world besides their own, at a pace their busy lives allowed, would lead to the award of a doctorate. None had been counseled to begin consideration of a dissertation topic. I discussed the terms of study for the PhD gently but firmly. All but one of my visitors left the chairman's office visibly unhappy. Upon Bernard Phillips' return he did not express his displeasure with me but, without speaking of it, called each of them to say that by no means did they need to drop out. The one I spoke of returned to taking classes and in course earned an honest doctorate. What it taught me was that our chairman had received approval from the dean and president for the nine hires described above by dint of the rapid growth of the graduate student body in the study of the world's religions.

The chairman had made another important move in the year preceding his semester's absence, namely getting approval for an expert in individual or personal ethics to complement John Raines in social ethics. The opening had been advertised through the American Academy of Religion (previously named the National Association of Bible Instructors, its acronym the Hebrew word for prophet, *nabi*). Applications arrived through the winter and spring. We all read them and by vote invited the most likely candidate to come east for interview. Hindery made the same favorable impression in person he had on paper and mentioned early in the exchange that he had recently taken steps to resign from monastic life and from the exercise of priestly ministry before he began the job search. Hoping now that this would not be a barrier to his being considered, he was assured that it would not. He returned home and was shortly thereafter offered a faculty position. Dr. Phillips, upon his return from foreign parts, took our corporate action amiss, despite reminding him that it was he who had gotten permission from the dean for the hire and that the waters might have closed over the slot then and in the indefinite future if we had not acted.

Something of much greater importance occurred in the academic year 1968-69. Being ever alert to expansion possibilities, Bernard Phillips learned of the intention of the plan of the Reconstructionist wing of American Judaism to found a rabbinical seminary in Philadelphia. Proximity to the research library of Dropsie College was the initial reason for the choice of location but also relevant was the fact that the founder of the movement, Mordecai Kaplan, then in his high nineties, had a trusted son-in-law, Ira Eisenstein, who lived in the city. A president of the new institution, Arthur Gilbert, had already been chosen and a handsome old brownstone on the west side of north Broad Street was purchased. Negotiations with Gilbert moved rapidly—several of us faculty were in on the discussions—and it was agreed that applicants for admission should have college records that showed them capable of PhD study at Temple concurrently with their pursuit of the Doctorate of Hebrew Letters in a five-year course. The arrangement was so ordered and resulted in the department's having some of its most distinguished students for the College's first ten years at least. After that, increasing numbers chose not to become academics in the study and teaching of religion, and availed themselves of degree possibilities elsewhere in the University.

Shortly after the initial student body of six arrived for dual enrollment three women joined them. This was at a time when neither the Reform nor Conservative U.S. seminary was entertaining female candidates for the rabbinate. Similar developments occurred at the same time on the Christian and the Muslim fronts, in the latter case by Professor al Faruqi's successful recruitment of students from around the Islamic world. In these years the Episcopal Church Seminary in West Philadelphia was planning a move to fuse with the Episcopal Divinity School in Cambridge, Massachusetts, while the Divinity School of Yale University was rumored to be interested in the student body and certain faculty members of the Jesuit seminary in Woodstock, Maryland. The seminary had announced its closing and relocation. Dr. Phillips arranged a luncheon meeting of three or four colleagues with the noted ecumenist theologian George Lindbeck, a Lutheran layman like Rudolf Bultmann, for exploratory purposes. The meeting was thoroughly cordial in a professional way but Phillips's hopes were dashed early in the meal when Lindbeck, who might not have known the reason he had been asked to come from New Haven other than ecumenical exchange, mentioned that his faculty was about to explore the possibility of an invitation to the entire Jesuit enterprise to come to New Haven. That came to naught when it was discovered that "our Fathers who art in Woodstock" intended to move to upper Manhattan with a view to its proximity to Columbia University. That seminary had two faculty members who had served as *periti* (skilled theologians) at the Second Council of the Vatican that had adjourned three years before, and a slightly overaged student body by a Catholic norm in virtue of a two-year novitiate rather than the normal one year and a day, and a three-year interruption between philosophy and theology studies for pastoral work, usually high-school teaching. Yale Divinity School was just as well off that its idea came to nothing because the Jesuit move to the metropolis was marked by the sharp decline in seminary enrollment that marked the post-Conciliar era countrywide. There was a diminished interest of men preparing for the priesthood in theological study in favor of part-time pastoral work on the streets of a great city. The Missouri Province of Jesuits had the same experience in bringing their seminary from eastern Kansas into St. Louis. Other factors played a part, starting with the *Zeitgeist* and the urban cultural milieu.

Meantime, word spread around the country that Temple's religion department was such a place for study in the setting of a major city. Student applicants grew in number and quality along with faculty members and course offerings. A major factor was the support for the study of religion and the religions shown by now-

Chancellor Gladfelter and President Anderson. The same was true of the dean of the College of Arts and Sciences, George Johnson, appointed in the fall of 1967 even though he had not yet completed work for his Columbia PhD in English. Johnson's energetic inquiry into Phillips' requests for new appointments and follow-up once they had been made was very much part of the department's growth and development. Its neighbor religion department at the University of Pennsylvania received no such encouragement from its chairman's academic superiors. Smaller in number of faculty, its professors of religious traditions other than the Christian or Jewish were Americans trained in such study at American universities. The contrast with those at Temple, who professed an academic exposition of religions to which they were committed, was marked. Bernard Phillips' recruitment principle caused the unhappy chairman at Penn to describe Temple's expanding department in print as "a religious zoo." In those early years of growth, it was commonplace to hear outsiders describe Temple University as having a program in comparative religion. That term, whatever it may mean, was surely wrong, if for no other reason that no professor knew any religion other than his own in sufficient depth to make a comparison. Each felt free in the classroom to teach about the religion he knew best without a belaboring of the excellence of that tradition bordering on its superiority. Early professors of Jewish and Islamic faith at Temple found it hardest to adhere strictly to such limits, especially with undergraduates seated before them who had grown up in a culture ignorant of or grossly misinformed about the religion in question. These college students did occasionally hear the special glories of a religion proclaimed. That was also true of a teaching assistant who had recently espoused Hare Krishna thought and was training students to intone *Omm* in class and dispensing sweet candy as a token of commitment to Vishnu under that name. He was told to desist.

As the standard of admissions to the program rose, especially of those from other countries who had English as a second language and the native-born who naïvely assumed they "knew their religion," there were corporate faculty decisions requiring comprehensive examinations at the end of course work for the MA or dropping students from the program at that time on the basis of poor performance. The word to students that caused the most anguish at that boundary marker was that some would be awarded the master's degree but not be allowed to continue for the doctorate. Such decisions were the work of the fairly high-powered faculty Professor Phillips had begun to assemble from 1964 on. They were not in the spirit of his ideal that exposure to the world's religions at the depth of classroom lectures was sufficient for the award of a degree. Such serious differences did not come up for discussion in department faculty meetings. They came to light only when the director of graduate studies promulgated such stringencies. The faculty members were well aware that the quality of the degrees they awarded was on the line. The more perceptive graduate students had the same concern. The defense of academically weak students by some instructors who had been chosen by them as their major professor became public knowledge. The chairman's fairly relaxed grasp of academic standards for the highest degree also came clear.

The result of all this was a fairly turbulent academic year, 1969-70, with some student agitation and discussion at the faculty level regarding the direction of reform at the top. This caused some faculty tension, unexpressed verbally among faculty head and members. One recently appointed lecturer in Hindu studies, Mrs. Dasgupta, still on leave from her southern state university, became the chairman's chief protagonist. She did not hesitate to harass her new colleagues verbally for their failure to come to his defense. A couple of meetings were called by the graduate student body to which their professors were invited. They were asked to do something about the situation. These were young professionals who thought their future in the job market might be imperiled. The faculty was in no mood to act. Finally, Dean Johnson, to whose attention the entire unpleasantness had been brought by student leaders demanding a change at the top, called a meeting of the department faculty on an April afternoon. He announced that in light of the department's turbulence which could not be allowed to continue, he had asked for and received the chairman's resignation. He proceeded to an election by secret ballot but without the previous nominating procedure. Opening the ballots before him, he announced the group's election of Gerard Sloyan without disclosing the tally.

The next four years passed with a faculty and student body silent about the above events, the founding chairman deeply wounded and communicating with his colleagues singly or corporately only through messages in mailboxes. His only presence on campus was to visit his own mailbox and his classrooms. The ensuing period was one of considerable faculty activity of a new sort. That began with frequent department faculty meetings, for a year or two as often as weekly, and always in a large assembly room in Sullivan Hall. The company which included two graduate student representatives discussed all questions except at the times when student progress toward degrees was under discussion. The price of pure democracy was long and often tedious meetings in which all had their say. In that period, the appointments of Charles Wei-Hsun Fu in Chinese Buddhist studies (he had been on the faculty of the University of Ohio in Athens) was accomplished, as was that of Bibhuti Yadav, a graduate of and lecturer in McMaster University at London, Ontario, in Hindu thought. Yadav succeeded a short-term incumbent, Santosh Sengupta, hired early in Sloyan's chairmanship. With the resignation of one of our professors of Judaism, Jacob Agus, a position was offered to Allan Lazaroff who accepted it but stayed for only two years. In his place Gerald Blidstein did the same, whose move was first to a Canadian faculty (in Montréal), then to Bar Ilan University in Beersheva, Israel. A colleague was needed for Isma'il al Faruqi in

Islamic thought and life and, after year or semester-long appointments of scholars from Egypt, Sudan, and India, and all with British university educations, a satisfactory settlement was made in the person of Hassan Hanafi, a native of Cairo. During the same period Professor al Faruqi made numerous trips abroad recruiting young teachers at college level from Malaysia, Indonesia, Nigeria, South Africa, and one from the Seychelles. Three women, one from the Republic of South Africa, were among them, anxious for US study and a degree. He also had the gift of persuading their home institutions or governments to fund them fully throughout their Temple years. New Reconstructionist Rabbinical students continued to come and enroll for the doctorate, while a new source was the Republic of Korea. These tended to be Protestant men who came to do divinity studies at Chestnut Hill's Westminster Theological Seminary (Conservative Presbyterian), and who applied to Temple after that course. An occasional Korean or Chinese Buddhist student also went the PhD route. Certain curricular revisions in Temple's undergraduate college in that period stipulated that one course in philosophy or religion would satisfy bachelor's degree requirements. This made the religion department happy that it had sufficient regular faculty and teaching assistants among the graduates to cover all the sections. The latter students came to be so numerous that some were part-time instructors in neighboring Catholic colleges for family support while studying. An undergraduate religion major had also been devised, which drew some outstanding young male and female scholars.

Toward the end of Sloyan's four years in the chair, Professor Maurice Friedman announced that he had been offered a position at San Diego State University and Professor Robert Gordis the same at his alma mater, the Jewish Theological Seminary in New York. When Sloyan went on a semester-length sabbatical in spring of 1974 he asked Paul Van Buren to assume the chairman's duties in his place, having announced his retirement from that position after two terms and necessitating the choosing a successor. Fairly early in his four-month stay in Cambridge, Massachusetts, he received a telephone call telling him that Bernard Phillips had died suddenly in the night, choking on a throat lozenge. The department founder had had a successful operation long before to remove a diseased throat gland. This meant that any winter cold or bronchitis could be perilous, but nothing keeps "like" approaching the cause of an accidental death. The men who had made him walk the plank never ceased to love and respect him. It was a silent and truly sorrowing assemblage in a north Broad Street funeral home for a religious service days later that bade him to fare well in his new life. Everyone among them knew that he owed Bernard the gift of a turn in his life to a new direction. The dozens of Temple University students and graduates who had remained in the area gathered in an identical mood of respect and gratitude.

Two important happenings marked the summer of 1974. Anderson Hall and Gladfelter Hall had been under construction for a year and were ready for occupancy in fall. Professor Van Buren was the group's choice of chairman. The interviews for a position in the psychology of religion had been made and a candidate selected, the department's first female member. She was Dr. Lucy Bregman, a native New Yorker, whose undergraduate studies had been in Pembroke College of Brown University and whose PhD was from the University of Chicago Divinity School. She had served briefly on the Indiana University faculty when Temple invited her. Unlike the Hindery hiring of six years before, the selection of this new colleague *in absentia praesidentis* [in the absence of the Chair] gave the retiring *sedes* person nothing but delight. Under Paul Van Buren's leadership the department needed to replace the resigned Professor Hanafi and did so by acquiring an Egyptian academic who had been teaching in Riyadh and was happy to come to the United States. His wife held France's highest degree in the literature of that language and was seeking a teaching opportunity that Saudi academia did not afford.

Another challenge created by the Gordis and Friedman departures was the naming of a person at associate level in Jewish studies. Under Sloyan's chairmanship, Lazaroff, Blidstein, and an Israeli woman of academic achievement, Rivkah Horwitz, were successively found but none stayed longer than two years. Van Buren's search efforts were rewarded with his discovery of the availability of Norbert Samuelson, a Reform rabbi, who was in a non-tenured assistant professor position at the University of Virginia in Charlottesville.

With something like a new stability achieved, the department was in for a period unmarked by change, or so it thought. It could not have reckoned with an administrative move several levels above it. On the night before the public announcement of Temple's appointment of an academic vice president and provost, President Marvin Wachman, called the chairman at his home to apologize for an inadvertent omission, namely that the new appointee had to be named to a faculty position, not to an administrative one only. The person in question, Gerhard Spiegler, had been a member of Haverford College's religion department when its trustees had named him acting president while the institution's president, John Coleman, a sociologist, had taken a year's leave of absence to work as a streets sanitation employee, literally field research for a book he was writing. Spiegler served so well in that office that Temple took steps to hire him in that administrative office. Wachman's afterthought also meant that Spiegler was a member of the religion department of record but nothing more. He was never introduced to his new colleagues as such and they in turn never met him in the next two years. In a strange twist of political action of the worst kind, some influential Jewish Philadelphians concluded quite erroneously that this man of German stock with a slight trace of an accent must have been in his boyhood a Nazi sympathizer or, if not that, being a German gentile was quite enough. In their wild ignorance the agitators neglected to discover that Spiegler's birth and early youth had been in a German enclave in Lithuania and that he was a Baptist, not of the state Lutheran-Reformed Church. A large segment of that clergy had thought National Socialism in its early stages a good thing. Moreover, the agitators were ignorant of the fact that Spiegler's father had been actively opposed to the Hitler regime. The pressure on President Wachman was such, however, that he thought the wisest thing he could do to avoid public unpleasantness was to ask Spiegler to take his place as a full professor in the religion department. Its members could do no other than accept him but with a total uncertainty of his caliber in the field of religion study. This serendipitous gift, not from the sea but from suburbia, was one of the best the religion department ever received. That Gerhard Spiegler proved an excellent colleague in every way is a matter of record, even to his serving in the chair for two terms up to 1984. He was back in the ranks in the early 1990s when Elizabethtown College, a Church of the Brethren institution, called him to be its president. George Johnson had shortly before been named president of George Mason University, newly Commonwealth of Virginia related. It is simply a fact and not a claim to say that membership in or a close relation to Temple University's department of religion was part of their preparation for later duties.

I have tried to provide a window on the twenty-year period that followed the account of the founding years of the department provided by Professor Ernest Stoeffler. It revealed a period of intense activity by teachers and students engaged in the business of graduate and undergraduate education. All or most of the players in the venture had previously been transmitting or receiving their faith traditions among fellow religionists based on the assumption of their religious truth. Without abandoning their religious convictions, teachers and students alike were examining long-held convictions in such a way as to help outsiders to the various traditions understand and appreciate them. The inevitable result was an increased appreciation of one's own tradition as it came to be seen in a setting of others. But this was not the primary purpose of the exercise. Like all that goes on in college or graduate education, the purpose was the diffusion of knowledge and the dispelling of ignorance.

The Temple University department of religion did not consciously set out to be a pioneer in US higher education. It assumed somewhat naïvely that all private or religiously sponsored institutions were free to do what it had done, but for reasons unknown, had not. By the early 1960s there had been numerous challenges in the courts to the use of public moneys for the teaching or otherwise promoting of religion. President, and later Chancellor, Gladfelter undoubtedly knew the risk Temple was running as a public institution, but nothing deflected him from his purpose. Paradoxically, he was protected against any threat of suit by the numerous institutions public and private, which took a page from Temple University's book and began to do the same.

BREAKTHROUGH TO DIALOGUE

"IN THOSE DAYS THERE WERE GIANTS IN THE LAND"

MARCIA SACHS LITTELL AND RICHARD LIBOWITZ

In the late 1960s, Bernie Phillips assembled a faculty for the Temple University Department of Religion (TUDOR) that, in breadth of experience and depth of scholarship, rivalled any in the world. Drawn from throughout the United States, Europe, Asia, the Middle East and Australia, and ranging in age from young professors to individuals in mid-career, they were scholars, writers, teachers and political activists. None combined more roles than the stocky man with the hazel eyes who walked through the campus in Stetson hat, string tie and western boots, Franklin Littell. In his early fifties, Littell had been a Methodist minister, professor, college president and *Chief Protestant Religious Advisor* to the *Allied High Command* in post-war Germany. For twenty-five years, Littell would teach undergraduate and graduate students, prepare doctoral candidates, author books on a range of topics, found organizations and, upon his arrival at TUDOR, inaugurate a conference that continues to draw international panels of scholars to its annual sessions.

Littell came to Temple as a recognized authority in four distinct fields; Radical Reformation in Christianity, Religion in America, Religious Liberty, and the Holocaust. While his interest in each topic would continue, it was to the Holocaust that he would devote his greatest attention and efforts, serving on the American *President's Council on the Holocaust* as well as the Board of its successor organization, the *United States Holocaust Memorial Museum*, establishing the Church Relations Committee, and serving on the

Museum Content Committee. He became the first Christian to sit on the International Governing Board of Yad Vashem, Israel's Holocaust memorial and research institute, and served as the Lady Davis Adjunct Professor at Hebrew University in the Department of Contemporary Jewry.

With colleague Hubert G. Locke, Littell founded what is now known as the *Annual Scholars' Conference on the Holocaust and the Churches*, bringing together for the first time Jewish and Christian scholars from a variety of fields, as well as survivors, rescuers and liberators from the event known in Hebrew as the *Shoah*.

The threads that composed the warp and woof of Franklin Littell were many and varied. A student of Reinhold Niebuhr and Paul Tillich and close friend of Dietrich Bonhoeffer while at New York's Union Theological Seminary, he held strong beliefs in interfaith understanding and religious liberty. A pacifist as a young man, he had travelled to Germany in the summer of 1939 —a famous photograph records him in heated debate with an SS officer—and witnessed first-hand the staccato drumbeat preceding war in Europe. Following the war, he and his young family relocated to the American Zone of Occupation in Germany, serving for nearly ten years as *Chief Protestant Religious Officer* in the *High Commission for Occupied Germany*, a civilian with the operative authority of a General, concerned with anti-communist programs and the de-nazification of Germany's churches. He expanded his work to include the rehabilitation and reeducation of Germany as Director of the *Franz Lieber Haus* in Bonn, working with German Protestant leaders as well as laypeople. In 1949, he helped plan and administer the *Deutsche Evangelisher Kirchentag* (German Protestant Church Congress), an interdenominational convention which continues to meet biennially in Germany.

Upon his return from Germany, Littell became Professor of Church History at Emory University's Chandler School of Theology (1958-60), where he created America's first graduate seminar on

"The Holocaust and the Church Struggle." He also began writing a mimeographed newsletter, which was distributed widely in Europe and America. Littell left Emory for Dallas, Texas, to serve as Professor of Church History and Department Chairman at Southern Methodist University's Perkins School of Theology (1960-62). He then moved on to the Chicago Theological Seminary (1962-69), during which time he continued to teach his graduate seminar, while also serving as President of Iowa Wesleyan College (now Iowa Wesleyan University).

In 1969, Littell came to Temple University, bringing with him plans for a Conference on the German Church Struggle and the Holocaust, which he had been organizing with a fellow professor and clergyman, Hubert G. Locke. The meeting they were planning would be historic and unique: bringing together for the first time Christian and Jewish scholars to consider the historical, theological, and political implications of the Holocaust for both Jews and Christians, drawing upon the expertise and resources of scholars representing a variety of academic departments. Meeting at Wayne State University, papers were presented which opened up questions that had never before been contemplated in a setting of that type. The Holocaust was no longer to be viewed simply as a Jewish tragedy; the encounter with Nazi idolatry was a "watershed" or "alpine event" for Western Civilization as a whole and Christianity in particular. It was at this first meeting—which included the now famous debate between Holocaust survivor and future Noble Prize winner Elie Wiesel and radical theologian Richard Rubenstein—that Littell enunciated the demand that all work on the Holocaust must be international, interdisciplinary and interfaith. Now known as the *Annual Scholars' Conference on the Holocaust and the Churches (ASC)*, the meetings have convened at different venues throughout the United States and in Europe, for forty-six years, including three generations of scholars, as well as survivors, rescuers and liberators.

At the same time, Littell was organizing an annual *Teachers' Conference on the Holocaust* in Philadelphia, with the support of the Temple University administration, TUDOR faculty and graduate students. He brought together members of the Metropolitan Christian Council, the Archdiocese of Philadelphia, the JCRC of the Jewish Federation, and the President of every major university and college in the Philadelphia area. This led to the first Holocaust curricula and courses taught both in Roman Catholic schools and the School District of Philadelphia. In 1985, the *Teachers' Conference* was incorporated into the ASC. In 1974-75, the nation's first *Interfaith Center on the Holocaust* was established at TUDOR. This Center served as a model nationally and internationally.

During his quarter century at Temple, Littell continued to teach both undergraduate and graduate courses, preparing a new generation of doctoral candidates, including Mordecai Paldiel, the first individual to receive a PhD in Holocaust Studies at Temple, in 1982. He also maintained his research in religious liberty and insisted his graduate students—whatever their area of specialization—be fully trained to teach any aspect of world religions.

Franklin was an indefatigable traveler, lecturing throughout the United States and Europe and making forty-six trips to Israel, to study and speak, while still finding time to spend at the family summer home in Montana, where for years he recharged his batteries while in pursuit of wily trout in mountain streams.

An appointee to U.S. Presidential Commissions by both Democratic and Republican Administrations, honored by the Governments of Israel and West Germany, Franklin Littell never stopped "asking the right question," a term and task which became a mantra for his students and disciples. He continued his activism even after retiring from Temple, continuing to write and conduct seminars into his 90s.

Each generation seeks to stand upon the shoulders of those who have come before them; each seeks to continue the tasks that, of necessity, are left incomplete. Franklin Littell took three generations of students along new paths of concern, giving them the intellectual tools to continue along the trail he blazed. We are unlikely to see his like again. We—his colleagues, students and friends—were blessed to have known him and fortunate to continue his efforts.

BREAKTHROUGH TO DIALOGUE

THE TEMPLE RELIGION DEPARTMENT
An Unscientific Postscript on My Career in Philadelphia

SAMUEL LAEUCHLI

Sometime ago the Religion Department distributed a letter asking for recollections about the beginning and early history of our department. Since I happen to be in Philadelphia at present and images are returning quite frequently, I take the time to write down a few thoughts about these years at Temple, as I see them in retrospect.

It was 1967. I had been teaching at Garrett-Northwestern in Evanston for eleven years and was ready to move on. It was the 60s, jobs were plentiful, I had over twenty offers, even from prestigious places. Somehow none appealed to me. One night, Paul van Buren called from Philadelphia and asked if I would consider an interview at Temple. I took a plane and it turned out to be a decisive trip. We met in what was the department at the time, a rundown building on North Broad Street, long gone today. The place felt chaotic. Coffee cups and coke bottles lay randomly around. The bathrooms did not work. An intense discussion got under way, with John Raines, Tom Dean, Paul, and the bright, bizarre chairman.

After ten minutes I knew I would spend decades here. The dynamic was exactly what I needed and what I had been looking for. (I had turned down Stanford, Nashville and the Chicago Divinity School). It was not academia in the traditional sense (I may have read too much Faust, Kirkegaard and Nietzsche by that time) but the place breathed vitality. Of course, I would accept; the concept of a large interreligious graduate center looked inviting. Thus began my Philadelphia sojourn which would change my life so profoundly.

Things were not as simple as they appeared and as they sometimes look in blue-eyed retrospect. When I entered the place that fall, we doubled the department's number of faculty in one month. A task lay ahead that was long, tenuous, and tedious, and we certainly made many mistakes along the way. Immediately we were under attack. The Penn crowd laughed at us, considering us the Zoo principle of religious studies. Today that department in West Philadelphia is no longer ridiculed, but the bitter criticism rang for years around the country. And it was precarious. We had to design a curriculum, courses, structures for exams, and a concept for this kind of graduate education in religion. We had few models to look up and work against, establish how to proceed, determine what kind of faculty to hire, and figure out how to balance the claim of various traditions. We often disagreed passionately with each other. But we shaped a program.

Behind the disagreements we shared a vision, and often with conviction: that there was a need for interreligious studies which would not follow the normal path of graduate education. Normally a Catholic, Jewish or Protestant faculty hires this or that adjunct member from another tradition. Instead the very fabric of the faculty, in a secular university with the strict separation of church and state, was to consist of different traditions. The scholars would represent their own religion and do research and teaching from within their field. Only as we went along did we realize how threatening this kind of vision was to some people in the guild, church and synagogue alike, and how much the insidious accusation of a zoo department in fact hit the very nerve of what was at stake in this experiment.

We came to realize, practically from the first month, that in such a pluralistic enterprise one faces hard realities. It is very easy to criticize another tradition, for in the dynamic of every-day life we all prefer certain myths and reject others. We project what we dislike onto others. But it is another matter to face the ambivalence in my own world. How do we proceed, constructing this department of religion? Should we invite scholars who are primarily apologetic, defending their tradition, or do we dare to invite some that are also self-critical, thereby offending their constituency? Should the scholars invited to teach here mainly represent their religions or should they do their work as independent individuals, whether their traditions agree with them or not? Many came to defend their own turf. I found out soon that to take on your own past was at first a precarious, dangerous enterprise. What is the balance between critique and acceptance?

The department and the individual faculty members never got clear on that split, and perhaps never could come to a satisfactory conclusion. We just had to let the chips fall. We found ourselves in similar predicaments. At times we built bridges, at times we fought. No matter the ideas, the day to day living threw us into the dilemma between crusade and alliance, between individual freedom and social pressure, and there surely was enough of that as the years went on.

In many ways, I was one of the real losers in this struggle for balance. As I developed my own work and my own life, I realized that we cannot study and teach religion without facing the religious dilemma in our own tradition. It is very easy to criticize another tradition, but the work really only begins when we face the tragedy of our own. Christianity has a great story, a profound myth, a fantastic art, but it is also a very dangerous enterprise. It is creative, and it is very evil at times. The same would hold for Islam, Judaism and Buddhism. I never got through with this conviction. The colleagues always thought this was Kirkegaard and Faust and Nietzsche (as Charles Fu put it to me in the corridor, with his wonderful sense of humor). Only the past decade showed how tragic this lack of self-critique could become, even politically, in the realm of religious conflicts.

From the outset, the curse of the religious past was with us. On a specific issue, some of us might go with the Jewish contingent, or with the third world, only to reverse the front a week later. That kind of chaotic see-saw happened to everyone in decision after decision. Of course, we never saw it like that. The issues were always seen as objective, "crucial," and only in retrospect can we fathom that time and time again, age-old alliances and confrontations had come back to tyrannize us with the law of return.

An experiment it was, and we surely ached with growing pains. The first years many of us had hardly any time, inclination or even strength to write books. I had come to do research but found myself in an old-fashioned university structure. The man who in fact had put forth, and quite single-handedly, that concept of a radical cross-religious department was at the same time an old-fashioned patriarch who regarded this department as his domain of personal play. I imagine he woke up at night and said to himself, recalling Louis XIV, "This religion department, *c'est moi*! [Tis I]" He did as he pleased. One time when I was on the graduate committee, a student was let go because he could not even remotely construct an academic argument. He went crying to Bernard Philips who assured him: don't you worry, they just talk big, but I am the boss here, you'll get the degree.

We tolerated the French *"roi soleil"* ["Sun King"—Louis XIV of France] for two years but then it was enough. We were going to elect a new chairman. Yet we were counting on the wrong powers. Temple was still on the old patriarchic payroll; the dean chose the chairmen, the two had all the freedom they wanted, and between them shuffled the cards to their hearts' content. It took us three hard years to change it, and I lost three years of my life in a war. They were years of bitter battles. The chairman had been Jewish, had converted to Islam and then to Zen, and could play all three hands at his ease and admirable skill. My younger colleagues will probably hardly believe that what is today a normal course of procedures with committees and elections was viewed at that time by the potentates as a communist-like attack by infantile rebels against the sacred scheme of paternalistic academia. But we won.

And yet, it was this highly problematic first chairman who in great anger finally disowned the department and who had the original vision of a radical cross-religious faculty. We did not realize at that time that his venture carried along a critical stance toward the traditional academic enterprise itself, and it was only much later in my own career that I found strange sympathy toward his conviction. Bernard Philips saw, perhaps because he ended up a Zen Buddhist, perhaps because he realized with his sharp mind the *déja vu* of what he saw and read, that the problem of religious studies was ominously tied to the Sisyphusian task of academia. This was Faust all over again. Over lunch in those first years, he often struggled with the futility of academic studies. He had published only one article (my memory may not be quite correct on that) and he constantly attempted to connect the academic task with his Buddhist convictions.

The academic game will not bring us new insight, he would say, and he often quoted the famous French proverb *plus che ça change, plus c'est la même chose*. The more things change, the more it's the same old thing all over. Existentialism had been around ten times over in ever different masks, and so had modernism, historicism, realism and the rest. One day I quoted Goethe to him: that all the truth has long been said, the real task is to say it once again. Goethe never could find a satisfactory answer to his unease, but who can?

The late sixties and early seventies was a fascinating period. At times a few campus buildings were burnt down, but there was also an extraordinary interest in what we were doing. Some of us were trying to push more women faculty, and one day we got bombarded with an angry pamphlet against affirmative action. Faculty members, not only from Temple, would come to our lecture series. Nuns and priests that had or had not laid down their habits joined us. My first graduate student was a bright former priest. I recall one evening when a German Catholic theologian gave a lecture to a huge audience. We must have had 600 people, laymen and even bishops in the large auditorium. It was the beginning of the Reconstructionist Rabbinical College and some bright and vivacious Jewish students came to study with us. Many of these traditions were more open to interreligious cooperation than they are now. For me it was an unforgettable experience, coming from a narrow Protestant background, to teach students from all these different worlds.

We thought we had to establish what we foolishly regarded as "credentials"; we made mistakes and paid for them. One dear example: because we wanted to be "recognized," we needed "respected scholars." In common English, we wanted big names. As if big names ever guarantee, let alone further, quality! Here we got ourselves a New Yorker, apparently very well known. We paid him a phenomenal salary, twice what I made at the time. Well, one day I flew from New York to Paris, and the man next to me on the plane wanted to know all about that Temple enterprise. I told him proudly of the New York professor who was teaching with us. "He is not your professor," he laughed, "he is an extremely well-paid New York rabbi." I wanted to know how he knew. "Because I am on the board of his synagogue," he said. We determined that the man earned a phenomenal living; he was also on the faculty of Jewish Theological Seminary on Broadway and made what in today's money would be in the neighborhood of $200,000 a year. (It was one grand moment in my academic career that I was treated to champagne, over the ocean, celebrating the fact that we had been royally taken...)

It was for me a rich choice joining that department. To be sure, I first had very rough years coming, personally and professionally, and I went through death and defeat on more occasions than one. I had to reconstruct a life and a career, but in a way, I only did what the department itself was based on. For we actually reconstructed, recreated on the drawing board, or tried to recreate, a graduate approach to deal with religions on a new, different scale. I believe here lies one of the reasons why the department allowed me to go my own way, and finally, over a span of two decades, I found a new career of my own. My experience reflects the dynamic of the enterprise I joined. I made this my Odyssey, and the department turned out to be extraordinarily open. There were a few who looked with some unease at what went on, but the team as a whole supported my work graciously.

It was above all the Center City campus of Temple where I taught, over twenty years, perhaps a thousand students. That became my focus of teaching, and I have never been in Philadelphia on a visit without someone stopping me downtown. Dr. Laeuchli! Or: Sam! The other day in the Warwick, a woman stopped us in the coffee shop, and just before a former student in history came running out of a camera store he had just opened, to greet me.

One time last year, as I was teaching in Hamburg, one of my German colleagues spoke with some bitterness about my experience with the Temple department. In Germany I would have had to teach for the rest of my life what I had been asked to teach in the first place, while my colleagues in Philadelphia allowed me to construct this work on symbol, myth and ritual. This gave my life a precious new meaning. For me, America has an important openness toward such changes. (Strange, that a Swiss philosopher postulated only recently that unless we change our field once or twice, something has gone wrong with us.) Whether he is right or not, he spoke not merely to my situation but to an important difference between American and European attitudes toward change and intellectual evolution. As I only then began to guess, it had been vital for me to come to America.

Of course, it was not always easy to do all this at Temple. The university was not exactly an ideal place to do graduate education. The presidents and the board of trustees were often hard to tolerate. We had to establish our right of existence. One of the professors of anthropology tried for years to put us out of business, pontificating in the Senate that "religion" had no place in a university and was no respectable graduate field. The trouble with him was not only that he was intellectually quite limited, but he had an "in" with the dean, and also so much hot air it would burn your face to come close to him.

My early day of glory in the university at large may have been one afternoon on the graduate board, in which I cast the only vote of 24 against dropping language as a graduate requirement. Though you could not really blame them, not many of the professors in that outfit could construct even a small talk in Spanish, French, or German.

That scene on the graduate board brings up a grotesque footnote. At that meeting, one especially nauseating professor ridiculed me in front of everybody. You did not have to know languages to get a Nobel Prize in science, he laughed. I came across him a few years later, after his department had finally succeeded in getting rid of him. He lived across from my father-in-law and was arrested one day for trying to aim a gun at his neighbor's wife. She had let her cat cross his garden. It was a repeat of the scene at the graduate board, the scientist with his huge paunch and baby face, aiming at enemies with the entitlement of a disturbed academic.

Indeed, it was not always uplifting to deal with Temple. I was turned down one day for a grant and asked one of the powers in the house for the reasons. Apparently, I had used the concept of "hermeneutics" wrongly. It was only after I talked to him for a while that I came to realize the issue: the committee thought "hermeneutics" was something invented recently by some Princeton anthropologists, and they had no idea, let alone had read any of the texts, that the concept had been around for 200 years since Schleiermacher in theology, philosophy and history. It was a bit painful to be exposed to that sort of ignorance.

In that context belongs another painful experience of mine. There was a strike, long after the department had gotten under way, and I had always been quite socialist and union-oriented in my outlook. As

I participated in the strike debates, I suddenly no longer knew what was worse for me, a corrupt president, an incompetent board or a disturbingly vicious faculty. I made enemies for the rest of my stay turning against a union in which I saw the same grabbing for power I had detested so much in the musical chairs of presidents and deans.

And yet, another quite different aspect of Temple has become very important for me over the years. Our department was created in the campus located in the midst of North Philadelphia. It was not a prestige school; we were confronted from the very beginning with the race issue, with poverty and ghetto, and the American dilemma of education. My own evolution cannot be separated from that cultural locus of Temple. I came out of elite schools, a highly sophisticated environment of a 600-year old university. At Temple I became introduced to an entirely different educational atmosphere. It is simply not true that these students were "stupid." I learned to meet and teach and connect with students whose limited education might produce scorn to visitors from Oxford and Tübingen, but whose insight, native intelligence, and intuitive creativity could not be matched by famous scholars in my field.

What seemed like a cultural desert, at times hard to tolerate, displayed at the same time a stunningly honest, authentic, and independent platform of intellectual search. I met extraordinary students, and I still meet them as they greet me on the streets of the inner city when I return. Temple made me at times angry because of its lack of cultural depth, but I discovered at Temple the unexpected power of the intellectual adventure. It freed me not just from the Ivy League myth of America, but from my own background with all its Latin and Greek prestige and three-thousand-year-old historical weight.

And so I experienced in three decades the emergence of an experiment. Later on, students and faculty often spoke with awe about this early history of the department, dreaming that this was the greatest of times. They are partly correct, and they are also quite wrong. I would like to spend the rest of this little presentation outlining to which degree such an evaluation of our history contains vital elements, and to which degree I see serious shortcomings.

We had a vision, and the political evolution of religions since then indicates that the need for such an approach is urgent and remains so. The risk by our first chairman to assemble individuals who represent their tradition, rather than have people talk about other traditions, was a real contribution to a new kind of study. The religious world is parochial, but so is often the academic study of religion. The fundamentalism of academia is no less a problem than the fundamentalism of traditions. Paul Feyerabend spoke so much to my experience.

To bring people from various traditions together was on first sight a step in the right direction, although it was initially viewed with contempt. Just to sit in a faculty meeting with Islamic, Jewish, Buddhist colleagues, to listen to and discuss with them, making decisions, not just regarding how they structure a doctoral exam, but how they cope with a task - all that was a new experience for me. The adventure was not necessarily in finding the right formula for studies and exams but in the very encounter with traditions that view the religious task differently than I do.

But here began the dilemma. In the first years we had exciting lectures, forums, and retreats which tried to break up our mythic ghettoes in which we exist. But as the time went on, the excitement lessened considerably, and I believe therein lies the real problem in what we tried to achieve during those years. Perhaps we were too naive. Interreligious dialogue does not suffice when fifteen people are sitting around a table talking. The walls are too high, the conflicts too serious, the talks too superficial. Narcissism is too destructive a human force. Interreligious dialogue turned out as much a phantom as the religious fanaticism we fought so much.

But the problems lay deeper. We did not, at first, have great ambitions, we simply wanted to be here with each other. We tried and tried again. At times we did not know how to go on, and knew that we were on thin ice. The shortcomings and tentativeness of the department's early times plays an important role in my recollections. We worked chaotically. But as we went on we began to have airs. We thought the task of our department was important. We began to forget how precarious it all was. Experiments do not succeed that way.

Nothing pinpoints the dilemma of our department as much as the murder of Ismail al Faruqi and his wife. It was a tragedy, and we went to the funeral in West Philadelphia shell-shocked. However, more died in that week than this couple from Lebanon and Denmark. Part of our department died too, the department as we had designed. I believe our naiveté was finally called on the carpet. The conflict with the murdered man had become more and more serious, and we were numb and blind to it. But what could we have done? He had called us imperialists, bigots, Westerners, and colonialists, and he had contempt for us, the Christians no less than the Jews. Something in him hated us. He told me once, "we shall drive them into the sea." To some degree, we all were the "Them." He was the voice of the dark.

We went on believing we could talk about religion as if it were an interesting academic discipline when, in fact, it was a matter of murder, violence and crime. The age of George Bush was already on the rise. No dialogue. I had to go to Ismail's funeral to be once more reminded of reality. Some returned afterward to teach as if the tragedy had never taken place. Living a bizarre flashback, Evelyne, my wife, came home one day some years later and told me that while visiting a prison, she had met a guard who had been present when Ismail al Faruqi had met his future murderer, as he was beginning to convert him to Islam.

Watching the scene from Europe where I have been living the last years, the conflict between religions has increased, but it has always been there. It is my tradition that started the crusades, one of many holocausts in our past, and I cannot visit Burgundy, which

Evelyne and I do quite often because of its spectacular art, without also hearing at moments Bernard of Clairvaux preach these crusades. And I could not get out of my mind, there at Bernard's famous abbey of Fontenaye, the description of how the blood of the people of Jerusalem flowed like a river, and how the Christian soldiers were standing in that blood. In the witch hunts we dealt with the murder of perhaps half a million innocent women, healers, and saints, and we had to face finally the murder of millions of Jews and gypsies. I cannot teach my Christian history without facing its criminal past. The problems are always seen on the other side. Today Islam has become, for many Europeans, the new enemy, as if we had not displayed the same violence for a long time.

We thought very naively that if we invited someone from a different tradition, he would deal with its own dark dynamic. It did not happen that way. People came to defend their fortress. It is easy to see the crime on the other side but we did not always have either the wisdom or the freedom to consider people who would see the issues on their own. Teaching religion, we forgot time and time again, is teaching superb imagery and models for society and consciousness. But it also means teaching murder. The violence of the Christian right, the slaughter in Algeria, the deadlocked situations in Bosnia and Northern Ireland, the murder of Rabin, and the war against Iraq have all made our early convictions somewhat naive. Religions are much more problematic than we academics imagined; indeed at times one is inclined to label them evil. All we need to do is look around us. The darkness of religion is more present than we thought at the time. Our "Dialogue": they will, if not murder you, ostracize you in many parts of the world if you only hint at a segment of what we used to dialogue about, in a fundamentalist church of South Carolina as well as in a street of Teheran.

And I am not just talking about the slaughter in Algeria or Afghanistan. To be sure, the fear of the ecumenical task has greatly diminished in some parts of the world, but the fear has also spread.

One of the German professors, a visiting scholar, will not be replaced in Hamburg, although he was the only Catholic member in an exclusively and painfully Protestant faculty. In a sense, the dream we had that by talking to each other we might create a more humane religious world has not worked out. The story of our department only reflects what is practiced in Belfast, Gaza, Bosnia, Or even in the Vatican.

And yet, the vision has deeply influenced my life and my work. Although no longer with doctoral candidates, the task has remained the same. For me the meeting of religions, the confrontations and dialogues must go through the immense pain we have inflicted on each other, in the hope that the mythic power behind our traditions is capable of healing, if only in small parts, what the studies and discussions have long failed to heal. To teach religion is to teach a tragedy, and our department has taught me its healing potential as well as its destructive force. To see the problems in the other person's religion is cheap; to see the violence of my own is a form of initiation.

As I learned at Temple, the task crosses social classes and ghettoes. Again, the learning experience for me was the sixteen years at Temple University Center City (TUCC). In my classes I taught people who walked in from North Philadelphia as well as medical doctors. In fact, one time a student came to me and asked me proudly if I realized that there were three MD's and four PhD's in the course. What he did not see was that there were also people from the streets of Philadelphia in that course: a sheriff from New Jersey who first thought we were all insane, an extraordinary dancer near a breakdown, who one night gave us a stunning performance, a black playwright who finally told me he had never before taken seriously a white Christian's convictions because they appeared to him so evil. For me, TUCC was Temple at its best.

Whenever Evelyn and I are introduced in Germany at a lecture or seminar, as we frequently are, I do not fail to give credit to

Philadelphia, to the American dynamic of psychology, race, and culture, and to the grace of having been immersed for 30 years in the Religion Department of Temple University. If my task is to teach a tragedy of religion, society and the individual, it is also to teach, no matter how tentatively, moments of catharsis and joy and the often hidden promise and mystery behind that tragedy. Temple made it possible for me to discover both.

FROM CATHOLIC ETHICS TO COMPARATIVE ETHICS

RODERICK HINDERY

I was interviewed and hired as Assistant Professor in Religious Studies at Temple University in 1968 in view of my specialization in Christian ethics and Catholic moral theology. After studies at the Catholic University of America, I had earned a doctorate in moral theology at the Lateran University's new special institute in Rome for the reform of moral theology, the Academia Alfonsiana. My friends and classmates there included the now well-known Charles Curran. Among our mentors were Francis Xavier Rhynne Murphy, Domenico Capone, and Bernhard Häring.

Inspired by Häring's fascination with the power of mass suggestion, especially during the time of the Third Reich, I began to realize that the Nazis' horrific physical atrocities against Jews and others were linked to their astounding emotional and ideological manipulations of European populations, including intellectual and religious elites. While doing doctoral research near Dachau in the summer of 1961, I was deeply moved while reading William Shirer's *Rise and Fall of the Third Reich,* especially his documentation about Goebbels' and Hitler's use of mass suggestion.

After I returned to teach moral theology at Conception Abbey in Missouri in 1962, which at that time included several hundred seminary collegians and theology students, I was able to convince Bernhard Häring to teach courses there in the summer of 1962. During that and subsequent summers, other academic institutions in the US also took advantage of his considerable charisma and talent, including when he taught at Temple University in spring of 1968.

From 1962 to 1968 my interest in the suffocation of critical thought and feeling by the power of ideologies and mass indoctrination had to yield to competing needs to discuss church reform, before, during and after the Second Vatican Council. When I first spoke out publicly (*National Catholic Reporter*, 1964), saying that religious dialogue should include moral subjects like the morality of artificial birth control, some bishops, including John Cardinal Cody, became upset with my statements. At the same time, others at Conception Abbey and Seminary were so focused on additional disputes about homosexuality, celibacy, and sexuality in general that I was scarcely able to draw attention to issues that I thought were more important, such as war and peace, global poverty, and the function and impact of propaganda within and beyond religious institutions.

After I joined Ignatius Hunt, Thomas Merton, and others on the board of the National Association for Pastoral Renewal to promote discussion about the merits of optional celibacy, my esteemed role model Bernhard Häring wrote me with displeasure that such dialogue was premature. Few then realized that such turmoil in our limited milieu reflected wider and necessary debates about the democratization of laity with clergy and of women with men in the church as well as much larger cultural debates about war and peace, poverty, justice, liberation ethics, sexual ethics, and the interaction of religions in general.

Amid these competing currents and my own personal need to move beyond a celibate and monastic way of life, I asked and received dispensation to marry canonically within the Catholic Church. I thought I would then become freer from matters of religious reform to reexamine social democratization and related moral issues from a broader context of the ideological mindsets and propagandas which had continued to distort these issues. With that background I inquired about positions at a few universities, including Temple, where I hoped that I could merge my specialization in religious ethics with a focus on mass media and propaganda. Luckily my inquiry about such interdisciplinary interests was forwarded by Temple's Vice President for Academic Affairs, (Anderson) to the Department of Religion where I was hired in 1968.

I taught graduate and undergraduate courses in the Department of Religion (1968-1982, 1985-1986), and Management (1977-1981). Major themes in my courses focused on comparative religious ethics, ethics and communications, and ethics in business and the professions. With an eye to interreligious dialogue, however, the Department of Religion had encouraged my teaching and research in comparative ethics rather than in ethics and communications.

My wife, Sheila Hindery, scholar and most compelling of colleagues, increasingly desired to live near her parents and brothers and sisters where she grew up in southern California and the Southwest. To that end, after I took early retirement from Temple in June 1986, I taught courses in religion, ethics, and professional ethics at CSUN and ASU. My family and I were thereby able to live near and interact with Sheila's parents and family before her parents and two siblings died from various illnesses. Although I missed the interreligious and occasional interdisciplinary dialogue I had shared at Temple, my graduate teaching in professional ethics at CSUN's *Masters in Public Administration* program enabled me to reactivate my earlier interest in the power of propaganda and the mass media. After retiring from teaching in 1997, I wrote a book, published several articles, and set up a website about topics related to *Propaganda vs. Critical Thought,* subjects which fascinate me more now than they did during my doctoral studies in Europe.

I. Religious Dialogue, Other Departments, New Hires, Early Teaching

Much of the early and subsequent developments within Temple's Department of Religion can be viewed as a window or microcosm for what was going on in other colleges and universities. Temple's

Department of Religion led important academic ventures into a discipline variously referred to as "comparative religious studies" or "interreligious dialogue."[1] Wary that comparative attempts might require enormous labor and risks, or imply assumptions of superiority, some of the Department's faculty sought dialogue less directly than others. Scholarly exchanges ranged from bold and explicit efforts to learn and compare structures of religious traditions to mere tolerance for juxtaposed research, interaction by osmosis, or wishful thinking.

Motives also varied. In a landmark article for *The Humanist,* for example, the Department's initial Chairperson, Bernard Phillips, evaluated religious traditions in terms of their proximity to personal experience. For Phillips religions shared a common *Tao* or *Zen* (flow). Zen meant not merely a species or apex of one religion such as Buddhism, but the core of religions and of human life in general. Others, like Isma'il al Faruqi, remained convinced that their traditions, in his case Islam, possessed a fullness of wisdom which other religions only reflected or absorbed in lesser degrees. Paul van Buren, who was minimally impressed by the historical accuracy of Muslim claims, early on appeared to compare traditions from more detached historical perspectives.

Beyond the framework of motives for comparative study, Leonard Swidler sought scholarly conversations in which dialogue was visibly interactive and in which scholars could perceive their own traditions more clearly and fully in the light of other traditions. In the spirit of Joachim Wach's phrase, *"Wer kennt eine religion, kennt keine,"* (Whoever knows only one tradition, knows none), declarations about one's own tradition were to be stated clearly and

---

[1] See Leonard Swidler, "The Study of Religion and Interreligious Dialogue," *Journal of Ecumenical Studies*, 45, 3 (Summer, 2010), pp. 349-351, where the two are carefully distinguished.

honestly, with an eye for commonalities as well as differences, and with a scholarly openness to other religious perspectives.

Whatever departmental differences existed about theoretical ideals and motives for comparative studies, practical approaches were similarly varied. They ranged from comparison and dialogue by mere juxtaposition to explicit jousting at faculty forums. Some students were directed by their mentors to use comparative methods and dialogue far less explicitly than others. If any structural comparisons or dialogue were to occur, they were often left to the ingenuity of individual students.

Other departments at Temple University were as unaware of the use of comparative methodology in the Department of Religion as they were in their own disciplines, such as philosophy or anthropology. Jacob Gruber, the Chair of Anthropology at Temple in the 1960s, challenged the Religion Department's *raison d'etre,* its right to exist within academe. Gruber may have feared, and perhaps projected, that some religious faculty confused study *about* religions with the study and advocacy *of* religions, that they fell short of scholarly objectivity and methods, and that they threatened the separation of religion and the state in a secular university.

Gruber's anxiety exemplified similar worries among scholars of other disciplines, not only at Temple but at other academic settings. Scholars reacted defensively in the measure that they felt insecure about their own scholarly objectivity and methods. Yet at the same time, they probably realized that departments of religious studies were not the only academic locations where advocacies functioned ideologically rather than scientifically, or were sometimes tolerated with uncritical complacence.

As I concluded in a recent article, "Advocacy in Academe: Academic vs. Confessional Theology,"[2] it is not only religious

---

[2] Roderick Hindery, "Advocacy in Academe: Academic vs. Confessional Theology," CSSR Bulletin, 32, 1 (February 2003), pp. 18-19.

studies or theology which have sometimes "misfired in confessional or proselytizing modes, but any or all theories which have functioned ideologically—from existentialism to postmodernism, from Marxist and other socialist models of production and allocation, to capitalist models of so-called "free market." Academics become ideologists to the degree they propose their assertions narrowly and infallibly. They "represent not inquiry, but indoctrination. If they substitute emotional intensity for evidence and logical deduction, they become not professors of learning, but proponents of propaganda."

Early critics of Religious Studies at Temple were partly correct. Some scholars of religion obviously promoted their own traditions. Claude Welch, a professor of Religious Studies at the University of Pennsylvania, criticized the Temple Religion Department's attempt to offer courses taught by scholars who had experienced the traditions about which they taught. This attempt he labeled "the zoo principle." His phrase did not necessarily lampoon the hypothesis that scholars function better if they have experienced from within the traditions which they describe externally. Rather it disclosed a wariness that experience, authentic or alleged, might be offered as a substitute for scholarship. Today his concern lives on in many universities. Then and now, this anxiety could be circumvented by heeding three caveats.

First, experiential familiarity with a given tradition is neither a necessary nor sufficient condition for scholarship, although it may enhance it, and, from a given religion's perspective, it may probe the tradition with greater wisdom. Second, the basic objective in academic discourse is neither to promote specific traditions positively, nor to evaluate them negatively, but to display them in the context of competing points of view. Third, even explicit and impassioned advocacy of religious traditions, religion, or agnosticism is compatible with scholarly fairness, if it occurs within context of critical thought, which allow interaction between opposing points of view. Isma'il al Faruqi, for example, used to promote vigorously the superiority of Islam over other traditions, sometimes irritating his colleagues at departmental meetings and forums. Coupled with his congenial personality and wit, however, his forceful advocacy did not wither opposing points of view. Instead it nourished them. Paradoxically, al Faruqi's blunt declarations fostered comparative study and discussion more than it impeded them.

In the Department's early years, new hires seemed to be acquired not only in terms of what Welch called the Zoo principle, that is, as scholars who had experienced the background of traditions about which they taught. They were also selected in terms of how well known they were and how gainfully they might attract future students and funding. Enormous risks lay ahead for academe, as increasingly, funding holds sway as a motive for the development of programs, departments, and affiliated centers and institutions. The acceptance of funding may entail hidden obligations.

II. What Was Special in My Experience at Temple, Reasons for Departments of Religious Studies, and Other Questions

During my early experience teaching at Temple, the vision and scholarship of several colleagues impressed me, especially Paul Van Buren, Bernard Phillips, Leonard Swidler, Maurice Friedmann, Isma'il al Faruqi, and (a few years later) Norbert Samuelson. Among visiting professors, Hasan Hanafi and Surama Dasgupta stood out for their scholarship and their enterprise. Working with them collegially was not only a privilege but an exciting venture.

In my efforts to take comparative religious studies seriously, I attended one or more classes taught by each of my colleagues in the 1970s. My dream was to complete or complement comparative religious studies by integrating them with comparative religious ethics. In my view religious ethics comprised a terrain of social issues where both religions and their scholars could encounter and learn from one another most directly and fruitfully. On the ethical landscape, scholars as well as practitioners could more effectively measure the practical impact and differences of various traditions. The scholarly works of Hans Küng on global ethics eventually became the most known arena where such practical dialogue has occurred. Amid competing visions of globalization, corporate hegemony, and social and environmental respect for indigenous peoples everywhere, much work in comparative ethics obviously remains.

My research in comparative religious ethics was important to me. After extensive research in several Asian countries, I felt fortunate to produce the first book (and numerous articles for various journals) which dealt with this new discipline—not only methodologically, but also substantively.[3]

However, as I indicated at the beginning of these pages, my primary dream was to revisit issues discussed in comparative religion and comparative religious ethics from two further perspectives which were not only interreligious, but a) methodologically interdisciplinary, and b) substantively reformulated from the perspective of propaganda versus authentic advocacy and critical thought. With the exception of an article I wrote, *Propagandas in the Church (Critic,* May-June, 1970, pp.39-43), I had put my work in this direction on hold twice, first to assist discussions about religious reform in the 1960s, and later to help develop the field of comparative religious ethics.

Eventually, after my retirement from teaching at ASU in 1997, I was able to produce a book I had long dreamed about writing: *Indoctrination and Self-deception or Free and Critical Thought?* Although Mellen Books' expensive pricing has made my book accessible to only a few, I have sought to expand further attention to issues I developed there by discussing them in articles published in the *CSSR Bulletin,* the *Humanist,* March-April 2003, "The Anatomy of Propaganda in Religious Terrorism," and in papers accessible at my

---

[3] Roderick Hindery, *Comparative Religious Ethics in Hindu and Buddhist Traditions,* (1978, new ed., 2004).

website *(Propaganda vs. Critical Thought, www.public.asu.edu/-sheilrodl).* These papers deal more concretely with issues about propaganda in religions, propaganda in departments of religious studies, and propaganda in other disciplines in academe.

Teaching at Temple in the 1960s and 1970s brought not only financial hardship to some of us newer faculty, but, because Temple was so popular with graduate students, a heavy share of work in multiple doctoral committees and other departmental committees. Many of the senior faculty bore their share of such work graciously. Others, like visiting, traveling, or commuting faculty members, whom Bernard Phillips referred to as prima donnas, left much to their colleagues. What made it all seem worthwhile was the palpable excitement which could be sensed in a department where ideas from many cultures and traditions collided in bursts of synergy.

Religious studies at Temple University in the early years of the department functioned as an exciting example and microcosm of the kind of cross-cultural and cross-disciplinary study in which academics dream to participate, where ideas from disparate cultures and traditions collide and explode with the energy of new paradigms. By the 1960s, politically and culturally, faculties of state universities in the United States had matured sufficiently to recognize that teaching *about* religions was not the same as the teaching *of* religions. With luck and hard work, the faculty at Temple's Department of Religion developed a blueprint for how other departments might reach similar evolution in paradigms.

With appreciation for sharing collegially at the Department of Religion, I would like to conclude these recollections with excerpts paraphrased from my article, *Advocacy in Academe: Academic versus Confessional Theology (CSSR Bulletin,* vol. 32, 1, Feb. 2003, pp. 18-19). "My years of academic adventure at Temple served as the furnace where these ideas were first fueled. Having nurtured and seasoned them gratefully, I give them back in the following lines.

"Economic and political ideologies, like confessional theologies, 'have no place in any academic discipline, department, or program, unless they appropriate scientific methods, e.g., a) by disclosing presuppositions; and b) by testing assumptions, arguments, and conclusions against competing positions.' Yet the scientific spirit is not dispassionate. Scientific endeavors invigorated by passion may actually work more efficiently and productively than proposals which are emotionally bloodless or anemic."

"Why should anemia reign in academe? If emotional expressions stimulate the desire for learning, why should ideas not be shouted from the rooftops? When positions are expounded both freely and fairly and with scientific openness to opposing positions, they can ring with passion. They can also eradicate the drudgery of religious and other ideologies in academe, which cloak enslavement to self-deception and indoctrination. This liberation of critical thought emerges not only as academically and socially productive, but ultimately as an adventure exciting in itself."

ISMA'IL AL FARUQI:
The Link Between Tudor and the Muslim World

IMTIYAZ YUSUF

Professor Isma'il al Faruqi (1921-1986) was a trailblazer of what he called Islamics or Islamic Studies in the modern age. Since the 1960s onwards, Prof. al Faruqi, along with Prof. Fazlur Rahman of the University of Chicago and Prof. Seyyed Hossein Nasr [after escaping from the Khomeini revolution in his native Iran, I arranged for him to join TUDOR, Swidler] now at George Washington University, were the first three prominent scholars of Islamics in the West. It was the time when Islamics was making an appearance as a field of study, research, and discourse in universities. Each of them made their specialized contributions to Islamic Studies in USA. Fazlur Rahman specialized in Islamic thought, Seyyed Hossein Nasr in Islamic mysticism, and Isma'il al Faruqi in the study of Islam focusing on the history of religion and interreligious dialogue, though he is more well known in the Muslim world for his theory of Islamization of Knowledge.

Trained in philosophy from Indiana University, he applied it to the study of Islam and religion at the al-Azhar University 1954-1958. In 1958 he took up the position of Visiting Fellow at the Faculty of Divinity at McGill University in Canada, where he came into contact with Professor Wilfred Cantwell Smith and Professor Fazlur Rahman of Pakistan, who was then teaching at the Institute. Both of them became friends and shared a common mission dedicated to raising the level of Islamic Studies in the Muslim world. Between 1961 and 1963, al Faruqi worked as visiting professor at the Central Institute of Islamic Research, Karachi, Pakistan. In the years 1964-1968 he was

Associate Professor of Islamic Studies at the department of religion at Syracuse University. In 1968, he was appointed Professor of Islamics at the newly established Department of Religion at Temple University, Philadelphia where he remained until his death in 1986.

Prof. Isma'il al Faruqi joined Temple University in 1968 when the university changed its status from a private institution to state-related institution in the Commonwealth of Pennsylvania. During this era, the study of world religions was just being initiated as a new area academic of study. Temple University's department of religion, then led by Professor Bernard Phillips, was launching an ambitious program in the study of religion where all world religions would be promoted as a foundational base for all branches of study.

Prof. Phillips appointed al Faruqi as professor of Islamics at Temple university after reading al Faruqi's seminal article on interreligious dialogue, "Islam and Christianity: Diatribe or Dialogue," published in the *Journal of Ecumenical Studies*.[1] Al Faruqi's academic and religious frankness expressed in this article landed him the job in the Department of Religion. Al Faruqi fitted in well with the general academic ethos of the department in which, "All or most of the players in the venture had previously been transmitting or receiving their faith among fellow religionists based on the assumption of their religious truth. Without abandoning their religious convictions, teachers and taught alike were examining long-held convictions in such a way as to help outsiders to the various traditions understand and appreciate them. The inevitable result was an increased appreciation of one's own tradition as it came to be seen in a setting of others. But this was not the primary purpose of the exercise. Like all that goes in university or graduate education, the purpose was the diffusion of knowledge and the dispelling of ignorance."

---

[1] Isma'il al Faruqi, "Islam and Christianity: Diatribe or Dialogue," *Journal of Ecumenical Studies*, 5, 1 (Winter, 1968), pp. 45–77.

In 1973, Prof. al Faruqi established the Islamic Studies Group in the American Academy of Religion (AAR) and chaired it for ten years. In other academic capacities he also served as vice-president of the Inter-Religious Peace Colloquium, The Muslim-Jewish-Christian Conference, and was president of the American Islamic College in Chicago, USA.[2]

Al Faruqi brought a comprehensive and blended approach to Islam which combined in it an Islamic rationalist approach to monotheism which was both modernist and activist, along an impartial approach towards the study of religion. In a way he was a modern successor to medieval Muslim scholars of comparative religion such as al-Biruni (973-1048 CE) and al-Shahrastani (1086–1153 CE).[3]

Prof. al Faruqi's contribution lies in four academic areas: Islamics, history and phenomenology of religion, interreligious dialogue, and Islamic educational movement in the modern age. His contributions to academia played an important role in the creation of Islamic Studies programs at the university level in United States and the Muslim world.

Both Isma'il and his wife Lamya (Lois) al Faruqi were inhumanly murdered in their home on 18 Ramadan 1406/27, May 1986, by an Afro-American convert to Islam whom he had befriended during his work with prisoners. Their deaths were unexpected and untimely.

---

[2] Richard C. Martin, "Isma'il R. al Faruqi and the American Academy of Religion: A Personal Remembrance," Imtiyaz Yusuf, ed., *Islam and Knowledge: The Concept of Religion in Islamic Thought : Essays in Honor of Isma'il al Faruqi* (London: I.B. Tauris, 2012), pp. 61-68.

[3] Eric J Sharpe, *Comparative Religion: A History* (London: Duckworth, 2003), p. 11.

Isma'il al Faruqi and the Study of Religion

Professor Bernard Phillips and his colleagues were clear in what they wanted to teach and research. They called their department a department of religion, not religious studies or comparative religion. Their focus was the generic role religion plays in human life, thought, and practice before being labelled as a particular tradition. The use of the term religion also meant distinguishing it from the approaches adopted in theological seminaries and those in social science departments. Yet their students were required to study at least three religious traditions in detail plus courses in scripture, philosophy, religion, social sciences, ethics, etc. The aim was to offer students from different religious or non-religious traditions and backgrounds a program that would cover the study of the phenomenon of religion in its whole gamut.

Isma'il al Faruqi's contribution to the study of Islam and religion has received lesser recognition than it deserves, for he has been largely judged in terms of his vehement support for the rights of the Palestinians in his homeland. For this, he was criticized, threatened and also prejudiced against. This anti-al Faruqi stance did not even go away twenty-one years after his death when in 2007, an attempt to establish an endowed Chair in the department in his honor was aborted at the university level and came to be well known as "the Islamic Chair issue"[4] controversy. The unfounded charges that the Chair was being funded by those having ties with terrorist organizations still remains fresh in the minds of the friends of al Faruqi and the department. It seems that al Faruqi still walks thumping as he did on the 6th floor of the Anderson Hall building.

---

[4] Lewis Gordon, "From the Editor: The Islamic Chair Controversy," *Temple University Faculty Herald* (vol. 38, no. 3, 2007), pp 1-6; available at www.temple.edu/herald accessed 29 March 2014.

Al Faruqi's pioneering contribution in the study of Islam as religion in what he would call "the stream of Being" is a rare area of study and research in the Muslim world—and if taught, it is mostly done within the framework of Islam being the final religion. That is why it is not surprising to read that al Faruqi's contributions were compared and judged as being less impressive than the contributions of Professor Fazlur Rahman of the University of Chicago and Professor Seyyed Hossein Nasr of the University of Washington—both of whom were specialists in Islamic Studies and not the study of religion.[5]

Professor Isma'il al Faruqi has been described as a scholar-activist, but not much has been written about his personality, thought, style, pedagogy, and academic vision.[6] This is largely because he has been viewed from an ideological perspective and because his views about his Palestinian homeland attracted more attention and comment.

Over the recent decades, al Faruqi's contribution has also largely come to be viewed as an ideological project of Islamization of Knowledge—a postcolonial Muslim enterprise in the area of the politics of knowledge, which is different from his view in which the process of knowledge means acquiring and advancing beyond previous contributions to knowledge similar to the contributions of Muslim scholastics, philosophers, and scientists to Islamic and world

---

[5] Sulayman S. Nyang and Mumtaz Ahmad, "The Muslim Intellectual Émigré in the United States," *Islamic Culture*, vol. 59 (1985), p. 289.

[6] Exceptions being the excellent introductions to the thought and works of al Faruqi by John L. Esposito viz., John Esposito, "Isma'il Raji al Faruqi" in John L. Esposito, *The Oxford Encyclopedia of the Modern Islamic World*, vol. 2 (Oxford University Press: 2001), 3-4; John L. Esposito, "Isma'il R. al Faruqi: Muslim Scholar-Activist" in Yvonne Yazbeck Haddad, *The Muslims of America* (Oxford University Press: 1993).65-79. David E. Sopher and Isma'il R. al Faruqi, *Historical Atlas of the Religions of the World*, illustrated edition. (Macmillan, 1975), 23–38.

intellectual history. It seems that al Faruqi's contribution got shortchanged by those who focused on his contributions from the view of their interests and disciplines and with a piecemeal approach overlooking its objective in its entirety.

Ziauddin Sardar and the *Afkar* group sought development of new disciplines rooted in a Muslim cultural context directed at addressing and solving problems specific to the Muslim condition, in other words, starting from *tabula rasa*.[7] Sardar criticizes al Faruqi's approach as being cosmetically Islamic but essentially a Western approach and that al Faruqi fails to decipher the Western political ambition to control the non-Westerners through knowledge, e.g., as in the case of the rise of anthropology of religion. Prof. al Faruqi replied to Sardar by saying, "You want us to reinvent the wheel?" Prof. al Faruqi's vision about knowledge was too grand to engage in or favor politics of knowledge; for him, engagement in the knowledge process was not merely an ideological project but a multidimensional civilization project.[8]

Today, twenty-eight years after his death, al Faruqi's legacy which calls upon the Muslim scholars and researchers to contribute to the process of knowledge in which Islam is one among many streams of human understanding of reality has been sidelined by narrowing its focus to the legalistic or ideological aspects of an Islamic worldview. It seems that al Faruqi's school of thought, with its core focus on the place of religion at the core of being as it illumes the path to knowledge, died with him, while a replaced process continues under the rubric of the Islamization of Knowledge project.

Whether celebrated and applauded by Muslim academics who liked his language, or criticized by who those who disliked his pro-Palestinian political stand, al Faruqi's contribution to the study of

---

[7] Ziauddin Sardar, *Desperately Seeking Paradise: Journeys of a Sceptical Muslim* (Granta: 2005), pp.199–200.
[8] Ibid., p. 200.

Islam as part of the study of the human history of religion and reality continues to be at a standstill or has been replaced by another focus. It seems that al Faruqi was understood less both in life and after his death.

Isma'il al Faruqi and Me

The thought of Isma'il al Faruqi represented the state of the Muslim mind and scholarship at the end of the colonial era and the Muslim world's entrance into the age of nation states. The Muslim mind was in search of Muslim identity in the modern age. It was an era in which the secular and religious nationalists represented by kings, military dictators, and presidents of secular, socialist, communist, and capitalist orientation came to power in the newly created Muslim countries. It was assumed that the Muslim world was passing from the traditional into modern liberal age.[9] There was an internal Muslim political contest over interpreting Islam in all spheres of life between reformists and traditionalists on Islam's compatibility with changing times. Isma'il al Faruqi had witnessed this quarrel at the Central Institute of Islamic Research, Karachi, Pakistan. The Muslim reformists were interested in developing new modern theories within the framework of an Islamic religious worldview, while the traditionalists opposed reform, and the secularists preferred to keep religion out of academia or adopt the Western intellectual paradigm as the model for knowledge.

The main question at the time of Muslim youth was that since the Muslim world was past its age of medieval glory, what should be the Islamic worldview of learning, research, and their applications in the postcolonial era.[10] It was about the intellectual crisis, the state of

---

[9] Daniel Lerner, *The Passing of Traditional Society: Modernizing the Middle East* (Free Press, 1965).

[10] Franz Rosenthal and Dimitri Gutas, "Knowledge Triumphant: The Concept of Knowledge," in *Medieval Islam* (Leiden: E.J. Brill, 2007).

education, and the future of the Muslim world, in the midst of such intellectual questioning that Isma'il al Faruqi offered a glimmer of hope through his plan called Islamization of Knowledge project.[11] It won the hearts and minds of many an inquiring youth, including me, then a graduate student in Islamic Studies at the Aligarh Muslim University in India, an institution founded by Sir Syed Ahmad Khan, an Islamic modernist in 1920.

After completion of my Master's degree I wrote a letter to Prof. al Faruqi expressing my desire as a student with no money to study with him for my doctoral studies. I did not expect a reply from him, and hence, I was surprised that he not only replied, but also in 1984 selected me to be one of his graduate students at Temple University. I studied with him for two years and was his last student assistant before his death in 1986. For twenty-six years since his death, I felt that we students of his had not done enough to honor his contribution to academia. I was thinking and dreaming of undertaking an initiative to fill this gap by producing a *Festschrift* in his honor, but, lacking resources, often wondered how to go about making it into a reality.

During the years 2009-2010, I was appointed visiting associate professor and the Malaysia Chair for Islam in Southeast Asia at the Alwaleed bin Talal Center for Muslim-Christian Understanding, Georgetown University, Washington, DC, USA. This opportunity came as a God given chance to fulfill my dream of producing a *Festschrift* as a step in making the scholarship and memory of Prof. al Faruqi a continuing legacy for academia. In this venture I received tremendous support from Professor John Esposito, University Professor and Founding Director of the Prince Alwaleed Bin Talal Center for Muslim-Christian Understanding, Georgetown University. Esposito is the first PhD graduate of Prof. al Faruqi and is also known as the "Don of the Temple Mafia," the group of TUDOR

---

[11] Isma'il R. al-Faruqi, *Al Tawhid: Its Implications for Thought & Life*, 2nd ed. (International Institute of Islamic Thought, 1994).

Muslim students from all around the world. The *International Institute of Islamic Thought* (IIIT), founded by Isma'il, trusted my ambition to contribute to making Prof. al Faruqi's contribution a living heritage.

Al Faruqi's Thought

Isma'il al Faruqi's approach to the Qur'an is ideational, axiological and aesthetical—three concepts which are central to the study of religion and philosophy.

a) Ideational—in the sense that it highlights the centrality of *tawhid*—monotheism as the core idea of Arabian consciousness in contrast to other civilizations.

b) Axiological— aluational adherence to Islam, i.e., faithfulness to the values of monotheistic piety, ethics, *ummatis*, and world affirmation. It is not national, racial, or ideological (for these degenerate into fanaticism) adherence to Islam.

3) Aesthetical—for al Faruqi the Qur'an is an aesthetical revelation, evident from the aesthetic character of its Arabic language which has been the source of the aesthetical expressions found in Muslim arts of literature, calligraphy, architecture, music, and painting.

Thus, for al Faruqi the theological, moral and aesthetical dimensions of Muslim life, thought, and action are infused with monotheistic consciousness, which stresses a duality between creator and creature.

Al Faruqi's view of Islam was Arabist without being Arab nationalist. His Arabism is religion-based and is opposed to the race-based nationalism of the modern age. In this view, monotheism is a gift of Arab consciousness to humanity. Of course, such a position stood opposite to an Orientalist view of the Middle Eastern religions of Judaism, Christianity, and Islam as separated entities. For al Faruqi, monotheistic based Arabism is the essence of Semitism. Prof. al Faruqi blended within himself different intellectual Islamic trends of rationalism, theological meticulousness, and historical criticism, with the goal of illustrating that monotheism represents the Arab (Semitic) Stream of Being made up of monotheistic moments, i.e., Assyria, Babylon, Judaism, Christianity and Islam. He preferred to call this stream Arab rather than Semitic, for the latter name is an invention of Biblical scholars over last 200 years. Acknowledging the work of Biblical scholars who had earlier established the shared linguistic and ethnic identity of Arabs/Semites a shared stream of being, al Faruqi saw his task as proving the same through establishing the shared religious and aesthetic unity of Arabic monotheism. Such an al Faruqi thesis came under strong criticism by Western scholars of the Middle East. Professor T. Cuyler Young of Princeton University described it as, "totalitarian Arabism (which) swallows up all that has been normally associated with Semitism."[12] Prof. al Faruqi replied, "I am trying to establish in a scholarly and academic way, the identity of the ideological or religious core of the ancient Near Eastern religions with that of Judaism, Christianity, and Islam. For the Semitic tradition is a unity, a stream of being, which had many moments, each of which was a development of what went before it, but never a repudiation or about-face. The later religions, i.e., Judaism, Christianity, and Islam are just as moments as the religions of Assyria and Babylonia, though they are the most mature and complex because of their being the last stages of the developing stream."[13] For al Faruqi, Judaism, Christianity, and Islam constitute a unity which he labelled as "the Arab Stream of Being."[14] Apart from the Western scholars, this theory also came under strong criticism

---

[12] Professor T. Cuyler Young's letter to Dr. Ismail al Faruqi, dated 5 November, 1963 in "Isma'il al Faruqi Papers Collection" at the International Institute of Islamic Thought, Herndon, VA, USA. Prof. Young was Chairman, Department of Oriental Studies, Princeton University, Princeton. USA.

[13] Isma'il al Faruqi's letter to Professor T. Cuyler Young, dated 11 November, 1963 in "Isma'il al Faruqi Papers Collection" at ibid.

[14] Ibid.

from non-Arab Muslim scholars, such as Fazlur Rahman, who remarked that al Faruqi was seen as, "an angry young Muslim Palestinian" and also "a guerilla scholar."[15]

In the area of Islamic thought, al Faruqi was much impressed by the Islamic rationalism of the Mutazili theologians like al-Nazzam (775–845), Qadi Abdul Jabbar (935–1025), the ethics of an eleventh-century group of philosophers of *Ikhwan al-Safa'* or "Brethren of Purity" and the *Tawhidi*—unitarian theology of Muhammad Ibn Abdul Wahab (1703–1792). Two common themes which run in the thought of these theologians and school of philosophy are *Tawhid*—God's oneness, and *adl*—justice. Being a Muslim and a Palestinian, these two topics were of paramount importance for al Faruqi. In fact, in the tradition of classical Muslim theologians, al Faruqi went on to write his own *Kitab al-Tawhid* in English for the sake of a new generation of Muslims, who are versed in English. It presents his philosophical and ideational view of Islam.[16]

Al Faruqi's Contributions: Islamics and History of Religion

Isma'il al Faruqi was the first Muslim scholar to engage the field of history of religion and relate it to the study of Islamics in modern times. Focusing on the connection between religion and geography during his appointment at University of Syracuse, he co-edited with his Syracuse colleague David E. Sopher the *Historical Atlas of the Religions of the World*, illustrated edition. (Macmillan, 1975)

This approach to the study of religion is called "cultural geography." It involves:

1. the influence of the environmental setting on the evolution of religious systems and particular religious institutions;

---

[15] Behrooz Ghamari-Tabrizi, "Loving America and Longing for Home: Isma'il al Faruqi and the Emergence of Muslim Diaspora in the United States," *International Migration*, 42, 2 (2004), pp. 61-68.
[16] Al-Faruqi, Al Tawhid.

2. the way religious systems and institutions modify their environment;
3. the different ways religious systems occupy and organize segments of earth space;
4. the geographic distribution of religions and the way religious systems spread and interact with each other.

In the field of history of religions, Prof. al Faruqi offered a Muslim perspective of religion based on the study and knowledge of the historical critical research of the ancient Near Eastern history and texts, and Muslim sources in the study of religion, such as the works of al-Biruni, Ibn Hazm (994–1064), al-Shahrastani, and Ibn Taymiyyah (1263–1328), upon which he improved and made his own contribution to the field.

Religion for al Faruqi was not a ritual act but dimension of every act.

> It is not a thing; but a perspective with which everything is invested. It is the highest and most important dimension; for it alone takes cognizance of the act as personal, as standing within the religio-cultural context in which it has taken place, as well as within the total context of space-time. For it, the act includes all the inner determinations of the person as well as its effects in space-time. And it is this relation of the whole to the space-time that constitutes the religious dimension.[17]

Al Faruqi saw the struggle between monotheism and polytheism as the central theme of the religions of the Arabian theater. For al Faruqi, a Muslim, the monotheists hold a "monotheic" ethical vision rooted in the Qur'anic view of *dīn* based on the principles of monotheism, universalism, tolerance, and life-affirmation, which will enable us to deal with contemporary challenges of materialism and ethno-religious

---

[17] Isma'il Ragi al Faruqi, "History of Religions: Its Nature and Significance for Christian Education and the Muslim-Christian Dialogue," *Numen*, 12, 1 (January, 1965), pp. 37-38.

conflicts. It will facilitate Muslim partnering in the dialogue between religions, cultures, and civilizations. He contrasts such a religious worldview with the "mythopoeic" religious worldview found in polytheistic religion, which are not able to transcend to an abstracted religious worldview.[18]

As far as I know, Prof. al Faruqi is the only Muslim professor in modern times who pleaded for an inquiry and research into pre-Hijrah Islam, highlighting its methodological importance for the study of and research about Islam. He also stressed that the neglect of this aspect in Muslim studies of Comparative Religions is the cause of the weak and marginalized state of Islamic Studies in the arena of knowledge.

> Islam is usually said to have begun with the Prophet Muhammad (may God's peace and blessings be upon him). It is considered that it was he who received the Holy Qur'an, who proclaimed God's religion in the Divine *ipsissima verba*, who launched the *ummah* on a glorious march in space-time. The institution of the Islamic calendar and its establishment as starting on the day the Prophet had set out to found the first Islamic community in Madinah, is the expression of this consciousness. Never before, so runs the implication, has Islam been a reality of history. Never before, has there been a community consciously committed to its pursuit and realization. Pre-Hijrah was, therefore, bound to be a period of "ignorance," of immorality and generally, of evil of every sort—in short, a genuine, all-round *Jahiliyyah* ("ignorance of divine guidance"). Pre-Hijrah was said to be a time when Islam was not: that is a cause sufficient to indict anything! Accordingly, our forefathers? *muhaddithun*, historians, literati or *'ulama*? deliberately applied themselves to the indictment of pre-Hijrah. Meccan pre-Hijrah furnished them with an arsenal of arguments which they hurled, with no mean relish, at all human pre-Hijrah history. The history of the Prophets was reduced to the Prophets' own, personal biographies, while the *Jahiliyyah* of Mecca became a fact of universal history. The darker the *Jahiliyyah* was painted, the brighter the advent of Islam through the Prophet Muhammad was supposed to be. Polytheism, stone worship, tribalism,

---

[18] Isma'il al Faruqi, *The Cultural Atlas of Islam* (Free Press, 1986), p. 80.

war, license, egoism, commercialism, vanity, illustrated in the notorious annals of a Basus War, the cynicism of an Imru' al-Qays [pre-Islam Arab poet], the irresponsibility of an 'Abd al-Mutalib [pre-Islam Arab leader] in front of Abraham, etc.?—all these were projected on to the whole canvas of pre-Hijrah. How could there have been, in this case, any reason to study pre-Hijrah?

Neither did our forefathers feel the need to study that aspect of pre-Hijrah which constitutes the religious history of Judaism and Christianity. In the Holy Qur'an, they read what seemed to them to be a ready-made answer to the question of what both Judaism and Christianity were or will be. Since the Holy Qur'an had given the news-events of those religions, the Muslims thought there was no need to investigate their history.[19]

This plea along with his other writings laid the theoretical and methodological foundations of his Islamic approach to the history of religion.[20]

Prof. Isma'il al Faruqi's scholarship was a combination of being a trained philosopher and historian of religion with a Muslim perspective. For him, study and research of religion was not a detached inquiry, but a critical engagement directed towards a critical study of the place of religion in human history.

Al Faruqi and Interreligious Dialogue

One factor which won al Faruqi a position in the Department of Religion at Temple University was his interest in interreligious dialogue; the above mentioned article, "Islam and Christianity: Diatribe or Dialogue" in the *Journal of Ecumenical Studies*, was a

---

[19] Isma'il R. al Faruqi, "Towards a Historiography of Pre-Hijrah Islam," *Islamic Studies*, 1, 2 (June, 1962), pp. 65-66.
[20] Al Faruqi, *The Cultural Atlas of Islam*, 80.

crucial element in his appointment at Temple University.[21] During the late 1960s, 70s and 80s, interreligious dialogue was a new academic venture conducted largely amongst limited groups of specialists and interested academicians. Professor Leonard Swidler, of the Department of Religion at Temple University played a pioneering role in the venture at the world level from his position at Temple University. He also engaged most of his colleagues in this task: al Faruqi was one of them.

Prof. al Faruqi was a pioneer and active participant in Islam's dialogue with other religions, especially Christianity in the West. As a citizen and resident of the West, Prof. al Faruqi engaged actively in interreligious dialogue since the 1960s when it was in its early stages in the West, following the dialogue initiatives of the World Council of Churches and the Second Vatican Council. One feels the presence of the dialogical aspect of Prof. al Faruqi's intellectual engagement present in his various dialogue documents, where he presents the meaning and message of Islam to the wider world community.[22] In this endeavor, he adapted Muslim epistemology to the changing times. He enthusiastically joined in dialogue with Christians, Jewish, Hindus, Buddhists, and followers of other religions. Here is a representative excerpt of his basic approach in interreligious dialogue.

> *Cragg:* What you are saying, then, is that God has sent prophets everywhere, but *ex hypothesis* these prophets must be consistent with Ilam.
> *Al Faruqi:* Yes, Islam as *religio naturalis, din al-fitrah*.
> *Cragg:* But that which in Buddhism is antithetical to Islam and to rationalism is not simply chaff mixed with wheat, if I may put it that way; it is the very wheat of Buddhism. By your analysis here it must

---

[21] Personal communication with Professor Leonard Swidler, 2010, in Philadelphia.
[22] Isma'il R. al Faruqi, *Islam and Other Faiths* (Islamic Foundation, 2007).

then have been a false prophecy which brought the Buddhist to that belief.

Al Faruqi: I won't say a false prophecy. I would say that a true revelation through an authentic prophet has been thoroughly falsified.

Fitzgerald: But by what historical criteria is the "true" prophet to be identified? And where is the "true" prophecy of which you speak within Buddhism?

Al Faruqi: I don't know, but it can be researched; the fact that I assume it to be there at the origin is at least a good step in the direction of ecumenical tolerance.

Ahmad: It is very possible that rudiments of the true prophecy are to be found even in some pagan religions. [23]

For al Faruqi, the aim of dialogue is to unite the religion of God and truth, bring about conversion to truth, and enable understanding of values and meanings. He also remarked that the methodology of dialogue requires criticism, internal coherence, historical perspective, noting the reality of religions, and not being dependent on absolutized scriptural figurizations which have occurred in all religions, including Islam. He concluded that the potential for the success of dialogue lies in the field of ethics.[24]

Regarding Islam-Christianity dialogue, al Faruqi remarked that the prospects for the exploration of common religious and moral ideas between these two religions are limitless. But he was pessimistic about it in the light of the Vatican II statement on Islam. He thought the document could have gone further, for Muslims still continue to feel excluded from the salvation plan. In al Faruqi's view, the interreligious dialogue between Christianity and Islam should start with the Nicene creed. It should also take into account the

---

[23] Isma'il al Faruqi, "'On The Nature Of Islamic Da'wah.' Christian Missions in the Muslim World," *International Review of Mission*, vol. LXV, no. 260 (October 1976): 391-400; 385-460.

[24] "Islam and Christianity: Diatribe or Dialogue," *Journal of Ecumenical Studies*, 5, 1 (1968), pp. 45-77.

ethical insights of modern humanity which holds life-affirming views, for whom the notion of justification is insufficient and whose moral mission on worldwide basis is still unfulfilled.[25]

Prof. al Faruqi joined in the dialogue enterprise at a time when it was in its infancy and was engaged in by few Muslims. He initiated Islam into interreligious dialogue in the contemporary age and as time passed others joined in and this legacy of his continues today.

From the Christian side it has been remarked that, "He has left much for Christians to ponder, and his efforts stand as a monument to one person's vision of what we all would long to see: a world community working in harmonious relationship to God and to each other."[26]

In relation to the role of an academic in interreligious dialogue, or on a public platform, or in his teaching profession, or as a Muslim scholar of Islam, al Faruqi knew where the lines separating these worlds were.

John Esposito told me an interesting story:

> There were two things he was not objective about. The one he did, and one he didn't. Long after I finished, he and I had lunch at the faculty club. I finally asked him one day, I said "You know, you have never, never asked me if I'd considered becoming a Muslim." I don't usually discuss this publicly, not that it matters, but I said I always wondered about that, because he had such a passion for Islam, not just for Islamic Studies. Isma'il was very interesting, he said to me "Well, I'm your professor and as an academic I can't do that." He said, "I'd probably love that you decided to become a

---

[25]Ibid, pp. 45-46; 71-77. For a detailed views of Isma'il al Faruqi on interreligious dialogue and other religions, see the contribution by Isma'il Raji al-Faruqi in Ataullah Siddiqui, ed., *Islam and Other Faiths* (Leicester: The Islamic Foundation, 1999).

[26] F. Peter Ford, Jr., "Isma'il al Faruqi on Muslim-Christian Dialogue: An Analysis From a Christian Perspective," *Islam & Christian Muslim Relations*, 4, 2 (1993), p. 279.

Muslim, but I'm a professor and so there's this fine line." So that was objective.

With Isma'il al Faruqi in the Classroom

Professor al Faruqi was a task master in the class room. He knew that the majority of the Muslim students in the department were not up to the mark of scholarship. He was also aware that his own prestige as a scholar and teacher was at stake if they did not perform well in their studies in his and other courses. Thus, he would not let us be at ease. I remember his remark on my first paper submission to him. He said, "this goes out of the window; do not simply quote the Qur'an verses to hide behind them; present an argument and make a reference to the Qur'anic verse."

On other occasion, he said, "you are here to learn and read; you are given a scholarship to read, read, read and write." I have not stopped since then.

Attending Prof. al Faruqi's classes was like taking a tour in the world of religions, learning about the contributions of top scholars and his positive or negative opinions about them. Yet he respected scholarship. The first course I attended with him was on the Qur'an, where in spite of personal and even scholarly disagreements with Professor Fazlur Rahman of the University of Chicago, the course text book was no other than Fazlur Rahman's best work, *The Major Themes of the Qur'an*.[27] Al Faruqi was magnanimous when it came to recognizing scholarship.

In another course on "Ancient Near Eastern Religions" he required us to read the top works of scholars' Ancient Near Eastern Studies and the original texts from that period. After the class, we naive Muslim students for whom Islam began and ended with Muhammad became familiar with names such as Gilgamesh, Enkidu,

---

[27] Fazlur Rahman, *Major Themes of the Qur'an* (University of Chicago Press, 2009, 2nd ed.).

Marduk, Ishtar, etc. After class we used to joke among ourselves about where al Faruqi was leading us. We thought we had come to learn about Islam from him. This was al Faruqi, the walking encyclopedia of religion, both in class and outside. He opened up new vistas for us.

He also introduced us to the field of the history of religion, a subject unheard of and not taught in the universities of the Muslim world or their theological seminaries, where often the study of other religions is seen as leading to unbelief. For al Faruqi, there were no limits to seeking knowledge. He was ready to enter every field and terrain to know and learn and he instilled this habit in me, making me ever restless to search and learn, where there is no limit to learning. The only limit is biological life time.

Conclusion

Al Faruqi held that Islam was not opposed to modern science and technology, whether it was based in past or modern paradigms. What mattered was whether it was axiologically sound in terms of values in the areas of ethics, aesthetics, and religion—as they impact our perceptions, decisions, and actions. He remarked, "Islam is not against science or technology, the charge of Islam is a moral one, given in the realm of ethics and religion, not science."[28]

For al Faruqi, teaching Islamics was a dual undertaking, "as a study of a stream of being, of life, and religio-culture under categories furnished by the data themselves, rather than drawn from the arsenal of prejudices built by a crusading, missionizing,

---

[28] Isma'il al Faruqi, "Islam and Modernism" in "Isma'il al Faruqi Papers Collection" at the International Institute of Islamic Thought, Herndon, VA, USA.

secularist, anti-Islamic, anti-Arab or imperialist West" directed towards discovering the meaning of being *homo-religiosus*.[29]

In his own judgment, the Department of Religion of Temple University was the ideal place for him to teach Islamics, pursue interreligious dialogue, and seriously address the spiritual problems facing humanity in modern age. I remember very well that in the 1980s after the death of Bernard Phillips he would often during class express his appreciation for the contributions and legacy of Bernard Phillips in setting up the department, and those of his colleagues, with whom he was united in the mission of educating the youth from all over the world.

Prof. al Faruqi has been accused and been labeled as being a Mutazili rationalist, an Arab nationalist, a philosophical rationalist influenced by Kantian deontology, a firebrand Islamist posing as an academic, an intolerant dialoguer, one who stole the idea of the Islamization of Knowledge from others,[30] the ideological father of the Islamization of Knowledge, a poor social scientist, a Palestinian nationalist, etc. In my view, he did not care. Rather, he rode above all of them. He did not have time for petty matters. He thought big and dreamed big.

It is good to remember his legacy, both personal and professional, at TUDOR, but it is more important to continue and develop it further. In my view, Prof. al Faruqi, while being concerned about the politics of knowledge, or power and knowledge, was not a politician when it came to seeking knowledge and doing research. Seeking knowledge and doing research for him had no bounds of time, space, or sources.

---

[29] Isma'il al Faruqi, "On the Nature of Religion, of the Department of Religion, and of My Role in the Department," "Islam and Modernism" in ibid.

[30] Syed Muhammad Naquib al-Attas, *Islam and Secularism* (International Institute of Islamic Thoughts and Civilization, 1978).

For Prof. al Faruqi, Islam was a worldview, a philosophy of action, and an educational undertaking whose universality had no limits or bounds. In my view, the rise and the fast spread of religious exclusivism among Muslims shows that along the way we have abandoned, lost, or forgotten his legacy in the areas of studying and research about the connection between Islam and history of religion and interreligious dialogue. Prof. al Faruqi was turned into a political ideologue of the Islamization of knowledge. In his life time, he did make comments on the state of politics and advised politicians, but there is more to his contribution than that.

Al Faruqi presented Islam as a religion, a worldview, and an integral part of the knowledge process, without engaging in apologetics, but by developing new theories about the role of Arabs and Islam in the religious stream of being in non-nationalist terms. His was an Islamic theory of aesthetics rooted in Qur'anic monotheism and the Islamization of knowledge, all of which remain his greatest contributions from his Temple tenure.

Without al Faruqi, the department of religion at Temple University would be a small world and without the department the Muslim world would not know of Isma'il al Faruqi. Students like me and many others would not have learned about the larger world of religion. It would be tragic to ever forget, ignore, or look down upon for political reasons the deep bond al Faruqi contributed, and built between the Department of Religion, Temple University and the Muslim world- an academic brand label that I and many other Muslim and non-Muslim students carry around the world.

BREAKTHROUGH TO DIALOGUE

PROFESSOR MAURICE FRIEDMAN: *WITH GRATITUDE*

KENNETH P. KRAMER

In the late summer of 1968, Temple's Religion Department's PhD program was relatively new. Its faculty was full of creative energy, and the students who came in the late 60s were full of a willingness to stretch, to grow, and to overcome previous limitations. I showed up after finishing Andover Newton Theological School (during which I realized I did not want to become a Baptist minister), Yale Divinity School (during which I realized that I wanted to study further the interface between religion and literature), and after spending a year teaching at Saint Andrew's Presbyterian College (during which I realized I wanted to continue teaching university level courses and therefore needed a PhD). I officially became a candidate for the PhD, or should I say, I jumped in and began swimming.

What happened?

Three professors in my graduate classes—Maurice Friedman, Bernard Phillips, and Richard DeMartino—would make all the difference in terms of the way my teaching and my writing would take shape. There's no telling who I learned the most from, although it was clearly Professor Friedman who would have the deepest and longest influence in my life. Bernard Phillips would be the first to expand my horizons from Christianity into the world of Asian religious traditions. Dick DeMartino would be the first to take me into the linguistic heart center of Rinzai Zen Buddhism. But it was Maurice Friedman who would point me to the dialogical philosophy of Martin Buber which was to serve me for the rest of my life. Each of them in his own way continues to live in the light that his teaching casts on my path.

1. On First Meeting Friedman

It was through the "Religion and Literature" program that he founded and directed at Temple, but also through the impact of his book *To Deny Our Nothingness*, that I first came to meet Maurice Friedman. My earliest significant memory of Friedman was learning in his seminars to avoid the temptation to reduce literature to "contents," "themes," or "symbols," and at the same time to develop a dialogical approach to religion and human experience.

"I have always felt," I recall Friedman saying in one of his graduate seminars, "that the two central statements in Buber's *I and Thou* were, first, 'all real living is meeting,' and second, what Buber says of the I-Thou relationship: 'by the graciousness of its comings and the solemn sadness of its goings, it teaches you to meet others and to hold your ground when you meet them.'" And then, switching his mood, he said, "It's not easy of course, not at all when the ground itself shifts." He laughed as if thinking of a funny situation that matched what Buber was describing. As it turned out, he was. When he then proceeded to tell us the story behind his laughter, it generated richer, more playful laughter. And that, I would discover, was how he conducted his classes—with a rich blend of the most serious existentialist thoughts intermixed with laughter-provoking remarks.

One of the most indelible memories that remains with me from Friedman's seminars was the way he illustrated the back and forth movement between two-sided "I-Thou" relationships and objectifying "I-It" relations. "Buber distinguishes between an I-Thou knowing and I-It knowledge. I-It knowledge comes again and again from I-Thou knowing. It is not, as we imagine, some objective reality in itself. Rather, it is a swinging back and forth between I-It and I-Thou." Extending his right hand, fingers down, he would trace an invisible infinity sign with his hand, his fingers turning upside-down as they traced their way back up the curve and then turning facedown upon reaching the top of the other curve. How powerfully life-changing Buber's words, along with Friedman's clarifications and applications, have become in my life! By focusing on the central significance of Buber's dialogical philosophy, Friedman's words encouraged me to engage with literature in ways that addressed me personally and which again and again drew me into dialogue with a speaking text.

As if in need of a fresh cup of hot coffee, when I arrived at Temple I lacked any specific direction toward a dissertation topic. I remember mentioning, in a conversation with Friedman, who was my dissertation advisor, that other graduate students in the English Department, where I was also taking courses, had encouraged me to write my dissertation on some obscure figure in order to avoid duplicating existing studies. Friedman, however, encouraged me in a different direction. "You ought to do something that is really meaningful to you, to write about someone who really addresses your humanness." This sage advice led me to write my dissertation on T.S. Eliot's *Four Quartets* as meditative poetry which, more than thirty years later, led to the publication of *Redeeming Time: T.S. Eliot's Four Quartets* (2007).

There was a lot of camaraderie and a lot of freedom in those days. When me and another student, Dan Shea, proposed a conference in religion and literature at Temple to Friedman, not only was he wide open to the proposal but he gave us free range on planning it. In fact, perhaps one of Friedman's best qualities was that he was always available, yet willing to stay behind the scenes when not needed. As a result, with the help of other students and faculty, Temple's Religion Department was able to host "God and Man in Contemporary Literature." Along with other notable speakers, Elie Weisel gave the closing address. The conference also presented the world premiere of Friedrich Dürrenmatt's play "The Meteor."

I'll never forget that in the discussion period following Stanley Romaine Hopper's presentation, "Eclipse of God and Existential Mistrust," Friedman empathetically refuted Hopper's suggestion that "Thou" was Buber's name for Tillich's "God beyond God." Friedman stated that Buber's "Thou" cannot be separated from the I-Thou relationship. To do so is to completely misunderstand "Thou." Years later, when working on my first Buber book, I asked Maurice "what does one need to know before reading *I and Thou* that will assist a person in their attempt to understand it more completely?" In response, he said, "it must be understood first that Thou is not an object but relationship. If this is not understood, the rest of the book will not be understood." I understood then why what he had said years earlier to Hopper was so important. Identifying Buber's "Thou" with God in Himself unfortunately is a fundamental misunderstanding that scholars, theologians, and general readers continue to make.

Or there was the time that the Religion Department sponsored a major lecture by the world-renowned writer/psychologist Victor Frankl. I remember nothing of his presentation. What I have never forgotten, however, was the way Dr. Phillips introduced him by quoting the opening lines of Confucius' *Analects:* "When a brother comes from afar to share what he has learned, what greater delight." More than thirty years later, the combination of Phillips' legacy and Friedman's influence is evident as I think back on my teaching career.

2. Phillips' Confucius and Friedman's Buber

In order to most accurately describe it, I'll let two eminent educators who have deeply influenced me speak. First, Confucius as Phillips taught him: he collected, internalized, and taught humanistic attitudes and in the process, developed a pedagogy of clarifying concepts and names. According to Phillips, Confucius' genius was to selectively preserve the classics, to transmit them with reanimated meaning and thereby to restore an ancient harmony between the teacher, the taught, and the teaching. Prior to Confucius, moral superiority of conduct and character was restricted to the feudal ruling family. For Confucius, however, the birth and background of a person were less important, for anyone could cultivate and refine one's humanity through personal effort and training. His aim was to repair the then present disharmonies in China by applying ancient wisdoms to help humanity rebalance itself.

Confucius said, "To learn and at due times to repeat what one has learned, is that not after all a great pleasure?" He followed this with, "He who by reanimating the Old can gain knowledge of the New is fit to be a teacher."[1] Confucius' genius was to selectively preserve the classics, to transmit them with reanimated meaning, and thereby to restore an ancient harmony between the teacher, the taught, and the teaching.

Second, Martin Buber as Friedman taught him: One of Buber's major contributions to the educational process was his introduction of the teacher's main tool—dialogue. Like Confucius' pedagogy of reanimation, Buber's educational approach is shaped by reciprocal interactions between and among teacher, taught, and teaching. That Buber's dialogical pedagogy is honest, exact, original, and even life-impacting seems obvious. But this book touches upon something less obvious: real teachers, Buber tells us, participate in "the secret history of the world."[2]

The first thing Friedman taught about Buber's philosophy of education is how radically perceptive it is. While books and essays have been written on it, it can be summed up in two words:

---

[1] *The Analects of Confucius,* trans. Arthur Waley (New York: Vintage Books, 1938), I, 1; II, 11.

[2] Martin Buber, *Mamre: Essays in Religion*, trans. Greta Hort (Westport, CN: Greenwood Press, 1946), p. 63.

"relationship educates."[3] Buber indicates that almost nothing is more important or more revitalizing than the space between us. And here's his major breakthrough: real learning happens neither because of the teacher's brilliant articulations nor the student's fidelity to the task alone, but the reciprocal bond of trust between the two.

That bond, of course, generates and is generated by genuine dialogue. When dialogue is direct, personal, mutual, and honest, it allows meaningful speech to occur. Characteristics of educative dialogue, according to Buber and Friedman after him, are:

- turning toward others courageously, and trustingly;
- being "fully" present to another's self-disclosure;
- listening attentively both to what is spoken and unspoken;
- imagining what the other is thinking, feeling, experiencing;
- responding responsibly without withholding oneself; and
- confirming the other as your dialogical partner.[4]

The central significance of genuine dialogue for Friedman is its "spokenness", or rather our being spoken through it. I did my best—still do—to embody these principles as naturally as possible.

1. Second Meetings

In 1971, the year I defended my dissertation on T.S Eliot, Friedman wrote in the preface to *Touchstones of Reality: Existential Trust and The Community of Peace,* that "none of my books is more

---

[3] Martin Buber, *A Believing Humanism*, trans. Maurice Friedman, (New York: (Simon and Schuster, 1967), 98. Buber writes that what he means by educating is no "content of an utterance, but the speaking voice; no instructing, but the glance, the movement, the being-there of those teaching when they are inspired by the educational task. Relationship educates ... provided that it is a genuine educational relationship."

[4] Kenneth Paul Kramer, ed., *Dialogically Speaking: Maurice Friedman's Interdisciplinary Humanism,* (Eugene, OR: Pickwick Publications, 2011), xvi.

my own than this one," and that a contemporary person needs "not 'faith' in the traditional sense of the term but a life-stand—a ground on which to stand and from which to go out to meet the ever changing realities and absurdities of a Techtronic age."[5] What is that life-stand? Two chapters toward the book's end describe it for me: "The Partnership of Existence" and one that speaks of the tools necessary to actualize that partnership, "Existential Trust: The Courage to Address and The Courage to Respond." It was dialogical courage that Friedman taught at Temple and that had begun to become a major component of my relational life-stand.

Over the years following the Temple days, I kept in irregular touch with Friedman, especially through his books. In my own classes, I used dialogue journals to help students reflect on their understandings of the course material. The purpose of a journal was to offer teachers and students alike a method for understanding not just course material but also the student's relationship with it. In this sense, the journal records a double dialogue—outer as well as inner. To my surprise, when I was reading Friedman's book *The Confirmation of Otherness*, I came to realize that he too used a journal in his undergrad classes at San Diego State University. He called it an academic journal that had four reciprocal elements:

1. Quote a personally significant passage from the reading or class discussion.
2. Rewrite it in your own words, not paraphrasing, but imagining the other person's viewpoint.
3. Respond to it from where you stand; enter into dialogue with it at any level, intellectually and/or emotionally.

---

[5] Maurice Friedman, *Touchstones of Reality: Existential Trust and the Community of Peace*, (New York: E.P Dutton & Company: 1972), 15.

4. Apply your dialogue to a recurring issue in the course, or in your life.[6]

While I'm not sure how Friedman used this tool, when I used it in my classes after completing these four steps, I asked students (who were willing) to share entries with the class in order to further refresh our dialogue with the course materials.

My second meeting with Friedman really began when in 1993 I visited him in his home in San Diego, ostensibly to record an interview about his views on death and dying. "If you were bedridden with no chance of recovery," I remember asking him, "would you ever consider physician-assisted suicide as a way to end your suffering?"

"This is a question," he responded, "that I cannot answer ahead of time." Then he said something that I often quote in similar conversations: "It depends on what resources would be available to me at that time." This response is a telling example of how Friedman has appropriated Buber's dialogical philosophy into his life, and how I then appropriated his appropriation.

Once at San Jose State University, using lottery funds designated for education, I invited Friedman to San Jose State where we had a dialogue in my large Death Dying and Religions class. Troubled by a question about the difficulty of dialogue, I asked him, "What is needed is a workable solution; a solution that truly considers every person in their particular situation. This force, however, is not without limits. What about the limits of dialogue?" He responded:

> There are several limits: one is time; one is hunger; and one is that you do what you can in a situation. There are even tragic situations where there are simply not enough resources on either side for a genuine meeting to take place. You don't insist on the dialogue and you don't assume it will always happen—you are simply open

---

[6] Maurice Friedman, "The Confirmation of Otherness," *Family, Community, and Society* (New York: Pilgrim Press, 1983), 157.

for it. If I could make dialogue happen, that wouldn't be dialogue. That would be willfulness. So, I have my radius. I can prevent it, though. There can be a one-sided prevention of dialogue. I can do it simply by saying—"nothing's going to get through to me." But when there's a *willingness* for dialogue, then—and you used the word earlier—one must "navigate" moment-by-moment. It's a listening process.[7]

1. Mutual Confirmation

A year before this, after he had retired, I was asked to give a lecture commemorating his career by the Lipinski Institute for Judaic Studies at San Diego State University. I gladly accepted. But what is there to say about a scholar whose comprehensive text *Martin Buber: The Life of Dialogue* and his translations almost single handedly introduced Buber to the West, and whose two volume biography of Buber's life and work is, according to Martin Marty, the place where all future Buber scholars must begin. What is there to say about a scholar whose writing on the human image and touchstones of reality offers us interreligious and psychotherapeutic applications of Buber's work, and who co-founded the Institute of Dialogical Psychotherapy in San Diego. When all his publications—over twenty books and more than two hundred articles—are added to his teaching and world-wide lecturing, he has accomplished enough to fill two careers. I wanted therefore to cover the breadth of his achievements. At the same time, I felt the need to add a few personal memories from his teaching career.

When I asked myself what fundamental attitude was beneath his life and thought, which tied it all together, I was obliged to begin with his own self-description. Friedman writes that in some ways as he grows older the aspect that speaks more and more to him is Buber's philosophical anthropology. It is crucial thus to understand

---

[7]Kramer, Dialogically Speaking, xxiii.

that the central subject of this science is neither the individual nor the collective but the dynamic between person and person. To be a philosophical anthropologist, one has to be able to bear solitude; one has to delve the human from within; one has to become a problem to oneself; and then one must discover all the varieties and cultures through which we express ourselves. The reason philosophical anthropology goes beyond cultural anthropology for Friedman is that it asks the question not just about human beings but about the human—about our wholeness and our uniqueness, and most importantly about our dynamic inter-relatedness with others.

There was one class—"Religion and Psychotherapy: The Problem of Confirmation"—that was different from the others. It is the only one in which, aside from the reading list, he handed us another sheet which began with Buber's statement defining "confirmation." Then Friedman listed a series of provocative questions that we worked on during the semester's readings and discussions. Look at the questions and imagine what it might be like to dwell with them, returning to different ones throughout the course. It was here, for the first time, that I learned the value of living with unanswered questions, of remaining open to the way life events take shape around the questions. For this reason, I've saved his list.

RELIGION AND PSYCHOTHERAPY

Prof. Maurice Friedman

(Temple University, 1970)

The Problem of Confirmation

"Sent forth from the natural domain of species into the hazard of the solitary category, surrounded by the air of a chaos which came into being with him, secretly and bashfully man watches for a Yes which allows him to be and which can come to him only from one human person to another."

Martin Buber, The Knowledge of Man

1a: How do I find the calling through which I can become myself in response to the World's call?

1b: How can I live authentically in the tension between personal, social, and existential confirmation?

2a: What part does our confirming one another in dialogue play in our realizing our personal uniqueness?

2b: Can I make you present through experiencing your side of our relationship without empathy or identification?

2c: Can I accept you as you are, yet refuse to confirm you when you are unfaithful to the person you are called to become?

2d: Can I expect my child or my student to confirm me as well as I them?

2e: Ought the student experience the teacher's side of the relationship, the patient, the therapist's?

3a: Are the social roles I play and the groups to which I belong the means or the alternative to my being confirmed as a unique person?

3b: When is the interhuman conflict an obstacle and when a getaway to mutual confirmation in depth?

4a: Is there an existential confirmation that we experience through and beyond the personal and the social?

4b: Does the courage to address and respond make possible the "courage to be," or the other way round?

4c: Can existential trust accept and overcome the social and existential mistrust that robs us of the courage to respond?

In a strangely wonderful way, Friedman's teaching and writing as a philosophical anthropologist reached its culmination in the reality of confirmation. Living with these questions, each person in different ways becomes a problem to him or herself. Yet, the list also points to a way out—confirmation—which for Buber was "a Yes that allows a person to be," and for Friedman happens when I communicate a willingness to continue our dialogue beyond acceptance and affirmation and into the future despite disagreements. As students and as persons, Maury's confirming dialogical approach continued to induce our self-discovery and our mutual confirmation. This is how existential trust can overcome existential mistrust. Through mutual contact, mutual trust, and mutual concern for all the issues being discussed, a path is opened into the future. As a result, each person can move more deeply into the direction that he or she is called to move.

For instance, after visiting several of my classes at San Jose State University, Friedman surprised me as I drove him back to the airport by saying, "Ken, you have created a real learning community here." His remark was a confirming one because I knew that by "the learning community" he meant a community of learners who mutually confirmed the otherness of each person (students and teacher). For him the learning community is an ever-regenerating community of people who are willing to be present to and for one another, willing to discuss multiple points of view, and willing to challenge and be challenged by one another. A learning community thus happens when open-minded dialogue occurs.

1. Friendship with Buber

Friedman's presentation of Buber's words has become vital to my spiritual health. Why? Because the existential trust of which he speaks is nothing to believe in. Because life is so malleable and fickle and always in transition that I am constantly carried forward into new forms of being human. Because I am again and again asked to relearn who I am, rediscovering in the process that I am not a solitary individualist. I consciously choose to address and respond courageously to whomever encounters me (whether religious or religionless) with dialogical respect. Am I always successful? No. Rather, "it's a direction of movement," as Friedman used to teach. Though never perfect or complete, what makes me truly human in the moment is the all-time effort of building with others a common world, a common speaking, and listening.

I was deeply honored, therefore, when Maury, in his middle 80's, asked me to write the foreword (as he had done for three of my Buber books[8]) for his last Buber book, then called *All Real Living is Meeting: My Friendship with Martin Buber*, which he later changed at my suggestion to simply *My Friendship with Martin Buber*.[9] He had told me over the years that he had been working on this dialogical memoir. When he, with some difficulty, sent me the manuscript (in 2008), I saw that it needed deep editing and that Friedman's typing skills were diminishing. In the following year, I offered to become his book's representative to get it edited, find a publisher, and handle all correspondence with the press. That process lasted until 2013.

The book is filled with wonderfully honest details of their relationship including, on Friedman's side, moments of distancing from and contending with Buber. Although Friedman did not meet Buber until after six years of immersion in his work, their first face-to-face encounter (on October 31, 1951, in New York) was both memorable and instructive for Friedman. Buber looked deeply into his eyes while taking his hand. Friedman's initial response was to

---

[8]Kenneth Paul Kramer, *Martin Buber's I and Thou: Practicing Living Dialogue* (New York: Paulist Press, 2003). Kenneth Paul Kramer, *Martin Buber's Spirituality: Hasidic Wisdom for Everyday Life* (New York: Rowman & Littlefield, 2012). Kenneth Paul Kramer, *Learning Through Dialogue: The Relevance of Martin Buber's Classroom* (New York: Rowman & Littlefield, 2013).

[9] Maurice Friedman, *My Friendship with Martin Buber* (New York: Syracuse University Press, 2013), ix-xiv.

feel how totally "other" Buber seemed. His eyes were of a depth, gentleness, and directness that Friedman had never before encountered.

For this reason, in 1961, a year after Friedman had spent four months in Jerusalem with Buber, he asked himself, "What did I experience when I looked into Buber's eyes?" Upon reflection, Friedman realized that when he looked into Buber's eyes, he understood that Buber really included him, and for this very reason also placed a demand on him to be fully present. As Friedman indicates, this was by no means an easy demand! And why? Because, as Friedman well knew, Buber's "inclusion" meant making present, and meant imagining what the other person was thinking, feeling, and experiencing (not as detached content but as a living process) without surrendering one's own stand. Once, when Friedman said to Buber that inclusion must be very difficult, Buber responded, "It's not difficult at all, it's a grace."

Yet what was Buber's perception of Friedman? Fortunately, the book provides us with several glimpses of how Buber viewed Friedman. For instance, in the summer of 1955 Friedman taught a course in Contemporary Religious Thought for the Department of Religion at Columbia University. Due to the success of this course, in 1956 Friedman was considered as a possible regular faculty member in the department. Buber agreed to write a letter recommending Friedman for the position. "I am going to tell you what I think of Maurice Friedman," Buber wrote to the department. "I do so at his request, but I rather like doing it," Buber added, continuing:

> This he could do only by true understanding, his best quality indeed. He understands the ideas he meets, and he understands even the persons who thought them, as persons who thought just these ideas and not different ones. I am sorry to say what he had to do in this case with a somewhat resisting subject, but he succeeded to grasp it adequately. His best faculty is to express and to explain what he has understood . . . . I have the impression that I have told you

what perhaps no other could tell you about the man. It is because for all these years I have been a witness and now I have come to give evidence.[10]

These interrelated characteristics—his best quality and his best faculty—continue to deem Friedman's work of the highest academic value.

Unfortunately, before the book reached publication, Maury died in San Diego. I say unfortunately because he would have especially enjoyed its packaging. The book's back cover offers a one-sentence recommendation by my late friend, Mishael Caspi, retired professor of Judaic and Islamic traditions at Bates College, Maine. I once introduced him to Maury after a talk Friedman had given at San Jose State University. In praise of the book, Mishael wrote, "Friedman's work will shine a light reaching directly to the reader's hearts, a light which cannot be hid, enlightening those seeking new ways to study Buber's thought and serving as a renewal of his philosophy." How perceptive. How grateful.

In light of Mishael's laudable words, I can't think of a better way to end this little essay than to refer to the dedication in *Learning through Dialogue: The Relevance of Martin Buber's Classroom*:

> For Maurice Friedman
> Esteemed teacher, mentor, friend
> Who "dared, despite all, to trust."

---

[10] Ibid., 98.

BREAKTHROUGH TO DIALOGUE

DEAD MAN LIVING
RICHARD DEMARTINO (1922-2013)

STEVE ANTINOFF

I never say anything but no one pays any attention so I keep repeating it.
—*DeMartino*

Forty-four years ago, when I first walked—late—into Richard DeMartino's evening class on Religion and Literature, this chart was written on the board:

- *Real Man*
- *Man's Man*
- *Ladies' Man*
- *Great Man*

(And then, under two drawn chalk lines to indicate an ultimate category):

- *True Man*

The first words I ever heard him speak were: "A great man is not necessarily a true man." He offered Charles DeGaulle as a case in point.

Students of course wanted to know whether DeMartino was a true man, or true Self, in the Zen sense of the term—that is, was he enlightened? Since it takes one to know one, though we had our opinions, we could not with certainty discern. What those drawn to him *did* know was that DeMartino was a *man*, a man first and a teacher second. His manliness—tough and full of charm—was nonetheless rooted in something far more intriguing: his nonchalance that suffused the classroom with the sense that he taught from a place not ensnared in the problem of existence he set before us and which several students were forced to acknowledge as our own.

He once brought back from one of the rare conferences he attended a quote from one of the presenters. "All philosophy must be political." "What I think the speaker meant," DeMartino added in class, "is that all philosophy must be existential." Whether or not this was the intended meaning of the quote, it is without question DeMartino's own position. He was existential to the core. A man of supreme intellect, he would say, in speaking of Zen, "Intellectual understanding doesn't cut any ice." Those of us who repeatedly took or audited his classes were driven to know because we wanted *to be*. In DeMartino we found someone whose first premise is that academic knowledge in philosophy and religion had to be in the service of the life-and-death struggle to resolve the fundamental problem of living and dying.

DeMartino was never impressed with himself for being a professor. He was pleased by the actor Spencer Tracy's line, "Take your work seriously but don't take yourself seriously." Though he published rarely, he wrote and thought obsessively, often citing a diary entry of the Japanese philosopher Kitarô Nishida, "I was born cursed to think." In faculty meetings, on busses, on trains, and over meals, he would revise what he'd written into a yellow legal pad pulled out of the cheap double-handled gym bag that accompanied him everywhere. At least once he was denied promotion for scant publications. But when it came to his writing he said, "I hurry for no one." When the research project he proposed to gain time off from teaching was rejected, and the department chair suggested he reapply in the future and mention he knew Japanese, DeMartino refused to make the addition, telling me in the most forceful tone, "I cannot promote myself. And I won't."

BREAKTHROUGH TO DIALOGUE

§

In the early years when class ended he always sat in a front row desk and copied his blackboard notes into his yellow legal pad. This gave me easy access to him once the other students had cleared out. I would ask him questions. Without permission, I soon began walking him back to his $60 per month apartment at Broad and Dauphin, interrogating him till he disappeared behind the door. In response to one inquiry he pointed across Broad Street to a third-floor pool hall. A man was visible in the window chalking his cue. DeMartino said, "See that guy up there. He thinks if he can just hit the seven ball into the side pocket everything will be all right. It won't be all right." When I once remarked on the difficulty of breaking through to enlightenment he grasped hold of the high iron railing that fenced off the Hardwick Hall dormitory, hoisted himself chin and chest against the bars, and said, "To step back from the gate and tell yourself 'I haven't broken through' accomplishes nothing. All you can do is press your head back against the gate and keep banging."[1]

§

DeMartino was my teacher and friend for more than four decades; the most significant person in my adult life. I attended his lectures as a university student, and for many years after. I was not a disciple. He had none. He once said (not referring to himself), "No master wants a disciple. He wants you to be the master." He quoted Krishnamurti from a radio interview: "Masters and disciples corrupt one another." Early on, at a Temple University event at which he was

---

[1] DeMartino's apartment life when I met him was not without adventure. Once he was held captive, alone, inside the local laundromat. On another occasion he was held up in his foyer at knifepoint. DeMartino told his attacker: "You can kill me. But I've got to get to class." The attacker insisted DeMartino buy a watch for five dollars. When he declined, the stranger lifted DeMartino's wallet, extracted a five-dollar bill, returned the wallet, and handed over the watch.

serving as a panelist with the visiting Japanese Zen philosopher Keiji Nishitani and the Religion Department's Maurice Friedman, I smiled at him from my front row seat. He responded with the tersest smile possible and looked away, leaving no doubt as to his warning: "Don't dare try to attach yourself to me. The Self that you are looking for cannot be attached to. I am as elusive as it is." When—in an upsurge of emotion—I tried to embrace him in front of the Temple center city campus the night before my departure for a Japanese Zen monastery, he got me in a judo hold, spun me 180 degrees, and pushed me in the direction of my home—his way of telling me, "You are alone!" This hardness was an expression of his warmth. He answered every question I ever posed to him in all of my letters from Japan, every question posed in Philadelphia, on the street and on the phone, however late the hour. In my thousand plus encounters with him between 1969 and 1999, when his Parkinson's put an end to my post-retirement visits to his Long Island home, he never once denied his help, and never once did harm, even when he slammed me, or forced me to slam into him, which was often. He seemed to have trodden each step of my path long before I had. He never lied. I never once knew him to act without integrity or compromise a principle. He could be fierce, funny, explosive, gentle, cantankerous, or stubborn. But if you observed him with care in these alterations, his mood never changed. Since his death in January my overriding impression is how interesting and entertaining he was, and how much fun to be around. He was serious when you needed him to be deadly serious about serious things.

§

He was ruthlessly serious with himself, too, although, following Chuang Tzu, he hid his universe in the universe and few noticed. If cursed to think, DeMartino always transcended being a teacher, a garment he easily removed, as though it had never been worn, once he retired. He described himself as a "vagabond student" or as a "bum," which he esteemed as a true art form. He said, "Until my forties I never had a penny." Key to his twenties was his two wars. He enlisted in the Naval Reserve and was sent to the Navy Japanese Language School in Colorado to learn Japanese—"much better than learning how to fire a cannon." Simultaneously, as he once told me, "I was fighting a war of my own." This second war was the problem of time and its attendant problem of first cause that tore him to shreds. By 1944, stationed at Pearl Harbor, he was volunteering for night duty so he could attend courses in Eastern philosophy during the day. From University of Hawaii Professor Charles Moore he first heard the name of the great Zen personality D. T. Suzuki. He was part of the invasion force at the battle of Tinian Island, serving as a Japanese language interpreter. An episode he recounted from the aftermath of that battle–both the story and the way DeMartino told it– –is informative of his character. The U.S. Navy surgeon attached to the invading force was obliged to amputate the leg of a Japanese local wounded in the invasion. He invited DeMartino to be present during the operation. Noting his reluctance, the surgeon heartily added, "It's like slicing a ham!" After the surgery DeMartino was obliged to break the news of the amputation to the young man's mother. "I explained to her it was the only way of saving her son's life. I'm sure she thought I was lying until her dying day."

He arrived in Japan shortly after the atomic bombings and spent several weeks in their vicinity (so that almost 50 years later when we were in New Mexico he passed on a trip to Los Alamos on the grounds he'd already been exposed to enough radiation for one lifetime). Moving eastward to Tokyo he was struck by the docile acceptance by the Japanese of the U.S. occupation; at 3 in the morning he walked the streets among the recent enemy in complete absence of fear. About to be discharged and sent back to the States, he was offered a job as Historical Consultant to the Defense Panel of the International Military Tribunal for the Far East (the Tokyo War Crimes Tribunal). This enabled him to stay on in Japan, which led in his meeting with D.T. Suzuki in 1947. He told me, "For the first six months I visited him I didn't know what the hell he was talking about. But I sensed he had the answer I needed so I kept going back." Years later he added, with wonderment at the way life plays out, "Hundreds of people met Suzuki and moved on. I met him and stopped." For nearly two decades he studied with him, served as his chauffeur, his assistant, even as his pillow, for the aged Suzuki would slump onto DeMartino and nap, including the night Suzuki pressed him to drive fast from Los Angeles back to Claremont, then conked out on his shoulder while DeMartino negotiated with the cop who had pulled him over for speeding.

In the meantime, DeMartino was going through hell. He said that Suzuki had tears in his eyes when he saw the extent of his suffering. It was Suzuki himself who for years suggested, given DeMartino's temperament, that he study with the more severe Zen master Shin'ichi Hisamatsu, the critical figure in DeMartino's life. "The talk that I abandoned Suzuki for Hisamatsu was nonsense."

His characterization of his second teacher—"Hisamatsu cuts like a razor. It takes you three days before you realize you've been cut"— was borne out at their first meeting. A delayed reaction to their encounter, at a dinner in Kyoto where Hisamatsu swiftly turned DeMartino's struggle with the problem of first cause into a Zen koan, produced a cough and a fever that lasted over a year. Back in New York as Suzuki's assistant at Columbia, he locked the windows of his apartment, fearful he'd jump out of the building in his sleep. Soon enough he decided that if he was capable of jumping while asleep, he was equally capable of unlocking the windows, then jumping. Up flew the windows. "I decided if I was going to kill myself at least I was going to get a good night's sleep." I asked if his parents, also in New York, knew what he was going through. "I concealed it. It wasn't easy. Only [Phillip] Kapleau knew." He said, "1952-53 was a helluva year." In his classes, he "was just going through the motions." One day someone approached him and asked, "Are you ok?" To his utter surprise, he was.

§

I did a double-take when DeMartino in his last professional appearance in New Mexico described himself as a "terrible speaker." He was a magnetizing force in class. Chief testament to this was the number of auditors in his classes—one semester as many as 35% at the old center city campus on Walnut Street. Students brought their friends, lovers, and spouses. Former students passing through Philadelphia would drop in for a lecture or for the duration of their stay. He was admonished for this but ignored it. "What am I supposed to do?" he said to me. "Some of these students have been hanging around my classes for years." He also believed in auditing in principle. "It was the way I was educated." When I admiringly reported what I had learned from a documentary that J. Robert Oppenheimer was such a compelling teacher that a student went on a hunger strike outside the packed auditorium after being refused admission to his course, DeMartino reacted to Oppenheimer's rejection with distaste.

§

Armed with references to Sinatra, Humprey Bogart, New York cab drivers, and comics like Joey Lewis ("You only live once, but if you do it right—once is enough"), DeMartino was a man of the 1940s. Yet he perfectly fit the need of a certain type of student of a 1960s that he had no interest in being part of. He deeply appreciated our interest in Eastern thought. But he tore the wheat from the chaff with a hacksaw. To a student who espoused the bohemian freedom of Jack Kerouac's novel *The Dharma Bums*, he replied, "The true dharma bum must be free even at the president's ball in white tie and tails." When a student back from a year in a California Zen center insisted that enlightenment without seated meditation was impossible, DeMartino pressed her. "What if someone has no legs?" The student said that would be too bad. DeMartino responded, "You'd better go back to California and do more meditation."

He pandered to no one. I know of no beloved teacher less concerned with being loved. He was ruthless with our illusions. I recall the night he blasted us free hippies. "Look at yourselves—you're all wearing uniforms!" Virtually every male in the room, me included, wore blue jeans, a blue work shirt, and a beard. He admired us for our quest. The highest compliment I ever heard him pay a class was, "I can sense your interest is not merely academic." But he also said, "We're not here to make friends" and fought us hard lest our struggle be misguided.

§

On that one kindness rests what mattered in my education, in accordance with DeMartino's distinction between education and propaganda. "Propaganda permits only answers; education wants you to question." He could be gruff, cutting me down mid-sentence as soon as he intuited where I was heading. When I asked about the admonitions to practitioners mentioned in the Ming Dynasty book *Whips for Driving Through the Frontier Barrier of Zen*, he exploded: "The hell with their admonitions! Make your own admonitions. At this point, throw yourself into the koan and resolve it!" But he was always encouraging. When I despaired at ever breaking through, he conked me gently on the top of the head and announced, "You'll get there." When I said, "I think my struggle is further advanced than my ability to sit in meditation," he said, "I think so, too." When I confessed I was afraid, he said, "Originally there is nothing. From where does the fear come?" When I telephoned to tell him I had abruptly roused from sleep only to die in the middle of the night—an experience that happened so quickly I didn't have time to quake until I woke the next morning - he laughed and said, "If I told you how many times that happened to me . . ."

He was starkly honest about the difficulties of the Zen quest, especially knowing my body often betrayed me. "The first thing any good Zen master will tell you is to take care of your health." But he also said, "The point comes when you have to give up the body." When, at a seminar in New Mexico, a pregnant woman (whose husband was also in attendance) asked about the costs of the Zen quest—nervous that its demands would negatively affect the raising of her child—she was cheerfully assured by some of the participants that there were none. As soon as the session ended I walked over to DeMartino. His first words: "Of course there are costs."

I once asked, "The people in Auschwitz were desperate. Why didn't they break through?" He said, "To be in despair is not enough. The despair must be focused." To provide proper focus was his constant concern to anyone who came to him. Usually it was lacking. "Ninety-nine percent of the questions brought to me are psychological, not religious," he told me. And in class he said, "People stay up all night worrying about everything but the one thing they should be worrying about." Among my few keepsakes is a 1977 letter, when the physical pain of prolonged meditation had me over the cliff. He wrote, "With regard to your questions about zazen (cross-legged meditation), pain, active and passive,[2] etc., I think you are getting too entangled in all these questions. I think the more advisable procedure would be to focus on the root-source of the problem (or motivation) that made you go to Japan. Let the restlessness and untenability of this problem (or motivation)—at its source—be the motivating power and directing force of your *kufû*.[3] Above all, *do not rely* on anything—neither zazen, koan, pain, your teachers, Zen, me, or anything else. I'm sure you know that already."

§

---

[2] That is, whether to actively try to break through the Zen koan or passively allow the koan to gnaw from within until a resolution came of its own accord.

[3] Literally, "seeking and contriving." One's struggle on the Zen quest.

Zen Buddhism as "something," as an object or phenomenon to be attached to, meant nothing to DeMartino. In "The Human Situation and Zen Buddhism," he wrote, "For Zen Buddhism, finally, neither is in itself, nor does it offer any objective content to be studied as such psychologically, religiously, philosophically, historically, culturally, or sociologically. The only valid component of Zen Buddhism is one's own concrete life and existence, its basic contradiction and incompleteness, and, in distinction to the mere longing, the actual quest for reconciliation and fulfillment."[4] The sacred cows and traditions of Buddhism and Zen meant equally little. "So much of Buddhism is irrelevant," he would say. Or, "if Gautama said *that*, he was wrong." He questioned every internal contradiction he found in Eastern philosophy and practice. That's what he meant in saying, "If you go to Japan, go as an American." Told socks were not permitted in a monastery during a freezing week of meditation he countered, "The true Self is formless. Why this attachment to socks? Once I get used to the cold, I'll remove them." Against traditional interpretations of the Four Noble Truths, he said, "To say the cause of the human problem is craving is *very* superficial." He said, discussing compassion, "'Father, forgive them, for they know not what they do,' is more profound than anything in Buddhism." He rejected the epithet of "the Perfect One," even the designation "wise," as applicable to Gautama, insisting, "Enlightened people can make mistakes." He held that Awakening solves the root problem of human existence but wisdom in any concrete situation requires insights that awakening does not of itself bring. "Just because you're Jesus Christ doesn't mean you can play the violin."

§

---

[4] "The Human Situation and Zen Buddhism," in D.T. Suzuki, Erich Fromm, and Richard DeMartino, *Zen Buddhism and Psychoanalysis* (New York: Harper & Brothers, 1960), 153.

No teacher in my experience thought on his feet as well as DeMartino. He *wanted* to be argued with—it helped clarify his thinking. He would order course readings by authors who disagreed with him, challenging, "Read their stuff and shove my analysis back down my throat." In hundreds of debates in class he was virtually never bested. On the rare occasion a student did land a punch, DeMartino cracked up with delight. Self-deprecation was a permanent feature of his teaching style. "When I walk into a room it seems like somebody important just walked out. Once for any man, twice for a fool, no, no—once for any man, twice for a fool, three times for DeMartino." He always insisted, acknowledging it was difficult when things got hot, that we "argue ideas, not persons," and was starkly impersonal even in criticizing himself. Walking up 13th Street discussing his revision of "The Human Situation and Zen Buddhism"–which I had just proofread in manuscript—I pointed out that in describing the nature of the Zen resolution to the human problem, the newer rendering stated something the exact opposite of what DeMartino had written in the published version twenty years before. He halted on the sidewalk, evidently contrasting in his mind the two long sentences in question. Suddenly he shouted with icy brutality, "I was wrong!"

This impersonal dimension was not just integrity. It was what he called "Being without being," the Self that is not itself. Once, some students invited DeMartino to a campus showing of Jean Cocteau's film *Orpheus*.

"I have to attend a faculty meeting."

"We'll come and kidnap you."

"I won't even be there."

§

DeMartino's enterprise as a teacher spawned from Gautama's utterance. "I teach two things: suffering and liberation from suffering." The fundamental problem of the human person, the solution to that problem, and how to existentially arrive at the solution was the through line of his teaching career. He ceaselessly reminded that intellectual understanding was not to be confused with existential self-actualization. But while warning the former could get in the way of the latter, he firmly asserted that a clear intellectual understanding could be of real help in avoiding the myriad dead-ends and pitfalls lurking in the Zen quest. "If I didn't believe this," he told one class, "I couldn't accept my contract."

The contracts he did accept never earned him much money. He was already forty-one when Bernard Phillips, whom he had known both in New York and Japan, invited him to come to Temple as a teaching assistant and to take a doctorate at the same time.[5] He played the stock market[6] to pick up the slack, once had a million dollars on paper, and shrugged when the market plummeted. "What would I do with a million dollars?" he said. He lived simply, seldom leaving campus, stunningly self-contained. I recall two women coming up to him at the end of class in 1969, one asking for the both, "Isn't it difficult for you to live alone?" DeMartino replied, stuffing papers in his gym bag, "I'm alone, but I'm not by myself."

---

[5] He could have easily ended up not teaching. He told me that the psychologist Carl Rogers, who he met in Japan, had invited DeMartino to take a graduate degree with him at University of Wisconsin. He accepted the invitation but the funding fell through. In retrospect, he said, he was "glad not to have gone into that line of work."

[6] One of my earliest experiences of DeMartino was his ritual purchase of the Philadelphia Inquirer from a small newsstand across the street from his apartment. The proprietor would greet him. "What you got to say to the world, Professor?" "E!" DeMartino would bellow from his lower abdomen, demanding the late edition that listed the day's closing stock returns. The shared pleasure and affection in this brief, nightly exchange, and DeMartino's exaggerated retort from the belly (or *hara*) in the Zen style, suggested from the beginning of our acquaintance a past in Japan that would never be penetrated, and a person, however much he revealed of himself in class, who would never be known.

The three apartments he lived in ranged from small to tiny, with books and photocopies everywhere, and with chairs so cluttered with books that the extremely infrequent guest couldn't sit down. He stored a high cupboard with folded large brown paper shopping bags, ignoring my assertions that these were both unnecessary and a fire hazard, years later chiding me with glee when the bags ran out moving him to a new apartment before we could finish the job. He was a pack rat, a habit learned furnishing foxholes. (When we bagged the last books from his mantelpiece, what remained was a reflector from a bicycle fender I'd seen him pick off the ground several years before.) Watching DeMartino I learned that a true eccentric is not someone who simply behaves oddly, but who does everything according to a strictly thought-through logic others judge peculiar, if not irrational. It was his *logos*, as he called it, that drove him to stock up on identical radios that he liked and purchase a drawer full of identical blue dress shirts; that made him go nowhere without a shaker of garlic powder in his gym bag; that drove him to buy out the health food store at 2nd and Market of its entire stock of a powdered vitamin-protein supplement called "Superfood" because the company may one day cease production. (It did.) It was his *logos*, manifest in a cascade of commands, which slowed every attempt to clear the items out of his apartment when two students and I moved him to his last Philadelphia abode. It was his *logos* that prompted him to put on his overcoat in the interval between the inner and outer double doors of the various Temple buildings and to avoid sweating by donning it one step earlier while still technically inside, or catching a chill by waiting until he'd stepped outside.

§

I had had, at twenty, a negative *satori*—a sudden illumination, incontestable in its authority that pinned me to the wall. That concurrent with this event was DeMartino's in-class articulation of the conceptual framework of what had happened to me was the luckiest break of my life. His lectures were the full orchestra version of what he'd said in an early conversation after class. "You've run up against the problem at a young age. That's good. But the problem is not the final word. There's a solution." How to attain that solution was the core of our discussions for years. I was struck from the outset that rather than suggesting I meditate he said, "Set an hour aside each night, sit in a chair, struggle with the problem and take it from there."

DeMartino's views on meditation surprised, and sometimes displeased, the many students who asked him about it. He was never overly impressed with cross-legged sitting, though he'd done a lot of it.[7] He referred to those who saw it as the way to enlightenment as mere "meditation masters." For him, meditation *as normally practiced* was trapped in the same difficulties of any method: a method of necessity established a duality between seeker and path, between path and goal; therefore, no object-method, path, or means undertaken by the ego-subject could definitively overcome the duality of subject and object that constituted the human problem. But as always with DeMartino, one had to understand the precise nature of his attack. He never discouraged anyone from meditating. When he put to me the question he often put to meditators—*Why* do you meditate?—and I answered, "To meditate without a meditator," he accepted this with an only slightly grudging, "Well, ok." When I told him I reached a state where my body was inert he said. "*All right*, but that's not enough." He was fully aware of the physiological and psychological benefits of sitting meditation. "I don't deny that the full lotus posture is a very comfortable position." He said, "Anyone who embarks seriously on the Zen quest will have hundreds of peak

---

[7] A comical side of his meditation concentration: a Japanese *aikido* master who taught classes in "ki" (vital force) cultivation for a year at the short-lived student Drop-in Center could not budge DeMartino until he made him laugh; this invariably broke his concentration, whereupon Moriyama-sensei would give him a shove.

experiences." But Zen awakening, he insisted again and again, is not an experience, which is by definition transient.

A leading member of the Philadelphia Zen Center who asked DeMartino at a public lecture at the Ethical Society if he did zazen was nonplussed by his reply. "I do it and I don't do it, but the zazen I do and do not do has nothing to do with sitting." Against the strongly held view that Dogen's famous expression of his awakening—"Body and mind fallen off"—pertained to sitting meditation, DeMartino said, "You've got to be able to walk down the street without body and mind." When I pressed him in class on the necessity of meditation he said, "*Dhyana* (meditation in Sanskrit) doesn't mean sitting. It means to start from the 'I' (which is where we have to start)—the 'I' which is split, dualistic. *Dhyana* as a practice means overcoming the problem of the 'I,' however you do it. The purpose of zazen on the 'way to'[8] the resolution is to actualize the great doubt block (the existential deadlock of the thinking, feeling and doing of the ordinary 'I' which is the precondition for enlightenment according to the Rinzai school of Zen). I'm not denying formal sitting may be of help. But how do you actualize the great doubt block? In one sense, it's impossible. The great doubt block can be actualized only by plunging into the problem and sticking with it. But when the problem takes over you are no longer the active agent. You are grasped by the problem and as such are the recipient."

So long as there was a duality between grasper and grasped, sitter and meditation, cross-legged meditation was of slight religious consequence to him. "To be able to sit in zazen for six hours without moving is of little interest. But to suddenly realize you've been sitting in zazen for the last six hours (without having been aware of it)—that begins to be interesting."

---

[8] DeMartino always made a distinction between "zazen to" and "zazen from." The former involved the struggle to resolve a problem, the latter was anything an Awakened person did. For him, neither was confined to "sitting."

When I asked, "Hisamatsu said in his conversation with Tillich that true meditation must not only be objectless but subjectless. What relation does this have to those states of sitting meditation in which there is neither subject nor object?" DeMartino said, "I would say none."

A year later I asked,

"What is the relation between states of meditation and the great doubt block?" DeMartino said, "I would say there's no relation."

"But what about reaching the state in which there is neither subject nor object?"

"It's a trance. Or else a temporary self-transcendence, but one that is still within the matrix of the 'I.' Insofar as the subject-object structure is transcended there is some relation, as in any *ecstasis*. Looking back later, after awakening, one may see some relation insofar as there was an overcoming of the subject-object scheme."

He said, "As far as we know Hui-neng never sat zazen for even one second.

Shen-hsiu [the chief meditation monk at the same monastery in seventh century China] sat all those years and didn't get it."

In class, while critiquing meditation he would often glance my way. Yet, once, at the end of a class in which he attacked the over-reliance on sitting, he acknowledged, almost under his breath, "At the beginning, it is probably essential."

But when does the beginning end?

§

In his apartment, seeking his advice about a sculptor friend who was in a bad way, DeMartino said, "Sometimes the only thing you can do is to listen with love." He was no doubt influenced by

Tillich's beautiful passage on the three aspects of love—listening, giving, and forgiving—in *Love, Power, and Justice*, a book DeMartino regretted had no equivalent in Buddhism. Not long after this conversation, as I said goodbye to him in center city after some Sunday academic event, DeMartino said, "I'm about to make a hospital visit. If you don't have plans, I'd appreciate your coming along." DeMartino was a loner and had been—I once asked him—since his youth. I sought him out or ran into him on campus hundreds of times. When I fell into step he accepted my company as a matter of course but he never—prior to or after this request—actively sought my companionship. I of course said yes.

In the Hahnemann Hospital room, tended by his wife, was Leonard Barrett (professor in the Religion Department, Temple University), body slumped in a wheel chair, face drooping on one side, an obvious stroke victim. I knew him only as my teacher in an undergraduate summer course fifteen years earlier, and liked him. I recalled a lively dignified man, explaining that "Jamaicans are 90% Catholic and 120% Voodoo;" that it was not uncommon for someone to fake eating the communion wafer and secretly slipping it into a pocket for subsequent use in a potion; that hair was a spiritual property and if you came home and found the armpits and crotch cut out of your wash hanging on the line, chances are someone was putting a spell on you. During my sole conversation with him at the end of class he sporadically plucked lint from my shirt and slipped it into his blazer pocket- his charming, impish way of implying he too might have a spell in mind.

Looking up and seeing DeMartino at the door he slurred, "Look what nature is doing to me." They small-talked, DeMartino striving, unsuccessfully in his own mind, I thought, for something adequate to say. As the half-hour conversation neared its end Dr. Barrett said, "I will go back to Jamaica. The sun and sand and sea must be allowed to do their work."

"You're a wise man, Leonard."

"I cannot teach!"

"Sometimes you've got to tell the world to go to hell. That, too, is compassion."

§

But DeMartino also used to say, "To turn your back on the world is to turn your back on your Self," though *how* one turned toward the world could never be predetermined. "The bodhisattva can assume any form, even that of a prostitute." In passing illustration, he once mentioned a Japanese friend, a Zen-influenced doctor of deep compassion, who, feigning sleep, and not wanting to hurt the visitor's feelings, did not resist as his overnight guest snuck into his bed. The context in which he mentioned this tale I have never forgotten. The summer after my first stay in Japan I ran into DeMartino on Montgomery Avenue on route to auditing his class. I said, "You emphasize the once-and-for-all 'great death' of the ego and rebirth as the true Self as the solution to the human problem." Masao Abe (his close friend) told me, "You must kill yourself at every instant." Abe's demand has an overt ethical aspect. Is the moment-by-moment killing of the ego related to the great death?"

DeMartino started to respond but class was about to begin. I took a seat in the back of a Curtis Hall room. For the next ninety minutes his entire lecture was addressed to my question. Only at the end did he look my way and ask, "Did that help?"

One sentence of his lecture struck me above all. "You're not going to get enlightened by giving your worst enemy a bunch of roses."

§

The Zen master Hakuin has a poem: "By hiring that idiot-sage/Let us work together to fill the well with snow." DeMartino's devotion to his major writing project—*The Zen Understanding of the*

Human Person—was total, though he'd say, "There's a tidal wave of misunderstanding out there and my work wouldn't stem a trickle." In thinking and writing he was a perfectionist; in one sense this led him astray. When I inquired upon his return from sabbatical as to the progress he had made, he told me he had spent the entire summer on a footnote arguing against Bertrand Russell. Too many years were spent revising the first two chapters of this work. Illness came, and the essential last two chapters were never completed. How much this bothered him I cannot say. When the *Eastern Buddhist* rejected his dialogue with D.T. Suzuki that he edited and revised over a couple of years, he said, indifferently, "So it won't get published." Of his later writing he said, "If (his wife) Kathleen likes it, that's enough for me."

DeMartino's life as a thinker rested on this base: Zen has a right to wait on the mountaintop until sought out but can't exclusively remain there. It needs to reach into the modern world. To do so it must offer, in conceptual, not just existential terms, its particular understanding of human existence. Other religions, theologians, philosophers, psychotherapists, political thinkers and economists had their view, Zen should set forth its view. I believe this is one of the reasons his graduate seminars were comparative, i.e., Zen and Western Mysticism, Zen and Western Psychotherapy, Zen and Existentialism. He wanted to test Zen thought, and his, against all other positions.

Seminar students were obliged to choose one Western thinker, compare this thinker to Zen, and then to report in class their findings. This could be daunting, so daunting that when DeMartino seemed to be working on his own writings and not paying attention during the presentation, a student who didn't know him could be seduced into hoping that his cross-examination would be lax. But DeMartino had a strange gift. I once remarked, "You seem to be able to concentrate on many things at once." He corrected: "Not *many*, two." Unfortunately for us, two was all he needed. I first witnessed this when as an undergraduate he allowed me to enroll in his graduate course. One of the students invited a friend, an expert on the idol of them both, Wilhelm Reich. The guest presented an analysis of Reich for over an hour. DeMartino seemed oblivious, revising his own work in his yellow legal pad. When the speaker finished, DeMartino stood, thanked him cordially and, using the blackboards that enclosed the Beury Hall classroom on three sides, proceeded to destroy Reich point by point by point.

It was a devastating *tour de force*, undertaken with complete courtesy and with the "bit of the bloodless prosecutor" that a professor at Union, observing him in action in a course of Paul Tillich's, told him was part of his core. DeMartino often said, "You have to be tender with people." When arguing ideas, he was steel, but the one overt expression of affection I ever heard him give a class *en masse* was a semester-ending, "Think critically. I love you." I always felt elevated when he clobbered me. It gave me two gifts: a path to ultimate existence and the ability to stand on my own. When he nailed me—"You're too contemporary! You've got to smash that middle-class veneer! I've told you before, there's something egotistical in your quest"—I was not knocked down, but forward.

§

DeMartino stayed hidden in clear sight. One of his first insights, upon reading Max Lerner's essay "The Joiners," was that joining was not part of his nature, though he acknowledged he needed the group in order to live on its periphery. He loved Chuang Tzu's advice on the use of being useless in the Taoist sense of the term. He could have easily, given his years in Japan and the "credentials" these provided, employed the 1960s interest in the East to celebrity status. He quietly chose not to. "No genuine religious teacher has ever charged a penny," was one of his firmer assertions. He did not consider himself a religious teacher of any sort. But he fielded all questions, academic and personal, inside and outside class, from anyone who asked. Always he was his own definition of a Zen koan.

"A Zen presentation in the form of a Zen challenge." I never met that challenge and never could get past the cage his words built around me. That I am part of my recollections of him is unavoidable, but of no significance at all. The cage is important, though—others may fall into it, someone may break out of it—and I'll let DeMartino sing a few bars:

*Once, when I had been in bad intestinal pain for several months, I said to DeMartino:

"The pain is so severe I can't practice."

"What's your practice?" he demanded.

"Sesshin (severe weeklong monastic meditation retreats) and meditation are my practice."

"That's not your practice. Your illness should be the source of your practice, not an impediment to it."

*I told DeMartino I am going to Japan. He said: "Don't make the problem geographical."

*I once asked: Should I try to break through or let go? DeMartino said:

"If you're breaking through is different from your letting go something is wrong."

*On another occasion I asked:

"Should I try to break through the koan[9] or do I let it carry me across?"

DeMartino: "Let it carry you across."

"Like a mantra?"

"No, not like a mantra."

Years later, when I reminded him he'd once said, "Let it carry you across," he replied, "I shouldn't have said that either." (His implication: you can't actively break through the koan *nor* passively

---

[9] DeMartino's master Hisamatsu held that the fundamental koan, expressing the essence of all other koan, is: "Whatever you do, will not do. What do you do?"

let it carry you across. Without being active or passive—if will won't do and grace won't do—now solve it!)

First meeting after my first stay in Japan:

As I walked into his evening class the first Monday back from my first stay in Japan, DeMartino, discussing the Zen memoir *The Empty Mirror* said, "Perhaps Mr. Antinoff has something to say from his own empty mirror."

"Don't hitchhike," I replied, and did not speak again in class. When the students had filed out and we were alone I told DeMartino that arriving in California on a missionary plane from Asia, I'd hitchhiked across country, gotten into the wrong car on a desolate road in Appalachian Kentucky and wound up at 3 a.m. with a rifle pointed at my head. My reaction, after my stint in a Zen monastery? I shook from head to foot. "You should have broken through," DeMartino said softly. "Your self-preservation instinct must have taken over."

First meeting after my second stay in Japan:

I helped DeMartino carry his supermarket purchases back to his apartment. When we'd set down the shopping bags on his kitchen table we had our first talk in three years.

"I can't find the determination to cut off my arm like Huik'o."[10]

DeMartino nodded.

"But I am not unrelated to that act."

He nodded again. "If you are planning to go back to school, do what you need to do to get through your classes but keep the real concern at the forefront."

---

[10] Huik'o, according to the likely legendary Zen account, stands through the night in a snowstorm outside the cave of the so-called first Zen Partiarch, Bodhidharma. When the master warns him that the Zen path is unendurably difficult, Huik'o pulls out a sword, cuts off his arm, and presents it to his teacher.

"When I finish my course work I'll go back to Japan."

"No five-year plans! Take up the koan at the next available moment."

*He often quoted the dialogue between Bernard Phillips [first Chair of the newly established—1964—religion department at Temple University] and Hisamatsu:

Phillips:" If you follow a way you'll never get there."

Hisamatsu: "That's right."

Phillips: "But if you don't follow a way you'll never get there."

Hisamatsu: "That's right."

Phillips: "Then it seems you have a dilemma."

Hisamatsu: "That dilemma is the way you must follow."

I was ceaselessly asking him about method—"How do I solve the koan?"

"How do I actualize the great doubt block?"

DeMartino eventually said.

"You keep asking: 'How am I to follow the dilemma?' You keep trying to step out of the dilemma to ask how to get out of the dilemma. But I ask you, how would you improve on Hisamatsu's formulation? 'The dilemma *is* the way you must follow!'" And, "All you can do is keep your nose to the grindstone. On the other hand, the nose *is* the grindstone."

*Walking him back to the Broad Street bus from the Temple center city campus, I said,

"Hisamatsu says in his commentary on the first case of the *Mumonkan* (The Gateless Barrier): 'All routes must be brought to the extremity and extinguished so that not one remains.' But it is impossible for the ego to do that."

DeMartino nodded his head. "Now you're in the dilemma."

Suddenly, all he had been saying for years about the contradiction of a means to enlightenment became clear. I blurted out, "The great doubt block can only be reached when the contradiction between the impossibility of resolving the problem and the necessity of resolving it is brought to the point of final extremity."

DeMartino said, "Of course."

*In class he said:

"It's not enough to want enlightenment. You've got to need it. No one gets wakened without blood, sweat, and tears. Yet effort alone will not get you there either. There's a passive element. The effort of the ego can do nothing to actualize the non-being aspect. If you start from the ego, the Zen quest is not only difficult, it's impossible. The moment you start on the Zen quest you are in the wrong direction. But of course, not doing anything won't get you anywhere either."

*In America between my second and third stays in Japan, I told DeMartino of my meeting with Hisamatsu. I had prepared one question, not knowing if I'd have a chance for two. I asked, "Is the life-staking effort that Gautama made at the *bodhi* tree—Enlightenment or death—necessary?" Before I could recount Hisamatsu's answer DeMartino exploded, "*Of course* it's necessary."

*From 1976 to 1979 I used to keep Yampolsky's translation of Hakuin under my cushion during the sesshin. It was one of four books I took to Japan. When I read it during the break periods my heart would blacken at the gap between his courage and mine. DeMartino wrote at my mention of this: "Courage doesn't sound right. Gautama sitting beneath the *bodhi* tree wasn't an act out of courage. He had no choice."

*Regarding Hisamatsu's fundamental koan—"Whatever you do will not do. What do you do?"

DeMartino said,

"To answer it you must change the question mark into an exclamation point!"

On another occasion he said,

"To be I yet not I—what Hisamatsu means with his fundamental koan."

*When DeMartino was telling me of a critical period of his life, I asked him if at that time he was using a koan.

"No. It was a matter of life and death."

DeMartino said: "If you are still aware of your breathing you are not really working on the koan."

He said, "Insofar as one 'works on' a koan, one will never solve the koan. Insofar as one 'concentrates on' a koan, one will never solve the koan. Insofar as one 'meditates on' a koan, one is never going to solve the koan."

He said, "You can 'broaden and deepen' koan after koan through sitting, but you'll never break out of the matrix."

*Walking from Anderson to Gladfelter hall I said to him, "You're always on top of your content." DeMartino replied, "I have no content."

Once I said, "Every time I illuminate an aspect of you, I find I've simply exposed an even more illimitable darkness." He said, "You're not making very much progress, are you."

When I said that in trying to understand him these many years I was just scratching the surface, he said, "I always tried to remove those scratches."

*Most afternoons or early evenings DeMartino would walk the grassy slope on the east side of Paley Library. His exercise route always commenced with a single set of W's across the gently slanted lawn until he reached the one steep point of incline by the rear of the building. This he'd ascend and descend in 20-30 minutes, the cardiovascular part of his exercise routine. Each time I spotted him from the window of the Critical Languages office, where I worked as part of my scholarship requirement, I would sneak off from my job and question him. DeMartino had been saying in class, as he often did, that the ego knew itself to be a subject, and may even defend a violation of its subjectivity to the death, yet cannot know itself *as* subject but only as an objectified image of itself. The next day as we were climbing the library slope I asked if the true Self could know itself as subject. "Of course," he said, and without breaking stride he bent over, picked up a fallen leaf, righted himself, and presented it to me. "Here it is." I hesitated, then grabbed at it. Still in stride, he held the leaf before me for a few seconds, and as I reached for it more aggressively, he said, "Here. And not anywhere," and let it drop to the ground.

*One morning I groggily answered the telephone.
"Did I wake you?" asked DeMartino.
"No."
"Sorry about that."

"WE WASH YOUR FEET"
EULOGY FOR BIBHUTI S YADAV: JULY 10, 1943 - OCTOBER 10, 1999

THOMAS DEAN

I. Introduction

"Where has my B.S. Yadav gone? Where has my B.S. Yadav gone?" Over and over, in her shock and grief, his mother repeated this lament, like a mantra, at the foot of the simple wooden platform on which lied the body of her dead son. "Where has our Dr. Yadav gone? How can it be that our Bibhuti is gone?" Over and over, we, his colleagues, students and friends, in our own shock and grief, have been repeating this mantra these past days and weeks.

Bibhuti Singh Yadav was born fifty-six years ago on July 10, 1943 in Tulasipur, a small village of 300-400 people in northern India near the city of Benares, or as it is also called, Varanasi. He died—for his family and for us, all too soon—on October 10, 1999 at Lankenau hospital in Wynnewood, Pennsylvania. His death was due to irreversible injuries to the brain suffered as the result of a late-night fall on a street one block from his home in the Philadelphia suburb of Narberth. At the request of his family his body was returned to India where a traditional ceremony was performed and his ashes were returned to the Ganges, the sacred river of India.

We knew him, as for the most part we know each other, in the context of our shared work in an academic department in a large, impersonal, urban university. It was in that setting that we formed our impressions of him as an absolutely unique and unforgettable human being, a brilliant mixture of intellect and emotion, a thinker who demanded of himself and of others the highest intellectual integrity and rigor, a teacher, for those lucky enough to have attended his classes, who in every class session never failed to captivate and confound with his ever-surprising, ever-astonishing fund of totally original and profound insights into the texts he was interpreting, texts which for him were not only philosophy but central to life itself. It was my great good luck that he became the dearest of friends, an engaging, sometimes frustrating, but in the end irresistibly charming colleague with the sassiest tongue I have ever heard inside or outside the classroom.

II. His Background

Before talking about his career at Temple University, I would like to share with you a few stories about his life in the rural village in India where he grew up, where he received his first educational training and took his first intellectual steps. Perhaps we may see in them hints of the attitudes and philosophy of the man and thinker he was to become.

But first we should be clear about the name of the person we are talking about. All of us, with the exception of Dr. Gerard Sloyan, have been mispronouncing his name since the time he arrived among us. His given name was pronounced Vibhuti, not Bivuti. For whatever reason, perhaps its spelling on the printed page, we reversed the "v" and "b" sounds, and, so far as I know, he never complained. Two interesting facts for post-colonial reflection: his family name, which was the name of every person in his village, was Yadava, not Yadav. Somewhere between the time he left India and arrived at Temple, the final "a" was dropped. In any case, the name he was known by in the village and land of his birth was Vibhuti Singh Yadava.)

Among many such tales, here are three he told about himself.

Story Number One: How he got his early start as a future scholar of Sanskrit. When he was a young boy, his father would tie him by his hair to the low ceiling of his village hut and force him to remain there until he had mastered that day's lesson in the Vedas. Those of you studying for your foreign language exams, take note!

Story Number Two: Perhaps because of this, however, Yadav sometimes seemed uncomfortable teaching about Hinduism. Of course, he knew it backwards and forwards, having been born and indoctrinated into the tradition by his father, and having further studied and written on it in his doctoral dissertation. But he had noticeably more enthusiasm for Buddhism. Questioned on one occasion as to why he had such misgivings about Hinduism, he answered simply, "Let me tell you what Hinduism is. My father would get up every morning, very early, so he could go down to the river and offer the sun a drink before it got up to take its daily journey. That was Hinduism. I just can't imagine offering the sun something to drink in the morning; think of how it feels at noon!"

Story Number Three: Let's call this one "Yadav's revenge." One day, in his early adolescence, Bibhuti had once again gone with his father and the local priest to the river for the morning ritual. This time, however, our young hero climbed into a tree by the nearby temple and proceeded to urinate on that sacred edifice. His father was so outraged by this act of sacrilege that he threw his son out of the village. From then on young Bibhuti had to live with an uncle in another village.

It seems as a boy Bibhuti was already the Bibhuti Yadav we all came to know and love!

One non-intellectual footnote on his early years: apparently, Yadav was an accomplished athlete in his youth. He was widely regarded as the best wrestler in the village. In fact, it was well-known throughout the district of Ghazipur that Yadav was the youth wrestling champ. It is interesting to speculate what would have happened if any of his students or colleagues, in a moment of pique, had challenged Yadav to "settle things outside." Fortunately, the sparring matches we had with him were limited to the verbal sort. Those were daunting enough!

(The wrestling style is an ancient Indian athletic art that has been practiced for millennia. Rather than initiating the match on their knees, as do modern Olympic wrestlers, both contestants begin on common ground, on equal footing. Rules inhibiting life threatening holds or executions are well documented. It is apparently a veritable art form characteristic of kshatriya training. It was perhaps for this reason that Yadav sometimes gave the impression he was a kshatriya, though according to Bill Allen (Yadav's student and successor at Temple—Swidler) the village of the Yadavas is low caste, no higher than Vaishya.)

III. How He Came to Temple University

You may be interested to know how this rascally fellow ended up coming all the way from Tulasipur to *this* Temple. His first stop was at Banaras Hindu University in Varanasi where, as a brilliant student of philosophy, he received his BA in 1962 at the age of 19. He was awarded the Banaras Hindu University Medal for standing first in the Department of Philosophy. Two years later in 1964 he received his MA in Philosophy. This time he was awarded the R. N. Lal Gold Medal for standing first in the Departments of Philosophy, Indian Philosophy, and Religion. As a PhD student in 1964-65 and again in 1967-68 he was awarded the Gayekwada Fellowship for Research in Philosophy, a fellowship previously held by his doctoral advisor, the distinguished Indian philosopher, T.R.V. Murti, and by the internationally known philosopher and former president of India, Sarvapalli Radhakrishnan. After serving as a Fellow at the Center for Advanced Study in Philosophy at Banaras Hindu University from 1967 to 1970, he received his PhD in 1970 with a dissertation on "The Concept of Appearance in Madhyamika Buddhism and Advaita Vedanta." In 1971 Dr. Yadav followed his teacher, Professor Murti, to North America, where he served as a Teaching Fellow in the Department of Religion at McMaster University in Canada for one year before joining the Department of Religion at Temple University in the fall of 1972.

When Temple began looking for a scholar in the Indian tradition, our then-chair, Dr. Gerard Sloyan, approached a colleague he knew at McMaster. As a result of conversations that also involved Professor Murti, in a letter of March 2, 1972 four names were put forward. One, a senior scholar man, was ruled out by the fact this was to a junior appointment. The next was a research scholar of Sanskrit and Indian philosophy. After five years he seemed 'totally unaware of North America, systematically avoided course work outside his specialty" (7th C. Buddhist critiques of Hinduism), and avoided teaching opportunities the department provided for most students." He was discounted as well. The next name on the list was that of a younger man named "B.S. Yadava." The last line of the informant's letter was, "I have talked with Yadava about the possibility and he was very interested." Gerry promptly sent a letter on March 6th addressed to "Mr. J.S. Yadava" inviting him to Temple for an interview, and "B.S. Yadava" replied, in a telegram addressed to "Gerard Sloyan," giving his arrival time at the Philadelphia airport. Sometime between March and April, apparently for the first time, "B.S. Yadava" became "B.S.Yadav," because on April 17th Dr. Sloyan sent a letter officially inviting "Dr. B.S. Yadav," to join our faculty, and on April 26th "B.S. Yadav" wrote back accepting an appointment as Assistant Professor. The rest is history!

IV. His Academic Career at Temple University

From the beginning of his career at Temple Dr. Yadav won the praise of his colleagues. In the required departmental review for new contracts, Dr. Sloyan, reporting in the fall of 1972 only a few months after Bibhuti's arrival, wrote: "Dr. Bibhuti Yadav has been with us only three months but is showing good promise. He is interested in his students and courses, faithful to all obligations, and is thoroughly agreeable in all department and university matters. I think we did well in changing over from distinguished visiting professors of Hindu studies to this earnest young scholar." In his report of the following year, recommending a renewal of contract, Dr. Sloyan had even more to say. "Considerable enthusiasm was expressed by the members of the Faculty Personnel Committee.... all present (Professors Laeuchli, Littel, Stoeffler, Swidler, Sloyan, Van Buren) voted in favor of this contract. Dr. Yadav is intellectually very much alive and giving satisfaction to his students at undergraduate and graduate levels as he begins his teaching career. He is single-minded in fulfillment of his university duties. He has no major outside interests besides Temple University and the academic progress of its students. The widespread feeling among his colleagues is that he will grow with the years and the field of Hindu studies will be hearing from him."

I have to add one footnote to this story. Later that year, in a letter to the International Services office, Dr. Sloyan asked if someone would help Dr. Yadav in gaining an extension of his one-year visa as a visiting scholar. As Gerry commented of the Bibhuti we all know so well, "I shall appreciate any assistance you can give him. By his own admission, he is not a master of detail in practical matters like this one."

For twenty-eight years, Bibhuti Yadav served as a teacher of classical Hindu and Indian Buddhist philosophy in the Department of Religion at Temple University. In the spring of 1991 he taught at Elizabethtown College in Pennsylvania, where the former chair of our department, Bibhuti's friend and colleague Dr. Gerhard Spiegler, was serving as college president. In the summer of 1992 and again during the academic years 1993-1994 and 1996-1998 Dr. Yadav also taught in the Religion, Asian Studies, and Intellectual Heritage programs at Temple University Japan, the branch campus of Temple University in Tokyo. This past summer he returned one last time to teach at TUJ.

Of Bibhuti as a colleague, one faculty member perhaps summed it up for all of us: "Bibhuti Yadav scorned what was merely conventional in thought or words. He placed a high value on candor, and advanced his views with vigor and force; but his modesty and humor would invariably force their way through, and a debate with him was as delightful as it was challenging."

And of course his reputation preceded him to TUJ. The Dean there, upon hearing the news of his death, said, "All of us at TUJ are, of course, deeply shocked and saddened by his loss. I didn't know Yadav well before he came to TUJ—in fact, I must admit that he had a bit of a reputation of being fairly eccentric back on Main Campus. But I found him to be a delightful colleague, gifted teacher, compassionate human being, and impressive intellectually."

He was indeed all these—and more—much, much more.

V. His Research and Publications

Bibhiuti Yadav was a lucid writer, subtle, sophisticated and provocative, on classical Indian philosophy and modern Indian society. His articles appeared in leading scholarly journals in both North America and India. Among them was a series of brilliant essays in which he drew on resources in contemporary Western philosophy ranging from linguistic analysis, phenomenology and hermeneutics to deconstruction, critical theory and postcolonial thought to undertake a completely original rereading of classical Indian texts. But equally and more importantly, in these same essays he also showed how insights from classical Indian thought could be used to challenge explicit, and implicit, claims to hegemony found in Western philosophy and Christian theology, including those he suspected in calls for interreligious dialogue. On the other hand, almost from the time of his arrival at Temple, stimulated by his conversations with our former colleague, Norbert Samuelson, and some of his own graduate students, he became deeply immersed in an interreligious dialogue himself, one between Indian and Jewish thought. The result of this exchange extending over two decades was a remarkable essay that appeared just last year in which he gave a

Buddhist perspective on the German-Jewish thinker, Franz Rosenzweig.

As his more recent publications and presentations at professional conferences bear witness, his interests were not limited to technical problems in Indian logic, philosophy of language, epistemology and metaphysics, or essays critical or supportive of cross-cultural philosophy or interreligious dialogue. From early on he was also engaged in philosophical analyses of ethical, social, and political issues in contemporary India as may be seen in his essays on "Ayodhya: Modernity and the Anguish of Modern India" or on "Mispredicated Identity and Postcolonial Discourse," as well as in his lectures on "Text and Society" and "Religion and Caste."

In fact, he did not view his interests in technical philosophy as separable from his interests in what one might call applied philosophy. For example, in his proposal for a study leave for the academic year 1979-1980 to work on the topic of "The Paradigm of Projection in Buddhism and Vedanta" he writes: "Philosophy, I may surmise, is a methodology of the conceptual construction of reality, and culture, a collective style of becoming actual in terms of the once conceptual ". The paradigm of Projection has had a complex history, having different functions in different schools of thought and entailing conflicting forms of cultural and intellectual life. Philosophers have used this paradigm as a tool of reform and rebellion in Indian social history. My long-term objective is to see the connection between the paradigm of Projection and the ideology of social change, between conflicting constructions of reality and social dissents and protests.

"My approach is interdisciplinary, the rationale being that there is a dialectical movement between forms of thinking and forms of life, between philosophy and culture. History of culture, therefore, cannot be left to historians or social scientists, just as philosophy cannot be left to philosophers. My request to philosophers is to see that epistemology is not necessarily the methodology of making truth-claims, that psychosocial orientations get incarnated in philosophical paradigms of the world. And I request social scientists to see that in a cognitive and classical civilization, such as India's, philosophy was the dominant methodology of constructing the world, that philosophical paradigms were skillfully turned into myths whose function in turn was to create popular forms of life."

An interesting postscript: Dr. Yadav was awarded his study leave and returned to India for the year to do his research. Shortly after his arrival there, in November 1979 he sent the following note to our then-chair, Gerhard Spiegler: "Please pardon me for this delayed contact. Having lived abroad for years, I found it a little difficult to get adjusted here in Varanasi. In the near future I shall write for you a dissertation type letter establishing the relationship between Varanasi, where everything is possible everywhere, and its ontology, according to which it is not logically necessary that there be the world."

At the time of his death he was working on a two-volume project, *Methodic Deconstruction: Madhyamika Theory of Language*. It was to have been his fullest, most mature statement of the contribution of classical Indian thought to contemporary philosophy, culture and society.

V. His Teaching Career at Temple University

Professor Yadav was recognized by his students and colleagues, both on Main Campus and at TUJ, as an outstanding classroom teacher. He was nominated several times for teaching awards and in 1992 received the award of Distinguished Teacher from Temple University. Asked on the occasion of this award to comment on his teaching, he wrote:

> (I believe that teaching has to do with being-in-the-world, and the world is conceived in texts. A great text, be it the Republic or the Bible, raises questions that are

answered only in the process of raising them again and again. The recurrence of these questions entails the endless presence of the texts. Teaching has to do with letting the texts face the students. I have real pleasure in helping the students to connect the present with the past, showing them how thinking, like life itself, is a temporal act.)

"I was trained in Buddhist epistemology but have grown over the years. Teaching proseminars in Hinduism and Buddhism has been particularly fruitful, for students of different backgrounds have forced me to connect religion with politics, ethics, social theory, psychology and philosophy of history. I also grew up by doing cross-cultural philosophy of religion, for example, comparing the process thought of Ramanuja and Whitehead, and the philosophy of language in Heidegger and Bhartrhari. For more specialized students, I have offered individual seminars on eminent thinkers like Vasubandhu and Dharmakirti, Abhinavagupta and Kumarila, Shankara and Ramanuja. I have been fortunate in producing some good PhDs who are doing well in North American colleges and universities." (In fact, students who received their PhDs under his direction or on whose doctoral committees he served as a reader hold tenured positions in Asian philosophy and religious thought at major colleges and universities not only in North America but also abroad in Korea, Taiwan, and Hong Kong.)

"A significant dimension of my teaching is my background. Most students do appreciate critical and creative insights into their intellectual legacies, especially when they come from frames of reference other than their own. I believe teaching is still a vocation that can light up the minds and spirits of us all."

In a letter supporting his nomination, Violet Ketels, Intellectual Heritage Director, commented on Bibhuti's extraordinary ability to lead undergraduate students to intellectual discoveries they did not know they were capable of. "As IH teaching evaluations consistently show, semester after semester, students are awed by Dr. Yadav's erudition. They recognize and admire his intellectual breadth and depth. They picture him as an encouraging, stimulating, inspiring teacher. Many students report a sense of intellectual growth under his tutelage. They seem surprised by their mastery of complex ideas they did not suspect they were capable of grasping."

A letter written by Zoharah Simmons in support of Dr. Yadav's nomination also captured the way he succeeded in making the philosophy relevant to life. "He doesn't leave you in the 'stars' contemplating some of the great Indian philosophers and seers. He brings their thinking right down to us where we live."

For colleagues fortunate enough to have sat in his classroom the experience was similarly unforgettable. If I may be permitted, in my own letter of support for Bibhuti's nomination for the Distinguished Teacher Award, I was moved to say the following:

> The many experiences of sitting in his seminars, whether as a co-instructor or a faculty auditor, have been the most stimulating intellectual experiences of my (now rather long) career as, first, student and then educator, a career that covers sitting in classes of professors at the University of Wisconsin, Harvard, Columbia, and Heidelberg as well as Temple and TUJ.
>
> First of all, the man is absolutely brilliant. He is incredibly well-read in both his own field of Indian and Buddhist philosophy and religious thought as well as in modern and contemporary Western philosophy and religious thought. The range of materials he is able to refer to and relate constructively to his own thinking constantly took, and takes, me by surprise.
>
> More than that, he also gives the most original, thought-provoking and exciting rereadings of classical Asian texts I have ever come across by anyone working in the area of Asian or comparative, cross-cultural philosophy. In the process he brings ancient texts into completely original and critical inter-textual relationship to the most contemporary ('postmodern') texts of the Western intellectual tradition (Heidegger, Derrida, Foucault).

> Moreover, he does this in a way that is not 'trendy' but that proceeds from, indeed insists upon, the most rigorous historical and philological analysis of texts in their original settings.
>
> It's hard to describe the effect this has on one. I would emerge from a Yadav seminar with cramped hands and a head dizzy with more insights, more new ideas, more directions for my own reflections from one three-hour session than I had come up with in a career of thinking about many of the same subjects and thinkers myself. It was both exhilarating and daunting. My own thinking about Heidegger, for example, or about the contemporary philosophical relevance of ancient Asian texts has been forever changed by sitting in the classroom of Bibhuti Yadav.

Nevertheless, the persons in the best position to appreciate his brilliance as a thinker were not his colleagues but those students who were lucky enough to have sat in his classes, graduate seminars and undergraduate classes alike, for clearly he refused to give his undergraduates anything less of himself than he poured into his graduate courses. For outsiders to that experience, a hint of what his students experienced can be found in the one complete description of his courses that we have from his hand, a faculty report on his teaching which he filled out early in his career for the academic year 1973-74.

> Of the spring courses that I taught, one was graduate, the other undergraduate. The graduate course dealt with the *Vaisnava Thought of Hinduism*. Problems such as the concept of Logos, Eros, the conflict or compatibility of Logos and Eros, God, Body, Beauty, Being and Becoming, typology of human emotions (*rasa*) and aesthetic experience were raised and examined in a comparative way. Conclusion—if there is a conclusion—reached was: God is beautiful, man is beautiful, and that the meeting point of God and man—the world—is beautiful; that religious consciousness at the heart is aesthetic consciousness.
>
> The undergraduate course in the spring semester was: *Gita and the Gandhian Ethic*. Problems raised and examined were: nature and varieties of violence and non-violence; sources of violence and non-

violence (social, psychological, biological, etc.); conflict of duty and duty, duty and love, love and love; relation of ethics and politics; ethics and government; ethics and law; ethics, anarchism and the State; ethics, war and conscience; truth, beautiful and good; ethics of means and ethics of ends; human nature, historicity and hope according to Gandhi."

The graduate proseminar in the fall of 1973 was designed to cover an otherwise less known area of Indian thought, i.e., *The Heterodox Systems of Ajivikas, Theravada Buddhism and Jainism*. Situating these systems in a detailed background of the Upanishads, our task was to examine the nature and structure of their literature; method and mode of their metaphysical reasoning; nature and reasons for raising philosophical problems such as that of the sources, validity and limit of cognitive claims; function, use and limit of language; and then the logical need of silence. On the spiritual side, problems were raised such as: the justification for raising questions about the meaning of existence, and reasons for concluding existence (*samsara*) as meaningless passion caught in the circularity of birth, disease and rebirth, or existence as a useful passion leading to *Nirvana* and *Kaivalya*. Philosophical problems ranging from metaphysics as a psychosis to metaphysics as a medicine dealing with the conflict of Being and Becoming, Space and Point, Time and Moment, Universal and Particular, etc. were raised and examined.

I should state that this class was more challenging, more searching, than other ones; and problems getting better located and then being resolved as naturally as ice becoming water. And I, of course, sweating more pleasantly and more lively.

The other undergraduate course that I taught was the Honors one entitled: Religion and the Nature of Man . . . . Two fundamental theories about human nature were examined in greater detail. According to one theory, a) there is no human nature; b) everything is inherently a chaos; c) no natural order, nature is a prolonged accident; d) no social order, society is a system of corruption; e) happiness can never be a socio-cultural value; f) freedom or *nirvana* is not realization, it is fatigue and nausea; g) and search for order, human nature, and *moksha* is a psychological disease.

The other theory—more important and more responsible—says that a) the talk of human nature is humanly important; b) there is ontological order in existence which justifies man's moral nature; c) human nature is a dialectic of free action and necessary consequence; d) my being born as a human being is my moral responsibility, and that dying as a cheerful act is my possibility; e) my being historical is both a possession as well as a problem; history is quest of truth, beautiful and good.

Just to read these descriptions is an exhilarating experience. One can only imagine what the courses themselves must have been like.

In that same report he says of his research vis-a-vis his teaching:

I feel so intensively to write about problems I have perceived so ambiguously and so clearly at the same time. I must admit that hitherto I have been sweating all along in coming up to my aspirations as a teacher and expectations of my students in the class. I must add that I take my existence in the class very seriously; it is so satisfying and so fulfilling . . . I could not do much about my own research and publications. In a very important sense, my own honest dissatisfaction with what I write is to be blamed, notwithstanding my young shoulders sweating with heavy load of teaching.

Ten years later, in another faculty report, while noting that his students in Intellectual Heritage are very exciting, challenging, and demanding, he sounds a plaintive note of protest about the scheduling: "8:30 a.m. is too early to do serious thinking in the classroom."

To illustrate how deeply he believed this, and how effectively he put that belief into practice in his classroom, I would like to share with you stories I have received from students over the past few weeks. They are eloquent testimony to their shared conviction that they had indeed been in the presence of a most unusual and inspiring teacher. Those of you who know Dr. Yadav will know how to take some of these stories. Those who do not should listen carefully so as not to miss the quality not only of the passionate intellect but equally important the caring mentor beneath the surface features of the narratives. The voices that follow are those of his graduate students.

I'll always remember him for his brilliance, the warmth he showed when he could tell I needed it, and especially some of the speeches we got as students. The following, which I remember almost verbatim, came at the beginning of each seminar, when a student unwisely got around to asking about what he wanted out of a paper. He would say in a slow, low-pitched voice dripping with sarcasm:

"I do not want bullshit. I want you to write for me a very profound paper. Your paper for this class should be so profound that it keeps me up at nights, drinking cups of coffee at eleven and twelve and one o'clock, just meditating on your magnificent insights. And when I finally try to go to sleep at two o'clock, I will not be able to because your paper has become so much a part of me that I can see your face looking in at me through the bedroom window. I will then have to get up, and walk through the dark streets at three o'clock in the morning, still wrestling with your brilliance. If your paper does not do this to me, I will flunk you." Then, before dismissing the class, he would almost always admonish: "The one other thing you must do for this class is be cheerful. If you come in here and I do not see some teeth, I will be very unhappy."

He was always challenging to his students, always ready with some comment to keep you on your toes, always ready to have a cigarette or a beer with you, and always prepared to stick behind you and give you a boost when he could see you needed one.

I wasn't always on top of things or aware of his good intentions all the time, and I find myself feeling bad about any misunderstandings we had. But I always loved being around him, and I'll miss him a lot. If I ever have a chance to go to the Ganges, I'll take some special time out to have a chat with him there, and maybe even share another beer, slice of pizza or cigarette—the three things besides the people in his village, Nagarjuna, and basketball he seemed to love the most.

In another story, from Spring of 1986, a student said, "My first exam in graduate school, I'm terrified, I've been memorizing and studying for a week, not leaving my apartment for three days, smoking, drinking coffee, staying up late. I think I know my stuff and walk into the exam for the proseminar in Hinduism. Dr. Yadav breezes in, hair mussed, wearing a *doti* (an Indian shirt). He shakes his head with mischievous glee as he hands out the exam, looks around at us, and states (with completely serious face) You are all going to fail. I write like a maniac because there is something about this teacher that makes me want to go as far as I possibly can. Later he comes around to each person and gently asks whether we would like tea, coffee, or soda. He goes out, buys each of us a drink, and brings it to us individually as we continue to write. I will never forget this generous side of him. I will, more importantly, not forget the intellectual fire that he gave to his students. I wrote for five hours and got an A.

Yet another student said, "This past Spring, I walked into the hall where Dr. Yadav was, as always, having a cigarette. He had just read my third and fourth chapters, and commented to me, 'I am very impressed with Schopenhauer. He understood *maya* better them some of the Keveladvaitins. The material has been presented very well.' Tricked into thinking I had been complimented, I stepped too far and said, Oh, thank you very much. 'No,' came the immediate response, 'I am not happy with you, I am happy with Schopenhauer.'"

Another student said, I doubt this one will go in your writing, but: He had a very sarcastic and hilarious way of making sure his students really had no clear idea of what he thought of their work. It was a great pedagogical tool, as it kept everyone working hard. Once, I was standing with him in the hall, and a student of his walked out, and suddenly, this burst came forth. "Sir, come in here. Let me offer you a cigarette. No, you don't smoke, but smoke one anyway, this is a good day for you. Sir, I am happy to say that your dissertation proposal has been accepted. The committee really liked what you wrote for them. They think very highly of you, and they are expecting great things from your work." By now, the student was blushing uncontrollably, not anticipating such an unrelenting stream of praise to be coming from Dr. Yadav. But, after a very short, well-timed pause, his cadence slowed and he almost whispered,

But, let me tell you... I just have to tell you one thing . . . . This department stinks!

As already noted, Dr. Yadav sometimes communicated mixed signals about Hinduism, or at least certain of the classical religious texts like the Bhagavad Gita or the Upanishads. This discomfort apparently showed up in his advising too. As one student recalled,

I remember when I first told him about my dissertation proposal, he told me "You should not do anything with the Upanishads, the Upanishads are worthless. With your background, you should do a project that deconstructs comparative philosophy. Or at least do Nyaya or Nagarjuna or the grammarians. Forget about the Upanishads, *brahman*, *atman*, all that kind of shit!"

A student recalled, On another occasion, I was challenging him in a class about whether Nagarjuna was opting out of rationality with his skeptical silence. "Come on!" he pleaded with me. "You're such a law and order guy, you don't want to make room for anybody else in your house. But I like this house. I want to live in the house. I just want to be able to say that the house has problems." Astounded by the answer, I shut up. To get me to shut up in a class, well, that teacher must be enlightened.

I almost forgot what could almost pass for Dr. Yadav's motto. Very often in class, after lecturing on how fixation on conceptual forms of thought was contrary to Nagarjuna, hence to all true, Buddhist teaching, and could never possibly lead to enlightenment, he would say in summation: "Philosophy is the discipline of very, very sick people." I thought several times of having a door or desk tag made for him with this printed on it under his name.

I was told by one student over the phone the other day about how he referred to people close to him. One could tell that Yadav and they were going to get along when he started to refer to them as "The highest incarnation of absolute stupidity." That was a good sign. But if you were compared to a European, you knew you were in trouble. He once told me about one of the European students: "I don't know if I trust him. He's really brilliant, but he looks like Max Mueller." Apparently that was about the worst fate he could think of.

To read just one of many e-mail messages I received from undergraduate students at TUJ: "I really would like to take this opportunity to share my grief with the members of the Yadav family. I am still in a state of shock and I have a hard time believing his death. I took two courses from him in which we both discussed in depths about philosophy and religion. He was truly an extraordinary professor with profound and keen insights. I always had such a pleasure debating on philosophical issues with him. As a matter of fact, I have learned so much from him. I have also heard from my classmates that he was helping the school at his village, which makes me believe that he was a true individual that believed in education. On behalf of the TUJ students I believe that he has left a great impact in our lives and will always remember him for his great teachings. We will truly miss him.

Lastly, a graduate student said, "One memory that was striking to me, again during a seminar. Dr. Yadav was lecturing on Nagarjuna, and talking about how Buddhists have fooled themselves into thinking that discourse about the Buddha is about some transcendental reality. "To be enlightened is to know, as Nararjuna knew, that all talk is conventional talk, all talk is about the world, and the world is about social practice." One of the persistent dissenters in the class suddenly challenged him. "So, are you enlightened?" Without hesitating, with a completely straight face and completely without pretension, Dr. Yadav answered, "Yes. I think so." To this day, Dr. Yadav is the only person I have heard to actually make that claim. But it was just the way he answered. And I believed him. In a very concrete way and for a very long time, he had lived that answer.

Dr. Yadav's commitment to the seriousness of the intellectual work that went on in the classroom extended to his judgment of students' work. At times that judgment could be rigorous indeed. For some reason his file contains a particular devastating example, a four-page single-spaced critique fully half the length of the graduate student's fifteen-page double-spaced paper. I will cite just a few of the withering remarks.

> There is no evidence that you have any familiarity with the primary texts at all. Such an ignoring, or shall I say ignorance, of the texts, primary and secondary, does not constitute a graduate paper. I ask you to look at your grade as a gift . . . . You will recall that the class spent session after session on just one sentence or paragraph in a text. You will also recall that such an exercise was not for fun; it was quite boring. The intention was to uncover metaphysical underpinnings, to discover why a sentence was composed the way it was, and how, were it composed differently, a form of thinking

would collapse. Thus, our object was to practice contextual thinking, to discern correlations between ontology and etymology, between the notion of the Absolute and the verb of a sentence, and between metaphysics and grammar. Ignoring my repeated requests to be textual and contextual, you produced a paper which is full of simple assertions, theosophical fondness for the superficial, and readable over-simplifications.

Yadav goes on to detail the paper's lack of methodological clarity and lack of analytical detail, which "makes your paper superficial, confusing, even downright irritating." Saying, "Let me carry my observations a little further," he then proceeds to list eight questions of substance with which the paper should have dealt. Finally, he offers a few comments concerning your classroom performance:

'You did make observations in the class but they were incomprehensible and irrelevant. They invariably broke up the logical rhythm of the discussions, forcing the instructor as well as the seminar members to test the limit of meditative patience. The class lived through a discrete rebellion, tacitly shocked when you spoke and patently thankful when you kept silent. I urge that you avoid being a liability in seminars. Rejoice in the boredom of reading difficult texts, learn the skill of critical thinking, and be considerate to seminar members by doing your homework. One more thing: mysticism is a serious matter. It involves logical, linguistic, and metaphysical discipline. Try not to confuse it with theosophical superfluity.

(The grade was a B. You can see that it was indeed the act of a compassionate bodhisattva!)

On the other hand, he could be effusive in his praise of students who had learned these skills. In a job recommendation he wrote for one of his PhD graduates, you can hear a description of what Bibhuti practiced so brilliantly as a thinker and teacher himself.

Hermeneutical enterprise is (his) greatest asset. He is reflexively at home in the Sanskrit texts. Listening to the Vaisnava tradition, following the logic that significant saying is creative resaying (bhasya), (he) persuades the medieval text to speak for its worldview once again in the contemporary world . . . . (He) is a brilliant, articulate scholar born to enliven classrooms. He challenges his students to recognize and confront the theories and presuppositions which lie behind their society and themselves. His mastery of the material enables him to translate the issues of alien and ancient texts into the language of modern discourse. There is in him a creative blend of critical distance and empathetic immanence in the themes and issues under discussion.

High praise indeed, for the student—and for his mentor.

It was not only in the classroom that Bibhuti left his mark. He left an indelible impression as well in whatever community he happened to be living. Here I will cite only one story provided by Dr. Anthony Matteo, his colleague at Elizabethtown College in rural Pennsylvania. Bibhuti had run out of cigarettes. So he went to the campus store and asked the woman at the register (a devout fundamentalist Christian) for a carton of Marlboros. With great indignation, she informed him that Elizabethtown College was a "Christian" school and "we don't sell cigarettes." Bibhuti replied, "Christian School! You don't sell cigarettes! My good woman, do you know that St. Thomas Aquinas smoked?!" She responded, "Who is St. Thomas Aquinas?" Bibhuti retorted, "My good woman, you call yourself a Christian and you don't know who St. Thomas Aquinas is. I am not a Christian, I'm a Hindu, but I know that St. Thomas Aquinas is the greatest Christian philosopher and theologian who ever lived. You cannot continue to call yourself a Christian until you read the works of St. Thomas Aquinas."

IX. His Post-Retirement Dreams

Bibhuti once said he was trapped between two worlds, two cultures, and was the most miserable of men because he had no choices. There is a great deal of anguish and suffering in these words.

Increasingly in the last months after his stroke, he spoke over and over of early retirement and returning to Varanasi, taking his books and setting up an institute for research in Indian philosophy. I always tried to talk him out of it. "No, no, Bibhuti, you're just depressed because of that stroke. Give yourself some time to recover, and when you're feeling better, maybe then you can think about it again." I didn't want to take him seriously. Like all of us, I suppose, I wanted to hold on to him for as long as I could. I couldn't imagine life in the department without him. But I now think that he knew something I didn't know, that if he was going to realize his dream, he was going to have to do it soon. And so the saddest thing is not that he has left us, but that now he will never have the chance to realize his post-retirement dream.

X. Those He Leaves Behind

During his twenty-eight years of residence in America, Dr. Yadav followed a simple life-style, preferring to send a portion of his salary regularly to his family in India. He apparently did so from the very beginning, because in his file there is a letter from Dr. Sloyan to the Dean dated May 2, 1973, the spring of Bibhuti's first year at Temple, in which Gerry writes in support of Dr. Yadav's request for an advance on his May salary check. The reason: "He is returning to India to visit his father, whom he has not seen in four years, but also to arrange the marriage of a younger sister. The dowry system is such that he is using all his modest savings for the purpose." Bibhuti also sent regular donations to the elementary school in his home village where he had gotten his first introduction to the world of ideas. He is survived by his mother, brother, six sisters, and a number of nieces, nephews and cousins, all residents of Tulasipur.

XI. A Message for the Department of Religion

As they were preparing to begin the procession to the river for the cremation, Bibhuti's brother, Hanuman, as a last gesture before Bibhuti's body was placed on a bamboo stretcher, tore a page from his diary book and, referring to Bibhuti's middle name, Singh, which in Sanskrit means "lion," dictated to Bill Allen (his student and immediate successor) the following message addressed to the members of Temple University's Department of Religion:

> The philosophical lion of my family and this rural area society, and of this India, and as well this world philosophical lion, now at this time is going to heaven. But where is heaven? and where has he gone? I and nobody knows where is that place of happening.
>
> "Dying is necessary for a human being to beget a new life. A man always take his birth on this earth, and after that he also is put on the earth.
>
> "The bamboo is the last friend of the dead body, and there is nothing in this world, because the dead of this world also go out with empty hand. Thus goes Dr. B. S. Yadav with empty hand.

XII. Concluding Salute and Farewell

Now, as he had dreamed of doing, this unforgettable lion of India, *Bibhuti Singh Yadava,* has returned home at last, to his village of Tulasipur, to find rest and peace in the eternal Ganges.

Dear Bibhuti, our colleague and teacher, beloved mentor and precious friend, we, gathered here, thank you one last time for your life among us. We were honored and privileged to have known you, we were blessed by your presence among us. May we too, in the time given to each of us, measure up in some small way to the shining example of rigorous thought and inspired teaching which you so splendidly and courageously embodied until the very end. We salute you. We miss you. We bid you a loving and final fare-well. Master, we wash your feet.

Namaste

BRIEF REMEMBRANCES

ZALMAN SCHACHTER-SHALOMI

Unfortunately, Reb Zalman Schachter's health was not strong enough for him to write anything for this TUDOR history. He dictated some reflections, and I did my best to edit them from the machine dictation. In my reflections elsewhere in this volume I mention something of his being raised in Vienna, escaping from the Nazi onslaught, arriving in America, and our TUDOR seminar trip to Germany in 1980. (I first met Zalman when he spoke at the Hillel Society of the University of Pittsburgh in the early 1960s when I was teaching at Duquesne University in Pittsburgh. I count Zalman as one of the several "hires" at TUDOR I was fundamentally responsible for, along with Pat Burke, Gerry Sloyan, Frank Littell, Khalid Duran, Mahmoud Ayoub, Ismail Faruqi, and Seyed Hosein Nasr.)

Shortly after he arrived, Zalman and I offered a joint seminar on Jewish-Christian Dialogue. I recall how about half way through the semester, while he and I were sitting next to each other and he was telling another of his penetrating stories—"parables" in New Testament Greek!—I looked at him and suddenly was hit with the insight that if Yeshua (Jesus) had not been murdered in his thirties, but like Zalman had escaped the assassins, and had lived into his sixties, he would have been just like Zalman! Full of compassion, always overflowing inner joy that beamed from his face, telling stories that touched one's heart and mind…. I uttered a silent *wow!*— Len Swidler.

§

At my age (89 years) I find it difficult to offer an objective "Bericht" for my time at Temple University. My memory doesn't serve me so well for specificity and details, but I will do my best to recall as accurately as possible.

At the University of Manitoba I served as head of the Department of Judaic Studies and was also a member of the Department of Religious Studies. There, one of the courses I most enjoyed to teach was psychology of religion. My Master's degree from Boston University was in psychology of religion, (pastoral psychology). I had the privilege of studying with Dr. Howard Thurman, who was the head of the Chapel and who offered a course in spiritual disciplines and resources "with labs."

I found the experience of studying religion with the opportunity to experience personally what I read about in the books most rewarding, and at Manitoba I put this experience to use in labs which I held in one of the chapels of the affiliated Roman Catholic and Anglican colleges. When Professor Paul Van Buren (as Chair of TUDOR) invited me to come to Temple I was elated. Across Broad Street, the Reconstructionist Rabbinical College asked me from time to time to offer some sessions to their students. Here too the labs and liturgy were appreciated.

The Chapel of the Four Chaplains at Temple was a wonderful resource for my labs with the students. It had built-in a merry-go-round altar which made it easy to turn the platform on which the altars were situated by simply pushing a button, and Catholic, Protestant and Jewish settings were available. I held many labs there and recorded for the students a demonstration of Jewish sancta. (Unfortunately the three-altar merry-go-round is no longer in the Chapel of the Four Chaplains—which is located in a sort of crypt on the Baptist Temple—now refurbished and part of Temple University—on Broad Street.—Swidler)

At an earlier time, at a meeting on Sufism, I had met Professor Hossein Nasr when he still heading the University of Teheran. When the revolution occurred it was suggested [by Len Swidler, who had become friends with Nasr at the disastrous-for-Catholicism-and-

Cardinal Pignedoli Catholic-Muslim Dialogue held in Tripoli, Libya, in 1976—Swidler] to the then the head of the department to invite him to come to Temple where he would not be threatened. I felt great kinship with him because of my own connection with Sufism. Professor Phillips who was the head of the department and who had also written about Sufism before my coming to Temple and I had more difficulty communicating.

One of the greatest delights of my time at Temple University was when graduate students and professors traveled to Germany to interact with our counterparts. Our visits to Freiburg and Aachen still remind me of this glorious time. With several of those "Doktoranden" I continue to be in correspondence.

Princess Antonia's Lehrtafel: One of the most interesting things for me on that journey was a side trip to Teinach, a small town in the Black Forest where at the request of Princess Antonia her pastor, who was interested in matters of the Kabbalah, had commissioned a painting (part of the triptych) dealing with Jewish and Christian Kabbalah. We also had the opportunity to visit Wittenberg, then in East Germany. The people there were wonderful but because it was before the wall came down the environment was very depressing. The students and faculty were doing heroic work in an unfriendly environment (they focused on a relief of the Wittenberg church which has a very antisemitic sculpture).

I was the office neighbor of Professor Bibhuti Yadav and had many good conversations with him about the deep teachings of Hinduism.

I also spoke of my experience and my own religious life in conversations with Gerard Sloyan, with whom I also I also discussed the exercises of Loyola.

John Raines and I likewise had good conversations dealing with Protestant spirituality and denominationalism.

Since I was raised in Austria and experienced the early Hitler years, Franklin Littell and I had many good conversations. I liked that when he wanted to make a subtle distinction about something we were discussing at faculty meetings he would use two German terms to show the difference—i.e., Gemeinschaft and Gesellschaft.

I remember Sam Laeuchli well and liked him a great deal. He and I had wonderful conversations!

In relation to studies in Judaism Professor Norbert Samuelsson and I were like two hemispheres of the brain—he representing the left, rational hemisphere and I representing the right hemisphere. A similar situation existed between Professor Isma'il al Faruqi, a Sunni, and Professor Hossein Nasr, a Shiite Sufi.

In all these conversations, with my background in Hasidism and what I learned from psychology of religion and Dr. Howard Thurman, it became clear to me that I could not teach anything in psychology of religion to people who had no liturgical and devotional experience. Any reading that I assigned to the students—like William James' Varieties of Religious Experience—did not evoke any experiential response from the majority of the students. It felt to me that it is useless to manipulate the terminology of devotion, contemplation, and liturgy without the students having a referent in their experience. Another way was to offer exams in which I gave them a text from one of the people they had studied and asked them to bring to bear what they had learned in the course by explaining which question the author of the text intended to answer.

I was especially conscious of the fact that some of the students who needed to take a proseminar with me in Judaism would not be exposed to the "basics" of the tradition they were studying. (Rahner and Küng, for instance, would never tell a student what a novena and a rosary was—nor would Buber and Kaplan tell the students what Kiddush and Havdalah and Kosher laws are all about.)

I remember on the one hand students from Afghanistan and Jordan working with me on things in Judaism that were familiar to them from their own tradition. I still recall with some students who became very well acquainted with the New Testament Q and the

Torah JEPD authors, but were not able to bring that text-critical awareness to the Qur'an. (They would say after discussing higher and lower criticism, "But God says!")

Student numbers were of great importance for the budget entitlement of a university department. Somehow when I offered courses on "Death and Dying" we got large numbers of students. Once I tried a course on "Life and Living" and could not get the requisite number for even a small class.

In retrospect my time at Temple University, especially my interactions with the faculty, was one of the best of my teaching career.

SOME RECOLLECTIONS OF MY YEARS AT TEMPLE

SEYYED HOSSEIN NASR

I joined the faculty of the Religion Department at Temple University at a very difficult moment of my life. The Islamic Revolution had just taken place and I had left Iran with my family in a very difficult condition. After a short period in Britain, I became Distinguished Visiting Professor at the University of Utah in March 1979 and set out to start a teaching career in America. Several universities made me offers to join them including Temple University, with which I had not had much contact before. My old friend and colleague Isma'il al Faruqi was there and he had heard of my coming to America. He and Professor Swidler got in touch with me and offered a full professorship with tenure, as had some other major universities, but these men added that at Temple the Religion Department was interested in teaching religions from a religious point of view and not just from a historical, sociological or philological one. Len Swidler added that they wanted Christians to teach Christianity, Jews Judaism, Muslims Islam, etc. and that the Department was very much interested in the relation between religions and religious ecumenism. Having supported these goals all my life, I turned down the other offers and accepted Temple's offer in the Fall of 1979. I was full-time professor there from 1979–1984 and visiting professor during 1984–1985 while having accepted the University Professor of Islamic Studies chair at The George Washington University starting in the fall of 1984.

Moving to Philadelphia in 1979 posed, however, a challenge for me. My two children were going to go to college in Boston, where I had studied myself, and after the loss of my house, other properties and financial assets in Iran, I could not afford to pay for both their tuition and room and board in that city. The only solution was to make our home in Boston where they could live at home while going to school, and for me to commute between Boston and Philadelphia. My worries were diminished when I discovered that Prof. Van Buren of the Temple Religion Department had been doing the same for years. And so for five years I commuted between these two cities, spending the middle of the week in Philadelphia and from Friday to Monday in Boston, where much of my time was spent at the incomparable Widener Library at Harvard. I knew the Islamic, religion and philosophy sections of the library like the palm of my hand, and so this difficult situation of living in two cities allowed me nevertheless to complete the text and all the footnotes of my Gifford Lectures which I delivered at the University of Edinburgh in 1981. The text appeared a few months later as Knowledge and the Sacred. I remember vividly the kindness of the Department professors when, after three weeks in Scotland where I had just given the ten lectures and during the first departmental meeting at Temple, the chairman, Prof. Gerhard Spiegler, announced my completion of the celebrated lectures. Everyone clapped loud and long to the point of embarrassing me. The Department was proud that one of its members was the first from Temple University ever to deliver the prestigious Gifford Lectures.

Within a few months of beginning my activities at Temple, I developed a congenial relation with nearly all the members of the Department despite philosophical differences with many. For example, after Knowledge and the Sacred appeared in print, Thomas Dean wrote a strong criticism of it, but we remained good friends. The atmosphere of the department was such that while serious scholarship was expected of all, different philosophical and methodological perspectives were respected as long as the necessary scholarly criteria were met.

Before turning to some of my recollections about the faculty at our Religion Department, I want to say a few words about our graduate students. I was told that Temple at that time had the largest number of graduate students of any program in America in the field of religion. My experience showed that we had essentially three types of such students: regular students in quest of an academic program in religion; American students from a Christian or Jewish background whose interest in religion was not only academic but also existential; and Muslim students, mostly from the Malay world, but also some from the Indo-Pakistani Subcontinent, the Arab world and a few from Africa, Turkey and Iran.

For my own academic scholarly life, having students from the Malay world was a novelty and a new opening into a faraway region of the Islamic world, told from the perspective of a Persian. When I taught at Tehran University, I had numerous Pakistani, Indian, Arab and Turkish students, besides Western, Russian and Japanese ones, but never a graduate student from the Malay world. Through Temple this opening was created. Some of my Malay students at Temple became close to me intellectually and later translated many of my works into Bhasa Malay and Indonesian. Profs. Isma'il al Faruqi and John Raines were also closely connected to Malaysia and the three of us strengthened in different ways the relation between Temple and the Malay world. The fact that even now, thirty years later, my humble works are so widely read and debated in both Indonesia and Malaysia is due to a large extent to my years at Temple. My Temple students and my writings even changed the intellectual relation between the Malay world and Iran and the Persian intellectual tradition, resulting in the introduction of later Islamic philosophy into the Malay world. Today there are numerous works on Mulla Sadra and translations of his treatises into Malay which are taught in many Malay universities. When I came to Temple, practically no one in Malaysia had even heard of this great philosopher. So, Temple has played an important role in the intellectual life of both Malaysia and

Indonesia even in the domain of Islamic thought and I am very happy to have had a small share in it.

Let me now turn to some of the Temple faculty with whom I was particularly close. Among Christian professors, besides Prof. Spiegler with whom I carried out many discussions on the philosophy of religion, I was closely associated with two Catholic professors, Profs. Sloyan and Swidler. Sloyan and I shared great interest in contemporary Catholic thought, especially Gilson and Maritain. I had known both men personally and attended some of Maritain's lectures while I was at M.I.T. and Harvard. Sloyan and I also supervised jointly the Ph.D. thesis of several students. As for Swidler, our main common interest was ecumenism, especially Islamic-Christian dialogue. We did much together in this domain and it was he who got me to debate Hans Küng at Temple, a debate that was attended by a large crowd and its written text widely read. Among Protestant professors I had the greatest exchange and intellectual debates with Prof. Thomas Dean and to a lesser extent Van Buren. These discussions included the thought of some of the leading Protestant philosophers of religion such as Barth, Tillich and especially John Hick. I am a perennialist, a view that Dean opposed as one can see in the exchanges we had after my Knowledge and the Sacred was published. Yet, we carried out many fruitful discussions together.

When I was at Temple, we had two outstanding Jewish professors both with different interests. Yet I had close intellectual and human relations with both of them. They were Profs. Zalman Schachter and Norbert Samuelson. Schachter was a master of Kabbalistic and Hassidic studies and was even secretly initiated into a Sufi order in Jerusalem. As soon as he discovered that not only did I teach Sufism, but was attached spiritually to it, we became very close friends and spent much time together discussing spiritual and esoteric matters. Schachter was so devoted to the Kabbalah that he even decided to retire from Temple at the age of sixty-three based on his understanding of Gematria calculations.

Samuelson's main interest was Jewish philosophy, in which he had done some wonderful work. But that meant that he was also very interested in Islamic philosophy, to which classical Jewish philosophy is so closely related. It was Samuelson who asked me if I would teach an Islamic philosophical text in the traditional Islamic method. I accepted and, following his suggestion, chose a text of Ibn Rushd (Averroës). We held the classes at lunch time and seven or eight people participated. I chose a text that I would read in Arabic, then translate it into English, and finally comment upon it in the traditional manner also in English. Samuelson was the most regular attendant and devoured everything that was being taught.

Before coming to Temple and while in Iran, I visited India often and had also studied Hindu religion, philosophy and art while at Harvard. I had known such renowned Indian philosophers as Radhakrishnan and been personal friends with famous Indian philosophers of the next generation such as Mahadevan and Murty. I had also participated in many ecumenical activities and conferences in comparative philosophy in India. With this background of experience and acquaintance with Indian philosophies I was expecting to have a close rapport with Prof. Yadav and even hoped to teach a course with him on comparative Islamic and Indian philosophy since he was also philosophically minded. But his philosophical outlook was very different from mine and we never became close, nor did we ever teach together the course I had had in mind.

Thirty years have passed since I left Temple. I still keep in touch with many of my former PhD students who did their thesis under my direction, not only Muslim students, but also Catholic, Protestant and Jewish young scholars, nearly all of whom I am proud to say became productive scholars and teachers. After the murder of my friend al Faruqi, my contact with the department faculty became less frequent but I have kept in touch with a few of them, especially Swidler and, until he died, Schachter. I look back with great fondness upon my

Temple years. Although coming in the wake of the Iranian Revolution, the shattering of my previous life and the loss of all my property, including my library and the fruit of much research, the Temple years were academically and intellectually among the most fruitful of my life, a period when I was able to deliver the Gifford Lectures and publish their text as well as write many other books and essays in addition to training so many fine young scholars. The atmosphere of cordiality and conviviality with the faculty and students is still present in my mind and soul. Some have said that the years I was at Temple were the golden years of the Religion Department. I thank God for having been a humble factor during that period and take pride in having made a small contribution to it.

TEACHING ABOUT RELIGION ON MARK C. TAYLOR'S *NEW YORK TIMES/INTERNATIONAL HERALD TRIBUNE* OP-ED ESSAY

THOMAS J. DEAN

Mark C. Taylor, professor of religion and humanities at Williams College, gained initial prominence by bringing Continental postmodern thought, especially that of the French exponent of "deconstruction," Jacques Derrida, to bear on a radical rethinking of philosophy of religion and theology in its American context. One of the major contributions of Derrida's philosophy was its undermining of the binaries that have governed Western philosophical and religious thought. These include such familiar pairs as reason and revelation, faith and reason, and the post-Enlightenment distinction of religious and secular.

Taylor's op-ed essay in the *New York Times* of December 21, 2006, "The Devoted Student" (his essay also appeared in the December 22, 2006 *International Herald Tribune* as "Faith That Refuses Questions") deplores the increasing reluctance of college students, especially the "religiously correct," "to engage in critical reflection about faith." My comments are reflections on this essay, which Leonard Swidler attached to his email entitled "Of Concern" sent that same day to the Religion department listserv. (I will copy and paste Taylor's essay at the end of my comments, along with five letters written to the NYT replying to his essay.) In his essay Taylor recounts being called into the office of an administrator at another university where he was teaching. He was asked to apologize to a student who had complained that Taylor had attacked his faith by asking the student to reflect on the implications of Nietzsche's critique of religion for belief in absolutes (surely an implication of Derrida's thought as well). Taylor, to his credit, refused to apologize. Professor Swidler notes that "though this sort of thing does not happen at Temple, we should be aware of the issue."

I would like to comment on the substance of Taylor's essay, but before I do I would like to share two of my own experiences teaching religion at Temple over the years which, though not the same as Taylor's, were brought to mind by his story of that encounter.

The first happened in the first semester of my first year at Temple in the fall of 1966. I too was summoned to the office of an administrator—in this case our chair (and founder of our department), Bernard Phillips. Phillips was both a philosopher and one-man embodiment of the dialogue among religions for which the department has become known and for which Taylor now calls. (Phillips, who was Jewish, once told me he was a Zen Sufi Jewish mystic. I suspect that other religious traditions were part of his mix as well!) A student had complained about my teaching of our introductory course, which at that time was called "Religion and Human Nature." The course featured a range of texts both "secular" and "religious." Opening with Beckett's "Waiting for Godot" (!), it put readings on world religions in critical perspective with selections from Freud, Nietzsche and Tillich. The complaint was not that I had attacked the student's faith (this was before the rise of the media phenomenon of so-called Christian "fundamentalism"—a term which, like David Watt, I find singularly "unhelpful"). It was that I had not provided the sort of facts that could be taken down as "notes" and given back as "answers" in a blue book. It turned out the student was a chemistry major who had taken the course hoping to "learn" some-thing about religion in the form of "knowledge," like that in science courses. The department chair wanted to know what I had to say for myself. Unlike Mark Taylor I was fortunately spared the need to apologize (or to refuse), since the course was one the chair himself had designed explicitly to confront students with the challenge of thinking critically about the "data" of religion. He called me in because of the student's complaint, but I suspect he also wanted to see whether his neophyte instructor was teaching the course in the reflective manner he hoped it would be taught.

My second experience occurred many years later, well into the period of resurgence of what Taylor refers to as "religious correctness" or "religious fundamentalism." This was in one of those intensive six-week summer courses that met every day. Again, it was the department's introductory course, but one from which, unfortunately, the critical texts had been eliminated. You would think the Taylor-type problem had thereby also been eliminated. But on the first day of class, after I had finished my opening remarks, a young woman in the first row demanded to know, "Do you agree that of all these religions Christianity is the only true one?" As best I recall this was the first and only time in my thirty-plus years of teaching religion at Temple that a student had asked me such a question outright, though I imagine many over the years, perhaps more so recently, may have silently entertained it. (As many of you have probably experienced, they are not similarly shy about asking "What do YOU think about these matters?") Anyway, I gave the standard answer that in a state-related university that has to observe the separation of church and state, and in a department of world religions, not a department of Christian theology, answering that question was not something I neither could nor should do. She seemed silenced, if not satisfied. However, it turned out she was not to be so easily denied. The next day she came to class with a beautifully illustrated chart that unfolded into a two-page spread. Across the top were the major world religions, and down the side the topics dealt with by those religions. I looked it over skeptically, thinking it would feature a hopeless caricature of all religions other than Christianity. To my surprise the account of the religions seemed absolutely correct. But then I noticed the column of Christian answers was green, while the columns of the other religions were pink. Why the difference?, I naively asked. Because, she said, the Christian beliefs are the true ones, all the others are false. Despite my best effort to construct exam questions that, given the limitations of the course, would challenge students to think and not just "give back," she passed the course with flying colors (blue, I guess)—after all, she had that chart!

My two experiences were, thankfully, much less nervous-making than Taylor's. But the important lesson I take from Taylor's example is that if you are summoned by an administrator to account for your teaching, you must be ready to defend your professional integrity, scary though that may be. I was lucky. My administrator was enlightened. I don't know if, as a brand-new teacher, I would have been as brave as Taylor. Further, if you are challenged by a student, with patience, understanding, good will, and perhaps a big dose of luck, you may be able to get through even to the most "religiously correct." If you do, you may find in such encounters some of your most instructive and rewarding experiences as a teacher.

§

With that bit of comparative biography, I would like to turn to the substance of Taylor's essay. It says much that is good and that needs to be said. Those reading it will know what that is. He says it and says it well:

- It is important to confront the disinclination of students to "engage in critical reflection about faith" (I might add, this applies not only to the "religiously correct" but also to those "secular dogmatists" who have decided that all religion is bunk);
- It is not the case that only true believers are qualified to teach their religious traditions (or even, I might add, persons, whether believers or not, who are native to the culture of a

particular religious tradition—although that has been a strength of our department);

- It is important to bring the resources of psychology, sociology and anthropology to bear on the critical analysis of religion/religions;
- It is important to "cultivate a faith in doubt that calls into question every certainty" (including, I would repeat, the certainty of skeptics about religion);
- It is important to foster in students "an expansive understanding of what religion is and of the manifold roles it plays in life";
- It is important for students "to explore the similarities and differences between and among various religions";
- Finally, these are not matters of academic concern only, that "in an era that thrives on both religious and political polarization" it is imperative to "establish a genuine dialogue within and among all kinds of belief," lest the conflicts that fuel this polarization become "even more deadly."

I take Taylor's points to be indisputable for the teaching of religion today. However, as a philosopher of religion and someone interested in the normative task of "religious thought" (I use this term rather than "theology" if by the latter is meant religious thought in the context of theistic traditions), I would like to explore some of the critical issues his essays raises and, while it is not central to the thrust of his essay, take the opportunity to offer a constructive supplement of my own.

Taylor's essay raised questions for me in four areas in particular. I would like to begin by listing them along with comments about them by my friend and theological adviser, Burton Cooper (hereafter BC; TD for Tom Dean), formerly professor of Systematic Theology at Louisville Theological Seminary, now living in retirement in rural Vermont, where he continues to ponder and write about issues theological, social and political. His remarks, and my essay that follows, reflect a situation and way of thinking from an earlier time. Yet I, and I suspect he, would like to think they still might have something to say to the situation of religious polarization that, as Taylor notes, characterizes our current educational and political life.

1. "RELIGIOUS FUNDAMENTALISM" VS. "SECULAR DOGMATISM"

TD: Is the binary of "religious fundamentalism/secular dogmatism" an accurate reflection of the current situation?

BC: For many of us this is not, or at least we wish it were not, an accurate reflection. But we 'liberals' are so marginalized and fragmented today that politically we do not appear to count anymore.

TD: Whether it is or is not, does the use of this binary to describe the current situation contribute to public discussion and/or the solution of "dialogue?"

BC: Well, it is better than no dialogue at all. Perhaps the problem is not so much in the binary, which simply states the extremes, but in the ideological character of those expressing the binaries.

TD: What is the source of this binary, and how does that contribute to, or affect, our understanding of the underlying issues, and strategies for dealing with it?

BC: Is it not always easier to see things as 'black and white?' Evolutionary biologists would probably argue that such seeing has a positive adaptive function. To see things as 'grey' is so dull, and it means that we have to deal with ambiguities, complexities and pluralities.

TD: What fundamental assumptions or presuppositions do religious fundamentalists and secular dogmatists agree on— Supernaturalist concepts of God, faith, beliefs, etc.? How do these assumptions or presuppositions affect the possibilities of discussion, solution, dialogue?

BC: I think the secular dogmatists like the fundamentalist's concept of God. Both of them are ignorant of any theological ideas and developments since Calvin (and they know that only in simplified form). It is as if three hundred years of biblical and historical criticism never happened, let alone Schleiermacher, Kierkegaard, the early Barth, Tillich, Niebuhr, Bultmann, et al.

2. DOUBT AND FAITH

TD: What makes possible "doubt that calls into question every certainty"?

BC: sin AND finitude.

TD: In other words, our moral-cum-religious, socio-political, and intellectual hubris, fallibility, and unjust power structures.

TD: What kind of "faith" is presupposed by "faith in doubt?" What is the source of that "faith?"

BC: I think that "faith in doubt" is a bad expression, a misuse of the word "doubt." It is, no doubt, an attempt to express the idea that doubt is a good thing in that it leads us to uncover error and towards an increase in true knowledge. The reason we should be open to doubt is given in my preceding answer.

3. STUDY, CRITICAL ANALYSIS, OF RELIGION

TD: What does it mean to "study" religion? (Compare: to "study" physics, sociology, history, literature.) Does "study" have anything to do with the "truth" of religion/s?

BC: If you mean, "What does it mean to study religion in an academic setting?" then it depends what discipline is doing the study. The anthropologist, historian and sociologist are trying to determine what others believe. Some types of philosophy are still interested in the question of truth—and not simply of meaning. Systematic, Constructive and/or Philosophical Theology, of course, are concerned with truth, but those disciplines hardly exist anymore. (Take a look at the publications of religious publishing houses.)

TD: What is the "object" of the study in the "study of religion"? Religion/s, not, say, God or the equivalents in other traditions? (I have in mind John Hick's distinction in his little book, "Philosophy of Religion.") What limitation does this place upon and affect the "study" of religion?

BC: The object is understanding (the question of truth is parenthetical). It is assumed that religion can be taught and understood without faith. This is certainly true to an extent; the question is, to what extent? (Note the change from Department of Religion to Department of Religious Studies.)

TD: What does it mean to engage in "critical analysis" of, or "critical reflection" upon, religion? How does that relate to and what is its place in the "study" of religion?

BC: From a (believing) theologian's point of view, theology is the critical analysis of (one's) faith.

TD: Given the distinction between the study of "critiques of religion" (for example, Nietzsche's critique of absolute beliefs) and the adequacy of "critiques of religion," (I owe this helpful distinction to BC), what is the place of (normative?) assessment of the latter in "study" of religion?

BC: I assume that all critiques have their adequacies and inadequacies (the dialectical yes and no). It's the job of analysis to find them and state them.

4. TEACHING (ABOUT) RELIGION

TD: What is the goal of pedagogy in teaching about religion? To leave students "confused and uncertain" in their beliefs about the subject? (In his essay Taylor appears to equate engaging students in "critical reflection about faith" with leaving them "more confused and uncertain at the end of the course than they were at the beginning.")

BC: Only as a joke should this be thought of as a goal.

TD: Or is it to give them the tools they need to deal with issues critically, but also a little more clearly, confidently, and dialogically, as truthfully to themselves and the subject matter as possible?

BC: I wish. Yes, this is what all professors hope for.

§

Turning to my own further engagement with these question areas in Taylor's essay:

(1) Though, as noted, Taylor is a disciple of Derrida and deconstruction, he draws on certain binaries to advance his critical argument. For example:

- "religious correctness" or "religious fundamentalism" versus "secular dogmatists" or "secular dogmatism"
- "religious correctness" or "chauvinistic believers" versus "faith in doubt" or "critical reflection on faith"

And perhaps less problematically:

- "critical analysis of religion" versus "passing judgment on religious beliefs and practices"
- "study of religion" versus "practice of religion"

In a short essay in a public forum intellectual shortcuts like these are sometimes necessary. It could be that Taylor is using these oppositional phrases to describe the current sociological or political situation rather than to endorse such binary thinking as appropriate (BC). My concern, however, is that they could be taken by readers in a way that short-circuits the need for critical thought. If they are, that would not serve the public's need to understand and cope with complex issues. It would also risk detracting from Taylor's otherwise legitimate points and perhaps undermining his call for dialogue.

(2) A critique of "secular dogmatism" risks being an echo of the "religious fundamentalist" complaint. In effect it adopts their critique of the "secular." This could be problematic, because it could prevent coming to terms critically with what the "religiously correct" student would see as the "secular dogmatism" of an approach to the study of religion, that is, one that limits itself to the methodologies of psychology, sociology or anthropology. Social-scientific interpretations of religion, they might argue, "reduce" religions to "networks of symbols, myths and rituals" that "serve" many "functions," functions that, to be sure, make life "more secure" vis-v-vis life's "complexities and uncertainties." Those interpretations, however true in their own framework, nevertheless "eliminate" the question of any distinctively religious truth.

A "religious fundamentalist" might press the point. How can doubt that "calls into question every certainty" present a view of religion as making life "more secure" vis-a-vis "uncertainties"? The secularist might respond that the only "certainty" they wish to call into question is certainty regarding the more-than-secular or other-than-secular "truth" of religion, not certainty regarding the secular "functions" of religion. Not fair! The "religiously correct" student might respond. How "critical" can such doubt be if it does not also call into question the presuppositions of the secular methods used to study or interpret religion? Why is such "study" unwilling to confront the question of the truth of religion, but all-too-ready to pronounce confidently about the functions of religion? The secularist might respond that the social sciences are happy to admit that their methodological presuppositions preclude them from raising the question of truth—one way or the other. But if so, the "religiously correct" student might respond, they have no business asking students to engage in a "critical analysis" of religion that calls into question "every" certainty about religion—in particular, the certainty of more-than- secular, religious truth.

(3) There appears to be an unresolved issue, therefore, in trying to decide upon the nature and scope of critical analysis in the study of religion if it is cast in terms of the "religious/secular" binary. On the one hand, it seems to allow for asking students to consider whether, for example, Nietzsche's critique of religion calls into question their belief in absolutes. Asking them to reflect critically on (and here I take "reflect critically on" to include "making judgments about") the certainty of claims to religious truth, pro or con, would seem to be a legitimate part of the study of religion.

On the other hand, as a "secular" discipline, such study is said to refrain from "passing judgment on religious beliefs and practices." The guidelines for "any responsible curriculum for the study of religion" in this sense seem to spell out a more restrictive view of what is and is not permissible. Study of religion would "wrongly cross that line" if it attempted to pronounce on the truth of belief in absolutes, one way or the other. To the "religiously correct" it would seem that, in this latter regard, critical reflection on religion is permitted to go only so far. While it may challenge students to call into question their belief in absolutes, it does not provide critical space to go beyond a "faith in doubt that calls into question every certainty." The principle of not "passing judgment" on religious beliefs or practices would appear to bar the door to any critical assessment of claims to religious truth. It would seem to exclude, for example, the normative attempt to incorporate such doubt into what Paul Ricoeur calls a "second naivete," or what Paul Tillich calls "faith that takes doubt into itself," faith that can "include the doubt about itself."

In other words, there appears to be a confusion at this point in Taylor's essay between (to use the distinction noted by Burton Cooper above) the "study" of the critique of religion, whether that of Feuerbach, Marx, Nietzsche or Freud, for example, and the "adequacy" of that critique. Is there room in what is called the "study" of religion for a "critical," that is, normative assessment of the "adequacy" of critiques of religion?

The "religiously correct" student is raising the specter of that knotty and perennially embarrassing question of the place of critical reflection on the truth of religion in the teaching and study of religion in the secular academy—a topic that has bedeviled the American Academy of Religion since its beginning and that shows no sign of surcease. (The debate usually takes the form of asking whether the AAR is a proper venue for doing "theology," or whether the AAR should be restricted to something called "religious studies.")

In an essay entitled "The Problem with Secularism" that precedes Taylor's in the *IHT*, two European lecturers, Phillip Blond and Adrian Pabst, propose to tackle this question head on. Like Taylor, they critique both "religious fundamentalism" and "militant atheism," the latter described as "reductionist secularism" or "secular humanism," and the current bad boys being the "unholy trinity" of Richard Dawkins, "The God Delusion"; Sam Harris, "The End of Faith"; and Daniel Dennett, "Breaking the Spell: Religion as a Natural Phenomenon." Blond and Pabst go on to propose their own solution for deconstructing that binary. They juxtapose what they term "true religion," with "a genuine alternative to the prevailing extremes." They call for "a real intellectual return to religion" in the work of the academy. They appear to have in mind something like an updating of the tradition of natural or rational theology exemplified by the so-called "proofs" for the existence of God. While I side with them in calling for a normative philosophical engagement with religion, I don't think the answer is to be found in a revamped version of a rationalist medieval or Enlightenment theology. In the spirit of their essay, however, I would like to propose my own alternative to the religious/secular binary and consider what implications it might have for the place of inquiry into the truth of religion in the academic study of religion.

§

My "constructivist supplement" rests on a conviction of the truth of what I shall call a "meta-experience." It is a more-than-ordinary experience of something witnessed not only in religious but also in so-called secular or non-religious sources—literary, philosophical, artistic, or cosmological. It is a "meta-" or ultimate experience of something that cannot be captured in or reduced to the categories or methodologies of the social or natural sciences without being inaccurately described or misinterpreted—in short, inadequately "studied." But neither does it point to, or constitute evidence for, a transcendent entity of the sort referred to in the traditional categories of metaphysics or those theologies that use such categories—what Heidegger calls the ontotheological tradition of the West. Nor does it refer to the sort of supernatural being depicted in the "mixed" mythological categories of traditional theism. Its "object" is not only other than "the God of the philosophers," to cite Pascal, it is also, to use Tillich's expression (without endorsing his ontology), "beyond the God of theism." (These and the following claims are ones for which I would have to argue, and are the subject of a book-length manuscript on which I am working.)

This meta-experience cannot, without further qualification, be described as "religious," nor can it be excluded, without further qualification, from being a dimension of the completely "secular." Neither pole of that polarizing binary applies to it. While this experience can be seen as a critique of the limitations of both, it can also be seen as providing a "non-bisected" (H. de Vries) or "non-dual" (Buddhist) broadening and deepening of both. De Vries, in his recent book, *Minimal Theologies: Critiques of Secular Reason in Adorno and Levinas*, proposes to show that via a(*hermeneutica sacra sive profana*)t [hermeneutics sacred or profane] the biconditional "*sive*" can be read as "is and (yet) is not, is not and (yet) is"; or, "is, if and only if, is not." A similar hermeneutical strategy is employed by

Nishida Kitaro, founder of the 20th century Kyoto School of Japanese philosophy. Nishida developed a logic of "contradictory identity," what he termed a "logic of *soku hi*" ("soku" being a Japanese version of the Latin "*sive*," meaning something like "that is" or "*qua*," and "*soku hi*" meaning "*sive/non*"). Nishida's terminology was an attempt to provide a modern formulation of the paradoxical identity statement of the classical Indian Buddhist thinker, Nagar-juna: "*nirvana* is *samsara*, *samsara* is *nirvana*." Nagarjuna's proposition in turn was an interpretation of the *locus classicus* in Buddhist scripture: "form is emptiness, emptiness is form." Drawing on these paradoxical looking linguistic structures, I would characterize this meta-experience as "religious if and only if secular, secular if and only if religious." (Shig Nagatomo has written a very helpful essay on this biconditional logic, the formula of which is: "A is not A and therefore A is A; A is A because it is non-A." For de Vries's views see the appended material at the end of this essay. For Nishida's logic, see his "Last Writings: Nothingness and the Religious Worldview.").

The language required to express this meta-experience, if taken in its "religious" form, is better understood as poetry-plus, not science-minus. The language of religious myth would be one example. Such language is not that of science-plus, a super-science that claims access to a supernatural reality. The meta-language called for by such a meta-experience is rather like that of poetry. It is metaphoric. As poetry with a "plus," it is in fact "super-metaphoric"—the language of poetry further transfigured, language operating at the edges of language. We find it expressed, for example, in the poetic-mythic ruminations of the so-called "creation" hymn from the ancient Indian scripture, the Rig Veda: "There was neither non-existence nor existence then; there was neither the realm of space nor the sky which is beyond. What stirred? Where? In whose protection? Was there water, bottomlessly deep? Poets seeking in their hearts with wisdom found the bond of existence in non-existence. Who really knows? Who will here proclaim it? Whence was it produced? Whence this creation? The gods came afterwards, with the creation of this universe. Who then knows whence it has arisen? Whence this creation has arisen—perhaps it formed itself, or perhaps it did not—the one who looks down on it, in the highest heaven, only he knows—or perhaps he does not know" (Rig Veda 10.129). (A question for further reflection: What is the truth of metaphor, and how might the meta-truth of religious metaphor, if it is poetry-plus, differ from the metaphoric truth of poetry that does not pretend to speak of things ultimate?)

In its philosophical form perhaps the clearest formulation of this meta-experience is found in the cosmological-ontological question made famous by Leibnitz and more recently Heidegger: "Why is there something rather than nothing?" The question paralyzes and liberates; it stuns yet gives birth to thought. (Aristotle: philosophy begins in wonder.) It can only be responded to with tautologies—grammatical forms that are, literally, "same-saying" (*t'autos-logos*), that is, that say nothing, are empty. Yet paradoxically, they seem to speak volumes: being "be's" (*das Sein "west"*—from the German verb *"wesen,"* to be), the world "worlds" (*die Welt "weltet"*), time "times" (*die Zeit "sich zeitigt"*) [Heidegger's neologisms]. We find ourselves going in ontological circles, our heads spinning. Beyond this there is nothing more we can say. The question, or its literary, artistic or religious equivalents, however existentially compelling and seemingly ineliminable from human consciousness, is, logically speaking, unanswerable. And it is so for a unique reason. For the "question" is in fact unaskable. It is unanswerable precisely because it is unaskable. (See, for example, Wittgenstein's remarks in his "*Tractatus Logico-Philosophicus*," 6.5, 6.51, 6.52; I have appended them at the end of this essay.) It is rather a one-of-a-kind philosophical expression calling attention to the fact that the world is without further 'Why,' that the world's existence is ultimately a mystery, a mystery in which we also participate. It is a permanent question mark that hovers over, impassions, and gives ultimate meaning to our existence—even, Tillich observes, if only to decry its ultimate "meaninglessness," or, with Camus, if only to affirm our lives in the face of its "absurdity". In that sense it is a "question"—that is, an experience of the reality of a mystery—to which the religions are not so much "answers" as reflections, expressions, pointers, markers, reminders, and place-holders for an ultimate mystery. It is a profound reflection of our awe and wonder in the face of the ultimate ontological fact—the reality that something exists rather than nothing.

A sense of awe and wonder at the irreducible "that-ness"—the "is-ness" or, in Buddhist terms, the "suchness" of things—calls forth in the "heart-mind" an answering response of gratitude for the gift of being. (Burton Cooper observes that such a response is of course not necessary; others are possible: witness Ivan in Dostoevsky's *Brothers Karamazov*. Faith, he says, as the response of gratitude, should therefore itself be considered a gift—a testimony to the power of that mystery to move us.) That faith, that gratitude, can lead in turn to a co-responding ethic of caring—a commitment to be stewards of this earth, servants of justice, and speakers of truth to the powers and principalities of this *"saeculum."* [age]. It is the ultimate indicative issuing in the most fundamental of imperatives.

§

I am now living in retirement in Madison, WI, home of the University of Wisconsin, my undergraduate alma mater. Every day when as a student I marched up Bascom Hill to the main liberal arts building of the campus, I entered that hall of academe past a plaque donated by the university's board of regents. The bronze tablet, which is still there, states: "Whatever may be the limits that trammel inquiry elsewhere, the great State University of Wisconsin must ever encourage that endless sifting and winnowing by which alone the truth may be found." I loved and drew inspiration from that phrase:

"the endless sifting and winnowing by which alone the truth may be found." In fact, I drew fierce pride from the thought that as a student at that university I too could become part of the great tradition of the search for truth. The phrase struck me then and still does today as a fascinating paradox, inviting and freeing one for the tremendously exciting, deeply satisfying, and intellectually and ethically fundamental task of critical thought. It forces one to confront and answer for oneself the question: how can "sifting and winnowing" that is "endless" lead to "truth"? As a raw undergraduate I could not answer the question then, and am still not sure as a retired old professor whether I have today.

However, I would submit that if it is possible at all, it can surely only be if an underlying "faith in truth" precedes and gives rise to what Taylor refers to as "faith in doubt" (not even Hume, let alone Descartes, thought endless doubt was a sustainable intellectual or moral position)—only if the "search for understanding" is the expression of a "faith" that truth can be found (Anselm). This is so even if, paradoxically, that faith must endlessly wrestle, as Tillich observed, with the task of incorporating critical doubt within itself. That is possible, I suggest, if that faith is a response to the ultimate and inexhaustible mystery of the gift of being that calls into question all our finite claims to knowledge or beliefs, secular or religious.

It was Tillich who also argued that in the final analysis only religion can provide a genuine critique of religion. Only doubt that arises from within faith itself, radical religious doubt, can lead to anything resembling religious truth. Not Nietzschean doubt, not Freudian doubt, not Marxist doubt (the three masters of the modern hermeneutics of suspicion), nor the doubts of their modern or post-modern successors. However important those non-religious sources of doubt may be—and they assuredly are vitally important—they cannot in and of themselves reach as deep, cannot in that sense be as "radical," as the critique available only from within faith itself (here another modern master, another forerunner for Taylor of postmodernism, comes to mind: Kierkegaard). Why? I would argue that it is because the critique by these modern masters of suspicion is directed in part, and rightly so, against the modern Enlightenment "God" of supernatural theism and the associated definition of "faith," in modern philosophy of religion, as "belief in the absence of sufficient evidence." But this "God" of supernatural theism is a modern construction, a modern idol, and the supernatural beliefs associated with it are, similarly, perversions of genuine faith. I am reminded of the famous graffiti I saw scrawled on the wall of the entrance to the subway station at Columbia University in NYC: "God is dead: Nietzsche. Nietzsche is dead: God." Both are true! Nietzsche is right, but so are Tillich and Kierkegaard.

Taylor's advocacy of critical analysis in the study of religion, an intellectual practice based on a "faith in doubt" that "calls into question every certainty," is something that has to be affirmed ever anew for each generation of students. But the binary of "religious" and "secular" is not sufficient for that task insofar as it presupposes a modern episteme that is itself a secular one. It is not that the sciences of psychology, sociology or anthropology, or for that matter history, evolutionary biology or neuroscience, cannot raise critical questions about the functions of religion or religions. They can, they do and they should. Freud, Marx, Durkheim, Weber, Nietzsche, Foucault, Bourdieu *et al*—even "bad boys" like Dawkins, Harris and Dennett—have important and true things to say about the phenomena of religion.

The point I want to urge, however, is that by the choice and limitations of their categories and methods, they are precluded from raising—one way or the other—the normative question that, for any constructivist philosophy of religion or religious thought, is fundamental for a critical assessment of religion— and that is the question of the more-than-"fundamentalist," more-than-"secularist" truth to which the world's religions each in their own way bear witness.

It is a truth that speaks in the words of poets and the *logoi* of philosophers. It is a truth that takes material shape in works of art, architecture and music (Kurt Vonnegut, who died April 11th, said: "The only proof I need for the existence of God is music." Karl Barth, who began each day listening to Mozart, said "Mozart creates music from a mysterious center." He called the music of Mozart "a true miracle" that enabled one "to hear the joy of God's creation in all its worldliness," saying that "when angels are 'off-duty' they most likely play Mozart." Even that wonderful skeptic George Bernard Shaw said of Mozart that his was "the only music yet written that would not sound out of place in the mouth of God."). It is a truth incarnated in human form in religious superstars—saints, prophets, mystics, religious revolutionaries—and in the religious beliefs and practices of ordinary mortals the world over and from time immemorial.

But alas! In the classrooms and assemblies of academe it is the truth that dare not speak its name.

§

The preceding comments focus on the theoretical and pedagogical issues that form the bulk of Taylor's essay. But in the last paragraphs Taylor urges that, in light of the "both religious and political polarization" of our era, we need to take practical steps that go "beyond the academy." For these to succeed, it is necessary that "religious conflict be less a matter of struggles between belief and unbelief than of clashes between believers who make room for doubt and those who do not." But this will not be possible, he argues, unless there is "genuine dialogue within and among all kinds of belief, ranging from religious fundamentalism to secular dogmatism."

Taylor would seem right in arguing that there can be no progress in mitigating, if not overcoming, this polarization as long as it involves a clash between "belief and unbelief" — between "religious fundamentalism" and "secular dogmatism" — or for that matter, between rival "religious fundamentalisms" rather than one between those who do and those who do not make room for faith in their respective views. But is dialogue possible in either of these cases? For genuine dialogue to be possible a basic desideratum would seem to be openness and willingness to listen to, even learn from, the voice of the other, predicated on some sort of motivation to do so.

Certainly, as Taylor seems to suggest, for "religious fundamentalists" and "secular dogmatists" it is not clear what and why that would be. "Believers" disinclined to "make room for doubt" in their respective certitudes are, without doubt, less interested in dialogue than in hurling mutual anathemas. Dialogue does not appear to be a recipe for overcoming the polarization between those two camps. Indeed, the very notion of "dialogue" would already be suspect to partisans on each side of that ideological divide.

What about the other possibility, the one that Taylor puts forward? What about dialogue between "believers who make room for doubt" and "those who do not"? Can we expect that "those who do not," the aforementioned religious or secular "dogmatists," would be inclined to talk with those who do make room for doubt in their religious or secular views? Conversely, should we think that, despite their "liberal" openness, those who make room for doubt would be any more inclined to believe in the possibility, let alone efficacy, of "genuine dialogue" with "fundamentalists," religious or secular?

Doubt does not seem compatible with certitude. Dialogue would seem unlikely to satisfy either the doubters or the non-doubters. The language of "clash"—whether of belief and unbelief, or between those who do and those do not make room for doubt—would itself seem to clash with the language of "dialogue."

Socrates says to Crito in Plato's dialogue of that name, "Now those who believe this, and those who do not, have no common ground of discussion, but they must necessarily, in view of their opinions, despise one another." Applying this to our current situation, if the parties do not share a mutual commitment to the ground rules that make dialogue possibility, then as Socrates observes, dialogue would seem to be a non-starter.

It would seem, therefore, that dialogue is really only possible between those who are already open to learning from others, religious or secular—between those who in that sense have already incorporated "doubt" into their understanding of their beliefs, whether secular or religious. But of course such dialogue would not solve the problem of polarization, since it would rest on a built-in "liberal" (or Socratic) assumption of common ground that would be anathema to "religious fundamentalists" as well as to the most "illiberal" of "secular dogmatists" (folks who probably otherwise pride themselves on being "liberal" in their freedom from religious belief). The sampling of letters to the liberal New York Times appended below, following Taylor's essay, would seem to confirm this dilemma.

To be sure, practical cooperation is possible, even when dialogue is not. Scientists and evangelicals recently tried to come together on global warming and other issues concerning the environment. But even that cooperation ran up against a wall when fellow religionists demanded they stick to issues that were deemed more important than our planetary future—campaigns against the teaching of evolution, or in support of legislation banning abortion, same-sex marriage, and stem-cell research. (See, for example, the recent article, "The Evangelical Surprise," by Frances Fitzgerald in the April 26, 2007, issue of the *New York Review of Books*. Kurt Vonnegut, in his last collection of essays [publ. 2005] his poem, "Requiem," closes: "When the last living thing/has died on account of us,/how poetical it would be/if Earth could say,/in a voice floating up/perhaps/from the floor/of the Grand Canyon,/'It is done.'/People did not like it here." So it goes.)

It would seem, therefore, that we are at an impasse.

Of course, if Taylor's concern was limited to the classroom, we would have to agree that "genuine dialogue within and among all kinds of belief, ranging from religious fundamentalism to secular dogmatism," carefully conducted, is an important resource for sound pedagogy in the teaching of religion. As Burton Cooper observed in his reply to my comments, "does not the academy have to continue to work Socratically in the classroom even with polarized students? Not all the students are as fixed as they seem, though we do not know in advance who is capable of movement. Is not this the faith of the professor?" While Cooper is certainly correct, the problem is that Taylor is not limiting his call for dialogue to the academy. He is recommending it as a practical way to overcome religious and political polarization "beyond the academy."

Frankly, for the reasons I have suggested, I do not think the answer to polarization will come from the side of public dialogue "within and among all kinds of belief." Rather, as Taylor himself in a way suggests by linking religious polarization with its political expression, I believe the answer must come primarily from the side of politics, from the critique of and struggle for power in the public arena. As the November 2006 elections suggest, it may only be possible if political power is brought to bear against those leaders, religious and political, who for decades now have been manipulating religious and political polarization for illiberal and unjust domestic and foreign policy ends. Those who value truth that incorporates doubt should not be shy about challenging that manipulation by drawing on those resources, religious and political, that can bring together the religiously-motivated and the secular-minded in support of a liberal and moral counter-agenda. It is not enough to look to dialogue where, as Socrates pointed out, there is -o common ground. The solution lies elsewhere.

Taylor is right. The conflict will be "less a matter of struggles between belief and unbelief than of clashes between those who make room for doubt and those who do not." But "a genuine dialogue within and among all kinds of belief, ranging from religious fundamentalism to secular dogmatism," will make sense only to the degree that it can contribute to the efforts of progressive forces to undo the damage caused by religious and political polarization and open up a space for truth and justice in the public arena. I suspect Taylor would not disagree.

Philosophers may not always be the best strategists when it comes to the task of speaking truth to power, religious or political—though they should at least try! But in any case, this is a situation where those who study religion with the aid of the social sciences and those who bring the resources of social ethics to bear on religion and politics have a vital role to play—as Taylor says—beyond the academy. As "engaged intellectuals" they can serve as important resources for actors in the public arena, not only as agents themselves but as educators to the rest of us—to religious leaders and politicians as well. We can look to them for help in articulating and strategizing a renewed progressive politics.

Such politics must proceed from a critique (with Nietzsche and Taylor) of claims to absolute religious truth as well as claims to unchecked political power (Bush II). But the power of that critique, and the truth of that critique, can only be assured if it is grounded in a faith that engages in endless self-critique. Whatever the tradition, "secular" or "religious," it must take doubt into itself if it is to respond faithfully to, and express truthfully, the ultimate mystery and gift of being. Such faith stuns and paralyzes—calls into question all our finite "knowings", sayings and doings. And yet, paradoxically, it liberates and gives birth—to our endless curiosity and desire to know, to the joyful creation of linguistic and material works, and to the confidence and courage that enable us to speak out. In the words of that sage of the Midwestern prairie, Garrison Keiller, to go out and "do what needs to be done."

§

To return to where I began these comments—a pedagogical postscript. I can imagine that former students, if they chanced to read this, might be prompted to say, "Why didn't you tell us straight out what YOU thought about all these matters when you were here? Why did you wait until now to come clean? If you felt that, as students of philosophy of religion or religious thought, we should be asking the question of truth, why didn't you tell us your own views? How do you reconcile your practice with the plea you are making for inclusion of the question of truth in guidelines for the study of religion? Isn't this a contradiction? Or was it that you didn't know what you thought until you had the leisure in retirement to figure it out? (In that case, you are forgiven!)"

In my defense I can only plead that I saw, and see, no contradiction between withholding one's own views about the truth of religious beliefs and insisting on the importance and legitimacy—at least in classes whose subject is the philosophy of religion, religious thought, or religious ethics—of engaging in critical analysis and rigorous debate of the truth-claims of the various religions, something the tools and texts of philosophy are designed to do (e.g., Taylor's use of Nietzsche). Thanks to Dr. Phillips in my first semester at Temple, and thanks to the fact our department of religion is in a state-related institution, I felt I was under no obligation to argue for my particular philosophical or religious beliefs. Rather, I saw my job first and foremost to be one of stimulating students' own independent passion for that normative task and helping them to acquire the critical and constructive tools to think about questions of truth for themselves. In that sense I am in total agreement with the claim, included in Taylor's guidelines, that it is not the job of scholars in such a department to "pass judgment on religious beliefs and practices." To raise doubts about those beliefs and practices, yes. To require students to critically assess the normative claims to truth of various religions, yes. (It was mainly to clarify and stress this latter point that I was concerned to offer these remarks.) But to use the classroom to pass my own judgments on those truth claims, or to plead the case for my own, no.

Here a further consideration entered into and constrained my pedagogical practice, one that probably would have guided me even if I had been teaching in a religiously-related institution. I worried, perhaps unnecessarily, that if I did use the classroom to put forward my own views, the unequal balance of power between teacher and student might compromise their willingness to stand up to the instructor and their freedom and confidence to work out their own views. I may have been wrong about this. I may have done my students a disservice by not making full use of other pedagogical possibilities, and in so doing I may not have measured up to the responsibilities that accompany the awesome privilege of being a teacher. I am sure others would answer this question differently and hopefully much better than I did. My only consolation is that, fortunately, my students were exposed to other teachers employing other strategies designed to challenge their intellectual freedom and development. I continue to struggle in my thinking about what constitutes good "teaching" in the "study" of religion, although I am no longer in a position to do much about it. The best I can do at this point to atone for my past shortcomings is to offer this, as it were, "posthumous" confession. At least in retirement I no longer have to worry about a power imbalance. I'm out of power now!

§

I would like to thank Leonard Swidler and the Religion Department Listserv for giving me this chance to respond (at overly great length!) to Mark Taylor's essay. I would also like to express my thanks to Burton Cooper for putting up with my endless questions and patiently giving of his wisdom and advice. I hope others will read

Taylor's essay, if they have not already, and will find it as stimulating as I did. And of course I would be interested in their comments on his essay, my comments on it, or the material and comments appended below.

§

APPENDED MATERIAL

PLATO

For manifestly you have long been aware of what you mean when you use the expression 'being.' We, however, who used to think we understood it, have now become perplexed. (*Sophist*, 244a; cited on the opening page of Heidegger's *Being and Time*.)

KANT

Two things fill the mind with ever new and increasing admiration and awe, the oftener and the more steadily we reflect on them: the starry heavens above and the moral law within. (*Critique of Practical Reason*, opening line of "Conclusion.")

WITTGENSTEIN

Tractatus Logico-Philosophicus 6.5 For an answer that cannot be expressed the question too cannot be expressed.

The riddle does not exist.

If a question can be put at all, then it can also be answered.

6.51 Scepticism is not irrefutable, but palpably senseless, if it would doubt where a question cannot be asked.

For doubt can only exist where there is a question; a question only where there is an answer, and this only where something can be said.

6.52 We feel that even if all possible scientific questions can be answered, the problems of life have still not been touched at all. Of course there is then no question left, and just this is the answer.

§

After I finished these remarks, I came across a review of Hent de Vries' book, "Minimal Theologies: Critiques of Secular Reason in Adorno and Levinas," in the current issue (March 2007) of the *Journal of the American Academy of Religion*. Assuming his views are correctly reported (I have not seen the book), I have problems with some, as noted in my comments below. Nevertheless many of his constructive proposals seem congruent with my own. Consequently, I inserted his notions of a "non-bisected" concept of (secular reason and religious faith) and a corresponding "*hermeneutica sacra sive profana*" in a paragraph of my essay where they helped to support a point. I have copied certain passages from the review and commented on them in what follows. I have also included some notes from a review in the same issue of the JAAR of *The Frankfurt School on Religion: Key Writings by the Major Thinkers*, edited by Eduardo Mendieta. Hent de Vries, *Minimal Theologies: Critiques of Secular Reason in Adorno and Levinas* (Washington, DC: Johns Hopkins University Press, 2005), 720 pp., $24.95; reviewed by William David Hart, University of North Carolina, Greensboro, *Journal of American Academy of Religion*, 75:1 (March 2007), pp. 179-182, p. 179: De Vries' thesis: "theology, minimally understood, is an unavoidable supplement to critical thought; indeed, secular reason makes claims for which cannot give adequate account on its own terms. It depends on the 'other of reason,' on religious figures of speech that supplement its every claim. Secular reason is parasitic on or in symbiosis with theological minimalism, that is, the trace of reason's transcendent other."

TD: If de Vries means that religion is "the other" of a reason that is "secular" in a narrowly conceived sense, fine. But then that remark must be supplemented by the other side of a deconstructive biconditional: secular reason is also "the transcendent other" of religion as traditionally understood. If, on the other hand, de Vries means by religion, i.e., "minimal theology," a standpoint based on his proposal of a "non-bisected" concept of (secular) reason/ (religious) faith, then he should not speak of religion as "the other" of reason in a unidirectional way. For what de Vries labels "minimal theology" I prefer, therefore, to eschew the label "theology" and to speak instead of a reason, a rationality, whether viewed as secular or religious, that in any case articulates the truth of, and response to, an ultimate mystery.

P. 179: For de Vries, minimal theology is not negative theology. Adorno and Levinas are not "postsecular." As with Kant, their critique of the limit of reason is tied up necessarily with the absolute, the trace of the other of reason.

TD: Again, there seems a tension between a concept of the "limit" of reason, conceived of as "transcended" by religion, and de Vries' "non-bisected" concept of secular reason/religious faith.

P. 179: Vries' critique is directed against a "bisected" notion of rationality, i.e., a reason split by the faith/knowledge binary.

P. 180: Adorno and Levinas (and de Vries) want instead a concept of rationality that is broader and deeper.

TD: Good. In other words, a concept of reason that includes the ability to speak of the truth and rationality of a faith that expresses the ultimate mystery of being.

P. 180: Adorno and Levinas' theological minimalism points toward an absolute, a trace of the "other of reason," toward a reality that eludes conceptualization.

TD: If by "eludes conceptualization" de Vries means to fall back again into a concept of the "limits" of a secular reason narrowly conceived, this seems to conflict with his desire for a "non-bisected" concept of reason/religion. How are we to make sense of a concept of an absolute that is "other" to reason if we are trying to fashion instead a "broader and deeper" concept of reason, one by which the mystery of being can come to expression?

P. 180: "He uses a mode of interpretation (*hermeneutica sacra sive profana*) that is simultaneously sacred and profane, which pursues the sacred through the profane."

TD: This hermeneutic, and its corollary, a non-bisected or non-dual concept of the secular/religious binary—simultaneously "religious" and (yet) "secular", "secular" and (yet) "religious—seems to me de Vries' real contribution, rather than his talk of 'theological minimalism' as "the trace of reason's transcendent other."

P. 180: This hermeneutical method is irreconcilable with a positive theology that affirms what the transcendent (infinite, absolute, or God) is. Rather, it involves an *ascesis* so extreme that it also outstrips any negative theology, a theology that also, says de Vries, remains "mired in classical thinking"—what Heidegger refers to as ontotheology. It is an "extreme *ascesis*, to the point of atheism," i.e., one that involves no appeal to the kind of metaphysics Nietzsche called "Platonic-Christian."

TD: I would agree with all of this, except his resort to the term 'atheism.' Again that involves falling back into a "bisected" notion of the secular/religious (here 'theistic') binary.

P. 180: De Vries quotes Levinas: "A theology which does not proceed from any speculation on the beyond of worlds-behind-the-world, from any knowledge transcending knowledge."

TD: Exactly, except (again) for the term 'theology.'

P. 181: On this view, paradoxically it is the "conceptual, imaginative, argumentative, and rhetorical resources of the religious and theological tradition" that are "the unavoidable constitutes of critical thought as non-bisected rationality"

TD: Yes, along with many other modes of imaginative expression. But of course there is no "paradox" if we are operating from within the already paradoxical hermeneutic of "religious *sive* secular, secular *sive* religion."

P. 181: "Such rationality recognizes the ambiguity and undecidability (regarding the existence) of the absolute other, thus pushing the theological discourse of idolatry-critique to its extreme. Only in this minimalist sense as trace of the other of reason does the discourse of transcendence (as absolute, God, or infinity) retain any intelligibility."

TD: Again, yes, as long as we are careful not to allow use of the term 'transcendence' to be used unidirectionally to undo a non-dual sense of religious/secular.

P. 181: De Vries commends theological minimalism in/to "an intellectual context in which the academic study of religion (as theology and as *Religionswissenschaft*) can no longer justify its existence. It fails both the pragmatic test (it is redundant, not a distinctive discipline), and the test of principle (it is incapable of providing a theoretical defense of its existence). On the one hand, classical theology, ontotheology, or theology as the science of 'God' is no longer credible. On the other hand, *Religionswissenschaft*, the sum total of religious studies brackets all truth claims regarding the reality, existence, and nature of deity. Its approach to these questions (methodological atheism) is indistinguishable from other empirical disciplines where God and the gods are one cultural phenomenon among others. In its refusal to ask truth questions, it succeeds in providing only half of the truth regarding religion. In contrast, only a minimal theology can provide the other half of truth."

TD: As to the pragmatic test, unlike de Vries I would argue that the methodological pluralism in the study of religion is a strength, not a weakness, as in other departments where such diversity exists. On his second point, the theoretical issue, I agree with de Vries. It was one of the main points I tried to make in my reply to Taylor.

P. 181: This move "turns the table" on "religious studies" by attributing a greater rationality to a certain kind of "theology."

TD: That puts it a bit provocatively, but, again, apart from the use of the term 'theology' and keeping in mind a non-dual sense of secular/religion (perhaps one could say, a 'non-bisected' concept of religious studies/theology too?!), it is a point I was trying to make as well.

P. 181: The reviewer refers to this as a kind of "afterlife" of theology inside secular reason (represented by religious figures of speech).

TD: I am not sure de Vries sees his view of minimal theology as nesting inside of, rather than with, Adorno and Levinas, functioning as a critique of secular reason.

P. 181: The reviewer says de Vries ignores "philosophy of religion." "Philosophy of religion," for the reviewer, is something that can be "reduced" neither to theology nor religious studies.

TD: How does the reviewer define that enterprise? There are many varieties of philosophy of religion, of which de Vries' understanding of minimal theology could be viewed as one possibility (see M. J. Charlesworth, "Philosophy of Religion: The Historic Approaches"). On a certain understanding of "philosophy of religion" I would agree, but then it would seem that this is precisely de Vries' understanding of "minimal theology" as well.

P. 182: The reviewer says, philosophy of religion has always addressed truth claims about the reality, existence, and nature of God and gods.

TD: Does de Vries not, in one sense, leave room for that? But in another sense, does he not critique that view of philosophy of religion, for good reason?

P. 182: The reviewer says: de Vries' critique of the incoherence of religious studies as an academic discipline or field, which supposedly endangers it because it does not have monopoly on its object of study, is apropos—but then he adds, that is true of many other fields as well.

TD: So, is he approving of de Vries' critique or not? For myself, I do not think de Vries' critique on this point has any force, not only for the reason the reviewer adds—that many other "departments" are methodologically pluralistic as well, but also because, as noted above, I see this, unlike de Vries, as a strength, not a weakness, of religion departments and those other departments

P. 182: The reviewer says: "many of us, who are otherwise suspicious of theology, might very well call ourselves theologians, assuming the minimalist notion of theology that de Vries has identified, where certain figures of speech such as 'absolute,' 'infinite,' 'wholly other,' 'revelation,' and 'idolatry' haunt secular reason."

TD: "Theology," even in the setting of de Vries' minimalist usage of the term, still remains dependent, as I have been arguing, on its binary 'other,' "secular." It exists in tension with the more radical, 'non-bisected' aspects of his proposal. So rather than 'theology,' how about: "thinking about the truth expressed in figures of traditional religious speech in a way that does not 'haunt' but finds expression in other forms of speech as well, including so-called 'non-religious' or 'secular' ones"? (a mouthful!)

P. 182: The reviewer concludes: "Then, what again, is the difference that makes a difference between a minimal theologian and a philosopher of religion?"

TD: Again, that all depends on how one defines philosophy of religion. But it also depends on whether it is helpful to call the line of thought de Vries is pursuing "theology," at least if his intention, like mine, is to deconstruct the sacred/profane, religious/secular, faith/knowledge binaries on behalf of a broader and deeper, "non-bisected" or non-dual sense of these terms and their relationship to one another.

§

Eduardo Mendieta, ed., *The Frankfurt School On Religion: Key Writings by the Major Thinkers*, (Routledge, 2005), 405 pp. $27.95; reviewed by Jens Zimmerman, Trinity Western University, *Journal of the American Academy of Religion*, 75:1 (March, 2007) pp. 236-239.

P. 237: In contrast to "naive forms of secularism," these thinkers see "religion as an essential tool of cultural criticism, and they acknowledge theology, even if restricted to negative theology, as a legitimate form of reason."

TD: Of course de Vries, and I, see what he calls 'minimal theology' as a critique of negative theology as well.

P. 237: "If religion is to be integrated seriously once again into academic research, this integration will have to occur based on a redefinition of reason that is open to religion."

TD: Agreed, as long as religion is seen not as 'transcending' the 'limits' of reason, but as sharing in a re-constructed (non-bisected, non-dual) understanding of both.

P. 237: In the Frankfurt School "we find a non-secular critique of religion for the sake of religion."

TD: Tillich's point too, though he would add that it is for the sake of the secular too.

P. 237: The Frankfurt School's focus on "a religious critique of reason in a secular age" is reminiscent of Bonhoeffer's "religionless Christianity."

TD: A very interesting observation! Bonhoeffer was one of the main inspirations for the so-called "death of God" movement (along with William Hamilton, Thomas Altizer, and Bp. John Robinson) and the appeal to the "secular meaning of the gospel" (Temple's own Paul van Buren) in the intellectual, social and political revolutions of the 1960's.

Nearly a half century later we are faced with the need to launch a new critique. A new dialogue, yes, but also a new struggle, not simply for the sake of religion but for the sake of the broader "*saeculum*"—this time against the reactionary forces of "both religious and political polarization." If we do not, as Mark Taylor warns us, "the conflicts of the future will probably be even more deadly."

Mark C. Taylor, "The Devoted Student," *New York Times*, December 21, 2006; "Faith That Refuses Questions," *International Herald Tribune*, December 22, 2006.

More American college students seem to be practicing traditional forms of religion today than at any time in my 30 years of teaching.

At first glance, the flourishing of religion on campuses seems to reverse trends long criticized by conservatives under the rubric of "political correctness." But in truth, something else is occurring. Once again, right and left have become mirror images of each other; religious correctness is simply the latest version of political correctness. Indeed, it seems the more religious students become, the less willing they are to engage in critical reflection about faith.

The chilling effect of these attitudes was brought home to me two years ago when an administrator at a university where I was then teaching called me into his office. A student had claimed that I had attacked his faith because I had urged him to consider whether Nietzsche's analysis of religion undermines belief in absolutes. The administrator insisted that I apologize to the student. (I refused.)

My experience was not unique. Today, professors invite harassment or worse by including "unacceptable" books on their syllabuses or by studying religious ideas and practices in ways deemed improper by religiously correct students.

Distinguished scholars at several major universities in the United States have been condemned, even subjected to death threats, for proposing psychological, sociological or anthropological interpretations of religious texts in their classes and published writings. In the most egregious cases, defenders of the faith insist that only true believers are qualified to teach their religious tradition.

At a time when colleges and universities engage in huge capital campaigns and are obsessed with public relations, faculty members can no longer be confident they will remain free to pose the questions that urgently need to be asked.

BREAKTHROUGH TO DIALOGUE

For years, I have begun my classes by telling students that if they are not more confused and uncertain at the end of the course than they were at the beginning, I will have failed. A growing number of religiously correct students consider this challenge a direct assault on their faith. Yet the task of thinking and teaching, especially in an age of emergent fundamentalisms, is to cultivate a faith in doubt that calls into question every certainty.

Any responsible curriculum for the study of religion in the 21st century must be guided by two basic principles: first, a clear distinction between the study and the practice of religion, and second, an expansive understanding of what religion is and of the manifold roles it plays in life. The aim of critical analysis is not to pass judgment on religious beliefs and practices— though some secular dogmatists wrongly cross that line—but to examine the conditions necessary for their formation and to consider the many functions they serve.

It is also important to explore the similarities and differences between and among various religions. Religious traditions are not fixed and monolithic, they are networks of symbols, myths and rituals which evolve over time by adapting to changing circumstances. If we fail to appreciate the complexity and diversity within, and among, religious traditions, we will overlook the fact that people from different traditions often share more with one another than they do with many members of their own tradition.

If chauvinistic believers develop deeper analyses of religion, they might begin to see in themselves what they criticize in others. In an era that thrives on both religious and political polarization, this is an important lesson to learn—one that extends well beyond the academy.

Since religion is often most influential where it is least obvious, it is imperative to examine both its manifest and latent dimensions. As defenders of a faith become more reflective about their own beliefs, they begin to understand that religion can serve not only to provide answers that render life more secure but also to prepare them for life's unavoidable complexities and uncertainties.

Until recently, many influential analysts argued that religion, a vestige of an earlier stage of human development, would wither away as people became more sophisticated and rational. Obviously, things have not turned out that way. Indeed, the 21st century will be dominated by religion in ways that were inconceivable just a few years ago. Religious conflict will be less a matter of struggles between belief and unbelief than of clashes between believers who make room for doubt and those who do not.

The warning signs are clear. Unless we establish a genuine dialogue within and among all kinds of belief, ranging from religious fundamentalism to secular dogmatism, the conflicts of the future will probably be even more deadly.

§

"Faith and Doubt: Can They Coexist?" Five Letters, *New York Times*, December 26, 2006. Re: "The Devoted Student," by Mark C. Taylor, Op-Ed, Dec. 21, 2006

I agree with Professor Taylor that college students seem less inclined to "engage in critical reflection about faith" these days. Just two weeks ago I had an intelligent young man, a devout Catholic, tell me, "When these hard questions are asked about my faith, I simply refuse to consider them." Nevertheless, I strenuously disagree with Professor Taylor's remark that "the aim of critical analysis is not to pass judgment on religious beliefs and practices." Critical analysis is precisely about passing evaluative judgments on beliefs — determining whether they are coherent, rationally warranted, fallacy-free, immune from crippling counterexamples and so forth. To exclude religious beliefs from this critical enterprise is to fall prey to the "religious correctness" Professor Taylor rightly abhors.

BREAKTHROUGH TO DIALOGUE

David W. Shoemaker Toledo, Ohio, Dec. 21, 2006. The writer is a professor of philosophy at Bowling Green State University.

Mark C. Taylor sounds an important warning about the need for dialogue on religion. Of course, with such a dialogue, it would become clear that what some people consider "evil" is merely an expression of prejudiced opinion—something all major religions admonish. This is perhaps a key reason dialogue often doesn't take place. Many are against it, for it would expose the use of prejudiced opinion masquerading as religious belief. But just because this is so, we shouldn't stop trying to dialogue. As Professor Taylor points out, our world may depend on it.

Mary Anne Thomas Black Mountain, N.C., Dec. 21, 2006.

Whatever the sources, religious fundamentalism presents the paradox of an informed mindlessness. Within Christianity, the apostle Paul believes that certainty is impossible in this life: "Now we see only puzzling reflections in a mirror, but then we shall see face to face." But as Professor Taylor points out, secular dogmatism is equally irrational. Perhaps that is why our public school systems have never been able to respond imaginatively to the ample room created by the Supreme Court in the 1960s. The rulings on prayer in school and on Bible reading were accompanied by a clear invitation to consider the role of religion in the historical development of the country. How painful it is to acknowledge that the God-given gift of reason is depreciated where one would expect it to be honored.

(Rev.) Joseph D. Herring Alpharetta, Ga., Dec. 21, 2006.

Like Mark C. Taylor, I have long tried to encourage students to reflect critically about faith. My experience with the "religiously correct," however, was different from his. Several years ago, I remarked in a lecture to 150 undergraduates that I was an atheist. Every day for the rest of the semester I was besieged after class by a bevy of earnest proselytizers who sought to save me from eternal damnation. Sadly, they weren't at all interested in engaging in the dialogue that Professor Taylor rightly suggests is essential for genuine learning and for attenuating social conflicts.

Marc Edelman NY, Dec. 21, 2006 The writer is a professor of anthropology at Hunter College, CUNY.

Mark C. Taylor decries fundamentalism, but he reveals himself a fundamentalist when he writes that "the task of thinking and teaching is to cultivate a faith in doubt that calls into question every certainty." Doubt is the new religion, but does doubt doubt itself? What if there are truths worth living by, and dying for?

Peter McFadden Cold Spring, N.Y., Dec. 21, 2006

GRADUATE STUDENTS

TUDOR HISTORY

RODGER VAN ALLEN

My experience with the Temple University Department of Religion (TUDOR) began in a largely pragmatic way. Retrospectively, I can see it all fitting together providentially, which is not a word I use casually.

In 1964, I completed a master's degree in theology at Villanova University. I had pursued the degree over a three-year period while teaching one year at Monsignor Bonner High School and two years at Devon Preparatory School. The Dean of Villanova's College of Arts and Sciences was my professor for one of my last classes. In the class I had worked particularly hard on a research paper on the problem of evil, which I pursued by following the Syntopicon (a thematic reading guide) of Robert Hutchins Great Books series. I had read and processed many of the great minds on the topic, but by the end of my research and writing was quite aware that I had found no absolutely satisfying resolution to this question either in their writings or in myself. I shared both this survey and conclusion in an oral presentation in class. After class the Dean asked me if I had considered teaching on the college level. I replied "Yes, that was in fact my goal," and he said Villanova had a full-time opening that was mine if I could get released from my upcoming high school contract. Devon Prep was both cooperative and fully supportive.

Within a matter of a few weeks I had a full-time tenure track position at Villanova. I was also advised that for my longer career and job security, I should acquire the terminal degree in my field. I had already been thinking about a doctorate degree, possibly at Notre Dame, Fordham or Catholic University. I had made the best decision in my life in 1963 by marrying Judy McGrath and we celebrated the Villanova job with our infant son Rodger.

In the fall of 1964, I taught my theology classes and was tutored by Judy in French, a language I had never studied, in order to prepare for the language exams that would be a part of the doctoral process. Judy and I were both native Philadelphians, in fact from the same neighborhood, and the sense of these roots for family and friends and a viable job in my field made a move to South Bend, Indiana, unattractive. Likewise daunting was multi-years of commuting to New York or Washington.

Was there some way to acquire the doctorate right here in Philadelphia? Clearly that was the best of all solutions. In December of 1964 I made an inquiring call to the Temple University Department of Religion, and in early January I had an appointment with Dr. Bernard Phillips, Chair of the Department, to discuss the possibilities for my furthering my studies at Temple.

Middle-thirties, bearded, energetic and just back from his karate class, Dr. Phillips welcomed me most graciously, and we had a full and comfortable conversation in which he let me know that the Department did indeed have a doctoral program and that the program was poised to develop significantly. It had been linked with the Temple University School of Theology, but that had recently changed. We were well into our conversation when he informed me that I was the first of Roman Catholic background to ever approach their program. Vatican II had just concluded its third of four sessions, and the thought of being the only student from my faith tradition gave me no pause. Besides, I was internally jumping for joy at not having to leave Philadelphia.

Phillips explained that the Graduate Record Exam (GRE) was required, and that there was also an entrance exam for which there was a study guide. I had recently taken the GRE and had my scores with me. I happily took the study guide. He asked me about my teaching at Villanova and we discussed that for some time. He then paused and said to me: "Are you a good teacher?" I said that I hoped so, that I personally enjoyed teaching and that I hoped my students found their classes satisfying and worthwhile. He then said that while it was a bit premature there was a possibility that I could receive a half-time assistantship, with a stipend and a reduction in tuition, if I taught a class in Contemporary Catholic Thought for TUDOR. Commonweal editor Daniel J. Callahan had taught it once for the department, but he had found the commute from New York a burden. Dr. Phillips said he needed someone to teach this class. He said he needed to process my application and I needed to take the entrance exam, but assuming that progressed appropriately, would I be interested in the teaching and the assistantship? "Absolutely!" was my reply.

I returned to Judy in our garage apartment in Merion bursting with excitement. Judy was ironing in the bedroom where she could keep an eye on our son, Rodger. Suddenly our life and future seemed secure and in place thanks to Dr. Phillips and TUDOR.

In September I enrolled in the class offered by Dr. John Macquarrie, the distinguished Anglican systematic theologian, who commuted to Temple from Union Theological Seminary in New York. His class was crowded with almost thirty students. After the lecture portion of the first class, we all took a ten-minute break, and resumed with a question period. I knew very little of Martin Heidegger and even less of Rudolph Bultmann, both so significant in Macquarrie's scholarship and theology. Judging from the questions my classmates asked, it seemed they already knew a great deal and asked long questions with preambles that demonstrated what to my ear sounded like such competence that I almost wondered why they bothered to take the class. I sat there thoroughly intimidated and wondering if I could really "cut it" in these new circumstances. I had questions, but they were elementary it seemed to what I was hearing. Finally, with my heart pounding somewhat faster, I decided to ask one of my elementary questions. As I recall, I asked if he would just review for me an existentialist theology. Unlike the relatively short answers he gave to the previous questions, he showed delight with my question and shared a wonderful and lengthy reply that I could see had served not only me but the class as well. He not only answered my question, he gave me a life lesson. "I want to be the kind of professor who makes my students feel as good as he has just made me feel by the way he treated me and answered my question," I said to myself, and I've said it over again since then.

My class in Contemporary Catholic Thought was open for graduate or undergraduate credit. Eleven students enrolled. All were Protestant ministers except for me, a Jewish under-graduate and one Episcopal laywoman, the only woman in the class. Charles Yrigoyen was a Methodist who served as a campus minister at Ursinus. Stacy Meyer was pastor of a Methodist Church in Philadelphia. Robert Beaman was the associate minister of a Presbyterian church in New Jersey. All the students were interesting and quite capable. We read from Robert Caponigri's edited two volume *Modern Catholic Thinkers*; Avery Dulles', *Apologetics and the Biblical Christ*; John Tracy Ellis', *American Catholicism*; Hans Küng's, *The Council, Reform and Reunion*; Thomas Merton's, *Life and Holiness*; Thomas Corbishley's, *Roman Catholicism*; Robert McAfee Brown's and Gustave Weigel's, *An American Dialogue*; and of course, the documents of Vatican II. I taught the course two times and learned a great deal from my students. The atmosphere in the class was open and delightful for me and I hope for them.

In 1966 Dr. Leonard Swidler, historian, theologian and Catholic ecumenical pioneer came from Duquesne University to the Temple faculty, bringing with him the *Journal of Ecumenical Studies* and an infusion of Catholic graduate students. I had been comfortable enough as the lone Catholic, and had only had a couple of experiences where I felt treated like a papal ambassador, but I welcomed the arrival of Swidler and the new grad students. In fall 1966, he offered a course on Vatican I and in spring 1967 a course on

Vatican II. The two courses were excellent in every way, the most stimulating academic experiences of my life. Dr. Swidler's class was reading, discussion, and student reports, all in a lively way. I admired the way Swidler both taught and coached us, always gently raising the best critical question to any position. It was an exercise in intellectual grace that I've aspired to and tried to practice in my teaching. There were about twelve students in the Vatican I class and four or five more in Vatican II. David Efroymson was an especially impressive class colleague; widely read, articulate, zestful, and great fun. James Biechler was more reserved, but unfailingly worthwhile with his input. Both had about ten years on me, and a longer theological development. We became friends as well as fellow students. Others included Jack Malinowski, a capable scholar who taught at Saint Joseph's University and went to jail for tax resistance against the Vietnam War; Suzanne Toton, who took a Master's from Temple, moved on to Columbia for her doctorate and has taught with me at Villanova for many years; John Groutt, who wrote a dissertation on religious communes, and has spent a career as a teacher and administrator at University of Maryland, Eastern Shore; and John Mawhinney, S.J. who taught at Gonzaga and Loyola New Orleans before going to El Salvador for distinguished mission service.

In spring 1966, I received a phone call and visit at Villanova from John Esposito who was teaching at Rosemont College, who like me needed a doctorate. "How do you like Temple?" he asked, and my response was very positive. He enrolled and we carpooled to Temple and became good friends, Judy and I with John and his wife Jean. In 1967, I rented a truck and John helped Judy and I move our expanded family from our garage apartment to our house in Bala Cynwyd.

The numbers of graduate students increased rapidly with large numbers of Catholics among them. A number of faculty and student committees on just about everything emerged in TUDOR. I stayed out of that, as a full-time job at Villanova, graduate classes and family responsibilities (a girl in 1965 and the arrival of twin boys in 1967) made life very full. By 1969, Dr. Phillips, having apparently had his fill of student committee advice, reportedly said with some dismay, "These Catholics! They can't reform their church, so they want to reform my religion department!"

The professors with whom I studied in addition to Macquarrie and Swidler, were Henry J. Cadbury, Bernard Phillips, Ernest Stoeffler, Roderick Hindery, Elwyn Smith, Theodore Tappert, John Raines, and T. Patrick Burke.

Comprehensive exams in TUDOR were especially frightening as some of the new high-powered professors reportedly wanted to "thin the herd" of grad students. We were assigned numbers to be used on our bluebooks to give anonymity and objectivity to the grading process. I was grateful when informed that I had passed.

I was if anything even more relieved when I passed the German reading exam. I had never studied German. I took an intensive summer prep course at the University of Pennsylvania designed specifically for doctoral language exams. It was three and one half hours of class Monday through Friday with some five or more hours of homework each night. It was just three weeks in length, but it was hell. I bought a box of one thousand German vocabulary cards which I then reviewed until taking the test in the early fall.

I received a great suggestion for my dissertation topic from Dr. Swidler. "Commonweal's fiftieth anniversary is coming up in 1974 and no one has done a history of that. Sound good?" he asked. I was sold immediately. A one semester study leave from Villanova helped me to plow through what was by the finish one hundred bound volumes of the then weekly publication. I derived piles of thematically organized 3 x 5 cards as best I could. The editors of the magazine were extremely cooperative with interviews and I got good advice on the project from the remarkable Gerard S. Sloyan and a shrewdly insightful Dennis Clark. Len Swidler was the mentor and he was extraordinary. Racing to finish in the spring of 1972 before he departed for Germany for two years, I would write madly all week and bring it to him on Friday afternoon. He would then meet with me on Sunday afternoon at his home to review the week's progress. I have never heard of anything coming even close to this level of service and support of a dissertation mentor to their student. I was and am profoundly grateful. I've also tried to remember and practice this kind of service to my students.

Dr. Swidler was right-on in his estimate for a successful book from the dissertation. I had met Norman Hjelm, editor at Fortress Press, at a neighbor's dinner party in Bala Cynwyd. He was aware of the dissertation and when I met him by chance in the neighborhood hardware store that June, he asked if I had a copy he could read. I said yes and that I would be grateful for any advice he had about placing it for publication. A week later he called and asked how I'd feel about Fortress being the publisher? "Great!" I replied, and with the interest *Commonweal* also had in the book, 8,000 copies emerged on time for the 50th anniversary of the magazine.

Temple was a gift for me. As I said at the beginning, it was a choice I made quite pragmatically, but it really was providential. I can't imagine a better or more stimulating place to have studied. And the stipends for teaching and some extra research funding Dr. Phillips secured for me completely covered my doctoral education costs. I'm also grateful to the citizens of Pennsylvania. Temple went state-related in July 1965 and I began studies that September. Tuition was remarkably reasonable.

Most of all, I'm grateful for the people of Temple, especially Dr. Swidler. As professor and mentor, he has been a model and inspiration. I could go on, however, with stories of Gerard Sloyan, the best proofreader ever of dissertations, who befriended and helped me, the memorable Henry J. Cadbury, who knew my mother-in-law at Bryn Mawr College, Ernest Stouffer, kindly, organized, and impressive, and Theodore Tappert, who taught me so much about

Martin Luther. And the students, many of whom are still my friends almost fifty years later. Thank you, Temple.

TUDOR THEN: YOUNG IN THE 60'S

DAVID P. EFROYMSON

I first learned of the Temple University Department of Religion (TUDOR) from Joe Cunneen (RIP), the founder and long-time editor of *Cross-Currents*, in the spring of 1966. He told me that Temple had become a state-affiliated university (I am not sure of the exact terminology) in Pennsylvania, and that the university—including the Department of Religion—was in a position, with the new state money, to "beef up" its faculty. He added that, among others, Leonard Swidler, then at Duquesne, was to join the Temple Religion faculty in the fall, and would bring the *Journal of Ecumenical Studies* (*JES*) with him. I did not know Temple, and did not know Len, but I had been a subscriber to *JES* from the beginning, in 1964, when Len, his wife Arlene and Elwyn Smith created it and Len had begun his long tenure as editor. The Journal met a real need at that time, and by 1966 had already published several articles of lasting worth (e.g. Cullmann, Ratzinger, Markus Barth, and George Lindbeck, who was the best of the lot, I thought). If Temple were to house the Journal, then Temple and its Department of Religion had to be, or had to become, a "class" operation, so I wrote to Swidler to find out what I could. Swidler graciously answered, telling me what he knew about the department, and suggested that I apply and write to Bernard Philips, the chair, to find out more. I wrote to Philips, but waited some time for an answer, since he was off somewhere in North Africa conferring with a Sufi spiritual advisor.

I was eventually admitted late that summer, granted a tuition scholarship, and my wife Carol, our infant daughter, and I moved to Philadelphia for the 1966-67 academic year. The Religion Department offices were then, as I recall, in a large old row house on

Broad St., on the university campus. I would spend a good deal of time there that first year. The department moved once or twice after that, before its now permanent situation.

The faculty at that time was not large but growing: Bernard Phillips (World Religions) was chair; Ernie Stoeffler was the most "veteran" member (Pietism, Reformation, Historical Theology generally); Paul Van Buren (Calvin; Western Religious Thought), who had arrived the year before, was probably the most well-known; Swidler (Catholic Studies, theological ecclesiology and historical, focusing on the 19th and 20th century) had just arrived (September, 1966), as had John Raines (Ethics) and Tom Dean (Modern Western Religious Thought), the latter two with recently minted or nearly-finished Ph.D.'s. Richard De Martino (Buddhism) and Lowell Streiker (theory of religion; some Bible?) were also aboard, as I think was Alan Cutler (Jewish Studies). Phillips, Stoeffler, Van Buren, and De Martino are now all deceased.

Also worthy of mention was Hazel Topham, Departmental Secretary, who from my vantage point provided a good deal of stability to a rapidly-changing and sometimes chaotic situation. This may be the place to add the name of Nancy Krody, who arrived somewhat later as Administrative and Editorial Assistant to *JES*. She kept the wheels turning and the presses running for many years, and, as this is written, still provides more than any title can communicate. This is now (2013) some 47 years ago, so I ask to be forgiven for any I may have left out from that first year.

The next year (1967-68) saw increased faculty strength with the arrival of Gerry Sloyan (NT, especially, but some other aspects of Catholic studies as well), Sam Laeuchli (Patristics, Early Christianity), and Pat Burke (Catholic Studies, Medieval Theology, and more). Frank Littell (Western Religious Thought, Jewish-Christian Relations), Maurice Friedman (Jewish Studies and more), and Rod Hindery (Ethics) may have come that year, or soon thereafter.

Among the doctoral candidates already working at Temple were Rodger Van Allen, a Philadelphian, then a young teacher at Villanova, and probably TUDOR's first Catholic doctoral candidate, as well as Norma Arnold and another bright woman whose name I have forgotten. Arriving at the same time as I did were Jack Malinowski, who knew Swidler from Duquesne days in Pittsburgh (and who then began teaching at St. Joe's), Peter Schreiner, who knew Swidler from Germany, Paul Diener, and a host of others. Jim Biechler came from Wisconsin in the second semester of 1966-67. Jerry McBride (from the Chicago area, like me), John White (from D.C.), and George Sherman (from Los Angeles) followed soon thereafter. There may be an abundance of names listed here and afterward, but the Temple story was then—and now still is—the story of *people*, so I include the names of faculty and graduate students unashamedly.

The first courses I took (Fall, 1966) were generally solid, differed widely in content and teaching style, and got me back into the swing (and the fun) of academe. I took four that first semester: Bernard Phillips, on Non-Western Religions, the area about which I then knew least; Ernie Stoeffler, on (Doctrinal) Issues in Early Christianity; Paul Van Buren on the History of Western Religious Thought (that first semester, from Plato to Calvin; from Descartes northward, co-taught with Tom Dean, in the second semester); and Len Swidler, a Seminar on Vatican I (and Vatican II in the second semester). These classes were satisfying, frequently interesting, and once in a while, exciting.

Phillips was a straight lecturer, but he tried—sometimes insightfully—to relate the Hindu and Buddhist materials to basic human (existential) problems. I learned a lot, some from Phillips, more from what I read for the various papers. I wrote a required paper on Hinduism for which I read some *Upanishads*, the *Bhagavad Gita*, and some secondary scholarship; another on Buddhism for which were read some primary texts, Suzuki and Conze. As a final paper at the end of the second semester, Phillips required a longer one on the "Confrontation" of Religions." The reading for this paper was intriguing and stood me in good stead for a course on World Religions which I would later teach for a time at La Salle, and included works from Zaehner, Suzuki, Buber, and more.

Allow me to insert at this point that I mention here and below several papers I wrote, not because I think any reader much cares about what I wrote, but because, like faculty and courses (lectures, discussions), the research one has the opportunity to undertake, and the papers one writes, make up a great deal of one's graduate experience, and thus are a significant part of "TUDOR THEN."

Stoeffler mostly lectured, but tried to involve his students—all adults, none very young—in the issues as they arose. I was the only Catholic in that class, so every once in a while, he would turn to me—he meant it as a generous "ecumenical" gesture—for the "Catholic" position. Sometimes the question was strictly historical, and I would point out that there was no "Catholic" position (which Stoeffler, of course, knew at least as well as me). At other times the issue was in some sense doctrinal, and I would have to aver that there was a "Vatican" position but also another one (sometimes more than one), usually left-leaning and "reformist," which I thought was at least as Catholic and which, I thought, made more sense. In addition to an end-of-semester exam, Stoeffler wanted a research paper. And I thoroughly enjoyed the work on that essay. For several years, long before arriving at Temple, I had been interested in the penitential discipline of the early church. So I wrote on Tertullian and penance, using especially Tertullian's *De Paenitentia* and *De Pudicitia* and a good deal of scholarship on the issue.

I will insert here a personal note, but an important part of my Temple experience: I had never learned to type, so my wife Carol got me through the Temple seminars and courses by typing every one of my hand-written papers, including the dissertation, banging them out—usually in multiple copies—on a manual typewriter. I mention this here because the last sentences of that Tertullian paper were not finally hand-written and then typed until the wee hours of the morning of the day it was due, all this about two or three weeks before Carol gave birth to our second daughter. I owe her a lot, but the debt for this paper is incalculable.

Van Buren's course structure consisted in individual student presentations on the required or related readings, followed by comments from Van Buren and discussion. I offered a presentation on Aristotle (a chapter of the *Metaphysics*) as one rendition, and another, later, on Aquinas on the *Quarta Via* (the fourth "way" to the existence of God) in the *Prima Pars* of the *Summa*. Van Buren was generous in his response to these presentations, but suggested I might have been too negative about Plato on *change* as a trigger for what Aristotle had written, and too sanguine about what I thought Aquinas had achieved. *Sic transit* the glory of my insights. The research paper for that class was also enjoyable and to me, valuable: a serious look at Augustine, Aquinas, and Calvin on the fate of unbaptized infants and its connection to predestination. The paper provided me an opportunity to look critically at Augustine, to be more discriminating about Aquinas than I had previously been, and to learn something at firsthand about one of the "great" Reformers (who, on this issue, I thought was no better than Augustine).

Swidler had us first find and comment on relevant shorter writings that bore on the late nineteenth-century Catholic Church and the First Vatican Council. I enjoyed—and learned from—reading, presenting, and then writing about *"Janus": The Pope and the Council*, a collection of essays by the nineteenth century church historian Döllinger, critical of the creeping centralization of pre-Vatican I Rome. The longer paper was on the "Roman School" of theologians (Perrone, Passaglia, Schrader, and Franzelin) and their influential pro-papal positions around the time of Vatican I (1869-70). I learned a lot about nineteenth century Ultramontanism, but did not much enjoy writing the paper. For the Vatican II seminar in the

Spring, we had the benefit of the frequent participation of Rev. Bill Leahy (RIP), a bright young Philadelphia priest who had been in Rome for the Council, worked as a secretary for Cardinal Krol and the Council itself, and who made available to the seminar participants his mimeographed notes from the council discussions and debates. For my paper, I attempted to identify and weigh certain elements of three conciliar documents (*Dei Verbum*, on revelation; *Lumen Gentium*, on the church; and *Unitatis Redintegratio*, on ecumenism) which I argued were resistant to the larger reform dimensions of the Council.

I took my first seminar with Sam Laeuchli upon his arrival the following year (1967-68), and, thanks to the transfer of credit from previous (seminary) academic work, I finished my course work, after I had begun teaching at La Salle, at the rate of one seminar per semester with Sam thereafter. The first was on the early fourth century Spanish Synod of Elvira; the research took me to relevant Roman legislation and several parallel issues from early church history. There followed studies of Gnosticism, early Christology and Nicaea, Eusebius (and Constantine), and Augustine.

In addition to the regular seminars on campus, Sam also hosted Saturday morning meetings of his students at his home, sometimes assembling regularly—perhaps monthly—(working on a trustworthy and readable translation of the Latin canons of the Synod of Elvira, and working through the Greek of the Letters of Ignatius of Antioch), and sometimes only occasionally (on one or another of Sam's "projects."). The participants either already were or soon became my fast friends: Jim Biechler, Jerry McBride, George Sherman (RIP), John White, and later Mary Hansbury, in addition to me. This was Sam going above and beyond what was required of him, of course; but it was also enriching, fun, and to me, an important part of that early TUDOR experience. The same should be said of at least one of the discussion or dialogue groups initiated by Len Swidler, this one (early 1970s?) on Jewish-Christian dialogue, and involving, in addition to the interested members of the Temple faculty and alums, one or two from Penn and some Israeli scholars from what became the Annenberg Center.

The library holdings at Temple were less than ample at first. The projected new library had been planned, but not yet built. We used what was, as I recall it, the old Conwell Theological Library, in a building just east of Broad St., near the main entrance to the University. For the Vatican I seminar, we were able to use the Library of St. Charles Borromeo Seminary, with a pretty good collection of nineteenth century Catholic materials as well as Hefele's and Mansi's conciliar texts. At that time and a little later, I recall using—without charge—the excellent Library of the University of Pennsylvania, as long as we were somehow identified as graduate students. Now, however, the fee for borrowing privileges at Penn for non-Penn people has become prohibitive. Of course, since then, I have made good use of La Salle's fine collection, and the Temple Library holdings have increased exponentially.

For the record, there was one other fairly serious weakness. I thought that the registration system each of those early semesters was far from adequate. It was not well organized. Lines were long, the process unnecessarily time-consuming and generally a burden for all concerned, even for those registering for a single seminar or for an Independent Study. I'm sure that computerization has improved the experience since those days, but this part of my TUDOR adventure does not afford a happy memory.

Financial aid was certainly an issue. I applied and was admitted too late for any financial aid beyond the tuition scholarship. Carol and I arrived with one infant daughter, another on the way, and about $3000. Dr. Phillips felt sure that, if registrations for the Introductory Religion course (Religion 11?) held up or improved in the second semester, he would have no hesitation assigning me two sections. I had enough seminary course work and other experience to warrant it. As it happened, registration did increase a bit, and he assigned me two teaching sections, one on the main campus and one on the campus of Temple's Tyler School of Art, just north of Philadelphia. The section on campus was large, at least thirty or more students, mostly sophomores, and a few upper-class students fulfilling a not-yet met requirement. The section on the Tyler campus proved more engaging. Phillips told me he was sending me to Tyler because I looked like an army sergeant (brush haircut, etc.), and "Those artist kids need some discipline. Some drink coffee in class, and some don't wear socks!" Now adequately warned, I headed up to Tyler. In fact, these young men and women (art majors, fulfilling a Philosophy or Religion requirement) were mostly juniors or seniors, bright, creative, not at all rebellious, but perhaps a little cavalier about getting assignments in on time (it was, after all, 1967, near the peak of the "Sixties," a time which irritated so many people). I don't know how much discipline I imposed, but the students and I got along well, and they seemed to enjoy the course as much as I did.

These two sections were my first experience creating and grading exams, assigning, reading, and annotating papers, and adjudicating final grades. The responsibility was probably a little tougher than I had anticipated it would be, but I survived, learned a great deal, and may have been slightly more generous with final grades than I should have been. I will add here, though, that the experience provided infinitely better preparation for a teaching career than that available in those institutions that do not provide teaching opportunities for their doctoral candidates.

Back to financial aid: before registration numbers had come in, Phillips went out of his way to help in another way. Dr. Stoeffler wanted to resign from his "extra" job as Religion Dept. representative on the Temple Academic Advising Board. The system at that time was, for any student not yet (before his or her junior year) committed to a major, that he or she was assigned to the Academic Advising Board, and, with periodic meetings with the academic advisors, would choose course work (to fulfill curricular requirements) and eventually a major. It was important that each department have some representation on the board, to describe the department's varied offerings to students (and to other faculty members who asked). Phillips wanted the department represented, and with a relatively small and new faculty, he did not feel he could simply order one of the faculty members to take the job. So he offered it to me. I then had to learn the Temple curriculum requirements with the help of two faculty members (one from English, the other from History) who trained me. I think I spent two days a week in the job, and found the contact with students healthy. The teaching and academic advising took up significant time, so I had more than my share of "Incomplete" grades. My teachers were considerate, and I survived that first year. I continued the advising for two months during the summer of 1967.

The stipend for the teaching was, I think, $600 per section. The academic advising probably paid me $1200 for the spring semester, and perhaps another $1000 for the summer. While this was not affluence, we made it through.

One more note on Phillips, beyond financial aid: early during my teaching career at La Salle, Phillips lectured there on some aspect of interreligious dialogue. After the lecture, he invited me to accompany him to nearby Germantown Hospital, where Sr. Alice Rutherford (then a TUDOR grad student) was recuperating from some malady. His visit with Alice was revealing: he went not as TUDOR administrator, nor as teacher of Hindu or Buddhist traditions. He was there as human being, paying a welcome visit to another human being in need. This was a side of him I had not seen before, and it told me something new about him and about TUDOR.

Even more helpful was Len Swidler. During that first semester, he relayed to me various speaking requests he received and which he could not meet: one to speak in an evening class at Beaver College (now Arcadia University), and another, a "chapel lecture" at Lebanon Valley College. He recommended me, and I delivered the lecture (on

Metz and "Political Theology"). Lebanon Valley students were obliged to attend some three or four such chapel lectures each term, and I fear none of them cared much about Metz or Political Theology. I did speak to two religion or theology classes there as part of that "deal," and those ventures were far more lively and successful. Then, in the late summer of 1968, the Adult Education Centers of Chicago had scheduled a series of lectures (by Christian and Jewish scholars) on Judaism, Jewish-Christian relations, and Christian anti-Judaism, to bring educators up to date on the background of Vatican II's treatment of the Jews and Judaism in *Nostra Aetate*. The Loyola faculty member who had originally been scheduled for one set of lectures (on the history of Jewish-Christian relations) became ill. Sr. Rose Thering, O.P., who was running the operation, contacted Len to inquire if he could substitute or recommend someone. Len again recommended me, and I lectured at Barat College, in Lake Forest, Ill. The stipend paid for our first return trip to Chicago since 1965, and the lectures gave me the opportunity to gather some materials (on the history of Christian anti-Judaism) that I would build on for the rest of my scholarly life. The week I spent at Barat also provided a wonderful opportunity to get to know—however briefly—Irving ("Yitz") Greenberg, John Pawlikowski, and, more briefly because she was ill, Sr. Rose.

This is all not to turn this essay into an autobiographical adventure, but to underline the helpfulness and generosity of Dr. Phillips and especially Len Swidler. To conclude this part of the narrative: Len had recently met Bro. James Kaiser, FSC, and Rev. Mark Heath, O.P., from La Salle College. They were in the initial stages of an attempt to "professionalize" the Theology Department faculty by hiring PhDs (or those on the way to PhDs) to replace the few archdiocesan priests and Christian Brothers with MAs who were currently teaching most of the theology offerings—in large part to bring the department up to Vatican II standards. Len referred me to them, and I was hired at La Salle for the Fall 1967 term.

Thus developed my debt to, and more importantly, my friendship with, various members of the Temple faculty. Swidler probably became my closest faculty friend, but at this stage, I probably spent more time on early Christian issues with Sam Laeuchli, who would eventually direct my dissertation. Gerry Sloyan also became a good friend over the years. I got to know John Raines, Tom Dean, and Pat Burke, but not as well as those first three. It would be an exaggeration to call Dick De Martino (RIP) a personal friend, but we shared an office in the spring 1967 semester and had a chance to talk a lot, and I learned more about Japanese (Zen) Buddhism from him personally and from an essay he wrote than I did from any dozen books. I wish I had gotten to know Paul Van Buren (RIP) better before I moved on to La Salle. They were decent human beings all, and a pleasure to work with. It bears underlining that these friendships with Temple faculty were not at all atypical; they were the order of the day at TUDOR. From among them, Laeuchli, Sloyan, and Van Buren would make up my dissertation committee.

Before the dissertation, of course, there came language exams and a battery of comprehensive exams. My comps had been delayed because of a couple of "Incomplete" grades, which I took care of over time. The system of comprehensive exams was revised at least once during my time, and I took them according to what we called the "old" system. In this system, examinations were in six areas, at least one of which was to be in a religious tradition other than one's own, usually a religion of Asia. As I recall the system, a set of some six "comprehensive" questions for each area was agreed on by the candidate and the appropriate faculty member, and in the three hours allotted, the candidate would write on two (of three?) selected by the faculty member.

My examination areas were the following, together with a representative selection of the questions which were to be prepared. I hope the detail does not prove tedious, but I thought the system was a good one, the exam questions demanding and sometimes imaginative and fair, and I think they deserve at least a word here:

Hebrew Bible: Examiner: Robert Gordis, (and Lowell Streiker, if Gordis were unavailable). Sample questions: (A). The history of biblical eschatology; (B). Apocalyptic literature: its origin and development.

Patristics: Examiner: Sam Laeuchli. Sample questions: (A). The dilemma of Nicaea; (B). Why did the ancient church establish a system of penance?

Theory of Religion: Examiner: Lowell Streiker. Sample questions: (A). "The routinization of charisma" (Weber); (B). Mysticism: sacred and profane.

Religious Thought: Examiner: Sam Laeuchli. Sample questions: (A). The contribution and limitations of psychology and sociology as arbiters of *religious* reality; (B). God and human autonomy/freedom in Origen, Augustine, and one modern or contemporary philosopher or religious thinker (I chose Buber).

World Religions: Examiner: Bernard Phillips. Sample questions: (A). God as *person* and as *absolute ground* in Indian religions and biblical religions; (B). the contrast between the religions of Semitic origin and those of India and China.

Hinduism: Examiner: Bernard Phillips. Sample questions: (A). *Dharma* vs. *moksha* as ultimate in Hinduism; (B). The unity and diversity of Hinduism: is Hinduism one religion or many? (C). Critical analysis of one work from the scriptures of Hinduism

The exam sessions ran for three hours each: 9:00-12:00 and 1:00-4:00 on three days. Mine were in August, 1970. The exams were each read by several faculty members. I had spent time that summer reading fairly widely on the various issues, and actually looked forward to taking the exams and getting started on my dissertation.

The dissertation I finally wrote was entitled *Tertullian's Anti-Judaism and Its Role in His Theology*. I finished and defended it at the end of the spring 1975 semester, too late for a 1975 degree, so I am listed as "PhD, Religion, 1976." Other early dissertations were Jim Biechler on Nicholas of Cusa and Conciliarism (one of the first dissertations published by the AAR); Rodger Van Allen on the history of *Commonweal*; George Sherman (RIP) on martyrs and martyr trials in the context of Church vs. Empire; John White on Ignatius of Antioch; Jerry McBride on something on Tertullian or North Africa; and Mike Kerlin on Peter Berger, as I recall (a second PhD for him, but the first in Religion). Later, there were Regina Boisclair on problems with Judaism (and with women?) in the Lectionary; Mary Laver on Calvin and the Jews/Judaism and Pam Monaco on the history of Catholic reform movements. Sherman, White, McBride and I wrote with Sam Laeuchli; Biechler and Kerlin with Pat Burke; Boisclair, I think, with Sloyan; Laver with Van Buren; and Van Allen (I think) and Monaco with Swidler. There were others, some with distinguished dissertations and subsequent publications, but these people I know, and the "group product" is cumulatively pretty solid.

Other names of doctoral candidates from that early time and a little later, each of which merits listing, are: Mary Hansbury, Pat Boni, Karen Brown, Colleen McDannell, Tony Matteo, Stevan Davies, George Papademetriou, Silvio Fittipaldi, Ken Kramer, June O'Connor, Catherine Berry, Tom Dugan, Alice Rutherford, Steve Heine, Merlyn Mowrey, John Groutt, Barbara Hogan, Jo Ann Spillman, David Mandeng, and Leslie Desmangles. In addition to Jim Biechler, John White, Mike Kerlin and me, these also taught at La Salle, at least as adjuncts: Jerry McBride, Pat Boni, Merlyn Mowrey, Pam Monaco, Colleen McDannell, Steve Heine, Joel Reizburg, Barbara Hogan, Ken Kramer, and Silvio Fittipaldi.

The occasions and motivations which led various graduate students to TUDOR constitute a story in itself. I don't know anything like the complete story, but two examples may be of some interest. Mike Kerlin was a Christian Brother, a member of the religious order which ran La Salle. He already had a doctorate in Philosophy from the Gregorian University in Rome. But he was about to leave the Brothers, and, as the most junior member of the Philosophy Department, was a bit concerned about his job, especially in a time of retrenchment. He would have been one of the more senior members of the young Theology (later Religion) Department, so he took a couple of religion courses at TUDOR, got interested, and before long finished another doctorate, this time in religion, with Pat Burke. A little later Pam Monaco, then a campus minister at La Salle, began work on an MA in La Salle's small graduate program in Religion and Theology. The teaching part of her campus ministry job was important to her, and she soon became enchanted with the graduate-level study of religion. She spoke to John Raines, who taught from time to time at La Salle, and he encouraged her to apply to TUDOR. As she had with her dissertation, she completed a history of the principal Catholic reform movements with Len Swidler.

Conversations and discussions among faculty and graduate students that first year or two were, as far as any in which I participated, lively and fairly "egalitarian," (i.e., no faculty pontificating). Politics was fair game (the Vietnam War, the forthcoming presidential elections of 1968, and more), as was Catholic church reform—usually with Len Swidler at the heart of it—at least for the Catholics in the aftermath of Vatican II. For example, the papal encyclical *Humanae vitae* (condemning artificial contraception) provoked a good deal of discussion at the end of the summer of 1968 and thereafter, all of it critical. In spring of 1967, several of us were concerned about the threat of Egypt and Syria to "drive Israel into the sea." By the same token, Israel's subsequent spectacular success in the Six-Day War relieved most of us. In general, most of these discussions were left-leaning. I was not privy, of course, to faculty meetings and discussions. Perhaps a faculty participant in this enterprise will provide enlightenment.

After I had begun to teach at La Salle in September, 1967, I had a good deal less contact with the whole TUDOR operation, except for the Laeuchli seminars each semester for a couple of years. There were, of course, the Laeuchli Saturday mornings, and the sporadic Swidler dialogues and projects. I learned of the faculty vote to elect Gerry Sloyan as chair; his experienced administrative hand was needed to maintain—and sometimes even to impose—order, in a fluid, developing, and sometimes confusing situation. There were some hurt feelings involved, but with no intention of criticizing his predecessor, the decision seemed to me a good one. Further positive (and disciplined) administrative contributions came from Isma'il al Faruqi (Islam), later tragically murdered with his wife Lois, and then Bob Wright (Hebrew Bible, Pseudepigrapha), each of whom did a fine job as Director of Graduate Studies.

Perhaps it's worth adding a note about ventures which were not strictly TUDOR enterprises, but which added to the TUDOR experience for both graduate students and several faculty members. Rodger Van Allen, for example, was among the leading forces in the creation of the College Theology Society, and became the first editor, as I recall, of the Society's journal, *Horizons*, a journal which served many of us well. Len Swidler co-founded the Association for the Rights of Catholics in the Church (ARCC), which has its own fascinating history, and which was important to most of the Catholics here. His later efforts at writing a "Constitution of the Catholic Church" involved a few of us. Frank Littell (RIP) was co-founder of the Annual Scholars' Conference on the Holocaust (this before his arrival at Temple). The conferences had less connection to TUDOR, but provided a chance for many to deliver papers.

Faculty and students were a fairly diverse group in those first years, but not yet the widely cosmopolitan and wildly interreligious operation it became, and remains today. Then diversity came from women and men, old and young, Protestants, Catholics (mostly left-wing, but some from the middle of the road), a few Jews, a few atheists, priests, ex-priests, ex-nuns, etc. from all over the country. This was later complemented by a more wide-ranging mix of

Muslims, Hindus, and Buddhists, from Asia, Europe, and Africa. Since those early days, the department has seen periods of fairly spectacular growth, as well as periods of financial stress and at least partial retrenchment. My sense is that it has served its graduate students very well. Some first-rate dissertations have been written, and some fine teachers and scholars have been started on their way. The presence of several colleges and universities in the area helped provide teaching experience and temporary employment for some, and productive careers afterward for many.

In sum, my TUDOR experience was satisfying and at times, enriching. It might have been less satisfying had I come with less reading and experience under my belt. But it afforded me the opportunity to build on what I knew and, in some areas, to correct what I thought I knew. I wish I could offer a "grand narrative," but with only that first year of uninterrupted course work and study, what I have been able to assemble above is the best I can offer. Most of the seminars, together with the faculty members I came to know and the fellow grad students who became colleagues and friends, provided a solid preparation for the teaching career I loved at La Salle. I guess I was ready for TUDOR, and TUDOR was right for me. *Ad multos annos!*

TUDOR AND THE STUDY OF SOCIAL JUSTICE

JOHN J. MAWHINNEY, S.J.

I first heard of Temple's doctorate program in religion in spring 1966. It was my final semester of required Jesuit theological studies at Woodstock College (Woodstock, MD). Woodstock had invited Dr. Paul van Buren to give a lecture. After the lecture I asked van Buren privately about Temple's graduate program. He replied very straightforwardly that when he first went there he was unsure of it, but was now quite pleased with how it was coming along. His forthright response impressed me. I immediately arranged an interview with its chair Dr. Bernard Phillips.

How My Own Background Led Me to Temple

I was raised a very traditional and strictly observant Roman Catholic (1930s/1940s style). From eighth through twelfth grade, I attended a Jesuit preparatory school. There I became very impressed by the education of my mainly Jesuit teachers as well as by an older Jesuit, Father Vincent L. Keelan, to whom I went for personal counsel nearly every week during the better part of my last two years of high school. Keelan gave little advice but was a great listener.

I graduated high school in 1950 at seventeen. In my final semester I sought admission to the Jesuits, was accepted, and entered the Society that summer at seventeen. I have now (2014) been a Jesuit for 64 years.

My reasons for entering had nothing to do with becoming a priest and doing parochial and sacramental work—though I knew that in the course of events I would eventually be ordained. I just wanted to become well educated, teach, and help others by being a good "listener" like Father Keelan. I was also deeply interested in social justice—though at that time I knew essentially nothing about what that entailed.

From the moment I entered, I set my sights on a doctorate. In my first four years as a Jesuit we were required to continue courses in the foreign language (in my case French) we had started in high school. However, I knew that PhD programs required a reading knowledge of German. So, I immediately began teaching myself to read German on my own.

In my second year as a Jesuit my novice director intensely sought to raise our awareness on social justice issues such as racism against African Americans and the right of workers to organize themselves just as businesses organize themselves in the form of corporations.

In my fifth through seventh years as a Jesuit (1954-1957), I did the three years of required Jesuit philosophy studies. I began these studies with the naïve belief that they would enable me to refute all arguments against the Roman Catholic faith. I was quickly disabused of that notion by the inability of my Jesuit professors to give satisfactory answers to many questions I had. I especially could not understand why most of them totally rejected modern philosophical ideas so highly appreciated by intellectuals outside of the Catholic Church. They mentioned such thinkers, if at all, only in passing. Their main objective was to ensure that we, as future priests, would think in ways fully consonant with traditional Roman Catholic teachings as set down by the Vatican. We were not to develop any contrary ideas. All courses were strictly grounded in medieval scholasticism.

However, I discovered and studied on my own a five-volume work of the Belgian Jesuit, Joseph Maréchal (d. 1944). His work thoroughly discussed—in a very positive, constructive, and detailed way—the evolution of the philosophy of knowledge from the pre-Socratics through Kant and the German idealists. Maréchal did not reject medieval scholasticism but did give it a very revisionist interpretation. His work highly influenced the German Jesuit, Karl Rahner (1904—1984), by far the most renowned Roman Catholic theologian of the twentieth century, whom I would later study on my own.

During the next stage of Jesuit training (1957-1962) I taught philosophy in a Jesuit university. In this period, I found plenty of time to study and take some courses in modern Western thought. It was then that I began my intense study, in German, of Karl Rahner's philosophy of religion (*Hörer des Wortes,* and of knowledge, *Geist im Welt*).

In 1962, I began four years of required theological studies at the Jesuit Woodstock College (Maryland). Vatican II (1962-1965) was just getting started. However, in anticipation of Vatican II, the Woodstock faculty had already made a sweeping overhaul of the curriculum. Woodstock was reputed to have the best Catholic theology program and library in the U.S.

Several of its faculty had already achieved, or soon would, international reputations: John Courtney Murray (the major architect of the Vatican II document on religious liberty and specialist in church-state relations); Joseph A Fitzmyer (New Testament, Dead Sea Scrolls, and Aramaic); and Avery R Dulles (soon to be a well-known theologian and eventually a Cardinal). Two other very progressive Jesuits joined the faculty as professors of moral and pastoral theology about the same time I arrived as a student. Both thought well "outside-the-box" in their approach to their disciplines. We quickly became good intellectual friends.

Another factor contributing to the intellectual environment was that ten percent of the 250 student body already had doctorates from quite prestigious universities (e.g., Johns Hopkins and the University of Pennsylvania) in astronomy, physics, biology, chemistry, or math. In addition, a large number, including me, were told to prepare for doctoral studies in a wide variety of fields once we completed theology studies.

JOHN J. MAWHINNEY, S.J.

By 1964 several Jesuits were already in doctoral studies in some areas of religious studies at non-Catholic universities. However, all their universities had at least some historical connection with Protestantism. In summer 1965 I visited three universities to inquire about doctoral studies: Southern Methodist, University of Chicago and University of Iowa.

Choice of Temple's Religion Department

After hearing of Temple's doctorate program, I arranged an interview with the founding chair of the program, Dr. Bernard Phillips. I arrived just as he was coming out of his office with two other men. He at once introduced me. They were Drs. Leonard Swidler and Elwyn Smith. He introduced us and explained that both were joining the faculty the following fall (1966) and were bringing with them the Journal of Ecumenical Studies. (Swidler and his wife Arlene Anderson Swidler, the founders of this journal, and now Leonard Swidler and Smith, were co-editors.) Phillips invited me to lunch with them at Temple's Faculty Club. It was an exciting lunch. Phillips told us that the University had just approved the department's entire budget request for the next fiscal year and gave many details. It included a gigantic amount for expanding the religious studies holdings of the University's library as well as generous amounts for additional faculty and student fellowships.

After lunch, I met with Phillips privately. He expressed great interest in having Jesuits enrolled in the graduate program and said I would be the first. He offered me a fellowship and said a considerable amount of my academic credits would be transferable.

I liked the idea of being the first Jesuit and on the cutting edge of a relatively new department. The more important reasons that drew me to Temple were:

First, my interest in social ethics, approached not from a self-consciously religious standpoint, but from secular-humanistic perspectives so that I could dialogue with persons regardless of their beliefs or non-beliefs. I found I could do that at Temple.

Second, I wanted to broaden my educational experience by studying at a secular university without religious ties. Thus far, all my schooling had been in Catholic schools and, since the seventh grade, in Jesuit educational institutions. After entering the Jesuits, the institutions where I studied were not only Jesuit-founded but also admitted only Jesuits as students and were staffed only by Jesuit professors, none of whom had had advanced studies at secular universities except for two Biblical scholars.

Third, I had no interest in studying more Catholic theology. My main interest lay in the modern philosophy of religion and social ethics as developed in the Western tradition.

After meeting with Phillips, I quickly sent all transcripts and began my studies in January 1967. I have never regretted the decision.

What I Got From Temple

My intense study of Karl Rahner and modern approaches to scriptural studies had convinced me of the culturally and historically conditioned character of all knowledge and the need to apply a historical-critical method to all intellectual disciplines, including social ethics. The courses at Temple deepened and better grounded my understanding of this conviction.

My biggest challenge at Temple was to develop a different method of doing ethics. The Catholic tradition sees the major task of ethicists to analyze concrete "cases" through casuistry and thereby determine the moral right or wrong of particular actions and thoughts. In doing so, it tends to be very prescriptive and largely ignores the impact of societal structures on shaping how we live together ethically. True, the Catholic Church has many official documents on social issues, but they are quite abstract and general. Because they lack concreteness, they do not really challenge us to rethink specific social structures. The Catholic tradition also employs a rather out-of-date mode of thinking that is rather strange to our age. It relies heavily on natural law to provide the major premises from which to deduce universal, absolute, and timeless moral judgments. It shows very little awareness that understandings of natural law are culturally and historically conditioned, and so no absolute, timeless conclusions can be deduced from it.

By the time I got to Temple I had concluded that the only absolute ethical principle was "do good, avoid evil" or one that was rooted in some value like justice or the dignity of the human person. However, what we count as good, evil, just, and human dignity varies tremendously from one culture to another.

Even Christianity had for centuries sanctioned slavery, crusades against Moslems, discrimination against Jews, even the kidnapping of Jewish children if some household servant had baptized them, the arrest, imprisonment, torture, exiling, and burning to death of heretics—to mention just a few of the more indisputably unethical practices as we see them today. In the context of how people saw the world in that age, these practices may be understandable. However, it is unthinkable that we would tolerate such practices today. People's ideas about right and wrong do change—though that is not to say always for the better.

This is not ethical relativism (i.e., the assertion that morality is just a feeling and that there can be no objective moral judgments.). It is just that humans are finite and must continually search for the truth. As William James said, truth is a search for what seems to put us in better relationship with the whole of reality—as best as we can see it at any point in time and place.

BREAKTHROUGH TO DIALOGUE

A Number of Courses at Temple Gave Me Opportunities to Deepen My Thinking

One was Dr. Ernest Stoeffler's course on Reformation theology. Particularly interesting was his discussion of the numerous medieval and early modern understandings given by both Protestants and Roman Catholics theologians to how they conceived of Jesus' presence in the Eucharist. Although we students could repeat the words the theologians used, I doubt if any of us really understood at a deep level the language and thought categories that undergirded them. Their intellectual frameworks were too foreign to how we think today.

Many years later, a Catholic woman came to me somewhat upset because her Protestant husband had gotten up in church and received "Catholic" communion on the day of their daughter's first communion. I told her about my experience in Stoeffler's class and said I doubt if anyone today really understands the different formulations used in that day to explain the manner of Jesus' "real" presence in the Eucharist—even if they can repeat the words of the Protestant and Catholic proponents (which only a tiny handful can do). I suggested that her husband, like she, just considered the day of their daughter's first Communion a religiously important event. He just wanted to share the event with her. The woman seemed satisfied. It is unfortunate that different religious faiths do not allow Eucharistic sharing more often.

Dr. Samuel Laeuchli's course on Patristics also deepened my understanding of the culturally and historical character of human knowledge. In every class he showed slides illustrating how various ideas of the Patristic theologians were reflected in the paintings and architecture of their age.

In Dr. Thomas Dean's course on philosophies of religion I wrote papers on both William James and John Dewey. I saw some similarities between how Dewey and Karl Rahner spoke of religious experience. Dean encouraged me to publish the paper I had written, "The Concept of Mystery in Karl Rahner's Philosophical Theology." The highly prestigious Union Theological Seminary Quarterly (New York City) immediately accepted it for a special issue on some major contemporary Christian theologians.

In one of Dean's courses, I came across the first two volumes of Career of Philosophy by John Herman Randal, Jr. of Colombia University. This brilliant work gave not only an excellent exposition of the various philosophers' ideas and showed how their problems and ideas arose out of the cultural and scientific contexts of their times.

Dr. John C. Raines' courses introduced me to Protestant ethicists like the Niebuhr brothers (Reinhold and H. Richard) and James M Gustafson. They opened my eyes to other approaches to societal ethics.

Doctoral Dissertation

I chose John Raines as my dissertation director, and Tom Dean was on my advisory board. My dissertation was entitled "The Universalistic Thrust of H. Richard Niebuhr" (1977).

In speaking of Niebuhr's universalistic thrust, I meant that Niebuhr encourages open, responsive dialogue among all peoples and communities. Niebuhr rejected the idea that there was such a thing as a "Christian" God or that God had revealed "himself" (herself) more fully to Christians than to other people. God is the God of all people. S/he is ineffable mystery and can reveal "her/self" to humans in only finite ways, for humans are finite and can receive divine revelation only in culturally and historically conditioned and limited ways.

However, my principal reason for choosing to write on H. Richard Niebuhr was his ideas on the center of value and his symbol of the "the person-as-responder" as a generally more adequate way to do ethical reflection in contrast to the traditional teleological "person-as-maker," or deontological "person-as-the-law-abider" approaches used in Roman Catholic ethical thinking.

Since Temple

My academic commitment has been to make myself and others aware of societal structures and policies, both domestic and global, from a structural justice standpoint. My primary focus has been on U.S. foreign policy (geopolitical, economic, and military) and its impacts on other people and nations. Over the decades I developed my own ethical methodology that I call societal structural justice analysis. It relies on the social sciences disciplines, particularly political science, U.S. foreign policy history, sociology, cultural anthropology, and socio-political economics. I do not pretend to give prescriptive ethical answers but only to lay bare both to myself and to others what is and has been happening. I do not attempt to follow H. Richard Niebuhr closely, but my way of examining our global and domestic structures and responsibilities is very much influenced by Niebuhr's symbol of "the responsible self."

As I said above, I have never regretted my decision to go to Temple. Temple has helped me to see the world as it finitely is and to do my best to search for the ethically good in ever more responsive, responsible, and non-dogmatic ways.

BREAKTHROUGH TO DIALOGUE

CELEBRATING A GROUNDBREAKING RELIGION DEPARTMENT

JOHN L. ESPOSITO

I. Catholic Beginnings

The creation of Temple University's Department of Religion was the right idea at the right time and in the right place. Like all pioneering ventures, its new paradigm for a PhD program was greeted with some skepticism in the academy but with enthusiasm (and no doubt some trepidation) by many of its faculty and graduate students.

I went to Temple University some 45 years ago in 1968 to pursue a doctorate majoring in Catholic studies not realizing that my experience would be quite something else and lead me down a path that would transform my life. At the time, I was a young assistant professor of theology, teaching at Rosemont College. Like many of the Catholic graduate students in the department, I had been in religious life, a Capuchin Franciscan, entering at fourteen and leaving at twenty-four years of age. After a brief fling at corporate life and high school teaching, I earned an MA in Theology at St. John's University in Jamaica, New York. I was particularly attracted by the fact that, rather than follow the conventional path and earn my degree at a Catholic university or seminary, I could major in Roman Catholic thought at a secular university with prominent scholars like Leonard Swidler. Len and his wife Arlene were already celebrated scholars and mentors for post-Vatican II Catholics. But first I decided to enjoy the luxury of studying with a Protestant expert and took John Raines' course in which we read both major Protestant thinkers (which was new to me) and some Catholic theologians. John was a breath of fresh air. Bright and extraordinarily well read, but in contrast to many of my previous studies in philosophy and theology, he was also dynamic, enthusiastic and welcoming. The seminar, like no others I had attended, made theology, in particular social ethics, come alive. I realized John's personal influence when years later I reflected on the fact that when I bought a new book bag, it looked curiously like John's and then I started smoking cigars.

Although I felt I was off to a good start and would move on to take courses in Catholic thought as well, I first had to fulfill the requirement for all grad students, a one-year course in World Religions with Bernard Phillips. I never looked back and proceeded to take courses in Hinduism and Zen Buddhism. When Amiya Chakravarty suggested I expand my term paper into a dissertation, I went to see Bernard Phillips, the visionary founding Chair of the Religion Department, to discuss a major in Hinduism. Up until that point, I had not been sure which religion to major in but this opportunity convinced me. Teaching full time, married, I was nothing if pragmatic! Hinduism it would be. However, to my astonishment, Phillips suggested that I study Islam!

II. Why Study Islam?

Raised in an Italian America neighborhood in Brooklyn, eventually my family moved to a new state subsidized coop in Jersey City, N.J. that offered affordable apartments for working class people. Most of my friends and neighbors were Jews who like a minority of Christians had migrated from New York. I had heard about (though not with any great interest or understanding) the 1967 Arab-Israeli war on the news. Deeply moved and influenced by the movie "The Exodus," which at that time I thought was historically accurate, I could not imagine why anyone would want to deal with Arabs or study Islam. My initial response to Professor Phillips was a polite but resolute "No, thank you." Yet here I am so many years later, having devoted an entire career and a major portion of my life to the study of Islam and Muslim societies! How could a "No" become a life-long profession, even vocation?

A distinctive feature of the department was the attempt to have all the world's great religions represented. Faculty had to have been born in (not necessarily practice) or be converts to the religious tradition they taught. Having acquired a good number of the faculty in Christianity, Judaism, Hinduism, Buddhism and Chinese religions, Temple was now developing its Islamic Studies component. Isma'il Ragi al Faruqi, a Palestinian trained in western philosophy at Harvard and Indiana and finally in Islamic studies, was Temple's first Professor of Islamic Studies. Because he had just finished a book, *Christian Ethics*, Phillips thought we would work well together. I did not think so. I knew little about Arabs or Islam and what I did know (much of it, I discovered later, was the product of bias and stereotypes) did not attract me. However, Phillips was "gently adamant" and I, reflecting on the precarious position of a grad student, finally agreed to "take just one course."

Ismail proved to be a remarkable lecturer who made Islam and Muslim history come alive in a classroom. My educational experience was enhanced by the fact that most of the students in my classes were from the Muslim world. Many were taking courses in Christianity and Judaism. Ismail aggressively recruited students and did his best to raise the financial support they needed. The class also included an Arab American, James Zogby, who later went on to be president of the Arab American Institute and Victor Makarre, an Egyptian-American Presbyterian minister.

III. You'll Never Get a Job?

The reaction of friends and family to my decision to study Islam is reflected in a comment from a fellow grad student, who specialized in Roman Catholic thought: "Why go into that abra kadabra field?

you'll never get a job." His belief mirrored the realities of the time. There was little demand for Islamicists (scholars of Islam) since Islam was virtually invisible in the academy, whereas Catholic colleges would always need a theology department and theologians.

Then why did I stick with it? Looking back, it was the powerful influence of Ismail and my Muslim colleagues and the exciting new world that opened up for me. Having had a welcomed breather, through my studies of Hinduism and Buddhism, from my immersion, personally and professionally, in Christianity, I was now astonished to discover that there was another Abrahamic faith. We had always talked about the Judeo-Christian connection but never the Judeo-Christian-Islamic. Why not? If Muslims recognized many of the major patriarchs and prophets of Judaism and Christianity (including Abraham, Moses, and Jesus) and God's revealed books, the Torah and the Message (New Testament) of Jesus, why had I not been aware of this after all my years of liberal arts and theological training? In addition, I discovered a history, or better perspective on history, that I had never known, a new way of understanding history, from the Crusades to European colonialism. Thus, religion but also history, politics, and civilization, classical and modern, came alive for me.

Studying under Isma'il at Temple had many advantages, some of which I did not appreciate until much later in my career. Most important was an understanding of Islam that I gained "from within." At Temple I learned Islam not only both from texts but also the context of Isma'il and grad students who came from Nigeria and Egypt to Pakistan and Malaysia. This unique feature of the program provided immediate insight not only into the unity but also the tremendous diversity of Islam and its role in history, politics and culture. I learned not only from traditional Muslim and Orientalist scholarship but also from the perspectives of believers from Africa to Southeast Asia, enabling me to see and understand Islam as a living/lived faith. Isma'il al Faruqi was the most dynamic and engaging of lecturers. Like all great teachers, his energy and passion for his subject was contagious. My Muslim classmates were bright, inquisitive, earnest, devout young believers as well as aspiring scholars. Most were there not simply to study Islam but to study other religions, especially Christianity and Judaism.

Looking back, my circle of fellow students and Ismail's guided course of studies enabled me to engage the global Islamic community from the very beginning, long before I would begin overseas research trips. But there were also embarrassing moments. Ismail, who had studied Christianity closely, would make a comparative point, citing an epistle St. Paul from the New Testament, and would turn to me for the appropriate scriptural reference. Since I was a Christian and taught scripture and theology, it seemed perfectly logical to him that I would know the text, especially since he did. Struggling as I was at the time to learn the Quran and deal with other Muslim texts, his comparative ecumenism was an unwelcome source of additional anxiety. However, nothing was more humiliating than when Isma'il asked me when the great Muslim theologian al-Ghazzali died, noting that this was a date no one could forget. I sat there in stunned silence, wondering why he expected me to remember it. I have never forgotten the date—1111 AD!

Many questioned whether studying solely with Muslim professors provided me with an "objective" study of Islam. Clearly, the conventional wisdom and practice was accepted that it was more objective to study with a non-Muslim! Of course few seemed bothered, especially years ago, that most professors of Christianity or Judaism were raised in or identified themselves as Christians or Jews. Indeed, in the not too distant past, it would have been unthinkable to have a non-Christian or non-Jew hold such positions, but not so when it came to professors of Islam. Today, it seems difficult to imagine a time when Middle Eastern Studies Association (MESA) or the American Academy of Religion (AAR) did not have sections or panels on Islam and the role of religion in modern history and politics. The issue was reflected in their programs and even elected officers. Ismail had to apply and then convince the American Academy of Religions to have a permanent section on Islam. I remember being conscious that some non-Muslim scholars of Islam saw the Islam section as "Faruqi's Muslim camp" rather than as singular professional opportunity and accomplishment. Of course today, both the AAR and MESA as many other organizations like American Political Science Association (APSA) and American Historical Association (AHA) have extensive coverage of Islam, Islamic movements and politics. I was delighted when as a sign of the changing times I was the first Islamic scholar to be elected president of MESA, followed in subsequent years by friends and now current colleagues like John Voll and Yvonne Haddad. And of course I was doubly delighted to be elected President of the AAR.

I discovered comparable attitudes among government officials and policymakers who believed that contact with Islamic activists and organizations compromised objectivity in formulating policy! Thus, in contrast to many other fields, it was somehow more acceptable and objective to learn about the "other" through "outsiders," (including government representatives of authoritarian regimes and secular Muslim elites who often represented not more than 10-20% of the population) books, government cable traffic and newspaper clippings than through firsthand experience. It took years before I could fully appreciate and ask in response an equally valid question. Why did we presume that non-Muslim professors, who in the past were Christian ministers, missionaries or the children of missionaries, or non-believers, provided more "objective" perspectives? How could academic or government experts analyze, judge and recommend policies for peoples they assiduously avoided and did not know? Isn't our first obligation to understand as fully and accurately as possible, to be able to explain the faith, values, beliefs and practices of others to make informed judgments? If so, what better way to begin than by engaging Islam through Muslims themselves?

Isma'il and Lamia al Faruqi were central to my Temple experience; they took a personal interest in all of the students. Their home was always open for visits and celebrations. It was a wonderful older, very spacious home in the Philadelphia suburbs. Lamia's expertise in Islamic art was reflected in beautiful décor. Often, rather than meeting at his office, we would meet at Isma'il's home where advice was always complemented by incredible hospitality: great fruit drinks, meals, desserts... The friendship and hospitality were reflected in the fact that more often than not, my wife Jean would join us. He always managed to strike the right balance between directing and guiding me as a grad student but also recognizing and respecting that I was an assistant professor in my early 30s. As a result we would discuss many of his projects and he would involve me in his AAR Islamic Studies Steering Committee as well as the meetings at Muslim organizations, many of which he had helped to establish, like the Muslim Students Association (MSA), AMSS, and others. This was also a time when in America the notion of religious dialogue between Jews and Christians expanded to include an introduction for the first time of a trialogue of Jews, Christians and Muslims.

A little known fact was Isma'il's willingness to become involved in a project to free the American hostages held in our embassy in Teheran. I had been asked to undertake a project supported by a wealthy Unitarian Church to put together a delegation of Muslim scholars/leaders who would go to Iran and attempt to convince Ayatollah Khomeini to intervene with the captors and free our hostages. Isma'il, like many Muslims and non-Muslims alike, had been a supporter of the revolution. Although he was very concerned about who might really be behind the initiative (whether it might actually be the CIA or some other intelligence agency) that of course might discredit participants as government agents and undermine the project, in the end, he was willing to trust me.

Soon we were off to Geneva to attend an international Muslim meeting at which he and I worked hard to recruit and convince a small group of internationally prominent Muslims who would have credibility with Khomeini and the Iranians to join our efforts. After several days we were able to put together a group that would first fly to London to spend a few days discussing the approach to be taken and the best way to proceed. At 3 am the morning we were to leave, I was awakened by a phone call informing me that the Unitarian church that was supposed to fund the trip had gotten cold feet because there were no firm assurances of its success!

IV. From Brooklyn to Beirut

My study with Isma'il and experience at Temple proved invaluable when I began to travel and speak to the Muslim world. I was the first Ampart (American participant) sponsored by USIA, the cultural wing of the State department, to lecture on Islam in Muslim countries. Initially there was some internal debate. Was it wise to have an American, and worse a non-Muslim, attempt to do this in Muslim countries? Wasn't USIA's mission to promote American culture and what of the risk that this new venture would backfire?

To the delight of all, the experiment proved to be a success. Muslim audiences were often initially skeptical and suspicious of this American, non-Muslim scholar. Why was I there? What was my real agenda? Was I an American agent? The situation was compounded by the fact that in these early days, I had no "name recognition," no track record, no professional reputation and no books that preceded me. For most Muslims (and ironically for most non-Muslims) my choice of profession made no sense. Why was I interested in Islam and Muslims? Why had I made Islamic studies a career if I was not a

Muslim? Ironically these were the same questions family and friends had asked for different reasons.

My ability to understand and explain Islam "from within" countered the stereotype of indifferent or anti-Muslim western scholarship and the legacy of some well-informed but ill-intentioned Orientalists. This was not only personally gratifying but also important because I wanted to signal that there was indeed a new breed of scholars. We understand Islam, can explain it in a manner that Muslims find authentic, and are not motivated by missionary or political agendas. My credibility was enhanced not only by my demonstrated knowledge of Islam but also and most importantly by my academic pedigree, the fact that my mentor, Isma'il al Faruqi, was a prominent and respected Muslim scholar. The situation would be enhanced in later years as more and more of Isma'il al Faruqi's Temple's graduate students from the Muslim world returned to their countries. Indeed, at a conference that Georgetown's Center for Muslim-Christian Understanding organized on Southeast Asian Islam in Kuala Lumpur in the 1990s I was introduced as the "Don of Temple's mafia," a reminder that I had been the first PhD in Islam and more importantly of the many graduates from Southeast Asia who had earned their degrees and returned to important jobs in academia and in government.

Because of my Muslim teachers and colleagues, I had instant access when I traveled abroad to younger generations of Muslims and Muslim organizations, many of whom would become prominent figures in what would later be called the Islamic revival or Islamic fundamentalism. At the time they were not among those that area specialists, social scientists, or Islamicists (who tended to emphasize language, text, and a classical approach rather than modern or contemporary orientation, some might even say "fixation") studied. Among them were the Sorbonne educated Dr. Hasan Turabi, Dean of the University of Khartoum Law School. He would become leader of Sudan's Muslim Brotherhood, a prominent Muslim reformer internationally, powerful political leader in Sudan, and labeled the Ayatollah of Africa by his critics. Another Sudanese was Sadiq al-Mahdi, the Oxford educated great grandson of the Mahdi of the Sudan, the great Sufi (mystic) leader whose eighteenth-century Islamic movement was the genesis of the modern Sudanese state. Anwar Ibrahim, the charismatic founder of the Youth Movement of Malaysia, would become Deputy Prime Minister and a major reformist voice in Southeast Asia before his imprisonment by Malaysia's authoritarian Prime Minister Mahathir Mohammed. Khurshid Ahmad would for decades be a Vice President of the Jamaat-i-Islami in Pakistan, a father of Islamic economics, and a voice of Islam in the West where he established a major Islamic center, the Islamic Foundation, in Leicester, England. Abdurrahman Wahid, an Indonesian intellectual and religious leader of the Nahdlatul Ulama in Indonesia, whose 25 million followers made it one of the largest Islamic organizations in the world, would become a major opposition leader to the Suharto regime and Indonesia's first democratically elected president.

The most important lesson I have learned from my experience at Temple and as a student of Isma'il's and many years an academic is the most obvious and yet elusive. If you want to know what people believe, if you want to grasp the reality of everyday life, you have to combine text and context. Understanding the faith of others requires knowledge of the sacred sources of a religion (scriptures, creeds, dogmas, and laws) but equally important what people *actually* believe and do! Appreciation of the essentials of a religion cannot exclude awareness of the diversity of its forms and expressions and lived experience.

We celebrate the fiftieth anniversary of Temple Department of Religion and our experiences and memories for many reasons. But these all stem from a visionary experiment and accomplishment: 1) It created in contrast to obtaining a doctorate from a theological faculty in a seminary/university, a unique PhD at a secular university in the academic study of religion; 2) In contrast to most PhD programs with traditional specialty areas within a specific religion, Temple pioneered a graduate program that required a major in one religion and a minor in two others. This approach produced teacher-scholars for late twentieth- and twenty-first centuries, trained to teach a world religion course that would soon become a "bread and butter" course in most colleges and university departments of religion, as well as courses in several religions. This made its graduates particularly marketable in the 1970s and 1980s (and today) in two very different contexts. In response to significant student interest and demand, religion departments and even theology departments at colleges and universities moved beyond their usual focus on Christianity and Judaism and did so again in response to the global resurgence of religion in personal but also in domestic and global politics. And in those periods when retrenchment in hiring has occurred or when departments are belatedly "opening up" to introducing "other religions," Temple graduates have had a leg up with training and teaching abilities in multiple religions in contrast to those with more narrowly defined degrees which restricted their training and teaching abilities within a single religion's scripture, theology (historical, systematic, moral), or law. The Temple experience offers a "win-win experience," innovative program, many dedicated teachers, the study of several religious traditions which trained us to also think, see, and analyze comparatively, and, for many of us, a more marketable credential.

BREAKTHROUGH TO DIALOGUE

RECOLLECTIONS OF A STUDENT FROM EARLY TIME OF TUDOR

KANA MITRA

I was a student of TUDOR in a very exciting time of the department. It was a relatively new department. It had a very diverse faculty and student body. I shall try to briefly describe my personal story of the benefits I received and the challenges that I faced during my time at the department.

At that time the course requirements were broad. We had to study at least one of Abrahamic and one of the religions of the East, besides courses on methodology and social sciences. Of course, there was the language requirement.

Personally, I had a great admiration for Christianity. The first school that I went to was a Protestant Christian school. I studied the Bible there as a child. There was no conflict between the moral codes that I learned in school and in my Hindu home. The only conflict that I encountered was about one God and many gods of Hinduism. I asked my mother who did not have much formal schooling, about it. She said that all these gods of the Hindus are different manifestations of the one God. At that time I did not know of the Vedic statement, *ekam sat vipra bahudha vadanti*—"truth is one, people call it by various names."

My admiration for Christianity was not simply because of what I understood to be the Biblical teaching, but also due to my encounter with many Christians. Although I was born in British India, the Christians that I met were not the colonialists but kind and openhearted missionaries. I was deeply impressed with some Fathers of Don Bosco. Coming to Temple, my encounter was with similar types of Christians. As a matter of fact, I entered in the program in the department due to their influence.

In the course offerings, I studied more courses on Christianity than on any other religions. One challenge about Christianity was the doctrine of the "one way." I tried to under-stand it not simply intellectually, but I seriously made the effort to do what John Dunn said about "passing over." Through all these efforts, I could not feel any need, nor did I see any reason to join any church. In the course of my study of Christianity I was also reflecting deeply on my tradition and received many insights.

In the department there was also the opportunity for dialogue with different faiths. As a matter of fact the *JES*, the journal that is associated with the department, has dialogue as its mission. I am grateful for the opportunity that I received to listen to the great thinkers that dealt with the issue of plurality of religions. Of course, each of them dealt with the issue differently. I was very much attracted to Raimundo Pannikar's way of dealing with plurality. I wrote my PhD dissertation on him. The challenge of the one and the many was settled for me by the opportunity of studying at TUDOR.

Another challenge that troubled me that is still unresolved is the divide between Western and Eastern way of thinking. In the Western religious thought, "enlightenment" is a big challenge. What is the role of reason and scientifically empirical discoveries in religion? The traditional idea in the West was that religion deals with faith and if science or rationality challenges it, one has to reject one or the other. I am really simplifying it too much. My study did familiarize me with many maneuvers that are made by so many theologians to reconcile them.

In the case of Hinduism and Buddhism, scientific discovery or application of critical thinking is not really a challenge in the same way. Buddha remained silent on the questions about God and how everything began. Hindus have many stories including agnostic rumination. Darwin's research and thought did not pose a problem in the same way as it did to the Abrahamic traditions. Of course, everything being interconnected, these thoughts and discoveries influenced the East as well, but differently. Thus, it is true that a butterfly flaps its wings and a bridge falls down. In Hinduism and Buddhism reasoning is pushed to its limits so that intuitive wisdom may dawn.

The choice of the method for studying religion is a big challenge for everyone who wants to study religion as a distinctive aspect of human life and not to reduce it to a psychological, social, or any other aspect of human life. Human life is complex and includes so many aspects that are interrelated that it is almost impossible to study them separately. In our department there were some scholars who de-emphasized the sacred, which, in my judgment, is the distinctive aspect of religion. I did not have enough skill in communication to convey my concern in a way that could be understood. There was similar difficulty in communication about the teachings and ideologies of Hinduism and Buddhism.

During the early years of the academic studies of religion, efforts were to discover similarities rather than differences of religions. I wrote a paper comparing Buddhist Nagarjuna with Christian Karl Barth and could find similarities between these two who at first sight seemed to be absolutely different. These days the emphasis is on highlighting the differences that are absolutely irreconcilable. Religion is more like applied science than purely theoretical science. It has implications not only for individuals but also on a particular as well as global society. Religion has tremendous power that can be used either constructively or destructively. Finding similarities can be reconciliatory, without overlooking the differences. This is a difficult issue that needs serious consideration.

REFLECTIONS OF THE STRANGER IN THE LAND (LEV 19:34)

THOMAS L. THOMPSON

I. The Quickest

The reason I have been asked to contribute this essay is that I entered the doctoral program at Temple in September, 1975 and defended my dissertation in May, 1976. Nine months for a PhD! The twenty-year record, which Kunihiku Terasawa established in 2012, lends contrast to my fleeting passage. It bears witness to TUDOR's commitment to depth and competence, not to patience. My record bears witness to TUDOR's treatment of the stranger in the land.

II. Losing Ones' Innocence

I first met Leonard Swidler as my undergraduate history teacher at Duquesne University in Pittsburgh more than fifty years ago. Common interests in history and theology provided the basis for a cherished friendship. His commitment to ecumenism and critical theology (for Catholics!) was shared by my interests in intellectual history and European scholarship. While I was taken up with philosophy and literature and spent most of my time reading from Hegel and Husserl to Joyce's revolutionary streams of consciousness, Leonard signed slips for me that I might borrow Feuerbach, Marx, and Sartre from the library (at Duquesne University, a Catholic university, those volumes were locked in a library cage because they were on the *Index of Forbidden Books*, still in force until Vatican II in 1962-65—Swidler). My absorption in Husserl, the leftist Hegelians and existentialism transformed my flight from my immigrant Irish roots to a fully-functional, critical perspective of religion and its social controls, which helped me steer my interest in things religious, without having a corresponding piety. My access to the library's stash of forbidden books produced my first academic article on Feuerbach and existentialism. It dealt with a theme to which, upon retirement, I returned a few years ago in my lecture.[1]

Leonard urged me to pursue graduate studies in Europe—especially Tübingen—and, responding to this support, John Wright, then bishop of Pittsburgh, offered to sponsor my studies in the, to him, more palatable Oxford. Austin Farrer was, indeed, a far cry from Tübingen's Hans Küng, but his beautiful lectures on biblical allegory and his dogged critique of the gospel scholarship's chimerical "Q" has had a dominant, subliminal influence on my exegetical work to this day.[2] I fell in love with Oxford, but by Christmas, my Feuerbach article had reached England and was read. Messages crossed the Atlantic and my princely patron became "concerned." Blackfriars' Professor of Moral Theology read my article and set the topic of Thomistic ethics for my orals, followed with an offer I could not refuse: "If you decide to move to Germany, you can be sure you go with my blessing." I wrote to friends in Tübingen. This, however, met resistance from my patron. Reports of "disturbing intellectual tendencies" and "spiritual immaturity" had reached Pittsburgh. I was ordered to Innsbruck to study under the world renowned, but theologically known and measured, Karl Rahner. I would live with the Jesuits and "learn the importance of prayer, obedience and humility." A train ticket to Salzburg arrived by

---

[1] T. L. Thompson, "Towards a Theology of Existence," *Philosophy Today* (Summer, 1962), 1-15; idem, "Imago Dei: A Problem of Pentateuchal Discourse," *Scandinavian Journal of the Old Testament* 23/1 (2009), 135-148.

[2] See, especially, Austin Farrer, *A Study in St. Mark* (Westminster: Dacre Press, 1951); T. L. Thompson, The Mythic Past: Biblical Archaeology and the Myth of Israel (*Basic Books*: 1999) and The Messiah Myth: The Ancient Near Eastern Roots of Jesus and David (*Basic Books:* 2005).

post, with instructions to participate in a six-week summer course in German. As poor as I was, I was doubly dependent on "my bishop." I could neither stay in Oxford nor return to Pittsburgh. Checkmate! Necessity overcame pride and independence. I found merit in silence and boarded my train for a breathtakingly brilliant summer in Salzburg. Authenticity and integrity needs must wait the *summer* out.

III. Theology's Asparagus Bed

I am pleased to be able to say that my resolve held through the summer and into August, when, together with a friend, I hitch-hiked to Tübingen. I arrived on a Thursday morning with $5 in my pocket. We went immediately to the bulletin postings at the student cafeteria, where we found a room offered without cost, against 8 hours housework in the French military zone on the edge of town. The captain's wife who answered the door was surprised and uncertain, but as soon as I saw her living room spread with Iranian carpets, I was determined to convince her I was perfect for the role as her French maid! What female student would beat her carpets? Over lunch, we reached an agreement: I beat carpets every other week and on Saturdays, I would assist in preparing a full-course spread for her weekly dinner party (pots and pans and playing the silent waiter!). In turn, I lived in an attic room, with a bath in the hall, shared by the building's three other maids. Next, I needed a job. The German miracle had already begun and, a few houses away, house painters were painting a ground-floor apartment. I presented myself to the boss and told him I was a student and wanted work. For him, that was a contradiction. Students were allergic to work! More in *volapük*[3] than German, I convinced him that I was different. I just had time to rush to the stores before closing to buy overalls. The following

---

[3] Constructed language based initially on German
https://en.wikipedia.org/wiki/Volap%C3%BCk

morning at 6:30 AM I was in his truck and on my way to my life as an independent scholar.

I lived in Tübingen the following twelve years, the first half of which I divided between the university's Catholic and Protestant faculties, supported by an openness which allowed me to work closely with both Herbert Haag (Catholic Faculty) and Kurt Galling (Protestant Faculty) over the next six years, while attending lectures and seminars by such diverse scholars as Elliger, Gese and Kuschke, Käsemann, Michel and Schelkle, Küng, Ratzinger, Moltmann, Jüngl, Oberman, Greinacher and others. Theology had for me many voices as I followed the shifting perspectives of a common tradition, which was ever more complex than any single voice or conviction could acknowledge. My Catholic longing for a wider world fed happily in Tübingen's asparagus bed. Of course, the openness of Tübingen's theological garden was also fragile and passing and, at the end of this intellectually transforming decade of the 1960s, shared the fate of Isaiah's divine garden (Isa 5:1-7)! Its walls began to crumble soon after the publication of Hans Küng's *Unfehlbar?* in 1970.[4] Despite its question mark, *Unfehlbar?* was met with an implacable smear campaign, which closed the window of openness that Catholic theology had so briefly and breathlessly experienced in the 1960s.[5] The reaction of the 1970s turned decidedly in the direction of sectarian fundamentalism, with irrational presuppositions and intolerance towards critical thought, which have divided Catholic theology intolerably these past 40 years. Censorship returned and, until today, many Catholic authors can hardly be cited nor can their

---

[4] Hans Küng, *Unfehlbar?* (Zürich: Benzinger, 1970); see, especially, the *Taschenbuchausgabe* from 1989, with forward from Herbert Haag (Munich: Piper).

[5] Norbert Greinacher and Herbert Haag, *Der Fall Küng: Eine Dokumentation* (Munich: Piper, 1980).

books be distributed. Appointments to theological chairs in Austria, Switzerland or Germany continue to reflect papal interests.[6]

Two years after beginning research on my dissertation in the Catholic faculty in 1967, I was appointed as a research fellow in the inter-disciplinary project of the *Tübinger Atlas des vorderen Orients* (*TAVO*) and was housed in Kurt Galling's *Biblisch-archäologisches Institut* in the Protestant faculty. This happily isolated me from the witch hunt against Küng and his students. My participation in the *TAVO* project, where I was responsible for creating historical maps of the Bronze Age in the Sinai, Negev, and Palestine, radically shifted my research away from theology and towards history; to a geographical, anthropological, and economic analysis of ancient settlement patterns, which were based on regional archaeological surveys.[7] In this work, I needed to use a different kind of analysis, one which enabled me to discuss the contingencies for settlement and development in a pre-historic Palestine. This work took me to the Middle East for several months of research each year. Here, my daily very specific questions of agricultural potential through the analysis of the relationship between soils, water resources, and aridity and the changing patterns of settlement, changed how I looked at the project of early history of the ancient world.[8] Religion was only one aspect

---

[6] See the introduction of Herbert Haag: "Eine unerledigte Anfrage," to Hans Küng, *Unfehlbar?* (Munich: Piper, 1989), v-vi.

[7] In the early 1970s, such research was encouraged particularly by the surveys of Moshe Kochavi on the West Bank and Rudolph Cohen in the Negev and the Sinai. For their final published reports, see Moshe Kochavi, *Judea, Samaria and the Golan: Archaeological Survey 1967-1968* (Jerusalem: IES, 1972). Rudolph Cohen, and R. Cohen-Amin, *Ancient Settlement of the Central Negev*, vol. 1: *The Chalcolithic Period, The Early Bronze Age and the Middle Bronze Age I IAA Report 6* (Jerusalem: IES, 1999); Rudolph Cohen and R. Cohen-Amin, *Ancient Settlement of the Negev Highlands*, vol. 2: *The Iron Age and the Persian Period, IAA Report 20* (Jerusalem: IES, 2004).

[8] Thomas L. Thompson, *The Bronze Age Settlement of Sinai and the Negev*, BTAVO 8 (Wiesbaden: Dr. Reichert Verlag, 1975); idem, *Palästina in der*

of an anthropology which needed to be construed on the basis of archaeological and geographical evidence. The distance of my historical work on the Bronze Age from biblical literature was significant. My dissertation, which was increasingly centered in the associations' contemporary scholarship, had claimed between the patriarchal narratives of Genesis and Palestine's Bronze Age was radically transformed by my work on *TAVO*. This historical-geographical study of the Bronze Age was closely related to the archaeological evidence from that period. Methodologically, my dissertation moved considerably away from what was ordinary for theological dissertations, rooted as it was in an entirely different paradigm. I finished the dissertation in June of 1971, drawing the conclusion that the patriarchal narratives were not only entirely irrelevant to Palestine's Bronze Age, dated to a period postdating Israel's presence in Palestine, but also that they were essentially unhistorical, rooted in folklore and myth.

The conclusion of my dissertation drew me inevitably into the conflicts of the Catholic faculty. The dissertation was judged by professors Haag and Galling and was accepted *summa cum laude*. I was free to seek publication and prepare myself for my doctoral oral examinations, set for the early Autumn of 1972. The dissertation, however, attracted both interest and support, not only from the Protestant faculty, but also from the Catholic research center, the École Biblique in Jerusalem, who invited me to give an eight-hour compact course on my thesis to their students. This first public presentation of my dissertation was attended by professors Avraham

---

Frühbronzezeit, TAVO B II 11a (Wiesbaden: Dr. Reichert Verlag, 1978); idem, *Palästina in der Übergangszeit der Frühbronze/Mittelbronzezeit, TAVO B II 11b* (1978); idem, *The Settlement of Palestine in the Bronze Age, BTAVO 34* (Wiesbaden: Dr. Reichert Verlag, 1979); idem, *Palästina in der Mittelbronzezeit, TAVO B II 11c* (1980); idem, *Palästina in der Spätbronzezeit, TAVO B II 11d*.

Malamat and Shalom Paul of the Hebrew University, who offered both encouragement and advice for further research.

Unfortunately, this early interest encouraged Tübingen's Professor Joseph Ratzinger to read the work. In a discussion in preparation for my oral exams in dogmatic theology, he told me that a Catholic could not write such a dissertation in Tübingen. Then, in the examination itself, he confronted me with my dissertation's conclusion that the narratives of the Pentateuch were mythic and folkloric, rather than historical: "Where do you find revelation in the Book of Exodus?" In answer, I turned to the story of the golden calf in Exodus 32-34 to argue against any such historicized Bible implied by his question. It was not revelation so much as a story about revelation: Moses descended the mountain with two tablets, a revelation written by the very finger of God himself. However, when he heard the noise of the people and saw the calf and the dancing, Moses' anger reiterated Yahweh's (cf. Ex 32:19 with 32:10).[9] It grew hot and he "threw God's tablets from his hands and broke them" (Ex 32:15-19). The Torah comes, not with Yahweh's tablets, but afterwards, when Moses takes up two stone tablets of his own and replaces the originals. It is not Yahweh, but Moses who writes on these tablets "the words of the covenant, the ten commandments" (Ex 34:28). What we have is not revelation, but myth, transmitting a parable and an allegory. What we think of as divine revelation of the *Torah* does not present us with an objective or historical God, but merely an author'sunderstanding of God, transmitted through human and limited experiences.[10] God is a god of tradition, but neither of history nor event. In the *Torah*, he is Emanuel, i.e., God as he was

---

[9] Thomas L. Thompson, "Imago Dei: A Problem in Pentateuchal Discourse," *Scandinavian Journal of the Old Testament* 23/1 (2009), 135-148.

[10] Thomas L. Thompson, "How Yahweh Became God: Exodus 3 and 6 and the Center of the Pentateuch," *Scandinavian Journal of the Old Testament* 8/1 (1994), 1-19.

known to Israel (*'ehyeh 'imak*: Ex 3:12; Isa 7:14; Matt 1:23).[11] The revelation in the parable of Exodus 34 as of Exodus 3 is Moses. That we may call it "revelation" is ever an assertion of faith.

Within the context of an examination in dogmatic theology, this answer was disastrous and doomed to confirm his judgment that such a PhD could not be accepted in Tübingen. I answered his challenge, knowing the answer's consequence and thereby effectively marking the coming confrontation of critical Old Testament studies and its theological past with a clarity that still surprises me. In my naïve effort to reiterate the biblical text's voice, my oral examination projected the coming debate in Old Testament studies which decisively changed our perspectives of the Bible so thoroughly. I hardly was prepared for such conflict. In looking for a publisher, my dissertation was quickly rejected by the monograph series of both the Catholic *Biblical Quarterly* and the *Society of Biblical Literature*, the former, because it lacked a proper recommendation and the latter for its critique of "Biblical Archaeology." Kurt Galling then recommended it to Georg Fohrer for publication in the *Beihefte zur Zeitscrift für die alttestamentliche Wischenschaft* and it was published in early 1974 as: *The Historicity of the Patriarchal Narratives: The Quest for the Historical Abraham*.

The earliest, largely negative, reviews of my dissertation[12] concentrated on the temerity of my break with the scholarly consensus of archaeologists and American biblical scholars. At the same time, the methodological distance between the stories of the Pentateuch and the world one met in writing a history of Palestine's Bronze Age was so great that it influenced my work on the settlement

---

[11] Ibid.

[12] The very earliest of which I am aware was John Huesman's presidential address to the Catholic Biblical Association in the summer of 1974: "Archaeology and Early Israel: The Scene Today," published in *Catholic Biblical Quarterly* 34 (1975), 1-16.

patterns of the Bronze Age deeply. As the efforts of Haag and Galling, together with friends and colleagues, to find a compromise with the Catholic faculty eventually failed, the development of my work on the Atlas project engaged the whole of my attention. My dissertation's concluding demand that we develop our history of Palestine independently of biblical narratives required just such a project! There were no large arm movements, but I began with a limited and modest effort to construct a brief narrative of change, based on the data we had for transhumance pastoralism in the Sinai and the Negev.[13] The more ambitious but still limited regional history of Palestine's early agriculture was projected for my Palestine study.[14] As my work on the Atlas project moved towards its first publication, I turned my thoughts towards returning to the States. My former wife Prof. Dorothy Irvin was offered a teaching post in Philadelphia, which began in September of 1974. I stayed on in Tübingen for a few months to finish the *TAVO* supplement to the Sinai and Negev maps and made arrangements to work on the monograph for the Palestine maps from Philadelphia.

IV. Love Notes from an Admirer

Once in Philadelphia, Leonard urged me to come to Temple and finish my PhD there. I was reluctant, with little trust in theologians. How would Temple be different from Tübingen? Leonard pressed his argument, with all the persuasive guile of an experienced ecumenist. A meeting with Robert Wright (Hebrew Bible—Swidler) and Gerard Sloyan (New Testament—Swidler), promised the acceptance of my dissertation without prejudice, though it was already published and could not be influenced in any significant way by the examiners. We also agreed that, upon fulfilling a two-semester residency and other requirements for the PhD at Temple, I would be allowed to stand for

---

[13] Thompson, *The Settlement of Sinai and the Negev*, 5-30.
[14] Thompson, *The Settlement of Palestine*, 5-67.

the oral doctoral examinations and dissertation defense. We also agreed that I be examined in ancient Near Eastern Studies, Hebrew Bible and New Testament and attend appropriate courses in Hebrew Bible, New Testament and Islam during the 1975/1976 academic year. The absence of a specifically church-related discipline won my trust.

My "Catholic" teacher, Gerard Sloyan, was taken up with historical Jesus studies (particularly in regard to the suffering and death stories of the gospels), though he also gave much time in popular lectures and articles criticizing the Catholic obsession with sex. This earned him many harsh reviews from the Catholic right. I admired his reading of the passion narratives and not least his treatment of the rhetorical and stereotypical thematic elements in these narratives, which later influenced my own study of some of the central themes in the ancient Near Eastern myth of the Messiah.[15] I was even more impressed by the openness of students and other teachers at Temple to the kinds of questions Gerry raised, not only within a Catholic perspective, but as an integral part of Temple's ecumenical discussion. This same openness impressed me in Bob Wright's lectures, which engaged most of my time. His research—engaged in a new translation of the Psalms of Solomon and its Hellenistic context—was about as far from my Bronze Age as one could imagine. His method of handling translation and exegetical problems were evidence-based and so distant from the theological concerns so dominant among the Catholic professors in Tübingen. In this rather stressful period of my life, I was grateful to Bob for his consistent support and advice as the mobbing of my *Historicity* grew both in volume and rhetoric in the winter of 1975-1976.[16] I was most

---

[15] Thomas L. Thompson, *The Messiah Myth: The Ancient Near Eastern Roots of Jesus and David* (New York: Basic Books, 2005).

[16] Typical was the lecture of Dean McBride of Yale at the Philadelphia regional meeting of the Society of Biblical Literature in the spring of 1976.

impressed in my brief stay at Temple with the lectures of the Palestinian professor of Islamic studies, Isma'il al Faruqi. As a Muslim and Palestinian, he walked a narrow, mine-filled path, connecting him to his colleagues, a path which uncertainly joined Islam to Judaism in mutual respect. It was a path which I had first begun to explore when working in Palestine with *TAVO*, moving each day for months between East and West Jerusalem and seeing daily far more than I wished. I often wondered whether his frequent preoccupation with Christian ethics was the result of a strategic decision to find some "neutral" ground, from which he could engage Christianity and Islam's Jewish roots with respect. Al Faruqi, in his critique of Zionism in its revision of Judaism and its highest values, supplied me with a key for addressing a problem which infested every aspect of my work in regard to biblical narrative and the history of Palestine, where the Zionist history of origins has not only been in conflict with modern critical scholarship, but also has intentionally distorted that narrative and history.

Al Faruqi was quite unhappy with my *Historicity*—though he liked what I was doing with Palestine's history. Bob and I often disagreed and Gerry found my Greek decidedly unimpressive. I must confess a bout of panic on my very last day as student. Arriving early in the morning for the oral defense of my dissertation, I learned that Professor James Ross, a well-known archaeologist from Virginia Theological Seminary, who had specialized in the Middle Bronze Period over the previous 25 years and a prominent member of the "Albright school," was to take part in my oral examination as my "opponent." My panic gradually receded as we proceeded through a debate that covered most aspects of the dissertation. Now, many years later, I look back on this sometimes heated debate with gratitude. It prepared me well for the much harsher debates which continued for ten years. Temple was never boring. Its openness and acceptance of so many differences created habits and expectations which I have never abandoned.

V. A Stranger in His Own Land

Following the publication of John Van Seters' *Abraham in History and Tradition*,[17] with its clearly independent evaluation of the relation of the patriarchal narratives to the Bronze Age and a bold revision of the dating of the Yahwist tradition in Pentateuchal criticism to the sixth century BCE, the debate concerning Israel's origins and Pentateuch's origin stories intensified. But it also began to influence an increasingly wide range of issues, most noticeably support for the historicity of biblical origin stories in Pentateuch, Joshua, and Judges, which were set within a pre-monarchic period. Already in 1977, J. Maxwell Miller and John Hayes published a comprehensive collection of articles reflecting a considerable "paradigm shift" in Old Testament studies. With its title, *Israelite and Judean History*,[18] this book not only separated the history of Israel from that of Judah, but questioned every "period" of what had been considered Israel's early history, from Abraham through the United Monarchy. Of equal importance, these essays all accepted the separation of biblical and archaeological analysis, which I had stressed in the conclusions of my *Historicity*. This was now expanded to a demand for the independence of Palestinian archaeology from biblical studies, that is, an end to biblical archaeology.[19] The field had changed, and new perspectives had begun to govern our research.

---

[17] J. Van Seters, *Abraham in History and Tradition* (New Haven: Yale University Press, 1975).

[18] J. H. Hayes and J. M. Miller, *Israelite and Judean History* (Westminster: Philadelphia, 1977).

[19] Thompson, *Historicity*, 320-321; idem, "Historical Notes on Israel's Conquest of Palestine," *Journal for the Study of the Old Testament* 7 (1978), 20-27; idem, "The Background of the Patriarchs: A Reply to William Dever and Malcolm Clark," *Journal for the Study of the Old Testament* 9 (1978), 76-84; see also W. G. Dever, "Retrospects and Prospects in Biblical and Syro-Palestinian Archaeology" *BA* (1982), 103-107.

Not all greeted such changes with a welcome. The patterns which the opposition took reflected the divisions which had long plagued Hebrew Bible studies. Those most opposed to such change were conservative Catholics, American and Israeli, from evangelical conservatives to Jewish and Christian Zionists, but also including the "Albright School," committed to the traditions of "Biblical Archaeology." After completing my work on the *Tübinger Atlas* in 1977, I found myself unemployable in the American universities for nearly a decade. This long period of drought, however, was interrupted by an invitation from the Catholic Biblical Association as annual Professor at the École Biblique for the Fall semester of 1985. Unfortunately, the École paid a considerable price for inviting me. It was during this stay that accusations of antisemitism were first linked to my *Historicity* book. Such slander increased when I extended my work with the École a further six months to develop a pilot proposal for analyzing modern toponymic changes in Palestine and concluded that the Israeli committee on place names must be criticized for its systematic de-Arabicization of Palestinian toponymy—often at serious cost to the region's ancient cultural heritage.[20]

When I returned to the States in June, 1986, I received a National Endowment Fellowship in January 1987 to write a monograph on the history of Palestine, which was to dominate my research through the following years.[21] While spending nine weeks of research at the Oriental Institute library of the University of Chicago, I shared my lunch hour with Gösta Ahlström, who was finishing his *History of Palestine*. He shared my ambition of writing a history that was

---

[20] Eventually published with F. Goncalvez as *Toponomie Palestinienne: Plaine de St Jean D'Acre et Corridor de Jérusalem* (Louvaine-La-Neuve: Institut Orientaliste, 1988), 90.

[21] Eventually published as: Thomas L. Thompson, E*arly History of the Israelite People from the Written and Archaeological Sources* (Leiden: Brill, 1992).

independent of the biblical mythology.[22] His recommendation enabled me to take a one-year appointment to teach at Lawrence University in Appleton, Wisconsin. This was followed by a tenure-track appointment at Marquette University, which began in September, 1989. At Marquette, I finally felt that I had come home—not only to the American Midwest of my childhood, but to a Catholic University, where I could draw on the whole of my experience in my teaching and writing. I was happy there, working with my students and developing a graduate seminar, where students were drawn into discourse with visiting scholars and important new works. When I came up for tenure in 1992, I felt assured of support from most of my colleagues.

I did not calculate the effects of my *Early History,* when it first appeared, early in 1992. It was released with an extraordinary review on the front pages of two London papers: *The Independent on Sunday* and the *Sunday Times* and that review spread everywhere you might imagine! It was lengthy and detailed and took pains to present the main themes of this monograph, which had begun with a 170 page *Stand der Forschung* on the Old Testament scholarship's failed efforts to write a history of either Palestine or Israel! I struggled, without success, to understand either the decision of these two editors of prominent British newspapers or the results of that decision as they affected me. The central goal of the monograph—beyond the argument about our failure to write an adequate history—was the sketch of a regional and archaeologically based history of Bronze and Iron Age Palestine, as independent of the biblical narrative as I could manage. It drew some conclusions which were hard to dismiss: 1) that it was unlikely an ethnicity as expressed by the biblical "Israel" could have existed before the Persian period; 2) that the biblical concept of Israel as a people was dependent on a self-understanding

---

[22] G. Ahlstrom, *The History of Ancient Palestine from the Palaeolithic Period to Alexander's Conquest* (Sheffield: JSOT Press, 1993).

of exile; 3) that there was no substantial historicity of the narratives from Genesis to 2 Kings; and 4) that the Bible is best understood as a literary product of the late Persian or early Hellenistic period. "The Debate," full of heated conflict, charges of willful distortion, incompetence and antisemitism followed immediately and dominated much of the field over the next decade. Immediately, it resulted for me in a denial of tenure.

Elijah's angels, however, cared for me. In mid-May, 1993, having concluded my last lecture at Marquette, I arrived in Copenhagen to take up Eduard Nielsen's chair of Old Testament studies.

VI. Changing Perspectives in Old Testament Studies

I was 54 years old when I arrived in Denmark. My points of contact were few and fragile, and I knew little of the land, its language or its traditions. I was a stranger—exiled from my own country and identity—and could hardly guess how I was to cope in a country I did not understand. I had met three of my colleagues—but could not say that I knew them. I did know that the theological faculty's primary teaching role was the training of priests for the Danish *Folkekirke,* within the Lutheran tradition, but I also knew that it was, nevertheless, independent of that church. Indeed, my own appointment confirmed that independence. I knew little else, as what I had read was much like what I had learned of the language: theory—without basis in reality. I do not think I could have then imagined that I would come to adopt Denmark as my "Fatherland."

It was not long before I could realize that Danish theology was without *mullahs*! Thoughts were neither controlled nor forbidden. Indeed, everyone had their opinion—and expected the teacher to have one too! Such a lack of sectarianism in the teaching and discourse in theology—which I had first experienced at Temple— including an acceptance of religion as well as of its absence was, in Copenhagen of the 1990s, a reality within a strikingly homogenous culture, open to a multi-cultural world. Such openness and freedom of thought, speech, and skepticism in regard to any special status, widespread disinterest in controlling others, and the freedom of students to control their own research and intellectual development were freedoms based in social principles which my colleagues shared as part of their culture. Many of the principles I had first experienced in Kurt Galling's Institute and in my work for the *Tübinger Atlas,* as at Temple, and had come to understand as necessary components for any freedom of research, were fundamental to the theology faculties in Copenhagen and throughout Scandinavia. As I integrated myself in Denmark, learned its language, and made it my home, I tried to make such principles my own—in writing and research, in lectures, seminars and examinations and in my relationships to both colleagues and students. I have become more Danish and, indeed, less American and less Catholic. Such loss is necessary if one wishes to participate in a wider, less sectarian and less controlled world.

One of my earliest projects after taking up my post in Copenhagen has been the editing of the academic monograph series, *Copenhagen International Seminar.* It is dedicated to the publication in English of works, which open new lines of research related to biblical studies, particularly undertaken by younger scholars of various scholarly traditions. I am pleased, with this series, that we have been able to support a number of first publications. We have also been able to bring some of the richness of Danish and Scandinavian scholarship to an international audience. We have also been able to publish a significant number of scholars, who are not themselves theologians—but anthropologists, archaeologists, historians, classicists and literary critics —and have brought some of their insights into biblical studies. In 2011, the *CIS* series expanded with the sub-series, *Changing Perspectives.* These publications of volumes are oriented towards the changes in perspective which have come about in the field of Old Testament studies over the past half-century and are dedicated to reflecting on the history of scholarship. I have tried to define the series as involving the republication of collected articles, which have either themselves changed perspectives within the field of Old Testament studies or which have significantly changed the perspective of their author.

I need to discuss one final development in my scholarship, which directly developed from the openness and integrity which I learned to cherish so deeply while at Temple. In 1995, my notorious 1992 book, *Early History,* was pirated by a Beirut publisher, translated into Arabic, and published. Because of this publication, I soon became engaged in mediating the changes which were developing in biblical studies and archaeology by giving and publishing a considerable number of lectures and articles in the Middle East, in Beirut, Damascus, Amman, Aleppo, Riyadh, Abu Dhabi, Ramallah and Jerusalem. This continued my engagement in Palestinian issues, which had first begun with my work on the projects of the *Tübinger Atlas* and *Toponomie Palestinienne.* It now took on more contemporary and more politically explicit implications. How grateful I have been for my discussions with Isma'il! What I had once argued so passionately for in my *Historicity of* 1974 and *Early History* of 1992—a history of Palestine, independent of the Bible's ethnocentric allegories—now had an engaged audience, which demanded a response with all of the integrity I could muster. In the years which have followed, personal relationships have gradually formed a commitment to an, as yet, unfinished project. (1) The translator and publisher of many of my books into Arabic, Ziad Mouna of Cadmus Publishing, (2) the great medieval and literary scholar and founder of East-West Nexus, Salma Khadra Jayyusi, who once planned with me and hosted a conference of, (primarily, western scholars on ancient Jerusalem and edited its results with me, and (3) Basem Ra"ad, the former dean of al-Quds University, have convinced me of the need for writing an ancient

History of Palestine for all Palestinians,[23] dedicated to the cultural heritage of the whole of Palestine's indigenous population, who, today, are Samaritans, Jews, Christians, Muslims and Druze: all with roots in Palestine's ancient past. It is a suitable project, I think, for a TUDOR alumnus.

---

[23] In the conception of this project I am indebted to Ilan Pappe, *A History of Modern Palestine* (Cambridge: Cambridge University Press, 2006), xix-xx.

LOOKING FORWARD

LEONARD SWIDLER

Over half a century ago TUDOR created a breakthrough in the study and teaching of religion, focusing on Dialogue and Critical-Thinking both from the inside and the outside. It was a part of the tsunami of positive change that was the "Sixties." In the religious field, doubtless the biggest breakthrough was that of the Second Vatican Council (1962-1965), which in a five-fold Copernican Turn committed the Catholic Church toward 1) freedom, 2) self-reform, 3) a focus on this world, 4) an embrace of a sense of history/change, and 5) dialogue with the Other. TUDOR, including its link with the Dialogue Pioneer *Journal of Ecumenical Studies/Dialogue Institute* was there at the same time, especially in its embrace of Dialogue/Critical-Thinking in the hiring of its multiple religious faculty, its multi-religious students, and commitment to critical scholarship.

The rest of American academia slowly followed TUDOR, and eventually the rest of the world also began to follow, embracing Dialogue. Breakthroughs in dialogue following in the 60/70s, especially intra-Christian, then Jewish-Christian, Christian-Marxist, Jewish-Christian-Muslim, then Hindu, Buddhist, Confucian . . . . A second major break toward Dialogue occurred with the fall of Communism and the end of the Cold War in 1990. The wave of Dialogue increasingly moved outside of narrow religious circles. Yet a third breakthrough began after the initial shock of 9/11 when the Muslim world began to flood into the Dialogue.

Clearly the world has always needed Dialogue. In 2016, the world is increasingly becoming aware that it desperately needs Dialogue—and not only in the area of religion, but also in all aspects of human life, including with the rest of nature.

Although all of the giants who launched TUDOR on its extraordinary path have either left teaching or this life (though I hardly count as "a giant"), they have not only produced an extraordinary model of how to study and teach religion in a dialogic and critical-thinking manner, but they have also shaped hundreds and thousands of leaders on all levels of the world who are not only carrying on the insights and breakthroughs they learned from those giants, and their successors.

Small select set of examples: One TUDOR PhD became the Foreign Minister of the third largest democracy of the world, Indonesia (Alwi Shihab); another became over many years a leading Member of Parliament of South Korea (Sunggon Kim); another became the Head Pastor of the largest megachurch in their world—over one million members!—Yoido Full Gospel Church in Seoul, Korea (Young Hoon Lee); another became the President of the *American Academy of Religion* (John Esposito)....

Further, those new leaders are also standing on the giants' shoulders and seeing new vistas, reaching for new goals, moving toward an ever-beckoning horizon, endlessly, toward the Infinite.

EPILOGUE

TERRY REY

PROFESSOR AND CHAIR OF THE RELIGION DEPARTMENT

How auspicious—or providential, or coincidental, or some combination thereof—that this scholarly experiment about the holy, the Department of Religion at Temple University, was launched in Pennsylvania, which itself was launched as a "holy experiment." The Quaker visionary William Penn staked his entire amazing life and considerable fortune on founding a society in the New World based on the principle of religious tolerance, with Philadelphia as its epicenter, thereby forging a colony unlike any the world had ever seen. His experiment was a first in American history, to boot. Exactly 200 years after Penn's initial landing, another visionary, this one a Baptist named Russell Conwell, arrived in Philadelphia in 1882 to pastor Grace Memorial Baptist Church and to mine "acres of diamonds" among the surrounding working class by providing them with a university education, also a first in American history. That church no longer stands, having been levelled, somewhat ironically, to make space for Anderson Hall, the building in which the department has resided since the early 1970s.

America's incomparably vibrant national religious diversity is arguably the result of the establishment clause of the First Amendment to the United States Constitution which prohibits the state from making any laws "respecting an establishment of religion," and the result of the spirit of entrepreneurship and ingenuity that its people have always possessed,[1] spirits that clearly drove Penn and

---

[1] R. Stephen Warner, "Work in Progress Toward a New Paradigm in the Sociological Study of Religion," *American Journal of Sociology* 98, 5, 1993, 1044-1093.

Conwell. That Amendment was written and passed in Philadelphia in the late eighteenth century, of course, where there were Quakers, Episcopalians, Catholics, Pietists, Lutherans, Presbyterians, Baptists, Methodists, Jews, Unitarians, and a whole assortment of religious others. That Amendment and the subsequent 1963 Supreme Court decision Abington School District v. Schempp which concerned one of Philadelphia's oldest suburbs would have far reaching effects for Temple University and its Department of Religion, and for the field of religious studies more generally. The justices ruled that the study of religion in a public school was acceptable as an integral part of the study of human history and culture.

Just two years later, Temple, which had been founded as a Baptist-affiliated college that eventually housed an interdenominational school of theology, gained state accreditation. As negotiations to transform itself from a private to a state institution unfolded, the implications for the school of theology were clear: It could no longer reside at Temple, hence its departure in 1958 and merger with a Baptist seminary in Massachusetts, which today is known as the Conwell-Gordon Theological Seminary. Thus, Temple's Department of Religion is in some respects the result of the First Amendment and Abington v. Schempp, as is the very field of religious studies.

In some respects, yes, but only some. The timing was uncanny, and the times were turbulent, as many youth in America questioned the values of their parents and their nation. Some turned to drugs and/or Eastern spirituality for alternative understandings of how we are to live as the war in Vietnam frayed America's soul, or whatever passes for it. But, in more substantive respects, the department owed (and owes) its legacy and reputation to the visionary insights of its founders, especially Ernest Stoeffler and Bernard Phillips. Stoeffler was a German church historian and Methodist minister, and Phillips was an American Jew who practiced Zen meditation. With no blueprint to employ in designing the department, they drew upon the spirit of perennialism that was then on the rise and quickly set out to populate its faculty with insiders; with, that is to say, expert scholars who practiced the faith traditions about which they wrote and taught. Hence, John Raines soon joined to teach Protestantism, Leonard Swidler to teach Catholicism, Bibhuti Yadav to teach Hinduism, Charles Fu to teach Chinese religions, Ismail al-Faruqi to teach Islam, and so on. By the late 1960s, there were over twenty scholars on the department faculty, with dozens of doctoral students in their seminars and with the first doctoral degrees minted in 1971. Two of the earliest dissertations focused on Protestant medical ethics and on Buddhism and Western psychology, respectively.

Over the following two decades, the doctoral program remained robust. It was likely the largest in the emergent field of religious studies and became especially renowned for its work in Islamic studies thanks chiefly to the tireless efforts and international connections of al-Faruqi. Often overlooked in considerations of Temple's marked contributions to the understanding of Islam is that soon after arriving at Temple, Phillips converted to Islam and was central to Thomas Merton's engagement of Sufism. In fact, the department's founding chair brought his North African sheikh to Merton's Trappist monastery in 1967. This meeting with the monk, one of the most influential and eloquent figures in the history of American religion, was a notable moment in the department's early years. An American Jew, a Muslim, and former Zen Buddhist guided an African sheikh to a Catholic monastery in the deep South to meet with Thomas Merton... quite impressive, to say the least.

Yet, the "world religions" model that had served the department so well over the years, along with the foundational intellectual assumptions that it provided for the centering of interreligious dialogue in its curriculum, fell under increasing suspicion–not just at Temple, but throughout the field–with the rise of postcolonialism, postmodernism, feminism, critical race theory, and other "hermeneutics of suspicion."[2] Such theoretical inquiries raised compelling questions about who has the authority to speak for any faith tradition and about the role of colonialism and white privilege in the very notions of what constitutes a religion and the academic study thereof. The field of religious studies had been exposed, so to speak, for its white liberal Protestant bias and its deep reliance on not just the intellectual (and often religious) assumptions that drove colonialism, but also to some degree the finances that resulted therefrom.[3] This hits close to home for Temple University, given how extensively the birth of the independent United States of America relied economically on slavery as reflected by the fact that the majority of the signers of the Declaration of Independence were slave owners. Its main author, Thomas Jefferson, owned over 600 slaves, and the text was drafted and ratified just two miles from where Temple University is today. True to course, the Department was founded by white men and governed by mostly white men until 1974, when it hired its first woman scholar, Lucy Bregman.

Tumult thus churned the department in its early years as the founders sought to chart a new course in the study of religion. Tumult also had by then a long and vibrant history in America, and when the department was founded in the 1960s, it witnessed new forms thereof that manifested when students rose up to protest neo-imperialism in the tragic Vietnam War. At a 2006 meeting of the American Academy of Religion in Philadelphia, Temple's Department of Religion hosted a special gathering to celebrate the 50th anniversary of its doctoral program (perhaps a bit belatedly). Several of its

---

[2] The quoted term is from Paul Ricouer, *Freud and Philosophy: An Essay on Interpretation*. Trans. Denis Savage. New Haven: Yale University Press, 2008 (1979).

[3] Tomoko Masuzawa, *The Invention of World Religions, or, How European Universalism Was Preserved in the Language of Pluralism*. Chicago: University of Chicago Press, 2005; Susan Buck-Morss, *Hegel, Haiti, and Universal History*. Pittsburgh: University of Pittsburgh Press, 2009.

pioneers offered remarks about their experiences, including Franklin Littell, Gerard Sloyan, John Raines, Leonard Swidler, and Patrick Burke. The latter, an Australian who had been trained in Catholic theology in Germany, made the following arresting observation: "I arrived the day before and had an apartment on Broad Street, near Temple. I woke up the next morning and looked out my window, and there was a tank on Broad Street." A tank! Welcome to America, Professor Burke! This was just two years after Columbia Avenue burned during race riots, and one year after Martin Luther King led marches around Girard College to protest segregation.

Alas, the Department was founded during a "time of trial" for the nation,[4] and many wondered what solutions or solace could be found in the world's religions. Temple sought to discover and provide answers in the study of religion then, as it does still today, another time of trial. The university would not exist were it not for Conwell's religious faith and his efforts to mine "acres of diamonds." Its mission statement calls on its' intellectual community "to create new knowledge that improves the human condition and uplifts the human spirit."

But what is that spirit? Does such a thing even exist? That it might be universal and could be sought through the comparative study of religion is one of the central assumptions upon which the field of religious studies–and nowhere more so than Temple–was founded. Although a few of the founders of Temple's Department of Religion, especially Raines, would take postcolonialism and postmodernism seriously, its implications for our field have recently begun to shift the direction of its course and mission. Twelve years ago, the department underwent periodic program review, and the unified opinion of three distinguished external scholars was that our model, while pioneering, was no longer justifiable or sustainable

---

[4] Robert N. Bellah, "Civil Religion in America," *Journal of the American Academy of Arts and Sciences* 96, 1, 1-21.

chiefly due to the impact of postcolonialism and postmodernism. The department's response was to develop "areas of scholarly concentration" (Religion and Society; Textual and Historical Traditions; Religion and Human Difference) and to begin moving away from the "world religions" approach, and this has been quite fruitful, attracting talented doctoral students and fomenting interdisciplinary discourse that has resulted in some stellar publications (Temple's Religion faculty far out-publishes that of any other public university – at the risk of self-promoting).

The problem is, though, that with the downturn in public interest in the humanities and social sciences–the theoretical and methodological bedrocks of our field–few undergraduate students currently choose to major or minor in religious studies. Though the department's doctoral program remains as strong as any in the world (really), one must thus wonder about its future, which seems from my perspective as its present chairperson to be under a bit of intellectual and realistic duress, as is the entire field. When one of its most influential and oft-cited scholars, Jonathan Z. Smith, can opine that "religion" is "solely the creation of a scholar's study" and "has no independent existence apart from the academy,"[5] the entire point of places like the Department of Religion at Temple University lies in the shuddering balance.

Surely most people of faith like me would take issue with Smith's rather sweeping generalization, but it is the case that as a category and object of analysis "religion" is a recent concept. Semantics aside, undeniably religion has been an awesome social and cultural force in human history, and this alone should justify the academic study thereof. The pursuit of the common truth amid faith traditions may no longer be the field's driving orientation, and the notion of "world religions" may have fallen out of favor. But

---

[5] Jonathan Z. Smith, *Imagining Religion: From Babylon to Jonestown*, Chicago: University of Chicago Press, 1982, xi.

Inshallah, there will always be people who are trained and paid to think full time about what religion is and how it shapes the course of human history, helping us expose its colossal dangers, and enhance its compassionate founts. Thankfully, the Department of Religion at Temple University has trained several hundred scholars to do precisely that, and today they teach, or have taught, at universities, colleges, and seminaries around the world. Though its future is uncertain, as is that of the humanities and social sciences in general, the department's legacy is remarkable. One wonders what Penn and Conwell would think were they to find so many Muslims in Philly today and in our seminars here. Onward with the holy experiment.

For more books from iPub Global Connection, please visit:
https://www.ipubcloud.com/featured-authors/

We welcome and encourage reviews and feedback on this and our other books. Please visit our website and join the dialogue.
www.iPubCloud.com
info@iPubCloud.com

www.ingramcontent.com/pod-product-compliance
Lightning Source LLC
Chambersburg PA
CBHW050849160426
43194CB00011B/2086